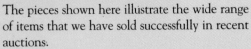

MILLER'S
Art Nouveau & Art Deco
BUYER'S GUIDE

Consultants
Judith and Martin Miller

Contributing Editor
Eric Knowles

Project Editors
Jo Wood
Lynn Bonnett

MILLER'S ART NOUVEAU & ART DECO BUYER'S GUIDE

Created and designed by
Miller's
The Cellars, High Street,
Tenterden, Kent, TN30 6BN
Tel: 01580 766411

Consultants: Judith & Martin Miller

Contributing Editor: Eric Knowles
Project Editors: Lynn Bonnett, Jo Wood
Editorial Assistants: Wendy Adlam, Marion Rickman
Production Assistants: Gillian Charles, Karen Taylor
Advertising Executive: Elizabeth Smith
Advertising Assistants: Melinda Williams, Joanne Daniels
Index compiled by: DD Editorial Services, Beccles
Design: Jody Taylor, Matthew Leppard, Darren Manser
Additional photography: Ian Booth, Robin Saker

First published in Great Britain in 1995
by Miller's, an imprint of
Reed Books Limited,
Michelin House, 81 Fulham Road,
London SW3 6RB
and Auckland, Melbourne, Singapore and Toronto

© 1995 Reed International Books Limited

A CIP catalogue record for this book is
available from the British Library

ISBN 1-85732-685-7

Bromide output by Perfect Image, Hurst Green, E. Sussex
Illustrations by G.H. Graphics, St. Leonard's-on-Sea
Colour origination by Scantrans, Singapore
Printed and bound in England by Bath Press, Avon

Miller's is a registered trademark of
Reed International Books Ltd

ACKNOWLEDGEMENTS

Miller's Publications would like to acknowledge the great assistance given by our consultants:

GENERAL INTRODUCTION
Eric Knowles, our contributing editor, is a director of Bonhams, a major London auction house. A leading authority on 19th and 20th century Decorative Arts, he appears regularly on the *BBC Antiques Roadshow* and is the resident antiques expert on *Crimewatch UK* and on BBC Radio 2's *Jimmy Young Show*. He has also contributed to a number of publications including *Miller's Understanding Antiques, Victoriana to Art Deco,* and *Miller's Checklists, Victoriana, Art Nouveau* and *Art Deco.*
Bonhams, 65-69 Lots Road, Chelsea, London SW10 ORN

BRONZE & IVORY FIGURES
Audrey Sternshire, after a very brief teaching career, began dealing in Antiquarian books in 1973, concentrating on Victorian Children's books and Art Reference. She soon developed an interest in Art Nouveau and Art Deco particularly sculpture which became her passion. She has contributed many articles on Bronze and Ivory for various publications, including *The British Art and Antiques Yearbook,* and has been a consultant on Decorative Arts for other Miller's Publications titles.
AS Antique Galleries, 26 Broad St, Pendleton, Salford, Manchester M6 5BY.

DECORATIVE GLASS
Patrick & Susan Gould started collecting glass in the early 1970s. By 1973 their passion for collecting focused on Studio Ceramics and Art Nouveau and Art Deco glass and they opened their first stall in the Portobello Road arcades. When Gray's Mews opened in 1978 they moved their shop there where they have remained ever since.
Patrick & Susan Gould, Stand L17, Grays Mews Antiques Market, Davies Mews, Davies Street, London W1Y 1AR

DOULTON
Mark Oliver started his career at Phillips (London) in 1981. After working in the saleroom he became a Doulton specialist in 1989. Mark has lectured on Doulton in the US and has contributed several articles on Doulton for collector's club magazines. In 1991 and 1992 he was responsible for two very successful Doulton exhibitions and auctions at Phillips in New York.
Phillips, 101 New Bond Street, London W1Y OAS

FURNITURE
Fiona Baker joined Phillips (London) Art Nouveau and Art Deco department in 1979 after graduating from Cambridge. Her speciality is furniture and she has contributed many articles on Art Nouveau and Art Deco furniture to leading antiques magazines.
Phillips, 101 New Bond Street, London W1Y OAS

JEWELLERY, SILVER & METALWARE
Keith Baker has been head of the Art Nouveau and Art Deco Dept at Phillips (London) since January 1976. His knowledge covers a wide field but his specializes in metalwares, silver and jewellery, particularly from the British Arts and Crafts era. He has written many articles on the subject for various collectors magazines and has given lectures worldwide.
Phillips, 101 New Bond Street, London W1Y OAS

LOUIS COMFORT TIFFANY & TIFFANY STUDIOS

Marybeth McCaffrey is an associate of J. Alastair Duncan, Ltd, in New York, and has been with the firm for ten years. She has travelled extensively in the Far East and Europe to appraise collections of art, and has assisted in the research and preparation of fourteen books on the Decorative Arts, as well as numerous catalogues and exhibitions, both in the United States and Japan.
J. Alastair Duncan Ltd, 1435 Lexington Avenue, New York, NY 10128, USA

POTTERY & PORCELAIN

Mark Wilkinson joined Christie's at the age of 16 as a sales clerk. He rapidly completed a stint in Motoring Art and Ephemera before taking over the Toy department. He now runs the 20thC Decorative Arts department and his keen involvement has resulted in spectacular pottery and porcelain sales particularly of Clarice Cliff. Mark also has a personal passion for Art Deco ceramics and is an avid collector.
Christie's (South Kensington) Ltd, 85 Old Brompton Road, London SW7 3LD

INDEX TO ADVERTISERS

CONTENTS

KEY TO ILLUSTRATIONS

Each illustration and descriptive caption is accompanied by a letter code. By referring to the following list of contributors, Auctioneers (denoted by * and Dealers •) the source of any item may be immediately determined. In no way does this constitute or imply a contract or binding offer on the part of any of our contributors to supply or sell the goods illustrated, or similar articles, at the prices stated. Advertisers are denoted by †.

A   *   Aldridges of Bath, The Auction Galleries, 130-132 Walcot Street, Bath BA 5BG. Tel: 01225 462830

AA   No longer trading

AAA   No longer trading

ABS   •   Abstract, 58-60 Kensington Church St, London W8 4DB. Tel: 0171 376 2652

ADC   † • Art Deco Ceramics, The Stratford Antiques Centre, Ely Street, Stratford-upon-Avon, Warwickshire CV37 6LN. Tel: 01789 297496

AG   *   Anderson & Garland, Marlborough House, Marlborough Crescent, Newcastle-upon-Tyne, Tyne & Wear, NE1 4EE. Tel: 0191 232 6278

AGr   *   Andrew Grant, St. Mark's House, St. Mark's Close, Worcester WR5 3DJ. Tel: 01905 357547

AH   *   Andrew Hartley, Victoria Hall, Little Lane, Ilkley, Yorks LS29 8EA. Tel: 01943 816363

AJ   No longer trading

AOS   † • Antiques on the Square, 2 Sandford Court, Sandford Avenue, Church Stretton, Shropshire SY6 6DA. Tel: 01694 724111

APO   •   Apollo Antiques Ltd, The Saltisford, Birmingham Road, Warwick CU34 4TD. Tel: 01926 494746

ARE   •   Arenski, 185 Westbourne Grove, London W11 2SB. Tel: 0171 727 8599

ARF   •   Art Furniture (London) Ltd, 158 Camden Street, London NW1 9PA. Tel: 0171 267 4324

ASA   † • A. S. Antiques, 26 Broad St, Pendleton, Salford, Manchester M6 5BY. Tel: 0161 737 5938

AW   No longer trading

BA   No longer trading

Bea   *   Bearnes, Rainbow, Avenue Road, Torquay, TQ2 5TG. Tel: 01803 296277

BEC   No longer trading

BEV   † • Beverley, 30 Church St, Marylebone, London NW8 8EP. Tel: 0171 262 1576

BKK   † • Bona Arts Decorative Ltd, 19 Princes Mead Shopping Centre, Farnborough, Hants GU14 7TJ. Tel: 01252 372188/544130

BLO   •   New Century Antiques, 69
NCA   Kensington Church St, London W8 4BG. Tel: 0171 937 2410

Bon   *   Bonhams, Montpelier St, London SW7 1HH. Tel: 0171 584 9161

BRI   •   Britannia, Stand 103 Grays Antiques Market, 58 Davies St, London W1Y 1AR Tel: 0171 629 6772

BWe   *   Biddle & Webb Ltd, Ladywood Middleway, Birmingham B16 OPP. Tel: 0121 455 8042

C   *   Christie's, 8 King Street, St James's, London SW1Y 6QT. Tel: 0171 839 9060

C(Am) * Christie's Amsterdam, Cornelis Schuystraat 54, Amsterdam, The Netherlands 107150. Tel: 013120 5755255

CA   •   Crafers Antiques, The Hill, Wickham Market, Suffolk IP13 OQS. Tel: 01728 747347

CAG   *   Canterbury Auction Galleries, 40 Station Road West, Canterbury CT2 8AN. Tel: 01227 763337

CAR   •   Carlton Gallery, 60 Burnston Road, Hull, Humberside HU5 4JY. Tel: 01482 443954

CDC   *   Capes Dunn & Co, The Auction Galleries, 38 Charles St, Greater Manchester M1 7DB. Tel: 0161 273 6060/1911

CEd   *   Christie's Scotland, 164-166 Bath Street, Glasgow G2 4TG. Tel: 0141 332 8134

CG   *   Christie's International SA, 8 Place de la Taconnerie, 1204 Geneva. Tel: 010 4122 311 17 66

CHa   No longer trading

CH   *   (Chancellors) now Edwards & Elliott, 32 High Street, Ascot SL5 7HG. Tel: 01344 872588

CIR   No longer trading

CNY   *   Christies Manson & Woods International Inc. (including Christie's East) 502 Park Avenue, New York NY10022. Tel: 01 212 546 1000.

CS   No longer trading

CSK   † * Christie's South Kensington Ltd, 85 Old Brompton Road, London SW7 3LD. Tel: 0171 581 7611

DEC   •   No longer trading

DID   •   Didier Antiques, 58-60 Kensington Church St, London W8 4DB. Tel: 0171 938 2537

DM   *   Diamond Mills & Co, 117 Hamilton Road, Felixstowe, IP11 7BL. Tel: 01394 282281

DN   *   Dreweatt Neate, Donnington Priory, Donnington, Newbury, Berks RG13 2JE. Tel: 01635 31234

DSA   No longer trading

DSH   (see AH above)

DWB   (See DN above)

E   *   Ewbank, Burnt Common Auction Room, London Rd, Send, Woking, Surrey GU23 7LN. Tel: 01483 223101

EG No longer trading

EH * Edgar Horn's Auction Galleries, 46/50 South Street, Eastbourne BN 21 4XB. Tel: 01323 410419

F No longer trading

FA • Frank Andrews, 10 Vincent Rd, London N22 6NA. Tel: 0181 881 0658

FHF * (Frank H. Fellows) now Fellows & Sons, Augusta House, 19 Augusta St, Hockley, Birmingham, B18 6JA. Tel: 0121 212 2131

G (See PSG)

GAK * G.A. Key, 8 Market Place, Aylsham, Norfolk, NR11 6EH. Tel: 01263 733195

GC No longer trading

GCA • Gerald Clark Antiques, 1 High Street, Mill Hill Village, NW7 1QY. Tel: 0181 906 0342

GIL * Gildings, Roman Way, Market Harborough, Leics LE16 7PQ. Tel: 01858 410414

GSP * Graves Son & Pilcher, Hove St, Hove BN3 2GL. Tel: 01273 735266

HAE • Hampstead Antique Emporium, 12 Heath St, London NW3. Tel: 0171 794 3297

HAM * Hamptons Fine Art Auctioneers, 6 Arlington Street, London SW1A 1RB. Tel: 0171 493 8222

HAR * William Hardie Ltd, 141 West Regent St, Glasgow G2 2SG. Tel: 0141 221 678

HCH * Hobbs & Chambers, Market Place, Cirencester, Glos GL7 1QQ. Tel: 01285 4736

HER • Heritage Antiques, Unit 14 Georgian Village, Camden Passage, London N1 8EA. Tel: 0171 226 9822

HEW †• Muir Hewitt, Halifax Antiques Centre, Queens Road/Gibbet St, Halifax, W.Yorks HX1 4LR. Tel: 01422 347377

HM No longer trading

HO (Hoddel Pritchard) now Clevedon

HOD * salerooms, Herbert Rd, Clevedon BS21 7ND. Tel: 01275 876699

HOW • Howards Antiques, 10 Alexandra Rd, Aberystwyth, Dyfed SY23 1LE. Tel: 01970 624973

HP * Hobbs Parker, Romney House, Ashford Market, Ashford, Kent TN23 1PG. Tel: 01233 622222

HSS * Henry Spencer & Sons, 20 The Square, Retford, DN22 6BX. Tel: 01777 708633

IM * Ibbett Mosely, 125 High St, Sevenoaks, TN13 1UT. Tel: 01732 456731

IS • Ian Sharp Antiques, 23 Front St, Tynemouth, Tyne & Wear, NE30 4DX. Tel: 0191 296 0656

JJIL • John Jesse, 160 Kensington Church

JES St, London W8 4BN. Tel: 0171 229 0312

JG No longer trading

KNG No longer trading

Ksh No longer trading

L * Lawrence Fine Art Auctioneers Ltd, South St, Crewkerne, TA18 8AB. Tel: 01460 73041

LAN * Langlois Auctioneers, Westaway Chambers, Don St, St. Helier, Jersey, JE2 4TR. Tel: 01534 22441

L&E * Locke & England, Black Horse

LE Agencies, 18 Guy St, Leamington Spa, Warks CV32 4RT. Tel: 01926 889100

LB • Linda B, Stand J20-1, Grays Mews, Davies St, London W1Y 1AR. Tel: 0171 629 5921

LBP No longer trading

LEX No longer trading

LF * 102 High St, Tenterden, Kent TN12 6DR. Tel: 01580 763233

LRG * Lots Road Chelsea Auction Galleries, 71 Lots Rd, World's End, London SW10 0RN. Tel: 0171 351 7771

LT * Louis Taylor Auctioneers, Britannia House, 10 Town Rd, Hanley, Stoke-on-Trent ST1 2QG. Tel: 01782 214111

M * Morphets of Harrogate, 4-6 Albert St, Harrogate, Nr. Yorks. Tel: 01423 502282

MA No longer trading

MAT No longer trading

McC * McCartney's, Portcullis Salerooms, Ludlow, Shropshire SY8 1PZ. Tel: 01584 872636

MGM * Michael G. Matthews (Bonhams West Country), Dowell St, Honiton EX14 8LX. Tel: 01404 41872

MJB * Michael J. Bowman, 6 Haccombe House, Netherton, Newton Abbot, Devon TQ12 4SJ. Tel: 01626 872890

MN * No longer trading

Msh • Manfred Schotton, The Crypt Antiques, 109 High St, Burford, Oxfordshire OX18 4QA. Tel: 01993 822302

MSL • Michael Stainer Ltd, St. Andrew's Hall, Boscombe, Bournemouth, Dorset BH6 6HF. Tel: 01202 309999

MT No longer trading

N * Neales, 192-194 Mansfield Rd, Nottingham NG1 3HU. Tel: 0115 962 4141

NCA • New Century Antiques,

BLO 69 KensingtonChurch St, London W8 4BG. Tel: 0171 937 2410

OCA • The Old Cinema, 160 Chiswick High Road, London W4 1PR. Tel: 0181 995 4166

OD • Offa's Dyke Antique Centre, 4 High St, Knighton, Powys, Wales LB7 1AT. Tel: 01547 528635

OL * Outhwaite & Litherland, Kingsway Galleries, Fontenoy St, Liverpool L3 2BE. Tel: 0151 236 6561

OO †•Pieter Oosthuizen, 1st Floor, Georgian Village, Camden Passage, London N1 8EA. Tel: 0171 359 3322/376 3852

OT No longer trading

P †• Phillips, Blenstock House, 101 New Bond St, London W1 OAS. Tel: 0171 629 6602

P(CW) * Phillips, Baffins Hall, Baffins Lane, Chichester, PO19 1UA. Tel: 01243 787548

P(M) * Phillips, Trinity House,
P(Re) 114 Washway Rd, Sale, Greater. Manchester, M33 1RF. Tel: 0161 962 9237

P(S) * Phillips Scotland, 207 Bath St, Glasgow G2 4HD. Tel: 0141 221 8377

PAR • Park House Antiques, Park St, Stow-on-the-Wold, Glos GL54 1AQ. Tel: 01451 830159

PB * Phillips, 39 Park End St, Oxford OX1 1JD. Tel: 01865 723524

PBJ * Phillips, l Old King St, Bath BA1 2JT. Tel: 01225 310609

PC Private Collection

PCh * Peter Cheney, Western Road Auction Rooms, Western Road, Littlehampton, Sussex BN17 5NP. Tel: 01903 722264/713418

Pea * (Pearsons) now Phillips, The Red House, Hyde St, Winchester SO23 7DX. Tel: 01962 862515

PGA • Paul Gibbs Antiques, 25 Castle St, Conwy, Gwynedd LL32 8AY. Tel:01492 593429

Ph • Phelps Ltd, 129-135 St Margarets Rd, Twickenham, Middx, TW1 1RG. Tel: 0181 892 1778

POW • Syliva Powell Decorative Arts, 28 The Mall, Camden Passage, London N1 OPD. Tel: 0171 354 2977

PSG • Patrick & Susan Gould, Stand L17, Gray's Mews, Davies St, London W1Y 1AR. Tel: 0171 408 0129

PWC * (Parsons Welch & Cowell) now Phillips, 49 London Rd, Sevenoaks, TN13 1AR. Tel: 01732 740310

RAG No longer trading

Re See Phillips P(M)

RG (Rowland Gorringe) now Gorringes Auction Gallery, 15 North St, Lewes BN7 2PD. Tel: 01273 472503

RIC †• Rich Designs, 1 Shakespeare St, Stratford-upon-Avon, CV37 6RN. Tel: 01789 261612

RID * Riddetts of Bournemouth, 26 Richmond Hill, The Square Bournemouth BH2 6EJ. Tel: 01202 555686

RO No longer trading

ROW No longer trading

RP • Robert Pugh. Tel: 01225 314713

RUM • Rumours Decorative Arts, 10 The Mall, Upper St, Camden Passage, London N1 OPD Tel: 01582 873561

S(C) * No longer trading

S(NY) *Sotheby's, 1334 York Avenue, New York, NY 10021, USA. Tel: 212 606 7000

S(S) * Sotheby's Sussex, Summers Place, Billingshurst, Sussex RH14 9AD. Tel: 01403 783933

SAI No longer trading

SBA * No longer trading

SBe See Bearnes (Bea)

SC No longer trading

SH No longer trading

SN No longer trading

STU No longer trading

SV • Sutton Valence Antiques, North St, Sutton Valence, Maidstone, Kent ME17 3AP. Tel: 01622 843333/843499

SWO * G. E. Sworder & Sons, 15 Northgate End Salerooms, Bishops Stortford, Herts CM33 2LF. Tel: 01279 651388

TA No longer trading

THA • Tudor House Antiques, 11 Tontine Hill, Ironbridge, Shropshire TF8 7AL. Tel: 01952 453783

TP †• The Collector (Tom Power), 9 Church St, London NW8 8EE. Tel: 0171 706 4586

TRU • The Trumpet, West End, Minchinhampton, Glos GL6 9JA. Tel: 01453 883027

TVA • Teme Valley Antiques, 1 The Bull Ring, Ludlow, Shropshire SY8 1AD. Tel: 01584 874686

TW * Thomas Watson & Sons, Northumberland St, Darlington, DL3 7HJ. Tel: 01352 462559

VAS • No longer trading

VIN No longer trading

VH • Valerie Howard, 2 Camden St, London W8 7LP. Tel: 0171 792 9702

W * Walter's, No 1 Mint Lane, Lincoln LN1 1UD. Tel: 01522 525454

Wai • Wain Antiques, 7 Nantwich Road, Woore, Cheshire CW3 9SA. Tel: 01630 817118

WHB * William H. Brown, Oilivers Rooms, Burkitts Lane, Sudbury, Suffolk. Tel: 01787 880305

WHL * W. H. Lane & Son, 65 Morrab Rd, Penzance, Cornwall TR18 2QT. Tel: 01736 61447

WIL * Peter Wilson, Victoria Gallery, Market St, Nantwich, CW5 5DG. Tel: 01270 623878

Wor See Canterbury Auction Galleries (CAG)

WW * Wooley & Wallis, Salisbury Salerooms, Castle St, Salisbury SP1 3SU. Tel: 01722 411422

ZEI †• Zeitgeist, 58 Kensington Church St, London W8 4DB. Tel: 0171 938 4817.

INTRODUCTION

Before I began my career in the world of fine art and antique auctioneering, I was a regular visitor to my local junk shops and second-hand shops. What to buy was never a problem: the shops appeared crammed full, with new stock arriving almost daily – in fact the biggest problem was what to leave behind after spending my budget. In later years some of the shops I had known took on a grander status by replacing the word 'junk' in their name with 'antique'. The stock itself remained much the same: a collection of Victoriana and pre-WWII items.

My personal interest at this time was focused on antique pottery and porcelain, which was starting to become more difficult to find. In contrast, pre-war pieces in the Art Deco style were relatively plentiful. Unfortunately, these items simply failed to excite me, and consequently I tended to ignore much of what I saw – until I decided to take a trip to my local museum in nearby Burnley.

Purely by chance my visit occurred at a time when the museum was hosting a travelling exhibition of Art Deco, organized by the Victoria and Albert Museum. This was definitely not the type of Art Deco ware I had become accustomed to seeing in the local shops: both the design and the quality of the craftsmanship were breathtaking. The exhibits featured were credited with the names of their makers and designers, many of which were unfamiliar and relatively exotic. It was here that I discovered the work of Maurice Marinot, Jean Despret, Ferdinand Preiss, Marcel Goupy and René Lalique.

That chance visit had a magical effect, and subsequently I was stimulated to achieve a better understanding not only of Art Deco, but of 20th century decorative and applied arts in general.

My understanding and appreciation of Art Nouveau began many years prior to my exposure to the best of Art Deco. Once again, it was a nearby museum that was to play an important role in educating my untutored eye. However surprising it may sound, the town of Accrington in Lancashire can boast probably the finest public collection of Tiffany glass outside the United States. The collection was assembled, and eventually bequeathed, by Joseph Briggs – a local lad made good. Briggs had travelled to New York in the 1890s, whereupon he found employment with Tiffany Studios working initially in the mosaic department. Over almost 40 years, Briggs rose to a top management position and became one of Louis Comfort Tiffany's most valued employees. It was Briggs who, prior to Tiffany's death in 1936, was responsible for winding up the company's affairs at the founder's instigation.

The collection is housed in the Haworth Art Gallery and Museum in Accrington, and on my first visit I remember being totally spellbound by the strange, often fluid, shapes, complemented by mesmerising iridescent decoration. My schoolboy imagination concluded that I must be witnessing the achievements of a transatlantic sorcerer. At the time I first saw it, the collection was spread throughout the numerous rooms of the Edwardian mansion with most pieces being unceremoniously positioned upon mantelshelves and sideboards, and readily available for hand-held inspection. Today the pieces are displayed behind toughened plate glass and protected by a regularly updated security system. The need to rethink the presentation was a response to the escalation in values, evident from prices paid for similar pieces in auction rooms in London and New York.

Since those early formative years, the demand for good examples of both Art Nouveau and Art Deco has continued to grow, and the prices paid today would have been considered unthinkable all those years ago. In recent years the market has proved to be just as fickle as those for the more traditional collecting areas. Japanese interest in French art glass, especially the work of Gallé, Daum and Lalique, resulted in prices spiralling throughout the late 1980s, only to end up 30 per cent and, in certain instances, 50 per cent down by as early as 1992. Today the market appears to be stabilising, with Daum glass in particular gaining in demand from Japanese, European and North American buyers.

The popularity of the Art Nouveau/Art Deco market was further enhanced by the knowledge that both styles found favour amongst those within the world of music and show business. The sales of collections assembled by Elton John and Barbra Streisand both achieved record prices and worldwide attention of the type normally associated with the sale of Impressionist or Old Master paintings.

Today Art Nouveau and Art Deco are both well-established collecting fields that continue to attract new collectors eager for both historical information and a sound knowledge of prices and trends. *Miller's Art Nouveau & Art Deco Buyer's Guide* sets out to equip both the new and the established collector with reports on the state of the market, what to look out for when buying, and warnings of possible pitfalls. With information provided by a team of highly respected specialists, this comprehensive guide combines expert and practical advice, making it an invaluable companion for anyone interested in Art Nouveau and Art Deco.

Eric Knowles

FEATURED DESIGNERS & MANUFACTURERS

Aalto, Alvar (1898–1976) Finnish Modernist architect and furniture designer. Director of Finmar and founder of Artek (1931), furnishing companies.

Argy-Rousseau, Gabriel (1885–1953 French designer of pâte-de-cristal glass objects.

Artificers' Guild (1901–1942) London-based metalworking firm founded by Nelson Dawson.

Ashbee, Charles R. (1863–1942) English architect and designer associated with the Arts and Crafts movement. In 1888, founded the Guild of Handicraft in order to perpetuate the ideals of medieval craft guilds. Ashbee and Guild marks are stamped.

Barnsley, Sydney (1865–1926) and Ernest (1863–1926) Furniture designers and co-founders of the Bath Cabinet Makers Co. Ltd. Pieces unmarked.

Bauhaus (1919–1933) German design school. Founded by the architect Walter Gropius, it included architects, engineers, designers, sculptors and painters, who sought to relate form to function and aesthtic qualities to the demands of machine production.

Bayes, Gilbert (1872–1953) English sculptor working in a style that combined Art Nouveau and medieval influences.

Bevan Charles (active 1860s) English designer and manufacturer of furniture, specializing in Gothic-revival style.

Bouraine, Marcel (dates unknown) French sculptor, best known for his Amazon figures in bronze. Mark: 'M.M.A. Bouraine'.

Brandt, Edgar-William (1880–1960) French designer and metalworker, best known for his fine wrought iron work, sometimes burnished or painted a silver colour.

Brannam, Charles (1855–1937) English art potter. Pieces are often signed and dated.

Breuer, Marcel (1902–81) Hungarian-born architect and furniture designer; studied interior design at the Bauhaus. Used wood and tubular steel in his designs. Moved from England to the United States in 1937. Unmarked, but his designs for Thonet and DIM have makers' labels and PEL and Standard-Mobel catalogues note some of his steel chairs.

Bugatti, Carlo (1855–1940) Italian furniture designer and craftsman.

Carlton Ware (est. 1897) Brand name used by Wiltshaw & Robinson, a pottery founded in 1897 in Stoke-on-Trent. Marks: 'W&R/STOKE ON TRENT' forming a circle which encloses a swallow, topped by a crown; 'Carlton ware' hand painted over name and address of firm.

Cartier (est. 1897) Paris jewellers. Opened in London (1903), New York (1912).

Century Guild (est. c1882) English Arts and Crafts society of designers, artists, architects and metalworkers, founded by Arthur Mackmurdo to restore responsibility for the decorative crafts to the artist from the tradesman. Marks: on metalwork, hammered; on textiles, printed initials.

Cheuret, Albert (dates unknown) French sculptor, working in Art Nouveau and Art Deco styles, producing functional work, featuring naturalist motifs. Mark: ALBERT CHEURET, incise cast.

Chiparus, Demêtre (Dimitri) (dates unknown) Rumanian-born sculptor who worked in Paris in the 1920s.

Christofle, Orfevèrie (1829) Metalworkers, founded in Paris.

Cliff, Clarice (1899–1972) English potter, designer and decorator. Art director at Wilkinson's Royal Staffordshire Pottery and its subsidiary, Newport Pottery. Cliff also decorated wares designed by other artists. Mark: black printed pottery mark, name of design and facsimile signature.

Colinet, Jeanne Robert (dates unknown) French sculptor. Mark: 'J.R. Colinet'

Cooper, Susie (b1902) English potter. Designed for A. E. Gray & Co. (c.1925), especially bright geometrical forms. Formed her own company in 1932.

Cotswold School Association of English furniture designers, led by Ernest Gimson and the Barnsley brothers.

Couper, James & Sons (dates unknown) Scottish glassmaking firm best known for 'Clutha' glass.

Crane, Walter (1845–1915) English painter, graphic artist and designer associated with the Arts and Crafts movement. Designed pottery and tiles for Wedgwood, Minton, Pilkington and Maw & Co. Painted monogram. Designed textiles for Morris and Co.

Daum Frères (1875–present) Nancy glassworks founded by brothers, Auguste (1853–1909) and Antonin (1864–1930); made fine vases and lamps. Marks: relief cut, etched or painted.

Décorchement, François-Emile (1880–1971) French glassmaker, exponent of pâte-de-verre and pâte-de-cristal.

de Morgan, William (1839–1917) English ceramic designer connected with the Arts and Crafts Movement. Founded the William de Morgan Pottery (1872) and other works. Marks: impressed.

Doulton & Co. (1815–present) Lambeth-based producer of commercial and industrial stoneware and porcelain figures, including saltglazeware. Marks: printed, impressed or painted. Doulton Lambeth Potteries, their art department, were pottery manufacturers founded by Henry Doulton and John Sparkes, head of the Lambeth School of Art.

Dresser, Christopher (1834–1904) Scottish-born botanist, designer and writer. Most famous for silver and metalwork designs for various firms, including Elkington, Coalbrookdale and Benham and Froud. Marks: on glass – etched; on metalwork – stamped.

Dufrêne, Maurice (1876–1955) French designer of furniture, ceramics, metal, glass and carpets. Later work included Modernist designs using tubular steel. Had a shop in Galeries Lafayette.

Elkington & Co. (c1830–present) English silversmith founded by George Elkington, who, with his cousin Henry, patented their electroplating process in 1840. Marks: stamped.

Ellis, Harvey (1852–1904) English-born architect and designer associated with Gustav Stickley.

Elton, Sir Edmund (1846–1920) English baronet and self-taught potter. Produced art pottery on his Somerset estate, first as the name Elton Ware. Mark: painted.

Farhner, Theodor (1868–1928) German jeweller: mass-produced fine jewellery in an abstract Art Nouveau style.

Finmar (est. 1934/5) Finnish furniture manufacturers headed by Alvar Aalto, producing items in laminated wood. Unmarked, although the Decorative Arts Journal shows the full range of their wares, and pieces made by Aalto in Finland are marked 'Aalto Möbler, Svensk Kvalitet Sprodurt'.

Foley (later Shelley) (1892–1925) Staffordshire pottery and producer of decorative earthenwares and bone china.

Follot, Paul (1877–1941) French interior decorator and designer and early exponent of Art Deco. Pieces unmarked, but some have characteristic 'Follot rose'.

Fouquet, Georges (1862–1957) Innovative French jewelry designer. Jointed his father's Paris firm in 1891 and took over in 1895, on his father's retirement.

Gaillard, Eugène (active 1895–1911) French furniture designer and associate of the Paris School.

Galliard, Lucien (b1861) French jeweller and silversmith, famous for fine hand-made work in unusual materials.

Gallé, Emile (1846–1904) French designer and glassworker; considered the greatest of glass craftsmen. Marks: on glass – large variety of etched marks; on furniture – signature in marquetry.

Goldscheider, Marcel (1855-1953) Viennese ceramics manufacturer; mass-produced Art Nouveau vases and later Art Deco figures.

Gropius, Walter (1883–1969) German architect, founder of the Bauhaus and director until 1928. Exponent of Modernism. His multi-combination modular furniture (1927) was highly influential.

Guild of Handicraft (1888–1908) British silverworking guild famous for exquistive silverware.

Gurschner, Gustav (b1873) Bavarian sculptor and metalworker.

Hagenauer (established 1898) Austrian foundry based in Vienna, known for its face masks and figures inspired by Negro art.

Heal, Sir Ambrose (1872–1959) English cabinet-maker and director of family firm, Heal & Son. He used many woods in his designs and, eventually, steel and aluminium. Mark: stamped or labelled company name.

Hoffman, Josef (1870–1956) Architect, designer, founder member of the Vienna Secession.

Hunebelle, André (active 1920s) French glass artist inspired by Lalique. Mark: 'A Hunebelle', impressed.

Hunt & Roskill (est. 1843) Formerly Storr & Mortimer. Important silversmith headed by Storr's nephew, the silversmith, John Samuel Hunt.

Hutton, William & Sons (1800–1923) English producer of silver, pewter and Britannia metal.

Jensen, Georg (1866–1935) Danish silversmith specialising in high-quality silverware and jewellery. Mark: stamped.

Knox, Archibald (1864–1933) Manx metalwork designer, notably of Liberty's Cymric range.

La Faguays, Pierre (dates unknown) French sculptor.

Lalique René (1860–1945) French master jeweller and glass maker, famous for his scent bottles. The Lalique works also made glass screens, lamps, innovative car mascots, fountains and lights. Marks: 'R Lalique' during Lalique's lifetime, the 'R' being dropped after his death.

Larche, Raoul-François (1860–1912) French sculptor known for gilt-bronze female figures.

Legrain, Pierre (1889–1929) Leading French Art Deco furniture designer, often showing an African influence. Used expensive and unusual materials.

Legras (1864–present) French glassmaking firm; produced cameo wares and commercial glass similar to Daum and Müller Frères.

Léonard, Agathon (b1841) French ceramist and sculptor. Made Art Nouveau-style biscuit figures and gilt-bronze statuettes.

Liberty & Co. (1875–present) English retail firm established by Arthuyr Lasenby to sell fine British-made goods and Oriental art and fabrics, later expanding to include ceramics, metalwork and furniture.

Lorenzl, Josef (dates unknown) Austrian sculptor.

Mackintosh, Charles Rennie (1868–1928) Scottish architect, designer. Formed the 'Glasgow Four' with Margaret Mackintosh, Frances Macdonald and J.H. McNair.

Mackmurdo, Arthur Heygate (1851–1942) English architect and founder of the Century Guild. Marks: hammered initials.

Massier, Clement (1845–1917) French ceramicist and producer of earthenware with iridescent or lustre decoration.

Mies van der Rohe, Ludwig (1886–1969) German Modernist architect and an innovative and influential furniture designer. Vice-president of Deutscher Werkbund, 1926; 1930–33 director of the Bauhaus; 1937 moved to America. Pieces unmarked.

Minton & Co. (1793–present, from 1873, Mintons Ltd) Staffordshire pottery; produced earthenware, art pottery and porcelain. Marks: printed.

Moorcroft, William (1872–1945) Head of Art Pottery Department of MacIntyre & Co. Best known for Florian ware vases. Mark: signature or monogram.

Morris, William (1834–96) English poet, writer, socialist and designer. Founded Marshall, Faulkner and Co. in 1861 (became Morris and Co.) to execute his designs for furniture, textiles and wallpapers.

Moser, Koloman (1868–1918) Austrian artist and designer for furniture, ceramics and glass; founder member of the Vienna Secession and co-founder of the Wiener Werkstätte.

Müller Frères (active c1900–36) French glassmaking firm run by Henri and Désirée Müller. Marks: etched or relief cut.

Murrle Bennett & Co. (1884–present) Anglo-German mass-producer of jewelry. Marks: stamped.

Nancy School A group of artists and designers inspired by the work of Gallé and Majorelle in Nancy towards the end of the 19thC.

Navarre, Henri (1885–1970) French glass artist. His sculptural, textured vases and bowls were influenced by Marinot. Mark: 'Henri Navarre'.

Olbrich, Josef Maria (1867–1908) Architect, designer and founder member of the Vienna Secession.

Orrefors (est. 1898) Swedish glassworks. From 1915 produced decorative glasswares designed by Edvard Hald and Simon Gate, amongst others.

Pèche, Dagobert (1887–1923) Austrian artist and designer of ceramics and metalwork, and co-director of the Wiener Werkstätte.

Poole Pottery (est. 1873) Originally Carter, Stabler & Adams. Partnership formed 1921 at Poole, Dorset. Traded as Poole Pottery Ltd from 1963.

Powell, James & Sons (c.1830–1980) Innovative London glasshouse, influential in the late 19thC. Acquired Whitefriars Glassworks in 1883. Designers included Philip Webb and Joseph Leicester. Marks: stamped.

Preiss, Ferdinand (1882–1943) German sculptor. Opened foundry in 1906. Mark: 'F Preiss'; foundry mark 'PK'.

Prutscher, Otto (1880–1949) Designer for the Wiener Werkstätte of distinctive glass, jewellery and silver. Wares unsigned.

Pugin, Augustus Welby Northmore (1812–52) English furniture designer whose work epitomises the Gothic revival in Britain. Produced solid and utilitarian furniture, usually of oak.

Quezal (1901–25) American glassmaking firm inspired by Tiffany.

Riessner, Stellmacher and Kessel (R.S.K.) (est. 1892) Bohemian ceramics firm; main contribution to Art Nouveau was the 'Amphora' range.

Rietveld, Gerrit T. (1888–1964) Dutch architect and furniture designer. Joined de Stijl, the Dutch artists' association, in 1919; the geometric forms, primary colours and revealed construction of his furniture epitomize the work of the group.

Rohlfs, Charles (1853–1936) American actor, stove maker and designer of furniture, particularly in oak. Mark: burned initials.

Rörstrand (est. 1726) Prominent Swedish pottery: producer of bold designs under the influence of French Art Nouveau.

Rosenthal, Philip (d1937) German potter and founder of the Rosenthal factory, producer of high-quality tablewares in the Art Nouveau style. Marks: printed.

Royal Dux (1860–mid 20thC) Bohemian ceramicists known for their classically-inspired figures.

Rozenburg (1883–1916) Pottery whose 'eggshell' porcelain is considered foremost Dutch contribution to Art Nouveau.

Ruhlmann, Jacques-Émille (1879–1933) French painter, master-cabinet-maker from 1925. Mark: branded signature.

Sabino, Marius Ernest (active 1920s and '30s) French glass architect inspired by Lalique. Mark: 'Sabino, France'.

Shelley Potteries (1872–1966) The name from 1925 of Foley, pottery firm established 1860 in Staffordshire, England.

Steuben Glass Works (1903–present) New York-based glassworks founded by Howkes family and Frederick Carder.

Stickley Brothers, L. and J.G. (1891–1910) George and Albert, brothers of Gustav, made oak furniture in a style popularized by Gustav, but of inferior quality.

Stickley, Gustav (1847–1942) American furniture designer; produced pieces with an Arts and Crafts feel, notably his range of 'Craftsman furniture'.

Stoor, Paul (active early 19thC) Most famous 19thC English silversmith. Best known for Neo-classical pieces in silver gilt.

Thompson, Robert 'Mouseman' (d1955) British cabinet maker who followed the principles of the Cotswold School. Work mainly in oak and largely undecorated. The figure of a mouse, usually in relief, but sometimes carved into a niche, became his trademark.

Thonet Brothers (Gebrüder Thonet, Thonet Frères) (est. 1853) Furniture manufacturers. Designed and manufactured bentwood furniture. Largely for export.

Tiffany & Co. (1837–present) American jeweller and retailer founded by Charles Louis Tiffany (1812–1902) and John B. Mill Young. Now established in Geneva, Paris, New York and London. Marks: stamped.

Tiffany, Louis Comfort (1848–1933) Founder of Louis C. Tiffany in the United States. Initially designed interiors but is now better known for glasswares, particularly lamps.

Toft, Albert (1862–1949) English sculptor of bronze figural pieces, mainly of ethereal, cloaked female subjects.

Van de Velde, Henri (1863–1957) Belgian architect and designer; worked with Samuel Bing and at Meissen.

Van Erp, Dirk (1860–1933/53) Dutch-born metalworker.

Vever (1821–1982) Leading French Art Nouveau retailer and jewellers.

Villeroy and Boch (1836–present) German producer of stoneware art pottery.

Voysey, Charles A (1847–1941) English architect. Designed interiors, wallpapers, textiles and furniture.

Wahliss, Ernst (1863–1930) Bohemian potter influenced by Michael Powolny.

Walton George (1867–1933) Scottish designer of interiors and furniture.

Walter Alméric (1859–1942) French Art Nouveau and Art Deco glass artist; worked primarily in pâte-de-verre.

Wiener Werkstätte (Vienna Workshops) (1903–32) Series of Austrian craft workshops founded by Koloman Moser and Josef Hoffmann, which sought to combine utility and aesthetic qualities in furniture, metalwork and building designs.

Wilkinson, A. J. Ltd. (est. 1896) English pottery company. Factories included Royal Staffordshire Pottery. Clarice Cliff was art director, although the company also produced the designs of other artists – for example, Vanessa Bell and Duncan Grant.

Wright, Frank Lloyd (1867–1959) American architect and designer, father of the Prairie School of architecture. Used pure forms, modern materials and modern techniques. Pieces are unsigned but usually well-documented.

Zach, Bruno (dates unknown) Austrian sculptor, best known for his erotic figures. Mark: 'Zach'.

Württembergischer Metallwarenfabrik (W.M.F.) (1880–present) Austrian metalwork foundry; produced decorative and domestic metalwork. Marks: stamped.

Zsolnay (est. 1862) Hungarian ceramics firm; helped the development of Art Nouveau in eastern Europe.

POTTERY & PORCELAIN

Over the last decade there has been a positive surge in all categories of collecting, with new areas and specialist sales appearing every year. One of the biggest growth areas has been in Art Nouveau and Art Deco pottery and porcelain.

Many factors have contributed to this onslaught of change. For instance, no longer are ceramic collections secretly hidden away in dusty cabinets, they are now being incorporated into the interior design of lounges and other rooms in the home. Collectors of Art Nouveau and Art Deco pottery and porcelain once had to hunt through antique shops and auction sales packed with many other collecting fields to find what they were looking for. Today there are specialist fairs, shops and auctions which cater exclusively to Art Nouveau and Art Deco collectors. In fact there is now an Art Deco fair somewhere in Britain every other week and there are auctions entirely devoted to Clarice Cliff pottery, Moorcroft pottery, Carlton Ware, and Studio pottery.

As a result, the auction houses have seen enormous changes in the last ten years. No longer are the London auction rooms the sole domain of dealers, the rich and the famous; rather, they are now viewed by a growing variety of people as a new and enjoyable way of purchasing art. Catalogues are now illustrated in colour, many have condition reports enabling clients to bid by telephone or in writing, rather than having to attend a sale personally. Once or twice a year collectors are now presented with a whole catalogue of Clarice Cliff ceramics for instance, which one can choose to bid for.

Another reason for the dramatic growth in popularity of pottery and porcelain is the rising number of publications which provide interested readers with valuable information and visual references. It can be difficult understanding pottery and porcelain if you cannot see the entire range produced – for instance, to an untrained eye a Clarice Cliff 5in (12.5cm) high conical sugar sifter (which can be worth as much as £1,800) hardly looks interesting when in a cabinet full of Doulton stoneware, but when seen reproduced in a book with twenty other sifters, all with different patterns to compare it to, its appeal can be appreciated.

Shrewd collectors now try to predict the next popular theme and stock-pile items in the hope there will be an exhibition or a book published on the subject which will help push up the price, as was recently experienced with Troika and Poole Pottery. It is generally at this point that auctioneers take an interest and in some cases organise a specialist sale.

Many of the new collecting fields now have special clubs (these were seldom found ten years ago) that publish newsletters and may arrange outings and conferences. The better known ones cater for collectors of Clarice Cliff, Carlton Ware, Shelley, Wade and Moorcroft.

Most Art Nouveau and Art Deco items collected in the UK are ceramic, unlike in France where they are glass (such as Lalique and Gallé). If you visit a British Art Nouveau and Art Deco fair, 80% of the items for sale will be ceramic and there always seems to be a 'newly discovered' factory to learn about. Some of the up and coming factories include Royal Winton, Troika, 1960s and 1970s Poole Pottery, Burleigh Ware and Rye Pottery.

Why are more people than ever before investing in Art Nouveau and Art Deco ceramics? Perhaps this is the result of the currently low Building Society rates and the uncertainty of shares. When one considers how long a building society investment of £100 would take to double, one can appreciate why so many people are turning to alternative investments.

Examples of good buys can be identified in retrospect by looking through old auction catalogues. For instance Clarice Cliff plates worth £600 today made £80 ten years ago. Not everything you buy will be a bargain, but if you do purchase an object you like you also have something to view and enjoy, and not just a bank statement or share certificate.

Most collectors find their bad buys are more than compensated for by their good ones and as one learns more about a subject so the good buys increase. The secret is to amass as much information as possible about a chosen category, using books, exhibitions, booklets, old auction catalogues, as well as visiting as many museums, collections, antique fairs and auctions as possible. Do not be afraid to talk to dealers or auctioneers about a particular field as it is in their interest to encourage new disciples to the fold. As one of the fastest changing and most exciting art markets, there is always something new to be learnt. Finally, take the plunge and experience how infectious collecting can be once started.

Mark Wilkinson

A Clarice Cliff Bizarre 'Crocus' pattern individual tea set, with 7 pieces, 1935.
£300–400 *GC*

A Clarice Cliff Bizarre 'Crocus' pattern vase. **£250–350** *HAR*

A Newport Pottery Clarice Cliff plaque, painted and moulded with stylised flowers, 12in (33cm) diam.
£200–300 *Re*

A Clarice Cliff 'Age of Jazz' two-sided plaque, modelled as 2 girls, one in an apple green ball gown, the other dressed in orange, dancing the tango with their respective escorts, facsimile signature 'Bizarre' and factory marks, 7in (17.5cm) high.
£4,000–5,000 *P*

A Clarice Cliff Bizarre shallow dish, with everted rim, 16½in (42cm) diam.
£300–350 *Bea*

A Clarice Cliff wall mask, printed marks, 7in (17.5cm) high.
£200–250 *CSK*

l. A Clarice Cliff breakfast set.
£100–120 *JAD*

A Clarice Cliff pottery tête-à-tête.
£200–400 *CDC*

Production Dates of Major Designs and Ranges

Design	
Original Bizarre	1928–30
Crocus	1928–39
Latona Range	1929–32
Inspiration	1929–32
Melon	1930–32
Trees and House	1930–32
Delecia Range	1930–33
Applique Range	1930–33
Autumn	1931–33
Summerhouse	1931–32
House and Bridge	1931–32
Gibraltar	1931–32
Chintz	1932–33
Secrets	1933–36
Coral Firs	1933–38
My Garden	1934–39
Rhodanthe	1934–38
Forest Glen	1935–37

A Clarice Cliff wall mask, printed marks, 7in (17.5cm) high.
£200–250 *CSK*

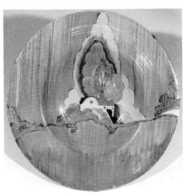

A Wilkinson Bizarre charger, by Clarice Cliff, with a dished centre, 18in (46cm) diam.
£2,000–3,000 *DSH*

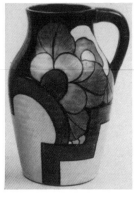

A Clarice Cliff Bizarre 'Lotus' jug, decorated in the Dahlia pattern, in black, green, pink, blue and yellow on a matt ground, rubber stamp mark, painted 'Latona', 12in (30cm) high.
£1,500–2,000 *CSK*

A Clarice Cliff Bizarre seven-piece cabaret set, with yellow and green geometric decoration on a cream ground, printed marks 'Bizarre by Clarice Cliff, Wilkinson Ltd., England', c1930.
£600–800 *C*

A Clarice Cliff mug, designed by Laura Knight, with female heads and an abstract design in orange, brown, blue and black on a cream ground, many printed marks including 'Bizarre by Clarice Cliff, Wilkinson Ltd.', and artist's facsimile signature, c1930, 6½in (16.5cm) high.
£300–400 *C*

l. A Clarice Cliff Bizarre 'Inspiration' vase, painted in the 'Blue Pines' design with dark blue and russet, printed marks, 10in (25cm) high.
£900–1,000 *CSK*

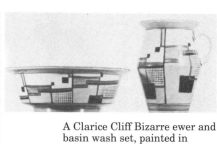

A Clarice Cliff Bizarre 'Lotus' twin-handled vase, painted in orange, black rust red and mauve, printed factory marks, 'Newport Pottery', 12in (30.5cm) high.
£500–800 *P*

A Clarice Cliff Bizarre 'Lotus' vase, with a geometric band between wide yellow and iron red bands, printed and impressed marks and 'Newport', late 1930s, 12in (30.5cm) high.
£500–800 *SS*

A Clarice Cliff Bizarre ewer and basin wash set, painted in strong bright colours, detailed with black, printed marks, ewer 10in (25cm) high, basin 15in (38cm) diam.
£2,000–3,000 *CSK*

A Clarice Cliff jar and cover, painted in blue, purple, yellow, pink, grey and black, with a vorticist pattern, black printed marks and facsimile signature, 1930s, 10in (24.5cm) high.
£800–1,200 *SS*

A Newport Pottery Clarice Cliff 'Applique' teapot and cover, 6in (15cm) high. **£1,000–1,500** *Re*

A Newport Pottery Clarice Cliff Bizarre 'Sunray' pattern confiture and cover of plain cylindrical form, printed mark in black, 3in (7.5cm) high.
£300–350 *HSS*

A Clarice Cliff breakfast set for one, painted in the 'Pansy Delecia' design with blue, pink and lilac flowerheads above a yellow, green and brown running glaze, printed marks, c1931, teapot 4½in (11.5cm) high.
£1,000–1,500 *C*

A Clarice Cliff tea-for-two set, painted with the 'Canterbury Bell' design, with a spray of orange flowers before green foliage with coloured rim borders, printed marks, c1930, teapot 4⅛in (11.6cm) high.
£700–900 *C*

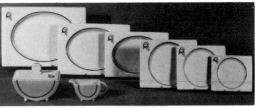

A Clarice Cliff 'Sunshine' tea-for-two service, painted with hollyhocks on a cream ground within yellow and russet borders, c1934, teapot 5in (12cm) high.
600–900 *C*

A Clarice Cliff 'Biarritz' 24-piece dinner service, deocrated in 'Modern' design, with a black printed stylised scroll and painted silver borders, printed marks, 1932. **£1,000–1,300** *C*

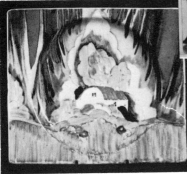

A 'Biarritz' plate, painted with a cottage in stylised garden and with tall trees before a streaked amber, grey and brown sky, printed marks, c1933, 9in (23cm) wide.
£300–400 *C*

A Bizarre 'Biarritz' pottery plate, by Clarice Cliff, painted in the 'Autumn' pattern, printed marks, 9in (23cm) wide
£300–500 *CSK*

A Bizarre 'Biarritz' pottery plate, by Clarice Cliff, printed marks, 9in (23cm) wide.
£300–400 *CSK*

A Clarice Cliff 23-piece honeyglaze tea service, painted in moss green with bright orange handles outlined in black, printed marks, c1938, teapot 4½in (11.1cm) high.
£1,000–1,500 *C*

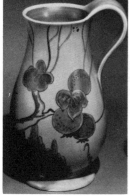

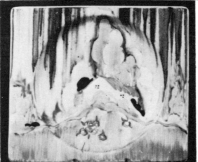

A Clarice Cliff oviform ewer, painted in the 'Oriental' design, on a turquoise ground, printed marks, star crack, 11in (27.5cm) high.
£80–120 *C*

A 'Biarritz' plate, painted with a cottage in stylised garden before a streaked amber, grey and brown sky, printed marks, c1933, 9in (22.9cm) wide.
£300–400 *C*

'Biarritz' refers to the rectangular shaped design.

A Clarice Cliff coffee service for 6, painted with striped borders of yellow, russet and black, 1933, coffee pot 7½in (18.8cm).
£600–700 *C*

A Clarice Cliff Bizarre vase, Wilkinson's Shape No. 370, with hand painted coloured design, 6in (15cm) high.
£600–900 *CDC*

A Newport Pottery Clarice Cliff Bizarre 'Patina' vase, 10in (25cm) high.
£300–500 *CDC*

A Clarice Cliff Bizarre vase, painted with orange fruit and purple, blue and green leaves between orange rim and foot borders, printed marks, moulded '370', 6in (15cm) high.
£800–1,200 *L*

A Clarice Cliff globular vase, painted with the 'Summerhouse' design, 6in (15cm) high.
£1,500–2,000 *Bea*

r. A Clarice Cliff Bizzare 'Fantasque' Lotus vase, painted with red, orange and yellow leaves in a coloured landscape, printed marks, 12in (30.5cm) high.
£1,500–2,000 *CSK*

l. A Clarice Cliff jam pot, decorated with pine trees.
£100–150 *BEV*

A Clarice Cliff 'Fantasque' coffee set, painted in orange, black and green, against a cream ground, printed factory marks and facsimile signature.
£1,000–1,500 *P*

A Clarice Cliff Bizarre one-person tea service, painted in green and black, with sponged green handles, comprising: teapot and cover, milk jug, sugar bowl, teacup and saucer, all with printed marks.
£250–300 *CSK*

l. A Clarice Cliff Lotus vase, painted in bright colours, with the 'Summerhouse' pattern, printed facsimile signature and 'Bizarre, Newport' marks, 9½in (24cm) high.
£300–400 *P*

r. A Clarice Cliff Bizarre jug, hand painted with 'Crocus' pattern, 3½in (9cm) high.
£50–80 *HM*

l. A Clarice Cliff Bizarre jug and bowl, hand painted with 'Crocus' pattern, 3in (7.5cm) diam.
£30–50 *HM*

A Clarice Cliff Fantasque plate, painted in black, orange, yellow, red and green, stamped marks, 1931, 9in (22.5cm) diam.
£300–500 *C*

A Clarice Cliff Fantasque ginger jar and cover, painted with cottages, printed marks 1932, 8in (20cm) high
£1,200–1,800 *C*

Four Clarice Cliff Fantasque octagonal plates, painted in the 'Secrets' pattern with cottages on a hillside, in a coastal landscape, printed marks, 1931.
£250–300 *C*

A Fantasque conical bowl, on 4 flange feet, painted in pure colours with 'Windbells' pattern, with stylised trees and harebells, printed marks, hair crack to rim, 1933, 9in (23.3cm) diam.
£600–800 *C*

A Clarice Cliff plate, painted with trees and flowerheads, printed marks, 9in (23cm.) wide.
£300–400 *C*

A Clarice Cliff Bizarre Fantasque Viking Longboat centrepiece, painted with 'Gibraltar' pattern in pink, blue, green, yellow and purple, with separate flower holder, printed marks, 15½in (40cm) wide.
£800–1,200 *CSK*

A Clarice Cliff coffee set, in orange, yellow, green, brown and blue comprising: coffee pot, cream jug, sugar bowl and 6 cups and saucers, printed marks, 1936.
£600–700 *CSK*

A Clarice Cliff Sungleam handled pitcher, decorated with yellow and orange 'Crocus' pattern, shape No. 634, 7in (18cm) high.
£300–350 *RIC*

A Clarice Cliff Bizarre Fantasque Lotus vase, painted in red, yellow, green and black, the neck painted orange, printed marks, 11½in (29.5cm) high
£1,000–1,500 *CSK.*

Two Clarice Cliff 'Crayon' plates, painted in pastel colours, printed marks, 1934, 9½in (24cm) diam.
£200–400 *C*

A Clarice Cliff coffee service for 6, on a tray, painted in orange, yellow and brown, printed marks, chips to one saucer, 1935, teapot 7½in (19cm) high.
£1,000–1,500 *C*

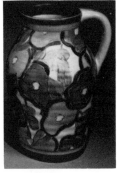

A Clarice Cliff Fantasque single handled Isis vase, painted with coloured foliage, printed marks, 1932, 9½in (24cm) high.
£800–900 *C*

A Clarice Cliff Lotus jug, decorated with 'Alpine' pattern, c1932, 12in (30.5cm) high. **£1,000–1,500** *AOS*

A Clarice Cliff cylindrical vase, decorated in geometrical pattern, 6in (15cm) high. **£325–375** *RIC*

A Clarice Cliff Dover shape jardinière, with 'Canterbury Bells' pattern, 8in (20cm) high. **£380–425** *RIC*

A Clarice Cliff ribbed vase, in 'Poplar' pattern, 7in (18cm) high. **£700–750** *RIC*

A Clarice Cliff vase, decorated with 'Alpine' pattern, c1932, 7in (18cm) high. **£220–270** *AOS*

A Clarice Cliff Inspiration floral vase, decorated with flowers in typical underglaze shades of blue, pink and buff heightened in orange and green enamel, printed mark, c1931, 6in (16cm) high. **£680–780** *S(S)*

A Clarice Cliff Tulip shape vase, No. 583, 5½in (14cm) high. **£300–350** *ADC*

A Clarice Cliff Bizarre jug, in 'Cottage' pattern, 6½in (16.5cm) high. **£150–200** *PC*

A Clarice Cliff Fantasque two-handled vase, 11½in (29.5cm) high. **£800–1,200** *Bea*

A Clarice Cliff fish group, 10in (25cm) wide. **£200–400** *ADC*

l. A Clarice Cliff Lotus vase, Patina design, painted in green, brown, orange and yellow, against a random slip textured ground of pink and honey, printed title, facsimile signature, 'Newport' and 'Provisional Patent No. 23385', 10in (25cm) high. **£400–600** *P*

A Clarice Cliff pottery vase, 16½in (42cm) high. **£350–400** *Bea*

A Clarice Cliff posy bowl, 8in (20cm) diam.
£90–120 *BEV*

A Clarice Cliff Bizarre part dinner
service, with 'Kew' pattern of a
red-roofed pagoda in parkland
scenery, comprising: 3 tureens and
2 covers, 3 sauceboats and stand,
6 grapefruit dishes and 8 stands,
5 meat dishes, 12 dinner plates,
8 dessert plates, and 7 small plates,
some damage. **£700–900** *Bea*

A Clarice Cliff part coffee service, painted in orange,
grey and black enamels, one saucer missing.
£2,000–3,000 *Bea*

A Clarice Cliff
Bizarre sugar
sifter, painted
with trees and
houses on a
mottled brown
ground, 5½in
(14.5cm).high.
£400–600 *Bea*

r. A Clarice Cliff
jam pot.
£75–100 *BEV*

A Clarice Cliff Crocus pattern 22-piece
matched part tea service. **£750–850** *SWO*

A Clarice Cliff Fantasque bowl,
painted with orange, red, black, green
and yellow, Farmhouse design, No.441,
printed 'F.B.F.S.N.P.' marks, c1930,
8in (20cm) diam. **£500–600** *MN*

A Clarice Cliff Bizarre muffineer set, decorated to
a design by Dame Laura Knight, of stylised head
and scroll motifs, painted in paink, brown,
orange, turquoise andblack, comprising: a salt
and pepper shaker, and a mustard pot and cover,
slight firing crack to salt, printed marks and
facsimile signature.
£600–700 *CSK*

A Clarice Cliff breakfast set, decorated with 'Secrets' pattern. **£600–900** *JAD*

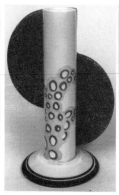

A Clarice Cliff vase, Shape 464, 8in (20cm) high. **£300–500** *JAD*

A Clarice Cliff Fantasque coffee service, painted in 'Summerhouse' pattern in red, yellow, green, black and blue, comprising: a coffee pot and cover, milk jug, sugar bowl and 6 cups and saucers, minor chips, stamped marks 'Fantasque Bizarre by Clarice Cliff, Newport Pottery, England', coffee pot 8in (20cm) high. **£1,600–1,800** *C*

A Clarice Cliff Bizarre tea service, painted with concentric light and dark brown rings on a cream ground, and a 'Crocus' pattern preserve jar and cover, some damage. **£170–200** *Bea*

A Clarice Cliff Bizarre Latona vase, boldly painted in blue with stylised pink, purple, blue and green flowers in panels, 12in (30cm) high. **£800–1,000** *OT*

A Clarice Cliff Bizarre pottery coffee service, each piece boldly painted in colours. **£350–400** *Bea*

A Clarice Cliff Fantasque vase, boldly painted in colours, 7½in (19cm) high. **£600–900** *Bea*

A pair of Clarice Cliff bookends, decorated with 'Crocus' pattern, 6½in (16cm) high. **£300–400** *Bea*

A Clarice Cliff Bizarre Lotus jug, painted in bright enamel colours, 11in (28.5cm) high. **£250–300** *Bea*

A Clarice Cliff Fantasque Lotus jug, boldly painted in bright enamel colours, 11½in (29cm) high. **£700–900** *Bea*

A Clarice Cliff Delecia jug. **£400–450** *HP*

l. A Clarice Cliff wall pocket, in the form of 2 budgerigars, painted in green, blue and yellow, 9in (23cm) high. **£70–100** *OT*

A Clarice Cliff Bizarre biscuit barrel, boldly painted in yellow and green against a blue and orange ground, with a wicker handle, 6½in (16.5cm) high. **£200–400** *OT*

A Clarice Cliff 'Blue Autumn' pattern coffee pot, with sinuous tree painted in blue, green and yellow above red grass, a cottage half hidden by purple cottages on the reverse, printed 'Fantasque, Bizarre, Clarice Cliff', 7½in (19cm) high.
£200–300 *Bon*

A complete set of Clarice Cliff Midwinter limited edition reproductions, comprising: 6 conical sugar sifters in 'Pastel Autumn', 'Pastel Melon', 'Crocus', 'Rudyard', 'House and Bridge' and 'Red Roof Cottage' patterns, a 'Summerhouse' wall plaque, an Umbrellas and Rain conical bowl and a Honolulu baluster vase, all in original boxes, printed factory marks.
£2,200–2,700 *CSK*

r. A Newport Pottery Clarice Cliff Bizarre pattern bowl, decorated with geometric shapes in shades of blue, green and mauve enclosing 2 leafy branches, printed mark in black, 9½in (24cm) diam.
£150–250 *HSS*

l. A Clarice Cliff Bizarre vase, painted in Rhodanthe design, oviform on ribbed foot, printed marks, 8in (20cm) high.
£300–350 *Bon*

r. An Applique Bizarre baluster vase, in the 'Blue Lugano' pattern, painted in colours, printed and painted marks, 12in (31cm) high.
£8,000–9,000 *CSK*

l. A Clarice Cliff Isis vase, in the 'Lumberlost' pattern, having red and white floral clusters with brown and green bushes nearby, under a canopy of red flowering trees, factory marks and facsimile signature to base, 10in (24.5cm) high.
£350–400 *P*

Three Clarice Cliff coasters, 'Delecia Pansy', 'Cabbage Flower' and 'Orange Roof Cottage' patterns, and 2 ashtrays in 'Rhodanthe' and 'Aurea' patterns, painted in colours, printed factory marks.
£300–400 *CSK*

A Clarice Cliff Bizarre 'Age of Jazz' figural group, modelled as a two-dimensional dancing couple, he in black tie and she in a bright green gown with red, yellow and black decoration, raised on a stepped rectangular base, factory marks and facsimile signature to base, 7in (18cm) high.
£4,000–5,000 *P*

'Age of Jazz' figures like this dancing couple are much sought after. These have a two-dimensional effect but are in fact freestanding plaques.

A Clarice Cliff Applique Bizarre pattern plate, Eden design, painted in colours with yellow, red and black banding, lithograph mark, 9in (23cm) diam.
£2,700–3,200 *CSK*

This pattern is previously unrecorded in the Applique range.

A Clarice Cliff Lotus 'Geometric' pattern jug, the ribbed tapering cylindrical body painted with a band of orange, blue and yellow triangular motifs, between orange and green bands, gilt printed mark, 11½in (29cm) high.
£600–700 *Bon*

A Clarice Cliff Bizarre cat, depicted with a cheerful countenance, painted orange with black spots and sporting a green bow tie, printed factory mark and facsimile signature, 6in (15cm) high.
£500–600 *P*

A Clarice Cliff 'Geometric' pattern comport, painted with a central star motif supporting 4 segmented triangles, in blue, yellow, red, green and purple on a cream ground, printed marks, 7in (18cm) diam.
£150–200 *Bon*

A Clarice Cliff Lotus jug, decorated with 'Geometric' pattern with green, blue and orange triangular motifs, between orange and green bands, black printed factory mark, 11½in (29cm) high.
£750–800 *Bon*

l. A Newport Pottery Clarice Cliff Bizarre Stamford shape part tea service, each piece painted with a small rectangular panel enclosing cottage with orange roof, yellow door and window among rolling hills with poplars beyond, on a cream ground within a wide green band, comprising: teapot and cover, tea plate, sugar basin, milk jug and conical tea cup with solid triangular handle, printed mark in black, inscribed '5954' in brown, damaged.
£250–300 *HSS*

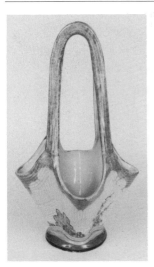

A Clarice Cliff basket, decorated with 'Fragrance' pattern, 13in (33cm) high.
£350–450 *AOS*

A Clarice Cliff cup and saucer, decorated in 'Football' pattern, c1929.
£140–190 *AOS*

A Clarice Cliff Melon bowl, 8in (20cm) diam.
£200–250 *AOS*

l. Two Clarice Cliff grapefruit dishes, Daffodil shape, 'Rainbow' pattern, 6½in (17cm) wide.
£65–75 each *ADC*

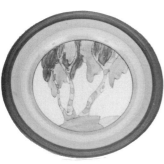

A Clarice Cliff plate, decorated with 'Rudyard' pattern, 9in (23cm) diam.
£325–375 *RIC*

A Clarice Cliff Chloris bowl, 9in (23cm) diam.
£100–150 *AOS*

A Clarice Cliff octagonal bowl, decorated with 'Woodland' pattern, 9in (23cm) diam.
£200–300 *ADC*

l. A Clarice Cliff plate, decorated in the 'Honolulu' pattern, painted in colours with green and black striped rim, printed factory marks, 9in (23cm) diam.
£250–300 *CSK*

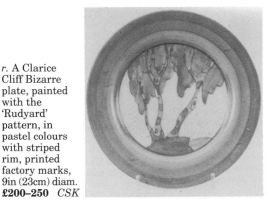

r. A Clarice Cliff Bizarre plate, painted with the 'Rudyard' pattern, in pastel colours with striped rim, printed factory marks, 9in (23cm) diam.
£200–250 *CSK*

A Newport Pottery Clarice Cliff Bizarre globular shaped vase, decorated with a landscape, castle, flowers and leaves, banded, impressed 'No. 370', 6in (15cm) diam.
£600–900 *L&E*

A Clarice Cliff Bizarre Café au Lait vase, the brown speckled ground decorated with 'Red Roofs' pattern, shape No. 358, printed marks, c1931, 8in (20cm) high.
£500–800 *S(S)*

A Clarice Cliff "Umbrellas and Rain' vase, shape no. 342, 8in (20cm) high.
£750–800 *ADC*

A Newport Pottery Clarice Cliff Latona vase, the globular body with a graduated ringed neck, painted with blue, pink, green, yellow and black flowers above a yellow band, black printed factory mark, c1930, 8in (20cm) high.
£400–600 *S(S)*

A Clarice Cliff vase, shape No. 342, decorated with 'Flora' pattern, 7½in (19cm) high.
£600–850 *AOS*

A Clarice Cliff 'Geometric' pattern two-handled Lotus vase, painted with a band of shapes within rectangular panels, in purple, orange, brown and yellow between orange bands, black printed factory mark, c1930, 11in (28cm) high.
£500–600 *S(S)*

A Clarice Cliff 'Geometric' pattern vase, shape No. 355, 8in (20cm) high.
£300–500 *AOS*

A Newport Pottery Clarice Cliff Latona candlestick, painted with stylised blue, pink, green, yellow and black flowers, with a yellow band below, black printed factory mark, remains of paper label, c1930, 8in (20cm) high.
£200–300 *S(S)*

A Clarice Cliff sabot, c1932.
£165–225 *AOS*

A Clarice Cliff Bizarre bowl, hand painted with 'Crocus' pattern, 9in (23cm) diam.
£80–100 *ADC*

A pair of Clarice Cliff vases, shape No. 451, in the 'Oranges and Lemons' pattern, on a white ground, 8in (20cm) high.
£1,000–1,500 P

l. A Clarice Cliff Bizarre plate, painted with the 'Delecia Pansy' pattern, 9in (23cm) diam.
£200–250 Bea

A Clarice Cliff Bizarre single handled jug, painted with 'Lightning' pattern in black, blue and purple, red, orange and yellow, printed factory marks and facsimile signature to base, 10in (25cm) high.
£2,500–3,000 P

A Clarice Cliff Bizarre Fantasque part tea set, decorated in the 'Pastel Autumn' pattern, painted in colours, comprising: milk jug, 5 cups and 6 saucers, 6 tea plates, and a sandwich plate, slight damage, lithograph marks.
£1,200–1,500 CSK

A Newport Pottery Clarice Cliff Berries part coffee service, the coffee pot painted with orange and red berries with blue and purple foliage, comprising: coffee pot and cover, 6 coffee mugs, 5 saucers, milk jug and sugar bowl, minor surface scratching, printed mark 'Fantasque', hand painted, c1930, pot 6½in (16.5cm) high.
£1,000–1,500 S(C)

l. A Latona Bizarre wall plaque, decorated in the 'Dahlia' pattern, painted in colours, printed and painted marks, 13in (33cm) diam.
£1,500–2,000 CSK

A Clarice Cliff Fantasque sandwich set, decorated in the 'Geometric Flowers' pattern, painted in colours, some damage, gilt rubber stamp marks, oblong plate 11½in (29cm) wide.
£750–1,000 CSK

A plate, designed by Ernest Proctor for Clarice Cliff, with a bride and groom on horseback, in pale green with silver lustre, 9in (23cm) diam.
£100–200 *BEV*

A Clarice Cliff Fantasque charger, decorated with 'Broth' pattern, with coloured star-like motifs on a bubble ground within an orange border, 17in (43.5cm) diam.
£1,500–2,000 *GSP*

A Clarice Cliff single-handled Isis jug, painted with the 'Forest Glen' pattern, in bright, warm enamel colours, 10in (25cm) high.
£900–1,200 *Bea*

l. A Clarice Cliff Fantasque sandwich plate, decorated in the seven-colour version of the 'Trees and House' pattern, in orange, yellow, blue, purple, green, rust and brown, minor wear, rubber stamp mark, 11½in (29cm) wide.
£450–500 *CSK*

l. A charger decorated to a design by Sir Frank Brangwyn, printed and painted in colours with a procession of figures of various nationalities in a tropical garden, hand painted inscription, 17in (43.5cm) diam.
£2,000–3,000 *CSK*

Adapted from the Empire panels originally intended for the Palace of Westminster, but eventually erected within the now Brangwyn Halls, Swansea, South Wales.

A Clarice Cliff Bizarre Fantasque two-handled Lotus jug, decorated with 'Football' pattern, in shades orange, yellow, blue, purple, green and black, printed mark, 11¼in (29cm) high.
£1,500–2,000 *HSS*

A pair of Clarice Cliff candlesticks, 3½in (9cm) high.
£150–170 *SAI*

A Fantasque Bizarre bon bon set, shape No. 471, decorated in the 'Windbells' pattern of blue foliate tree in stylised garden, painted in green, orange, yellow and blue, comprising: oval dish with overhead handle and 6 triangular dishes, minor wear, lithograph mark.
£500–800 *CSK*

A Clarice Cliff cruet, decorated in 'Orange Chintz' pattern, 3½in (9cm) high.
£200–220 *BEC*

A Clarice Cliff Bizarre single handled Lotus vase, painted in russet, grey and shades of green with white blossoms, printed marks, 12in (30cm) high.
£600–800 *CSK*

r. A Clarice Cliff Bizarre part tea service, with blue, orange and yellow flowers with green leaves, comprising a D-shaped teapot and cover, a cream jug and a sugar bowl, all with printed marks.
£200–400 *CSK*

A Clarice Cliff Bizarre jug and basin set, painted in bright red, green and blue stylised flowering plants, outlined in black and having yellow, blue and red banding, factory marks, 8in (19.5cm) high.
£800–1,000 *P*

A Clarice Cliff Original Bizarre jardinière, painted with a band of yellow and mauve diamond shapes outlined in green on a blue ground, printed marks, 9½in (24cm) high.
£300–350 *CSK*

A Clarice Cliff Bizarre Fantasque tea service, painted in 'Summerhouse' pattern in red, black and yellow, comprising a teapot, milk jug, sugar caster, slop bowl, a biscuit barrel, one cake plate, 6 tea cups and saucers, 6 side plates, all with printed marks.
£2,200–2,600 *CSK*

A Clarice Cliff Bizarre Inspiration two-handled vase, painted in the 'Persian' pattern, in turquoise, blue and pink, printed marks, 11½in (29cm) high.
£2,000–3,000 *CSK*

A Clarice Cliff Fantasque pottery jardinière, painted with the 'Melon' pattern, the lower body orange, 8in (20cm) diam. **£600–900** *P*

A Clarice Cliff Bizarre Sgraffito vase, painted in black, royal blue, silver and pale blue, printed mark 'Newport', painted '5995 Sgraffito', 9in (23cm) high.
£450–500 *P*

A Clarice Cliff oviform vase, 'Persian' pattern, painted in reds, blues, green and brown dissected by a central foliate band, signed 'Persian by Clarice Cliff Newport Pottery Burslem', 8in (20cm).
£130–200 *P*

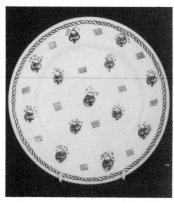

A Clarice Cliff plate, by Graham Sutherland, impressed mark, 1934, 9in (23cm) diam.
£100–150 *AOS*

A Clarice Cliff Athens shape jug, with 'Sliced Fruit' pattern, 8in (20cm) high.
£200–245 *RIC*

A Clarice Cliff plate, with Laura Knight design, from the Artists in Industry range, 9in (23cm) diam.
£550–750 *RIC*

A Clarice Cliff jug, in 'Gibraltar' pattern, 4in (10cm) high.
£500–550 *ADC*

A Newport Pottery Clarice Cliff Bizarre Inspiration 'Persian' pattern charger, decorated with quatrefoil flowerhead within a border of scrolls in mottled blue, green, apricot and lilac glazes, inscribed in brown, 13in (34cm) diam.
£500–700 *HSS*

A set of 3 graduated Clarice Cliff meat plates, each designed by Ernest Proctor and painted in pink, green, black and blue with abstract waves and coils, printed and impressed marks, 1934, largest 18½in (47cm) wide.
£600–700 *S(S)*

A Newport Pottery Clarice Cliff Fantasque Lotus jug, decorated with 'Melon' pattern, printed mark and facsimile signature in black, 11½in (29cm) high.
£550–650 *HSS*

A Clarice Cliff Athens shape 'Umbrellas and Rain' teapot, 7in (18cm) high.
£425–475 *RIC*

A Clarice Cliff Oceanic jug, with 'Windbells' pattern, 6in (15cm) high.
£225–275 *RIC*

A Clarice Cliff Athens shape teapot, decorated with 'Berries' pattern, 4½in (11cm) high.
£300–350 *ADC*

A Clarice Cliff Lotus shape jug, decorated with 'Goldstone' pattern, 6½in (16cm) high.
£120–140 *GAK*

A Newport Pottery Clarice Cliff teapot in the form of a teepee, by Betty Silvester, moulded with moss and leaves, the spout in the form of a Red Indian, the handle as a totem pole, inscribed under the base 'Greetings from Canada', 7in (18cm) high.
£600–1,000 *Bea*

l. A Clarice Cliff Fantasque Lotus jug, in orange, purple, green and blue, gilt printed on base 'Lawley's Norfolk Pottery Stoke', and 'Fantasque by Clarice Cliff', 11½in (29cm) high.
£500–800 *Bon*

A Clarice Cliff Bizarre oviform jug, painted in yellow and black, printed marks, 7in (18cm).high.
£500–800 *CSK*

A Clarice Cliff Bizarre Inspiration two-handled Isis vase, painted with bands of yellow, blue and turquoise stylised foliage outlined in brown on a turquoise ground, printed marks, 10in (25cm). high.
£3,000–3,500 *CSK*

A Clarice Cliff Bizarre part dinner service, comprising: 2 tureens and covers, a gravy boat, a pair of graduated oval dishes and 6 plates.
£250–300 *Bea*

r. A Clarice Cliff Fantasque single handed Isis vase, painted with blue, purple and orange blossoms amid foliage between yellow rim, printed marks, 9½in (24.5cm) high.
£300–350 *L*

r. A Clarice Cliff Bizarre ginger jar and cover, painted with bright colours, signed with factory marks on base, 8in (20cm) high.
£800–1,200 *P*

A Clarice Cliff Lotus shape jug, painted in bright colours, on a cream ground with coloured banded borders, printed facsimile signature, factory marks, Newport, 11½in (29cm) high.
£1,000–1,500 *P*

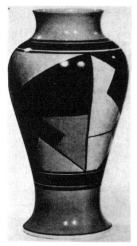

A Clarice Cliff Fantasque baluster-shaped vase, painted with bands of yellow, blue, orange and green, outlined in black between horizontal bands of orange, black, blue and green, printed marks, 16in (40.5cm) high.
£1,100–1,500 *CSK*

A Clarice Cliff Bizarre crocus pattern tea service, comprising: teapot, milk jug, sugar basin, 2 bread and butter plates, 10 cups, 12 saucers and 12 side plates.
£800–1,200 *Pea*

l. A Clarice Cliff Lotus shape jug, painted in bright colours, reserved against a cream ground with orange borders, printed facsimile signature and factory marks, Newport, 11½in (29cm) high.
£1,000–1,500 *P*

A Clarice Cliff Inspiration plate, painted with pink lilies, with black stems and black lily pads, on a green ground, black printed factory mark, 'Hand Painted, Bizarre, by Clarice Cliff, Wilkinson Ltd., England', 1931, 10in (25cm) diam.
£300–400 *S(C)*

A Clarice Cliff Inspiration vase, 'Persian' pattern, vibrant azure blue with spiral and ogee motif in turquoise, lavender and amber, signed 'Persian', printed Bizarre marks, 10in (25cm) high.
£800–1,000 *CNY*

A Clarice Cliff Fantasque plate, decorated in 'Melons' pattern, with a band of fruits in yellow and orange, with blue sections and green dots, minor damage, printed mark, 'Hand Painted, Fantasque, by Clarice Cliff, Wilkinson Ltd., England', 10in (25cm) diam.
£200–300 *S(C)*

A pair of Clarice Cliff 'Cottage' bookends, decorated in red on a green ground with a blue sky, one cracked, one chipped, black printed mark 'Clarice Cliff, Wilkinson Pottery', retailer's mark, 'Lawley's, Regent Street, late 1930s, 5½in (14cm) high.
£450–650 *S(C)*

A Clarice Cliff Bizarre single handled Isis jug, painted in 'Sliced Circle' pattern with bright colours, printed factory marks and facsimile signature, 10in (25cm) high.
£1,800–2,200 *P*

A Clarice Cliff pierced floral wall plaque, moulded in low relief with flowers, printed factory mark, 'Hand Painted, Bizarre, Newport Pottery, England, the property of Threlfalls Brewery', signed 'Clarice Cliff', c1930, 13in (33cm) diam.
£200–300 *S(C)*

A Clarice Cliff Apples Isis vase, painted with apples and grapes, in pink, orange, black, yellow and green, fitted as a lamp base, with electric fittings and shade, black printed factory mark, 'Fantasque, Hand Painted, Bizarre, by Clarice Cliff, Newport Pottery, England', c1932, 10in (25cm) high.
£900–1,200 *S(C)*

A Clarice Cliff Isis vase, boldly painted with trees in Latona glazes, 10in (25cm) high. **£470–520** *Bea*

A Clarice Cliff conical sugar sifter, decorated with pink pearls, 3in (8cm) high.
£200–250 *RIC*

A Clarice Cliff Tankard shape coffee set, decorated in 'Gay Day' pattern.
£650–750 *RIC*

A Clarice Cliff 'Solitude' pattern sugar sifter, 5½in (14cm) high.
£600–900 *RIC*

A pair of Clarice Cliff 'Autumn' design vases, 8½in (21cm) high.
£1,500–1,800 *HEW*

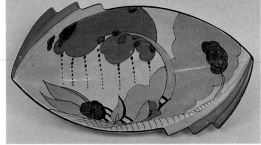

A Clarice Cliff bowl, Daffodil shape No. 475, decorated in 'Devon' pattern, 13in (33cm) long.
£650–750 *ADC*

A Clarice Cliff bowl, decorated in 'My Garden' pattern, 12in (31cm) diam.
£250–350 *ADC*

A Clarice Cliff jug, decorated in 'Orange House' pattern, 5in (13cm) high.
£425–475 *RIC*

A Clarice Cliff Isis vase, decorated in 'Woodland' design, 9½in (24cm) high.
£450–550 *RIC*

A Clarice Cliff baluster shaped vase, in 'Sliced Fruit' pattern, 15in (38cm) high.
£1,000–1,200 *RIC*

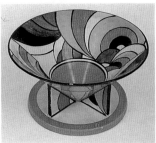

A Clarice Cliff footed bowl, c1930, 9in (23cm) diam.
£2,000–2,200 *HEW*

A Clarice Cliff Latona Red Rose stepped vase, 6in (15cm) high.
£450–550 *RIC*

A Clarice Cliff Athens shape teapot, decorated in 'Diamonds' pattern.
£450–550 *ADC*

A Clarice Cliff plate, decorated with 'Gibraltar' pattern, 9in (23cm) diam.
£600–800 *BEV*

A Clarice Cliff plate, painted with 'House and Tree' pattern, 9in (23cm) diam.
£500–700 *BEV*

A Clarice Cliff plate, painted with 'Idyll' pattern, 9in (23cm) diam.
£300–500 *BEV*

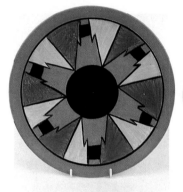

A Clarice Cliff plate, painted in 'Geometric' pattern, c1925, 10½in (26cm) diam.
£200–400 *BEV*

A Clarice Cliff plate, painted in 'Gardenia' pattern, 9½in (24cm) diam. **£400–600** *BEV*

A Clarice Cliff blue and yellow un-named plate, 9in (23cm) diam.
£200–400 *BEV*

A Clarice Cliff plate, painted with 'Orange Tree Cottage' pattern, 9in (23cm) diam.
£600–800 *BEV*

A Clarice Cliff plate, in 'Geometric' pattern, 7in (18cm) diam.
£200–300 *BEV*

A Clarice Cliff plate, painted in 'Autumn' pattern, 9in (23cm) diam.
£400–600 *BEV*

A Clarice Cliff plate, painted with 'Solitude' pattern, 9in (23cm) diam.
£400–600 *BEV*

Collecting Clarice Cliff Pottery

- Check condition carefully. Restoration is not always easy to detect.
- Look particularly at spouts and handles, check rims and bases for chipping or repainting.
- Look out for any slight variation in the colour where the pattern may have been touched up.
- Genuine Clarice Cliff reproductions do exist, but are clearly dated.
- On flatware, three circles or stilt marks around the signature where the pot stood in the kiln are signs of authenticity.

A Clarice Cliff Lotus jug, in the 'Blue W' pattern, 12in (31cm) high.
£2,500–3,500 *F*

A charger, painted by Clarice Cliff, from one of the Brangwyn panels (No. 7), designed for the House of Lords, 1925, first exhibited at Olympia 1933, 17½in (44cm) diam.
£2,000–2,500 *ARE*

A Clarice Cliff pottery biscuit barrel.
£250–350 *HCH*

A Doulton Burslem vase, by Fred Sutton, a portrait artist, c1900, 11½in (29cm) high.
£600–800 *HER*

A Royal Doulton figure of a Sealyham terrier, HN1030, 9in (23cm) wide.
£50–60 *PCh*

An Art Nouveau Gouda pottery vase, decorated in Chryso design, from Regina factory, c1920, 11½in (29cm) high.
£300–350 *OO*

A Clarice Cliff Lotus jug, in 'Applique Orange Lucerne' pattern, printed marks.
£5,500–6,000 *Bon*

A Doulton Lambeth vase, designed by Hannah Barlow and Eliza Simmons, c1891, 20in (51cm) high.
£2,200–2,500 *POW*

A Clarice Cliff castor, 'Inspiration' pattern, 5in (13cm) high.
£55–65 *PCh*

A Clarice Cliff wall plate, decorated in 'Applique Idyll' pattern, c1932, 10in (25cm) diam.
£1,400–1,600 *PC*

A Clarice Cliff candlestick, decorated in 'Applique Lugano' pattern, c1930, 8in (20cm) high.
£2,000–2,200 *PC*

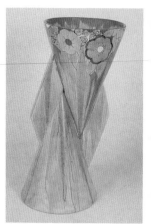

A Clarice Cliff Yo Yo vase, decorated with 'Delecia Lydiat' pattern, 18in (45.5cm) high.
£6,000–6,500 *PC*

A Clarice Cliff Sign of the Zodiac, 'Aquarius', 6in (15cm) wide.
£120–180 *RIC*

A Clarice Cliff Conical jug, decorated with 'Applique Lugano' pattern, c1930, 7in (17.5cm) high.
£2,500–3,000 *PC*

A Clarice Cliff Athens jug, decorated with 'Applique Palermo' pattern, c1930, 7in (17.5cm) high.
£2,200–2,500 *PC*

A Clarice Cliff vase, Shape 341, decorated with 'Applique Blossom' pattern, c1932, 5½in (14cm) high.
£2,500–2,750 *PC*

A Clarice Cliff vase, Shape 358, decorated with 'Applique Avignon' pattern, c1930, 8in (20cm) high.
£6,000–7,000 *PC*

A Clarice Cliff Lotus jug, decorated with 'Diamonds' pattern, 12in (30.5cm) high.
£1,200–1,800 *RIC*

A Clarice Cliff plate, decorated with 'Tulip' pattern, 9in (22.5cm) diam.
£150–250 *RIC*

A Clarice Cliff vase, Shape 264, 'Applique Caravan' pattern, c1930, 8in (20cm) high.
£3,000–3,400 *PC*

A fifteen-piece ceramic coffee set, painted mark by Clarice Cliff, Wilkinson Ltd., England, coffee pot 6½in (16.5cm) high.
£1,800–2,200 *C*

A selection of Clarice Cliff pottery.
£450–5,000 each *P*

A Clarice Cliff Bizarre charger, factory marks, 16½in (42cm) diam.
£1,500–2,000 *P*

A Clarice Cliff Fantasque Farmhouse vase, printed 'F.B.', 'F.S.', and 'N.P.' marks, c1930, 16½in (42cm) high.
£4,000–4,500 *MN*

l. A Clarice Cliff Bizarre jardinière, Applique pattern, printed Newport Pottery, marked, 7½in (19cm) high.
£4,000–4,500 *MN*

A vase, by Carter Stabler Adams, 14in (35.5cm) high.
£250–300 *AW*

A sugar bowl, designed by Susie Cooper, by A. E. Gray & Co. Ltd., marked. **£90–120** *AW*

A Moorcroft 'Anemone' design lustre vase, made for Liberty, c1909, 8in (20cm) high.
£800–1,200 *LIO*

A Moorcroft flambé squat vase, 'Leaf and Berry' design, c1932, 6in (15cm) high.
£550–650 *LIO*

A Moorcroft vase, 'Baraware' design, made for Liberty, restored, c1908, 3½in (9cm) high.
£250–350 *LIO*

A Moorcroft saltglaze vase, 'Fish' design, dated '1931', 14in (36cm) high.
£2,200–3,200 *LIO*

A Moorcroft MacIntyre vase, salmon and green 'Carnation' design, c1898, 12in (31cm) high.
£1,000–1,500 *LIO*

A Walter Moorcroft vase, yellow 'Hibiscus' design, c1960, 6in (15cm) high.
£130–170 *LIO*

A Moorcroft flambé vase, 'Waratah' design, 1939, 17in (43cm) high.
£7,000–9,000 *LIO*

A Moorcroft vase, matt glaze ochre 'Leaf and Berry' design, c1936, 4in (10cm) high.
£350–450 *LIO*

A Minton stick stand, 23in (58cm) high.
£400–500 *CAR*

A Moorcroft MacIntyre vase, Florian Ware 'Blue Tree' design, c1902.
£1,500–2,500 *LIO*

A Moorcroft MacIntyre vase, 'Pansy' design, restored, c1912, 10½in (26cm) high.
£400–600 *LIO*

A pair of floral skittle vases, inscribed 'W. Moorcroft MacIntyre Burslem', 12in (30.5cm) high.
£2,000–2,500 *W*

A Moorcroft oviform jardinière, with inverted rim, decorated with bands of peacock feathers, restored, signed in green, 8in (20cm) high.
£900–1,200 *CSK*

A Moorcroft flambé vase, signed, 10in (25cm) high.
£650–750 *CSK*

A Moorcroft vase, impressed and signed.
£200–250 *CSK*

A Moorcroft twin-handled pedestal fruit bowl, the interior decorated with pansies, restored, signed, 8in (20cm) diam.
£250–300 *CSK*

A William Moorcroft vase, banded 'Pomegranate' design, c1928, 17in (43cm) high.
£2,000–2,500 *RUM*

A Moorcroft jardinière, decorated with a band of foliage, damaged, signed, 8in (20cm) diam.
£400–500 *CSK*

A Moorcroft vase, decorated in 'Moonlit Blue' pattern, signed in blue, impressed factory mark, 10in (25cm) high.
£900–1,200 *CSK*

A Moorcroft bowl, on a Tudric pewter foot, the interior decorated with pansies, the exterior with buds and foliage, stamped marks, 8in (20cm) diam.
£250–300 *CSK*

A Moorcroft vase, restored, marked, 12in (31cm) high.
£900–1,200 *CSK*

A Moorcroft bowl in decorated in 'Claremont' pattern, Liberty mark, signed, 10in (25cm) diam.
£650–750 *CSK*

A Walter Moorcroft vase, decorated with 'African Lily' design, c1955, 12in (31cm) high.
£350–450 *RUM*

A Moorcroft vase, with everted rim, impressed factory mark, signed in blue, 10in (25cm) high.
£500–600 *CSK*

A Walter Moorcroft vase, 'Clematis' design, c1955, 5in (13cm) high.
£200–300 *RUM*

A pair of Moorcroft vases, 'Pomegranate' pattern, signed, factory mark, 10½in (26cm) high.
£450–550 *CSK*

A Moorcroft MacIntyre jardinière, marked.
£800–900 *CSK*

r. A Moorcroft bowl, decorated inside and outside, factory mark, signed, 8in (20cm) diam.
£250–300 *CSK*

A Foley Intarsio bowl, decorated with a Shakespeare scene, c1900, 11½in (29cm) diam.
£500–600 *AJ*

A Clarice Cliff bowl, decorated with 'Kandina' pattern, 8in (20cm) diam.
£450–500 *BEV*

A Shelley lustre bowl, signed by Walter Slater, c1920, 7in (18cm) high.
£150–200 *AJ*

A Bernard Moore bowl, initialled by Cicely Jackson, 9in (23cm) diam.
£250–300 *BLO*

An Austrian amphora, 9in (23cm) high.
£180–200 *BLO*

An Ault Grotesque jug, 7in (17.5cm) high.
£200–250 *BLO*

A Clarice Cliff Lotus jug, with 'Inspiration Caprice' pattern, rim cracked, 12in (30.5cm).
£1,000–1,200 *SWO*

A porcelain Limousine water jug, 8in (20cm) high.
£80–100 *BLO*

A Foley Intarsio jardinière, decorated in the 'Goose' pattern, c1900, 4½in (11cm) high.
£300–400 *AJ*

l. A Foley Intarsio jardinière on stand, by Frederick Rhead.
£2,000–2,500 *PC*

A Clarice Cliff step jardinière, 3½in (8.5cm) high.
£200–250 *BEV*

A pair of Liberty & Co. stoneware jardinières, designed by Archibald Knox, 16in (41cm) high.
£2,000–3,000 *C*

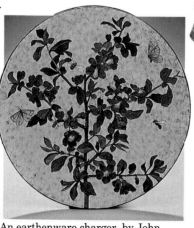

An earthenware charger, by John Bennett, signed, 1878, 14½in (37cm) diam.
£3,000–3,500 *CNY*

A Minton blank, painted by an amateur artist, exhibited in 1883, 10in (25cm) diam. **£100–150** *BLO*

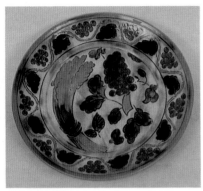

A Royal Doulton wall plaque, by
Frank Brangwyn, in 'Harvest' pattern,
decorated by hand, 13in (33cm) diam.
£250–350 *ADC*

A Martin Brothers salt
glazed porcelain Love
Birds group, dated '1902'.
£4,600–5,000 *S(NY)*

A Gray's Pottery Art Deco eight-piece coffee set,
in yellow and black geometric pattern.
£200–300 *PCh*

A Royal Dux two-
handled vase,
16in (41cm) high.
£350–450 *PCh*

A Susie Cooper charger,
signed and dated '1934'.
£600–900 *CAR*

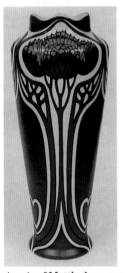

A Martin Brothers
bird and cover, c1913.
£1,500–2,500 *S*

A figure of
Bat Girl, 8½in
(21cm) high.
£350–500 *ASA*

A pair of Mettlach vases,
1904, 14⅛in (37cm) high.
£700–750 *POW*

A pair of Bermantofts
vases, by V. Kremer,
11in (28cm) high.
£1,000–1,500 *NCA*

A Bursley Ware tray, No. TL43, designed by
Charlotte Rhead, in shades of blue on grey,
9in (22.5cm) wide.
£75–85 *ADC*

A Charlotte Rhead
vase, 7in (17.5cm) high.
£100–120 *HEW*

A Royal Doulton vase,
by Frank Butler, c1906,
19in (48cm) high.
£1,000–1,250 *POW*

A Charlotte Rhead bowl, 'Rhodian' pattern, 10in (25cm) diam.
£90–100 *HEW*

An Art Deco group, by Lobel Riche, c1925, 14in (35.5cm) high.
£600–650 *POW*

An Austrian porcelain figure of a girl, by Ernst Wahliss, c1910, 17½in (44cm) high.
£900–1,200 *HOW*

A Charlotte Rhead posy bowl, 6in (15cm) diam.
£40–45 *HEW*

A Goldscheider ceramic figure, c1930, 14in (35.5cm) high.
£500–700 *ASA*

A Royal Dux porcelain female figure, Bohemian, c1910, 15½in (39cm) high.
£900–1,200 *HOW*

A pair of Katshütte figures of skiers, 11½in (29cm) high.
£600–900 *ASA*

A Royal Doulton figure, 'The Hornpipe', HN2161, 10in (25cm) high.
£300–350 *PCh*

l. A Royal Dux porcelain bust of a young woman, minor losses, impressed factory marks, c1900.
£1,500–2,000 *SNY*

An Austrian porcelain figure, c1900.
£900–1,200 *HOW*

A Rosenthal porcelain figure, depicting a snake charmer, c1920.
£350–550 *ASA*

A William de Morgan plate, 'Panthers' design, decorated on reverse, 9½in (24cm) diam. **£900–1,200** *BLO*

A Foley Intarsio tea caddy, c1900, 6in (15cm) high. **£300–400** *AJ*

An Art Deco Shelley 21-piece tea service, decorated in blue, black and silver block pattern, c1931. **£300–500** *AJ*

A Clarice Cliff 50-piece dinner service, with painted design. **£2,000–2,500** *Bea*

A Shelley Art Deco 21-piece tea service, 'Orange J' pattern, teapot missing, c1931. **£200–400** *AJ*

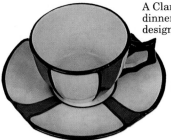

An Art Deco Quimper cup and saucer, signed, saucer 7½in (19cm) diam. **£25–30** *VH*

A Clarice Cliff tea set, 'Patina' design, comprising: milk jug, sugar bowl, cup, saucer and plate, teapot 5in (13cm) high. **£900–1,000** *BEV*

A pair of Dutch Villeroy and Boch vases, c1900. **£350–450** *BEV*

A pair of Villeroy and Boch jars, c1900, 7in (18cm) high. **£250–350** *BEV*

A Minton vase, Aesthetic influence, c1886, 12in (31.5cm) high. **£550–650** *BLO*

A Foley Intarsio vase, designed by Frederick Rhead, 9in (23cm) high. **£600–800** *PC*

r. A Moorcroft vase, 9½in (24cm) high. **£450–500** *SBA*

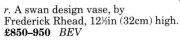

r. A swan design vase, by Frederick Rhead, 12½in (32cm) high. **£850–950** *BEV*

A Carlton Ware spill vase, decorated with an exotic bird in gilt lustre on a blue ground, 6in (15cm) high.
£80–100 *PCh*

A Foley Intarsio vase, designed by Frederick Rhead, c1900, 11in (28cm) high.
£400–500 *AJ*

A Shelley intarsio vase, designed by Walter Slater, c1912, 10in (25cm) high.
£350–400 *AJ*

A William de Morgan two-handled vase, Merton Abbey period, c1885, 41in (104cm) high.
£6,000–7,000 *POW*

An Art Nouveau vase, Rozenburg factory, The Hague, c1897, 7in (17cm) high.
£450–500 *OO*

A pair of Art Nouveau Florian Ware tapered vases, signed, early 20thC, 8in (20cm) high.
£850–900 *PCh*

A Dutch pottery jug, Arnhem factory, c1926, 10½in (26cm) high.
£200–250 *OO*

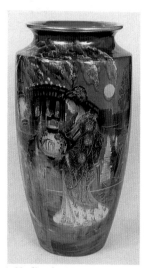

A Shelley lustre vase, signed 'Walter Slater', c1920, 15in (38cm) high.
£500–600 *AJ*

A Foley faïence trio, designed by Frederick Rhead, centrepiece 8in (20cm) high.
£550–650 *AJ*

l. A Rozenburg vase, 'Julianna' pattern, The Hague, c1910, 13½in (34cm) high.
£500–550 *OO*

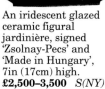

An iridescent glazed ceramic figural jardinière, signed 'Zsolnay-Pecs' and 'Made in Hungary', 7in (17cm) high.
£2,500–3,500 *S(NY)*

A Clarice Cliff Bizarre batchelor tea set, painted in greens, orange and yellow, printed marks. **£1,000–£1,500** *CSK*

A Clarice Cliff Bizarre Lotus vase, painted with the 'Honolulu' pattern, striped green and black trees with orange, red and yellow foliage, printed marks, 11½in high. **£1,500–2,000** *CSK*

A Clarice Cliff Bizarre Isis vase, painted in Applique Lucerne design, in orange, yellow, green and black, with a deep blue sky above, printed and painted marks, impressed 'Isis', 9½in (24cm) high **£3,000–4,000** *CSK*

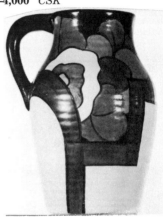

A Clarice Cliff Bizarre Lotus vase, 'Clouvre', the mottled matt lilac and blue ground painted in vermilion, lime green and yellow, painted and printed marks 11½in (29cm) high **£2,000–3,000** *CSK*

A Clarice Cliff Bizarre two-handled Lotus vase, painted in pink, green, yellow and blue, printed marks, 11½in (29cm)high. **£1,000–1,500** *CSK*

A Clarice Cliff Bizarre Lotus Latona vase, printed marks, 11½in (29cm) high. **£1,500–1,800** *CSK*

A Clarice Cliff Fantasque Bizarre tea-for-two set. painted in the 'Summer House' design, printed marks. **£1,500–2,000** *CSK*

A Clarice Cliff Bizarre coffee set, in orange, yellow, green, brown and grey, comprising: a coffee pot, 7 cups, 6 saucers, cream jug and sugar bowl, printed marks. **£500–800** *CSK*

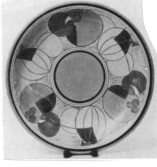

A Clarice Cliff Bizarre twin-handled Lotus vase, painted in a rich chestnut, blue, purple and green, printed marks, 11½in (29cm) high **£800–900** *CSK*

A Clarice Cliff Bizarre 'Golly' pencil holder, in green, orange and red, printed marks, 5½in (14cm) high. **£500–800** *CSK*

A Clarice Cliff Fantasque 'Melon' pattern wall plate, painted in vivid oranges, yellow, blue, red and green, factory marks and facsimile signature, 16½in (42cm) diam. **£1,000–1,500** *P*

r. A Clarice Cliff Fantasque Isis vase, painted in orange, green, brown and black between wide orange and yellow borders, printed marks, 9½in (23cm) high **£600–900** *CSK*

Original artwork for a Clarice Cliff advertisement, depicting several young ladies drinking coffee from a Tankard coffee set, gouache on paper, 22 by 28in (56 by 71cm). **£850–950** *CSK*

Two Clarice Cliff Circus plates, designed by Laura Knight, one centred with a horse and trainer performing in the ring, enclosed by an audience and clown border, in mauve, yellow, brown, black and green, another with a girl astride a horse, in same colours, with factory marks and facsimile signatures to base, both 9in (23cm) diam. **£500–800 each** *P*

A Clarice Cliff Bizarre 'Honolulu' patterned Lotus jug, Fantasque, hand painted by Newport Pottery, 11½in (29cm) high. **£1.200–1,500** *GAK*

A Clarice Cliff Inspiration 'Persian' pattern vase, shape No. 342, painted with abstract shapes in vertical and horizontal bands in turquoise, blue, orange and brown, factory marks and facsimile signature with 'Persian' to base, 8in (20cm) high. **£600–800** *P*

A Clarice Cliff Bizarre vase, decorated with 'Orange Secrets' pattern, oviform with horizontally ribbed neck, painted in vivid colours with cottages on a rolling hillside, factory marks and facsimile signature to base, 8in (20cm) high. **£500–800** *P*

A Clarice Cliff conical coffee set, in the Rising Sun design, painted in orange, mauve and yellow blooms with blue grapes against an orange and white sunburst ground, comprising: a coffee pot and lid, 6 cups and saucers, a milk jug and sugar bowl, factory marks and facsimile signature to base, coffee pot 7in (17cm) high. **£1,200–1,800** *P*

A Clarice Cliff Isis Lotus vase decorated in Green Japan design, with a summerhouse by a lake, an exotic orange and green leaved tree nearby with purple and black foliage, beneath a yellow sky, factory marks and facsimile signature to base, 11½in (29cm) high. **£700–900** *P*

l. A Clarice Cliff Bizarre cup, saucer and plate in the 'Broth' pattern, painted in colours with orange banding, rubber stamp mark. **£180–250** *CSK*

A Clarice Cliff tea service for 4, painted in the 'Crocus' pattern, some pieces marked, c1935.
£300–500 *C*

A Clarice Cliff Biarritz dinner service, the cream ground painted in green, black and orange, comprising: 5 meat plates, 12 dinner plates, 12 side plates, 12 dessert plates, 6 soup plates, 2 tureens and covers, and a sauceboat.
£500–800 *SS*

A Clarice Cliff Isis vase, painted with 'Gayday' pattern, with a border of colourful daisies between a yellow rim and brown and green foot borders, printed marks, painted marks, 1936, 10in (25cm) high.
£200–250 *C*

A Clarice Cliff Bizarre Fantasque vase, painted in red, blue, yellow and green against a cream ground, printed factory marks, 10in (25cm) high.
£800–1,200 *SBe*

A Clarice Cliff vase, painted with 'Honey Glaze' pattern, 8in (20cm) high.
£200–300 *ASA*

A Newport Pottery Bizarre candlestick, painted with a formalised landscape in shades of yellow, blue and green, printed marks, c1930, 5½in (14cm) high.
£600–700 *S*

A Newport Pottery Clarice Cliff vase, 7in (17.5cm) high.
£300–400 *CSK*

A Newport Pottery Clarice Cliff Bizarre vase, printed factory and designer's marks, c1930, 6in (15cm) diam.
£800–1,200 *SB*

A Clarice Cliff Inspiration charger, decorated with 'The Knight Errant', reserved against a green and turquoise ground, printed factory marks and facsimile signature, 18in (45.5cm) diam.
£3,000–4,000 *P*

A Clarice Cliff Bizarre vase, 10in (25cm) high.
£1,500–2,000 *Bea*

A Newport Pottery Clarice Cliff Bizarre earthenware wall plaque, painted in bright orange, yellow and red, c1930, 13in (33cm) diam.
£200–250 *SB*

STARTING A DOULTON COLLECTION

The serious collector of Doulton faces a choice: to concentrate on building up a representative collection from the different types of ceramics produced (stoneware, figurines, character jugs, series ware, to name a few), or simply to focus on one area. Once that choice has been made, the next difficulty is finding good quality items.

Over the past ten years, growing interest in Doulton has resulted in a decreasing supply of such items. Specialist magazines have nurtured a greater interest in Doulton not only in Britain but all over the world, and there are established collectors' clubs in the USA, Canada, Australia and New Zealand. Often there is demand for Doulton that has links with a collector's own country; for example, Hannah Barlow pieces decorated with kangaroos are nearly all exported to Australia.

Prices – most areas are governed by the simple laws of supply and demand. People who began acquiring pieces ten years ago are now concentrating on finding the rarer or missing items for their collections and hence creating more competition for these pieces. Over the past four to five years the recession has caused people to be more selective in what they buy – many would rather save to buy one expensive object than choose several lesser pieces at whim. When a private Doulton collection does come onto the market, prices can be very high as collectors like to see 'fresh' pieces for which they are willing to pay a premium. Other collectors who have been priced out of certain areas (for example, artist stoneware), have shown greater interest in the more affordable and mass produced stonewares such as Slaters Patent Ware and 'Natural foliage' ware.

Certain pieces have acquired great value because they are unique or have been produced in very short numbers. The 'Village Blacksmith' character jug, for example, surfaced at auction a couple of years ago. Dating from the 1950s, it was produced by the factory as a trial piece but was then discarded and literally thrown out. An employee who rescued it from a dustbin kept it at home for many years before placing it in a specialist Doulton sale where it realised £6,000 despite being badly damaged by a large crack.

The prices of figurines are also influenced by scarcity value: 'Top o' the hill', Doulton's most popular figurine (in production since the 1930s) can be bought for under £100, while rarely seen figures at the beginning of the HN series (Doulton assigned letters and numbers to their figurines) can command prices in the £2,000–3,000 bracket. The Art Deco figurines, such as the 'Butterfly Girl' and 'Sunshine Girl' which exude the frivolous mood of the 1920s continue to rise in popularity. The character jug market, on the other hand, has now levelled out from a rather over-inflated position in the mid-1980s.

Doulton collectors can be fascinated by colour and model variations, particularly in the figurine and character jug field. The price of a 'Cavalier' character jug, for example, might be £100 whereas the same jug with a small goatee beard would cost closer to £1,500, just because it was in production for only one year. Also, an item that did not sell well in its day may be very sought after today. 'The Bookworm' plate from the 'Professionals' series might set you back £200, while all the other plates in the series would cost only £60 each.

With the series ware, those pieces decorated with historical, literary or nursery rhyme subjects are very desirable, although sporting subjects (especially golf) are the most popular. Stoneware is collected by artist name, with the Barlows, George Tinworth and Eliza Simmance being the most sought after. Collectors will pay a premium for particular work by these artists, for example the Tinworth Mouse groups.

The golden rule when buying Doulton is to check condition carefully. Obvious damage such as cracks or chips will affect the value, as will restoration which can be more difficult to spot. Figurines may have had their heads knocked off and then have been restored around the neck, vases may have chips filled in or handles replaced. Do not forget that many of these items will have been around for over 100 years, so always make sure the auction house or dealer can confirm whether restoration does or does not exist – it might be so well done that you might still wish to acquire the piece but at a price level that takes this into account. For the more common item, damage or restoration might halve or even quarter its value, but collectors are much more tolerant of the faults to rarer pieces. A Tinworth clock with one or two small chips would hardly affect the value.

There is of course a wide variety of Doulton marks used throughout the long history of the company and collectors should familiarise themselves with these as they will help date a piece. Figurines often have a number to the top right of the lion and crown mark and if this is added to the year 1927 it will give a date of production for the figurine – hence a number five will mean it was was produced in 1932.

All Doulton products have a degree of hand crafting to them. Most involve the initial use of a mould and then a process of several stages of glazing and hand crafting down to the most intricate floral embellishment. Many of Doulton's greatest designers, such as Peggy Davies or Mary Nicoll, managed to create facial expressions of great character and all their studies have a sense of time, place and movement. At the very top of the range the 'Prestige studies' such as 'Princess Badoura' are produced to order and reveal a wealth of historical detail and flamboyant glazing through the intricate hand crafting they have commanded. The retail price reflects this – some £12,000!

Mark Oliver

A Royal Doulton musical character jug, 'Toby Weller', designed by L. Harradine and H. Fenton, D5888, printed marks, 6in (15cm) high. **£300–400** *CSK*

A Royal Doulton character jug, 'Old Charley', printed marks, 7in (18cm) high. **£600–800** *CSK*

A Royal Doulton character jug, 'Granny', designed by H. Fenton and M. Henk, D5521, printed marks, 7in (19cm) high. **£300–400** *CSK*

A Royal Doulton character jug, 'Paddy', designed by H. Fenton, D5887, printed marks, 6in (15cm) high. **£250–350** *CSK*

A Royal Doulton figure, 'Sunshine Girl', designed by L. Harradine, HN1344, printed and painted marks, 5in (12.5cm) high. **£1,000–1,500** *CSK*

A Royal Doulton figure,
'The Goose Girl', designed
by L. Harradine, HN559,
introduced 1923, withdrawn
1938, 8in (20cm) high.
£750–800 *LT*

A Royal Doulton figure,
'Ibraham', HN2095,
withdrawn 1955.
£250–300 *Bea*

A Royal Doulton figure,
'Farmer Bunnykins,
D3003, printed and painted
marks, 7in (18cm) high.
£1,500–2,500 *CSK*

A Royal Doulton figure,
'Abdullah', HN2104,
withdrawn 1962.
£200–250 *Bea*

A Royal Doulton figure, 'King
Charles', designed by C. J.
Noke and H. Tittensor, HN404,
cane missing, printed marks,
17in (43cm) hgh.
£300–400 *CSK*

A Royal Doulton figure, 'The
Jester', HN1295, withdrawn
1949, signed 'C. J. Noke',
10in (25cm) high.
£400–600 *LT*

A Royal Doulton figure,
'Carpet Seller', HN1464,
withdrawn 1969.
£150–250 *Bea*

A Royal Doulton figure, 'The
Alchemist', designed by L. Harradine,
HN1282, date code for 1937,
introduced 1928, withdrawn 1938,
11½in (29.5cm) high.
£600–800 *P*

A Royal Doulton figure,
'Miss 1928', designed by
L. Harradine, HN1205,
withdrawn c1938, 7in
(17.5cm) high.
£900–1,000 *LT*

A Royal Doulton figure,
'The Poke Bonnet', HN612,
9½in (24cm) high.
£350–400 *LT*

A Royal Doulton figure, 'Delight', designer L. Harradine, HN1772, printed and painted marks, 7½in (49.5cm) high, and 4 other pieces. **£120–150** *CSK*

A Royal Doulton figure, 'Easter Day', HN2039, withdrawn 1969. **£200–300** *Bea*

A Royal Doulton figure, 'The Wardrobe Mistress', HN2145, withdrawn 1967. **£200–250** *Bea*

A Royal Doulton figure, 'The Gaffer', HN2053, green printed marks to base, 7½in (19cm) high. **£200–300** *BWe*

r. A Royal Doulton figure, 'One of the Forty', designer H. Tittensor, HN677, introduced 1924, withdrawn 1938, 8½in (21.5cm) high. **£600–800** *LT*

l. A Royal Doulton figure, 'Mephistopheles & Marguerite', designed by C. J. Noke, HN775, withdrawn 1949, 8in (20cm) high. **£** *LT*

A Royal Doulton figure, 'Uriah Heep', HN2101, green printed marks to base, 7½in (19cm) high. **£150–200** *BWe*

A Royal Doulton pilot figure, of a girl with a pink skirt and a pail under her right arm, 7in (17.5cm) high. **£800–1,000** *LT*

A Royal Doulton figure, 'Sweet and Twenty', designer L. Harradine, HN1360, printed marks, 6in (15cm) high. **£150–200** *CSK*

A Royal Doulton figure, 'Quality Street', HN1211, introduced 1926, withdrawn 1938, 7in (17.5cm) high. **£600–700** *LT*

A Royal Doulton figure 'Midinette', designer L. Harradine, HN2090, printed marks, 7in (17.5cm) high. **£150–200** *CSK*

A Royal Doulton figure, 'Butterfly', designer L. Harradine, HN719, 6½in (16.5cm) high. **£600–800** *LT*

A Royal Doulton cabinet plate, painted and signed by W. E. J. Dean, dated '1916', 9in (22.5cm) diam.
£250–300 *TVA*

A Royal Doulton Holbein ware pottery vase, decorated by W. Nunn, in colours with 2 men seated drinking at a table, signed and impressed 'Doulton Ivory 1920B', printed mark in green, 9½in (24cm) high.
£200–250 *HSS*

A Doulton Lambeth plaque, decorated by Hannah Barlow, dated '1874', 9in (22.5cm) square.
£400–500 *Wai*

A Royal Doulton porcelain figure, 'Matador and Bull', designed by M. Davies, HN2011, printed and painted marks, 15½in (39.5cm) wide.
£1,500–2,000 *CSK*

A Royal Doulton figure, 'The Curtsey', HN334.
£450–500 *GSP*

A Royal Doulton Art Nouveau vase, artists' monograms for Eliza Simmance and Bessie Newbery, incised date code for 1909, 15in (38cm) high.
£500–600 *TVA*

A Royal Doulton jug, 'The Pied Piper', by H. Fenton, No. 252 of limited edition of 600, 10in (25cm) high.
£400–500 *P(M)*

A Royal Doulton Lambeth stoneware figure of Samuel, by George Tinworth, on an oval moulded base, impressed initials, 6in (15cm) high.
£450–500 *AH*

A Royal Doulton flambé model of a seated rabbit, restored, c1925, 4in (10cm) high.
£125–175 *TVA*

A Royal Doulton blue and white chamber pot, c1900.
£40–45 *OD*

l. A Royal Doulton figure, 'Henry Lytton as Jack Point', HN610, designed by C. J. Noke, introduced 1924, withdrawn 1949, 6½in (17cm). high.
£300–400 *LT*

r. A Royal Doulton figure, 'The Mendicant', wearing a draped costume and turban holding a tambourine and seated on a pile of red bricks, HN1365, printed Doulton mark, withdrawn 1969, 8½in (22cm) high.
£100–150 *TW*

A Royal Doulton figure, 'Angela', HN1204, designed by L. Harradine, introduced 1926, withdrawn 1938, hairline crack to base, 7½in (19cm) high.
£250–350 *LT*

l. A Royal Doulton figure, 'Yeoman of the Guard', designed by L. Harradine, HN2122, introduced 1954, withdrawn 1959, 6in (15cm) high.
£450–500 *LT*

l. A Royal Doulton figure, 'Moorish Piper Minstrel', on a plinth, no number, designed by C. J. Noke, withdrawn 1938, 13½in (34cm) high.
£1,000–1,500 *LT*

r. A Royal Doulton figure, 'Lady Jester', designer L. Harradine, HN1222, introduced 1927, withdrawn by 1938. **£600–800** *LT*

A Royal Doulton figure, 'Mask Seller', designer L. Harradine, HN1361, introduced 1929, withdrawn by 1938, 8½in (22cm) high.
£400–500 *LT*

Three miniatures, 'One of the Forty', decorated in gilt, designer H. Tittensor, no number, should be HN423, 2½in, 2in, and 3in (6cm, 5cm, and 8cm) high.
£950–1,100 *LT*

l. A Royal Doulton figure, 'Fox in Red Coat', seated, HN100, 6½in(17cm) high.
£500–700 *LT*

A Royal Doulton stoneware garden ornament, impressed 'C.M. & I', 11½in (29cm) high.
£500–600 *P*

A porcelain group of 'Spooks' modelled as two elderly gentlemen wearing long turquoise coloured cloaks and black caps, by C. J. Noke, HN88, printed and painted 'Royal Doulton, England' and 'Doulton & Co.' marks, 7in (18cm) high.
£1,000–1,200 *CSK*

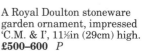

A Royal Doulton figure, 'Scotties', designed by L. Harradine, HN1281, introduced 1928, withdrawn 1938, slight damage, 5in (12.5cm) high.
£400–450 *WIL*

A Royal Doulton figure, 'Easter Day', designed by M. Davies, HN2039, introduced 1949, withdrawn 1969.
£160–200 *WIL*

A Royal Doulton figure, 'Griselda', 1947–53, 6in (15cm) high.
£200-230 *TRU*

A Royal Doulton figure, 'Memories', 1949–59, 6in (15cm) high.
£150–165 *TRU*

A Royal Doulton figure, 'Modena', HN1846, withdrawn 1949, cracked.
£120–180 *Bea*

A Royal Doulton figure, 'Bess', HN2002, 7½in (18cm) high.
£200–300 *TW*

A Royal Doulton figure, 'Dreamland', HN1481, base cracked, printed marks in green script, impressed date '1931'.
£850–950 *SC*

A Royal Doulton figure, 'Bonnie Lassie', HN1626, introduced 1934, withdrawn 1953, 5½in (14cm) high.
£250–300 *Bea*

A Royal Doulton figure, 'Francine', designed by J. Bromley, introduced 1922, withdrawn 1981, 5½in (14cm) high.
£50–70 *TVA*

r. A Royal Doulton figure, 'The Orange Lady, HN1759, introduced 1936, withdrawn 1975, 9in (22.5cm) high.
£150–200 *TW*

l. A Royal Doulton figure of a seated bulldog, with a Union Jack flag draped over its back, printed factory marks, 4in (10cm) high.
£150–200 *CSK*

A Royal Doulton figure, 'Butterfly', HN1456, 6½in (16.5cm) high.
£800–1,200 *CSK*

A Royal Doulton double-sided figure, 'Mephistopheles and Marguerite', HN775, 8in (20cm) high.
£700–900 *CSK*

A Royal Doulton figure, 'Angela', slight damage, painted title, HN1204, date code for 1929, 7in (17.5cm) high.
£400–500 *S*

A Royal Doulton figure, 'Negligée', a girl in a coloured slip and red turban, on a multi-coloured cushion, HN1219, printed and painted marks, 5in (12.5cm) high.
£400–600 *CSK*

l. A Royal Doulton figure, 'Columbine', designed by L. Harradine, BH1296, impressed date '2.9.29', introduced 1928, withdrawn 1938, 6in (15cm) high.
£400-500 *P*

A Royal Doulton figure, 'Geisha', by C. J. Noke, HN1292, impressed date '4.1.28', 7in (17.5cm) high.
£600–800 *P*

A Royal Doulton figure, 'Negligée', by L. Harradine, HN1272, impressed date '1.1.28', 5in (12.5cm) high.
£400-600 *P*

Make the Most of Miller's

Condition is absolutely vital when assessing the value of an antique. Items in good condition are more likely to appreciate than less perfect examples. Rare, desirable items may command higher prices even when in need of restoration.

A Royal Doulton figure, 'Covent Garden', HN1339, 9in (22.5cm) high. **£500–600** *Bea*

A Royal Doulton figure, 'Pierrette', printed and painted marks, painted title, HN731, impressed date code for 1927, 7in (17.5cm) high.
£350–450 *S*

r. A Royal Doulton figure, 'Marion', HN1583, introduced 1933, withdrawn 1938, 6½in (16.5cm) high.
£350–450 *Bea*

A Royal Doulton figure, 'Marietta', HN1341, printed Royal Doulton marks, 8in (20cm) high.
£400–450 *CSK*

r. A Royal Doulton figure, 'Columbine', in a pink and yellow dress, seated on a green column, printed and painted marks, HN1439, 6in (15cm) high.
£400–500 *CSK*

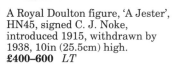

r. A Royal Doulton figure, 'Guy Fawkes', HN98, designer C. J. Noke, introduced 1918, withdrawn by 1949, 10½in (26.5cm) high. **£400–500** *LT*

'An Orange Vendor', HN72, designer C. J. Noke, introduced 1917, withdrawn 1938, 6in (16cm) high. **£350–400** *LT*

A Royal Doulton figure, 'In The Stocks', 1st version, HN14/4, designer L. Harradine, introduced 1931, withdrawn by 1938, 5in (13cm) high. **£1,000–1,500** *LT*

A Royal Doulton figure, 'A Jester', HN45, signed C. J. Noke, introduced 1915, withdrawn by 1938, 10in (25.5cm) high. **£400–600** *LT*

l. A Royal Doulton figure, 'Geisha', designer H. Tittensor, dated February 1927, 11in (27cm) high. **£1,500–2,000** *LT*

l. A Royal Doulton figure, 'Pierrette', HN644, 1st version, designer L. Harradine, introduced 1924, withdrawn 1938, 7in (18cm) high. **£400–500** *LT*

A Royal Doulton figure, 'The Beggar', HN526, designed L. Harradine, introduced 1921, withdrawn by 1949, 6½in (16.5cm) high. **£200–250** *LT*

r. A Royal Doulton figure, 'Harlequinade Masked', designer L. Harradine, introduced 1925, withdrawn by 1938, 6½in (16.5cm) high. **£700–800** *LT*

A Royal Doulton figure, 'Butterfly', HN719, designer L. Harradine, 6½in (16.5cm) high. **£600–700** *LT*

A Royal Doulton figure, 'Pierrette', pilot decoration, designer L. Harradine, introduced 1924, withdrawn by 1938, 7in (18cm) high. **£400–500** *LT*

A Royal Doulton figure, 'Judge and Jury', HN1264, designer J. G. Hughes, introduced 1927, withdrawn 1938, 6in (15cm) high. **£2,000–3,000** *LT*

A Royal Doulton figure, 'London Cry, Turnips and Carrots', HN752, designer L. Harradine, introduced 1925, withdrawn 1938, 7in (17cm) high. **£500–600** *LT*

A Royal Doulton figure, 'The Modern Piper', HN756, designer L. Harradine, introduced 1925, withdrawn by 1938, 8½in (21.5cm) high. **£500–700** *LT*

A Royal Doulton figure, 'Negligée', HN1219, designer L. Harradine, introduced 1927, withdrawn 1938, 5in (12.5cm) high. **£600–800** *LT*

A Royal Doulton figure, 'Gladys', designer L. Harradine, HN1740, introduced 1935, withdrawn by 1949, 5in (13cm) high.
£350–400 *LT*

A Royal Doulton figure, 'Veronica', designer L. Harradine, no number, should be HN1943, introduced 1940, withdrawn by 1949.
£200–300 *LT*

A Royal Doulton figure, 'Top O' The Hill', designer L. Harradine, HN1834, introduced 1937, 7in (18cm) high. **£50–100** *LT*

A Royal Doulton figure, 'Carmen', designed by L. Harradine, introduced 1928, withdrawn 1938, HN1267, 7in (18cm) high.
£350–450 *LT*

A Royal Doulton figure, 'The Awakening', 1st version, designer L. Harradine, HN1927, introduced 1940, withdrawn by 1949.
£900–1,000 *LT*

A pilot Royal Doulton figure of a boy carrying a lantern, in red coat and tricorn, not produced, 6½in (17cm) high.
£700–1,000 *LT*

l. A Royal Doulton figure, 'The Bather', designer L. Harradine, no number, model as HN1708 but with different decoration, with check robe, black costume and blue base, 7½in (19cm) high.
£400–600 *LT*

l. A Royal Doulton figure, 'The Mask', designer L. Harradine, HN7333, introduced 1925, withdrawn by 1938, 7in (18cm) high.
£700–1,000 *LT*

A Royal Doulton figure, 'Mantilla', designer E. J. Griffiths, HN2712, 12in (30cm) high.
£150–200 *LT*

r. A Doulton figure, 'Spring', designed by Richard Garbe, modelled as a partially draped maiden holding flowers to her bosom as she is swept upwards, her drapery resting on a circular plinth above a stepped square section base, cream-coloured glaze, in two sections with original screw and nut fixing, hand painted signature, 'Potted by Doulton & Co. Edition Limited to 100, No. 61, "Spring" by Richard Garbe ARA', moulded artist's signature and date '1932' on the plinth, 21½in (54cm) high overall.
£2,700–3,000 *C*

A Royal Doulton figure, 'Ellen Terry as Queen Catherine', by C. J. Noke, HN379, 12⅛in (32cm) high. **£600–1,100** *LT*

A Royal Doulton figure, 'Coppelia', HN2115, 7in (17.5cm) high.
£300–350 *WIL*

A Royal Doulton pilot figure of an Elizabethan lady courtier, holding a rose, 10½in (26.5cm) high.
£820–870 *WIL*

Doulton

A London pottery firm established in 1815, but important for its Art Pottery only from the 1860s, when it revived brown stoneware and saltglaze ware. Its leading potter was George Tinworth and the company had links with the Martin Brothers. In the 1870s the Barlow sisters decorated ware with animals and scenes. In the 1880s and 1890s, many different artists made or decorated fancy ware, 'siliconware' or enamelled china. In 1902 Doulton received the Royal Warrant. Royal Doulton figures were introduced in 1913, since when more than 2,000 designs have been produced.

A Royal Doulton figure, 'Clemency', HN1633, 7½in (19cm) high.
£200–250 *WIL*

A Royal Doulton pilot figure of a young lady in a red dress, standing by a sundial, 7in (17.5cm) high.
£960–1,200 *LT*

A Royal Doulton figure, 'Sonia', HN1692, 6½in (16.5cm) high.
£330–380 *LT*

r. A Royal Doulton miniature character jug, 'Pearly Girl'.
£3,100–3,300 *LT*

l. A Royal Doulton miniature character jug, 'Pearly Boy'.
£2,250–2,500 *LT*

A Royal Doulton musical mug, 'Old King Cole', with a yellow crown, fitted with a Thorens Swiss movement, No. D6014, 8in (20cm) high.
£750–800 *AH*

l. A Royal Doulton figure of a newsboy, HN2244, 8in (20cm) high.
£160–200 *LT*

r. A Royal Doulton character jug 'Old King Cole', with a yellow crown.
£500–600 *LT*

A Royal Doulton figure, 'Siesta', designer L. Harradine, HN1305, produced February 1931, 5in (12cm) high. **£800–1,000** *LT*

'Tulips', HN1334, introduced 1929, withdrawn 1938, 9½in (23cm) high. **£500–600** *LT*

A Royal Doulton figure, 'Lady Jester', designer L. Harradine, 2nd version, HN1284, introduced 1928, withdrawn 1938, 4in (10cm) high. **£800–1,000** *LT*

'Folly', designer L. Harradine, HN1335, introduced 1929, withdrawn 1938, 9in (22.5cm) high. **£800–1,200** *LT*

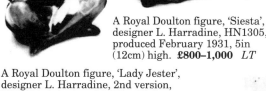

l. A Royal Doulton figure, 'Sweet Lavender', designer L. Harradine, HN1373, introduced 1930, withdrawn 1949, 9in (22.5cm) high. **£300–500** *LT*

A Royal Doulton figure, 'The Courtier', designer L. Harradine, HN1338, introduced 1929, withdrawn 1938, 4½in (11.5cm) high. **£1,000–1,500** *LT*

l. A Royal Doulton figure, 'Doreen', designer L. Harradine, HN1389, introduced 1930, withdrawn 1938, 5in (12.5cm) high. **£400–500** *LT*

'Iona', designer L. Harradine, HN1346, introduced 1929, withdrawn 1938, 7½in (19cm) high. **£1,000–1,500** *LT*

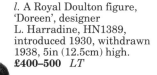

r. A Royal Doulton figure, 'Tildy', designer L. Harradine, HN1576, introduced 1933, withdrawn 1938, 5½in (14cm) high. **£350–400** *LT*

A Royal Doulton figure, 'Phyllis', designer L. Harradine, HN1420, introduced 1930, withdrawn 1949, slight damage, 9in (22.5cm) high. **£200–300** *WIL*

A Royal Doulton figure, 'Calumet', designer C. J. Noke, HN1428, introduced 1930, withdrawn 1949, 6in (15cm) high. **£400–600** *LT*

r. 'Teresa', designer L. Harradine, HN1683, introduced 1935, withdrawn 1938, hair cracks, 6in (15cm) high. **£350–400** *LT*

A Royal Doulton figure, 'Dreamland', designer L. Harradine, should be HN1473, introduced 1931, withdrawn 1938, 4½in (12cm) wide. **£1,000–1,200** *LT*

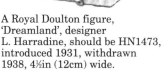
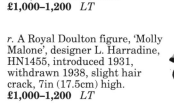

r. A Royal Doulton figure, 'Molly Malone', designer L. Harradine, HN1455, introduced 1931, withdrawn 1938, slight hair crack, 7in (17.5cm) high. **£1,000–1,200** *LT*

l. A Royal Doulton figure, 'Court Shoemaker', designer L. Harradine, HN1755, introduced 1936, withdrawn 1949, hair cracks to base, 7in (17.5cm) high. **£420–480** *LT*

A Royal Doulton figure, 'The Winner', No. 1407, 1930–38, 6in (15cm) high.
£1,200–1,500 *TP*

A Royal Doulton group, depicting a bay mare with her foal, No. 2522, 1938–60, 6in (15cm) high.
£350–450

A Royal Doulton figure, 'Town Crier', No. 2119, 1953–76, 8in (20cm) high.
£120–150 *TP*

A Royal Doulton 'Treasure Island' loving cup, from a limited edition of 600, c1934.
£400–500 *TP*

A Royal Doulton figure, 'The Organ Grinder', No. 2173, 1956–75, 8in (20cm) high.
£350–400 *TP*

A Royal Doulton figure of a seated collie, No. 47, c1920.
£300–400 *TP*

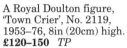

l. A Royal Doulton set of The Four Seasons, 2nd version, 'Autumn' HN2087, 'Winter' HN2088, 'Spring' HN2085, and 'Summer' HN2086, designer Margaret Davies, introduced 1952, withdrawn 1959, 6 to 8in (15 to 20cm) high.
£800–1,000 *LT*

l. A Royal Doulton figure 'Spring Flowers', HN1945, designer L. Harradine, introduced 1940, withdrawn by 1949, 7in (17.5cm) high.
£200–300 *LT*

A Royal Doulton group, 'Afternoon Tea', HN1747, 5½in (14cm) high.
£100–150 *HCH*

A Royal Doulton pilot figure of a lady in a blue and pink ballgown, damaged, 9in (23cm) high.
£900–1,200 *LT*

A Royal Doulton figure, 'The Squire', HN1814.
£1,200–1,500 *LT*

A Royal Doulton figure, 'Miranda', designer L. Harradine, HN1819, 8½in (21.5cm) high.
£450–550 *LT*

A Royal Doulton figure, 'Mariquita', designer L. Harradine, HN1837, 8in (20cm) high.
£800–1,000 *LT*

A Royal Doulton figure, 'Henry VIII', designer C. J. Noke, 2nd version, HN1792, No. 39 of 200, hair crack in base, 11½in (29cm) high.
£2,000–2,500 *LT*

l. A Royal Doulton figure, 'The Young Miss Nightingale', designer Margaret Davies, HN2010, 9in (23cm) high.
£400–500 *LT*

A Royal Doulton figure, 'The Corinthian', designer H Fenton, no number, should be HN1973, 8in (20cm) high.
£800–1,000 *LT*

r. A Royal Doulton figure, 'Pearly Boy', 2nd version, designer L Harradine, HN2035, 5½in (13.5cm) high.
£130–180 *WIL*

A Royal Doulton figure, 'Granny's Heritage', HN1873, 7in (18cm) high.
£300–400 *CDC*

A Royal Doulton figure, 'Promenade', designer Margaret Davies, HN2076, 8in (20cm) high.
£800–1,200 *LT*

A Royal Doulton figure, 'St George', designer Stanley Thorogood, ARCA, HN2067, 16in (40.5cm) high. **£600–800** *LT*

A Royal Doulton figure, 'Pearly Girl', 2nd version, designer L. Harradine, HN2036, 5½in (14cm) high. **£120–160** *WIL*

A Royal Doulton figure, 'Kathleen', designer L. Harradine, HN1252, printed and painted marks, 8in (20cm) high.
£350–450 *CSK*

A Royal Doulton figure, 'The Tailor', designer M. Nicoll, HN2174, 4in (10cm) high.
£500–600 *LT*

l. A Royal Doulton figure, 'Jolly Sailor', designer M. Nicoll, HN2172, 6½in (16.5cm) high.
£400–500 *LT*

A Royal Doulton figure, 'St George and the Dragon', designer W. K. Harper, 3rd version, HN2856, 16½in (42cm) high. **£600–800** *LT*

A Royal Doulton figure, 'June', designer L. Harradine, HN1691, withdrawn 1949, 7½in (18.5cm) high. **£250–300** *LT*

A Royal Doulton figure, 'Daffy Down Dilly', designed by L. Harradine, HN1712, introduced 1935, withdrawn 1975, 8in (20cm) high. **£150–200** *L*

A Royal Doulton figure, 'Romany Sue', HN1758, 1936–1949, hairline crack in shawl, 9½in (23.5cm) high. **£400–500** *Bon*

A Royal Doulton figure, 'Matilda', HN2011, printed and painted marks, 'COPR 1947', 10in (25cm) high. **£400–500** *SS*

A Royal Doulton figure, 'The Leisure Hour', designer Margaret Davies, HN2055, withdrawn 1965, 6½in (17cm) high. **£200–300** *LT*

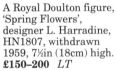

A Royal Doulton figure, 'Spring Flowers', designer L. Harradine, HN1807, withdrawn 1959, 7½in (18cm) high. **£150–200** *LT*

An unissued porcelain figure of a young girl seated in a chair wearing a blue dress feeding a baby, printed Royal Doulton England marks, HN 2252, 5in (12.5cm) high. **£550–600** *CSK*

A Royal Doulton seated figure, 'Linda', HN2106, withdrawn 1976. **£100–120** *Bea*

l. A Royal Doulton figure, 'Sir Walter Raleigh', HN2015, withdrawn 1955. **£300–400** *Bea*

A Royal Doulton figure, from the Seasons series, 'Winter', HN2088, introduced 1952, withdrawn 1959. **£150–200** *TW*

A Royal Doulton figure, 'Sleepy Head', HN2114, printed Royal Doulton England marks, 4½in (11.5cm) high. **£800–1,000** *CSK*

r. A Royal Doulton figure, 'Masquerade', HN2251, circle mark, lion and crown, c1960, 8½in (21cm) high. **£150–200** *TVA*

Four Royal Doulton character jugs.
From left.
'Parson Brown'. **£50–60**
'White-haired Clown'. **£300–400**
'Toby Philpot'. **£50–60**
'Vicar of Bray'. **£80–100** *MGM*

A Royal Doulton figure, 'The Perfect Pair', 7in (18cm) high. **£300–400** *PB*

A Royal Doulton pilot figure, believed to be entitled 'The Logsman', not produced, Block No. 1767, 6in (15cm) high. **£1,500–2,000** *LT*

A Royal Doulton flambé Buddha, signed 'Noke', 8in (21.5cm) high. **£600–800** *HCH*

Three Royal Doulton figures:
l. ''Ard of 'Earing', designer D. Biggs, D6588, registered numbers 913137, 45356, 9681, 811/63, 7½in (19cm) high. **£400–500**

c. 'The Clown', brown haired version, designer H. Fenton, registered number 810520, 6in (15cm) high. **£700–900**

r. 'Old King Cole', designer H. Fenton, 6in (15cm) high. **£100–150** *GC*

A Royal Doulton figure, 'Lord Nelson', designer M. Henk, D6336, introduced 1952, withdrawn in 1969, 7in (18cm) high. **£150–250** *WIL*

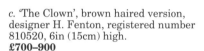
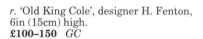

l. A Royal Doulton flambé model of a leaping salmon, 12in (30.5cm) high. **£300–400**
r. A Royal Doulton flambé model of a seated fox, 9in (23cm) high. **£300–400** *MGM*

A Royal Doulton 'Jester' wall mask. **£250–300** *MGM*

A Royal Doulton Lonsdale leaf and floral decorated toilet jug and basin. **£200–250** *PC*

A Royal Doulton Isaac Walton two-handled 'fishing pot', with transfer print decoration, and inscription 'And when the Timorous Trout...', 6in (15cm) high. **£80–100** *MN*

A Royal Doulton model of a bulldog, HN 1043, and a smaller bulldog. **£250–300** *Bea*

A Royal Doulton Kingsware 'golfing' jug, decorated with embossed golfing figures in period costume, printed factory mark, c1935, 9in (23cm) high. **£250–300** *WIL*

l. A Doulton figure of a mandarin, wearing a yellow tunic with circular motifs over a plain blue full length skirt, his jacket with larger motifs on a black ground, small chip to hat, dated '7.24', HN611, 10in (25cm) high.
£650–1,000 *S(C)*

A pair of Doulton Lambeth saltglazed stoneware bookends, one with a single monkey, the other with a monkey and infant, on a foliate base under a green glaze, stamped factory mark, Doulton, Lambeth, c1890, 6in (15cm) high.
£300–400 *S(C)*

A 1930s style Doulton dinner service, entitled 'Dubarry', comprising: 4 tureens and covers, 2 ladles, 5 graduated meat plates, 2 sauceboats, 22 plates and 2 petal edged plates, on a cream ground, with a geometric pattern of intersecting lines and semi-circles edged in green with a central motif of a stylised flower in orange, some plates worn.
£300–400 *P(M)*

A Doulton Lambeth stoneware vase, decorated by Edith Lupton, carved and glazed with flowers and grasses over a beige background with painted florets, dated '1887', 16in (41cm) high.
£450–550 *PCh*

l. A Doulton figure, 'Contentment', designed by L. Harradine, HN395, decorated mainly in yellow, light green and pink, 7½in (19cm) high.
£450–650 *S(C)*

l. A Doulton salt glazed stoneware vase, by Hannah B. Barlow, impressed factory marks and date, incised monogram 'BHB' and 'LAB' for Lucy A. Barlow, c1884, 12in (31cm) high.
£650–750 *S(C)*

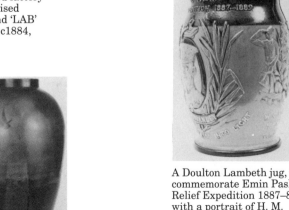

r. A flambé baluster vase, decorated in black against rich flambé ground, printed and impressed marks, 20in (51cm) high.
£150–200 *CSK*

A Doulton Lambeth jug, to commemorate Emin Pasha, Relief Expedition 1887–89, with a portrait of H. M. Stanley, 8in (20cm) high.
£250–300 *WIL*

Seven Doulton figures:
from left:
'Philippa of Hainault', HN2008, 9½in (24cm) high. **£350–400**
'Matilda', HN2011, 9in (23cm) high. **£400–500**
'The Lady Anne Neville', HN2006, 9½in (24cm) high.
£400–500
'Margaret of Anjou', HN2012, 9in (23cm) high. **£300–350**
'The Young Miss Nightingale', HN2010, 9in (23cm) high.
£350–450
'Mrs Fitzherbert', HN2007, 9in (23cm) high. **£350–450**
'Henrietta Maria', HN2005, 9in (23cm) high. **£400–500** *EH*

A set of 8 Doulton Dickensian
characters, printed marks, 4in
(10cm) high. **£200–250** *SC*

l. A Royal
Doulton figure,
'Little Boy Blue',
designed by L.
Harradine, 6in
(15cm) high.
£80–120 *TVA*

A Royal Doulton figure,
'Rosebud', designed by
L. Harradine, HN1581,
3in (8cm) high.
£300–400 *P*

A Doulton stoneware butter
dish, impressed and incised
marks for Florence Barlow and
Bessie Newberry, dated '1887'.
£250–350 *DWB*

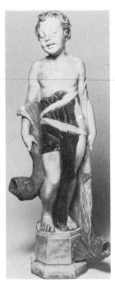

A Royal Doulton
polychrome glazed
stoneware fountain
figure, designed by
Gilbert Bayes,
impressed signature
'Gilbert Bayes', 1934,
42in (106.5cm) high.
£2,000–3,000 *C*

A Royal Doulton figure, 'Fortune
Teller', HN2159, introduced
1955, withdrawn 1967.
£200–250 *TW*

A Royal Doulton figure,
'The Puppetmaker', HN2253,
1962–73, 8in (20cm) high.
£150–200 *Bon*

A Royal Doulton character
jug, 'The White Haired Clown',
designer L. Harradine, D6322,
withdrawn 1955.
£300–400 *LT*

A Royal Doulton figure, 'The Shepherd',
M.17, miniature, withdrawn 1938, 4in
(10cm) high.
£300–400 *LT*

A Royal Doulton character
jug, 'The Clown', modelled
by H. Fenton, the red haired
version, printed mark and
title in green, c1940, 6½in
(16.2cm) high.
£800–1,000 *SC*

l. A Royal Doulton character
mug, 'Friar Tuck'.
£150–200 *M*

A Royal Doulton character mug,
'The Poacher'. **£60–80** *M*

A Royal Doulton character jug,
'Punch & Judy Man', designed by
D. Biggs, D6590, introduced 1964,
withdrawn 1969, 7in (17.5cm) high.
£200–250 *WIL*

r. A Royal Doulton character jug,
'Dick Whittington', designed by
M. Henk, introduced 1953,
withdrawn 1960, 6½in (16cm)
high. **£120–150** *P*

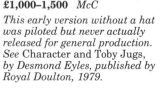

A Royal Doulton character jug,
'Drake', hatless version, date
code for 1940, 6in (15cm) high.
£1,000–1,500 *McC*

*This early version without a hat
was piloted but never actually
released for general production.
See* Character and Toby Jugs,
*by Desmond Eyles, published by
Royal Doulton, 1979.*

l. A pair of Doulton dessert plates.
£75–100 *AOS*

A pair of inverted baluster form salt-glazed stoneware vases, initials of Florence E. Barlow, assistant Eleaner Tosen, one rim chipped, c1902-5, 10½in (26.5cm) high.
£500–700 *CDC*

A Doulton fishing plate, 10½in (26cm) diam.
£100–120 *RP*

l. A Doulton Lambeth stoneware oil lamp, by Florence nd Lucy Barlow, with etched glass shade and chimney, impressed mark and initials, 25in (63.5cm) high.
£800–1,000 *DSH*

A pair of Doulton Burslem twin-handled vases, painted in green, pink, purple, white and brown with gilt highlights, against a background with gilt flowerheads on a light blue ground, printed and painted marks, 14½in (36.5cm) high.
£800–1,000 *CSK*

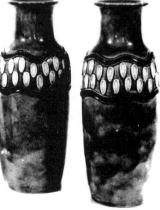

A Doulton Lambeth dish, decorated by Linnie Watt, painted in shades of brown, yellow and blue, damaged, impressed and painted marks, 6in (15cm) wide.
£250–300 *CSK*

A Doulton Lambeth stoneware tobacco jar and cover, with applied decoration, painted in shades of buff and blue, outlined in white slip, all on a stippled green and brown ground, impressed factory mark, incised artist's monogram, c1925, 6in (15cm) high.
£60–80 *WIL*

A Doulton Lambeth vase, damaged, impressed date '1885', monogram of G. H. Tabor.
£175–200 *SN*

A Lambeth vase, decorated in Art Nouveau style with mauve flowers on green ground, by Eliza Simmance, 14in (36cm) high.
£700–900 *LT*

A pair of saltglazed stoneware vases, grey-green with blue and ochre details, initials of Bessie Newbery, a supervisor at Doultons from 1911, c1912–18, 12in (31cm) high.
£200–300 *CDC*

A pair of Doulton Lambeth green and blue decorated tankards, 6in (15cm) high.
£150–200 *PC*

A Doulton Burslem vase, by W. Slater, with chrysanthemums in shades of yellow, blue, mauve and green on a mottled turquoise ground, signed, printed marks, 1890s, 19½in (49.5cm) high.
£600–800 *SS*

A pair of Doulton Burslem blue and white transferware soup plates, 'Madras' pattern, 10in (25cm) diam.
£15–20 *OD*

A Doulton vase, by G. H. Tabar, incised with blue flowerheads and dark green leaves and foliage on a green ground, impressed 'Doulton Lambeth 1881', 10½in (26.5cm) high.
£300–400 *CSK*

A Doulton Lambeth vase, by Hannah Barlow, decorated with an incised band of cattle, dated '1888', 7½in (19cm) high.
£350–450 *TVA*

A Doulton Lambeth stoneware group, modelled by George Tinworth, signed on base 'Doulton's Lambeth' and 'GT' monogram, 7in (17.5cm) high.
£2,500–3,000 *P*

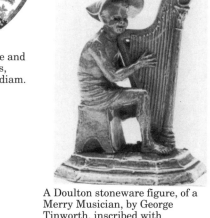

A Doulton stoneware figure, of a Merry Musician, by George Tinworth, inscribed with monogram 'T.G.', 4in (10cm) high.
£300–400 *Bea*

A Royal Doulton stoneware jardinière and stand, in muted colours on a green ground, hair crack to rim, 37in (94cm) high.
£800–1,000 *Bea*

A Doulton Lambeth stoneware globular vase, by Eliza Simmance, glazed olive against a ground of slip-decorated petals, artist's monogram No. 875, dated '1886', 10½in (26.5cm) high.
£400–500 *P*

A Doulton Lambeth pottery lemonade jug, by Emily J. Partington, with silver plated hinged cover and thumbpiece, decorated in low relief within oval buff reserve panels, on flower decorated green and blue ground, impressed mark and initials, 9in (22.5cm) high.
£500–600 *AH*

A pair of Doulton stoneware vases, decorated by Hannah Barlow, with bands of deer within stylised foliage borders, impressed mark and date '1885', 9½in (24cm) high.
£600–800 *SWO*

A Royal Doulton Chang vase, covered in a thick crackled mottled white, black, red, ochre glaze running over mottled shades of ochre, red, blue and black, printed marks 'Chang, Royal Doulton, Noke', 4½in (11cm) high.
£450–600 *C*

A pair of Royal Doulton baluster vases, with mottled green glaze and raised design of stylised flowers and foliage.
£300–350 *LRG*

A Royal Doulton teapot and cover, commemorating Lord Nelson, blue ground with brown glazed rope-twist handle and spout, with raised decoration of the head of the Admiral, the other side depicting *HMS Victory*, and inscribed around the neck, 'England Expects Every Man Will Do His Duty', monogrammed 'Ap.', 5in (13cm) high.
£110–150 *RID*

A Royal Doulton urn, with Grecian figures, 13in (33cm) high.
£250–380 *ASA*

A Doulton Studio ware vase, c1930, 7in (18cm) high.
£75–95 *AOS*

A pair of Royal Doulton toy vases, hand painted with a country scene, c1910, 1½in (4cm) high.
£200–250 *TVA*

l. A pair of Doulton Lambeth stoneware vases, decorated by Florence Barlow in green slip with black grouse, incised marks, monogram 'F.E.B.', 14in (36cm) high.
£600–700 *MJB*

A Royal Doulton vase, decorated with a continuous floriate pattern in blue, white and gilt, against a shaded ground, 18½in (47cm) high.
£220–270 *RID*

A pair of Doulton stoneware vases, 11in (28cm) high.
£200–300 *ASA*

Two Doulton stoneware candlesticks, by George Tinworth, signed, c1900, 8in (20cm) high. **£800–1,000** *HER*

A Royal Doulton earthenware suffragette inkwell, 3in (7.5cm) high. **£270–300** *GAK*

A Royal Doulton soap dish, specially designed and manufactured by the factory for the proprietors of Wright's Coal Tar soap, c1920, 6in (15cm) wide. **£80–100** *POW*

A Royal Doulton fish ashtray, in green, blue, brown and grey, 6in (15cm) wide. **£100–130** *POW*

l. A Royal Doulton Art Deco coffee set, cream ground with a yellow, green, blue and orange C-scroll pattern, slight damage and losses. **£80–100** *GAK*

A Doulton bulldog, 'Old Bill' in a steel helmet with a rucksack, khaki glaze. **£200–300** *HER*

A pair of Royal Doulton pottery vases, brown ground with raised blue and light brown floral and leaf pattern, 12½in (32cm) high. **£140–180** *GAK*

A Royal Doulton earthenware 56-piece dinner service, designed by Sir Frank Brangwyn, cream ground with green geometric panels with green, yellow and blue foliage motifs, minor damage, printed marks 'Designed by F. Frank Brangwyn R.D., Royal Doulton, England c1930', and a 23-piece part tea service, 'Harvest', designed by Sir Frank Brangwyn, incised and impressed decoration of fruit with foliage and sheaves of corn, polychrome on a cream ground, various printed Royal Doulton marks, minor damage, c1930. **£2,000–2,500** *C*

l. A pair of Doulton faïence vases, c1880, 11½in (29cm) high. **£400–500** *HER*

l. A Doulton Lambeth vase, by Hannah Barlow, with green ground and a band of ponies, 13in (33cm) high. **£400–450** *GAK*

A Royal Doulton glazed stoneware jardinière and stand, deep blue and mottled green glazed ground, minor damage, impressed lion, crown and circle mark, incised monogram 'MB' early 20thC, 42in (106cm) high. **£600–900** *S(S)*

A Doulton Lambeth stoneware vase, with decorated seaweed fronds in the Art Nouveau style in blue, green and white on shaded brown and green ground, initialled 'MVM' for Mark V. Marshall, 17in (43cm) high.
£260–320 *MJB*

A pair of Doulton faïence vases, by A. Euphemia Thatcher, assisted by Elizabeth Shelley, 1880, 11in (28cm) high.
£400–500 *HER*

A Royal Doulton Chang vase, 13½in (34cm) high. **£600–800** *LT*

A Doulton Series Ware vase, 'The Blue Children', with blue and white gilt rim, introduced in 1890, c1920.
£400–500 *HER*

A Doulton faïence moon flask, painted by Hannah Barlow, 1885, 11½in (29cm) high.
£1,000–1,200 *HER*

A Doulton faïence vase, by Mary Butterton, dated '1879', 22in (56cm) high.
£600–800 *HER*

l. A pair of Doulton faïence vases, by M. M. Arding, ochre base, blue ground, c1883, 11in (28cm) high.
£400–500 *HER*

l. A Doulton faïence vase, painted by Mary Butterton, with 3 circular panels of white peonies on a yellow ground, on a reserve of overlapping palmettes in shades of brown and yellow, the neck with a band of butterfly-wing design, painted monograms, damaged, 24in (61cm) high.
£400–600 *C*

A pair of Doulton Lambeth vases by Frank Butler, 14in (36cm) high.
£750–800 *LT*

A Doulton Lambeth stoneware jug, by George Tinworth, with green scrolling foliage and applied flowerheads, mounted with silver rim and cover, hallmarks for Sheffield 1873, impressed marks and incised 'GT' monogram to base, 11½in (29cm) high. **£350–400** *CSK*

A Doulton Lambeth baluster jug, by Hannah Barlow, brown, green and cream, with a silver rim and cover, hallmarks for London 1894, restored, incised and impressed marks 'HBB', 7½in (19cm) high. **£200–300** *CSK*

A Doulton Lambeth stoneware jug, by George Tinworth, glazed in green, blue, brown and white, mounted with a silver rim and hinged cover, with Hukin and Heath Birmingham hall marks for 1877, impressed and incised marks, 10in (25.5cm) high. **£500–600** *CSK*

A Doulton Lambeth stoneware silver rimmed lemonade set, comprising a jug and a pair of beakers, all moulded in relief, jug 9½in (24cm) high. **£300–400** *Wor*

A Doulton Burslem dessert service, comprising: 5 cake stands and 12 dessert plates, painted in pink, purple, light green, blue and gilt, damaged, printed and painted marks, plates 8½in (22cm) diam. **£800–1,000** *CSK*

A Doulton Lambeth stoneware jug and 2 beakers, by George Tinworth, glazed in green, blue and brown, each with white metal mount to rim, 'G.T.' monogram to body, impressed date '1882', and incised marks to base, 9½in (24cm) high. **£350–400** *CSK*

A Doulton Lambeth stoneware jug, by Hannah Barlow, incised with goats above a band of blue and green stylised leaves, Doulton Lambeth mark, dated '1878', incised 'HBB' and assistants, 8in (21cm) high. **£450–500** *CSK*

A Doulton Lambeth faïence wall plaque, 'First Come First Served', painted by Esther Lewis in naturalistic colours, impressed and painted marks, numbers '242', 17in (43cm) diam. **£600–800** *CSK*

r. A Doulton faïence jardinière and stand, moulded in high relief with foliate rococo designs, the baluster stand with fluted waist, painted in muted enamel colours, slight retoration to bowl, late 19thC, 18in (45cm) high. **£800–1,000** *Bea*

A Royal Doulton jug, by Mark V. Marshall, with blue and brown foliage, impressed 'Doulton Lambeth England', 9½in (24cm) high. **£300–400** *CSK*

A Royal Doulton Sung vase, ruby red, blue and green, marked 'Sung, Noke', monogram 'FM', 5in (13cm) high. **£300–400** *P*

A pair of Royal Doulton vases, decorated by Frank Butler, ochre, lavender and green, on a blue and buff ground, marked, artist's monogram, '991', assistant's initials of Jane Hurst, date code for 1906, 18½in (47cm) high. **£1,000–1,500** *S*

A Royal Doulton stoneware vase, by Francis C. Pope, with white flowers in relief, brown foliage on a purple ground, signed 'F.C.P.', No. 537, date code for 1916, 16in (41cm) high. **£1,000–1,500** *P*

A Royal Doulton Chang snuff bottle, with a crackled white glaze streaked in red, amber, blue, brown and green, marked 'C.M., Chang, Noke', monogram for Harry Nixon, date code for 1925, 2½in (6cm) high. **£250–350** *P*

A pair of Doulton Lambeth stoneware oviform vases, by Harry Simeon, blue, brown and mustard, impressed Lambeth faïence mark with 'Faïence' cancelled, signed 'HS', No. 369, 13in (33cm) high. **£1,000–1,500** *P*

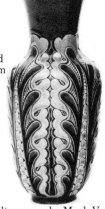

A pair of Royal Doulton vases, incised by Francis C. Pope, green and blue against a tan ground, impressed marks, artist's assistant's initials, No. 98, date code for 1904, 15in (38cm) high. **£800–1,000** *S*

A Doulton vase, by Mark V. Marshall, green and blue, impressed Lambeth mark, artist's and assistant's initials, No. 990, dated '1883', 10½in (27cm) high. **£300–350** *S*

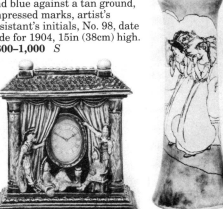

A Doulton Lambeth faïence vase, probably decorated by Margaret E.Thompson, impressed and printed marks, No. L7782, c1910, 10½in (27cm) high. **£600–800** *S*

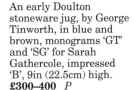

A Doulton Lambeth stoneware timepiece, by George Tinworth, modelled as a theatre, incised marks, 'GT' monogram, assistant's initials 'LB' and 'PK', 8½in (21cm) high. **£2,000–2,500** *P*

A pair of Doulton Lambeth faïence vases, decorated by Margaret E. Thompson, impressed and printed marks, No. L8095, artist's monogram, '14', c1900, 13in (33cm) high. **£1,200–1,500** *S*

An early Doulton stoneware jug, by George Tinworth, in blue and brown, monograms 'GT' and 'SG' for Sarah Gathercole, impressed 'B', 9in (22.5cm) high. **£300–400** *P*

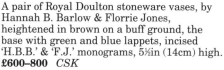

r. A pair of Royal Doulton stoneware vases, with panels of blue brown on a green ground. **£100–150** *MGM*

A pair of Royal Doulton stoneware vases, by Hannah B. Barlow & Florrie Jones, heightened in brown on a buff ground, the base with green and blue lappets, incised 'H.B.B.' & 'F.J.' monograms, 5½in (14cm) high. **£600–800** *CSK*

A pair of Royal Doulton stoneware vases, incised monograms for Eliza Simmance and Bessie Newberry, early 20thC. **£400–500** *WIL*

r. A pair of Royal Doulton vases, initialled 'WB', c1925, 13in (33cm) high. **£200–250** *TVA*

A pair of Royal Doulton vases, decorated in the Art Nouveau manner, in green and yellow on a gold decorated ivory ground, c1900, 10½in (26.5cm) high. **£400–500** *Bea*

A pair of Royal Doulton stoneware vases, decorated on a blue ground. **£200–250** *MGM*

A Royal Doulton Chang vase, covered in a thick multi-coloured crackled glaze, bearing the marks for Charles John Noke and Harry Nixon, 5½in (13.5cm) high. **£400–500** *Bea*

A Royal Doulton plate, depicting Porchester, signed 'A. Holdcroft', c1925, 10in (25cm) diam. **£120–140** *TVA*

A Royal Doulton 'Master of Foxhounds' presentation jug, No. 248 of a limited edition of 500, with original certificate of verification, 13in (33cm) high. **£400–600** *OL*

A Royal Doulton stoneware Dewar's whisky jug, with green collar, c1895, 6½in (16.5cm) high. **£100–150** *CA*

l. A Royal Doulton buff stoneware jardinière, by Hannah Barlow, with olive green glazed neck, incised with sheep in panoramic landscape, 9in (23cm) diam. **£400–600** *WHB*

r. A Royal Doulton stoneware jardinière and stand, painted with deep blue and mottled green, stand chipped, late 19thC, 37½in (95cm) high. **£700–900** *Bea*

l. A set of 5 Royal Doulton plates, with gilded rims, the centres painted with flowers and fruit, signed 'A. Piper', 9½in (24cm) diam. **£300–400** *P(Re)*

An early Doulton Lambeth stoneware jug, decorated by Hannah B. Barlow, with silver collar and cover, artist's monogram, London hallmarks for 1872, 11½in (28cm) high. **£500–600** *P*

A Doulton stoneware jug, of tapering form with skirted base, and a pair of beakers, incised by Hannah Barlow, impressed mark 'Doulton Lambeth 1878', and signed 'BHB', with silver mounts, London 1878, jug 9½in (24cm) high. **£600–800** *L*

A Doulton Lambeth biscuit barrel, with plated hinged top, decorated with a sheepdog and sheep by Hannah Barlow, impressed mark and date '1873', incised marks, 8½in (21cm) high. **£400–500** *DWB*

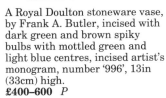

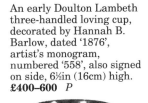

An early Doulton Lambeth three-handled loving cup, decorated by Hannah B. Barlow, dated '1876', artist's monogram, numbered '558', also signed on side, 6½in (16cm) high. **£400–600** *P*

A vase, by Hannah Barlow, incised with a band of donkeys and 2 children, impressed 'Doulton Lambeth, 10½in (26cm) high. **£300–400** *CSK*

A Royal Doulton pottery vase, decorated by Hannah Barlow, with a fox attacking sheep, 12in (30.5cm) high. **£600–800** *DSH*

A Royal Doulton stoneware vase, by Frank A. Butler, incised with dark green and brown spiky bulbs with mottled green and light blue centres, incised artist's monogram, number '996', 13in (33cm) high. **£400–600** *P*

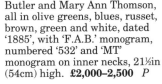

A pair of baluster vases, by Hannah Barlow, incised with lions, impressed 'Doulton Lambeth England' marks, 14in (35cm) high. **£1,800–2,200** *CSK*

l. A pair of Doulton Lambeth vases, decorated by Frank A. Butler and Mary Ann Thomson, all in olive greens, blues, russet, brown, green and white, dated '1885', with 'F.A.B.' monogram, numbered '532' and 'MT' monogram on inner necks, 21½in (54cm) high. **£2,000–2,500** *P*

A Doulton Lambeth faïence jardinière, painted by Florence E. Lewis, with a shaded green and lemon ground, artist's monogram, numbered '317', 13in (33cm) high. **£400–500** *P*

A Royal Doulton pilot figure of a botanist, 6½in (17cm) high.
£650–750 *LT*

A Royal Doulton loving cup, polychrome moulded in relief with the Three Musketeers, No. 395 from an edition of 600, printed marks, 10in (25cm) high.
£300–400 *Bon*

A Royal Doulton character jug, ''Ard of 'Earing'. No. D6588.
£500–600 *LT*

A Doulton bust of Churchill, one of only 3 made, c1940, 8½in (21cm) high.
£1,400–1,800 *ARE*

A Doulton jardinière, signed by George Tinworth, c1880, 12in (30.5cm) high.
£600–700 *HER*

A Doulton Lambeth biscuit barrel, by Florence Barlow, with plated swing handle and lid, the mottled brown body with incised acanthus scroll and star decoration, incised 'FEB' mark to base.
£150–200 *Bon*

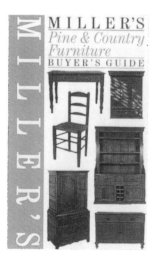

A Doulton siliconware owl, by J. A. Milne.
£400–500 *Bon*

A Doulton Lambeth stoneware Queen Victoria Jubilee commemorative jug, with a silver mounted neck, 7½in (19cm) high.
£150–200 *Re*

A group modelled as 2 frogs attacking 2 mice, on an oval mound base, entitled 'The Combat', by George Tinworth, 4in (10cm) high.
£1,000–1,500 *CSK*

l. A pair of Doulton ivory earthenware 'Galleon' jugs, each inverted ovoid body printed with 6 galleons in choppy seas, with dolphins on lower frieze, c1885, 7in (18cm) high.
£400–500 *TW*

A Doulton Lambeth stoneware bowl by Frank A. Butler, in green, pink and blue beneath a beaded band, with gilt metal rim, impressed Doulton mark, incised monogram 'FAB', dated '1882', 9½in (24cm) diam.
£200–300 *Bon*

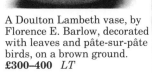

A Doulton Lambeth vase, by Florence E. Barlow, decorated with leaves and pâte-sur-pâte birds, on a brown ground.
£300–400 *LT*

A Doulton Lambeth stoneware figure, attributed to John Broad, impressed 'Doulton' on base, 18in (46cm) high.
£400–600 *P*

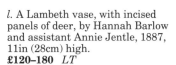

A Douldon character jug, 'Ugly Duchess', a designed by M. Henk, D6603, printed marks, 4in (10cm) high. **£160–200** *CSK*

A Doulton Lambeth stoneware commemorative vase, by George Tinworth, glazed in shades of brown, green and blue, incised 'GT' monogram, 9in (23cm) high. **£550–650** *P*

l. A Lambeth vase, with incised panels of deer, by Hannah Barlow and assistant Annie Jentle, 1887, 11in (28cm) high.
£120–180 *LT*

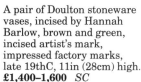

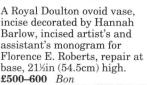

A Doulton Lambeth teapot and cover, by Hannah Barlow, incised with goats. **£400–600** *WHB*

A pair of Doulton stoneware vases, incised by Hannah Barlow, brown and green, incised artist's mark, impressed factory marks, late 19thC, 11in (28cm) high. **£1,400–1,600** *SC*

A Royal Doulton ovoid vase, incise decorated by Hannah Barlow, incised artist's and assistant's monogram for Florence E. Roberts, repair at base, 21½in (54.5cm) high. **£500–600** *Bon*

A Royal Doulton vase, by Hannah Barlow, monogram for Florence E. Roberts, 19½in (49cm) high. **£800–1,000** *Bon*

A Doulton Lambeth longcase clock, by Frank Butler, caramel ground with stylised acanthus leaves and stylised floret, heightened in blue, incised 'Doulton Lambeth 1884', artist's monogram, chip to hood, 12in (30.5cm) high. **£800–1,000** *Bon*

A Doulton Lambeth stoneware vase, incised by Hannah Barlow, brown on a buff ground, with green and blue incised leaves and florets by Frank Butler, artists' monograms, assistant's mark for Emma Martin, dated '1876', 15in (38cm) high. **£1,000–1,500** *P*

A Royal Doulton stoneware vase, by Frank A. Butler, 'F.A.B.' monogram, No. '347', 16in (41cm) high. **£400–600** *P*

A pair of Doulton vases, decorated by Frank Butler, 19thC, 17½in (44.5cm) high. **£1,500–2,000** *SC*

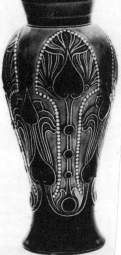

A pair of Doulton vases, tube-lined and beaded by Frank Butler, blue and brown on an olive ground, impressed Lambeth mark, incised artist's and assistant's initials, No. 3439, c1900, 11in (28.5cm) high. **£600–800** *S*

A Doulton vase, tube-lined by Frank Butler, glazed in blue and brown against an olive ground, impressed Lambeth mark, incised artist's and assistant's monograms, c1900, No. 58, 13½in (34.5cm) high. **£600–800** *S*

r. A Royal Doulton stoneware vase, by Mark V. Marshall, crushed strawberry ground decorated in lilac and pale green, artist's initials, numbered '96' and 'M.H.' possibly for Marion Holbrook, and date letter for 1902, 12in (30.5cm) high. **£800–1,000** *P*

A Royal Doulton vase, tube-lined by Frank Butler, impressed mark, incised artist's initials, No. 647, impressed date code for 1902, 17½in (44.5cm) high. **£600–900** *S*

A Doulton menu-holder, by George Tinworth, the base titled 'I See No Reason Why Gunpowder Treason Should Ever Be Forgot', olive and ochre, impressed Lambeth mark, monogram, repaired, 1880s, 4½in (11.5cm) high.
£800–1,000 *S*

A Doulton stoneware mouse group 'Waits', by George Tinworth, blue and ochre, impressed Lambeth mark, c.1880, 5½in (14cm) high.
£1,200–1,500 *S*

A Doulton vase, painted by George White, with the legend of Orpheus and Eurydice in Hades, signed, incised 'No. 1210' and date code for 1911, one handle repaired, 16in (40.5cm) high.
£1,500–2,500 *S*

A Doulton three-handled mug, commemorating the 'Hoisting of the Flag at Pretoria', green and blue glazes, impressed marks, 10½in (26.5cm) high.
£300–350 *CSK*

A Doulton Burslem vase and cover, by George White, signed, printed mark, repaired, c1910, 21in (53cm) high.
£800–1,200 *S*

l & r. A pair of Royal Doulton 'Blue Children' oviform vases, the bases marked 'Royal Doulton Flambé', 11½in (29cm) high.
£800–1,000 *P*
c. A Royal Doulton 'Blue Children' globular vase, date code for 1931, 7in (17.5cm) high.
£300–400 *P*

A pair of Doulton Lambeth stoneware vases, by Hannah Barlow, in shades of blue and green, slight chips to rims, incised and impressed marks 'HBB', and assistant's marks, 8in (20cm) high.
£500–600 *CSK*

A Doulton Lambeth musical mice group, 'Happy Violincello', by George Tinworth, traces of monogram, inscribed title, 5in (13cm) high. **£800–1,000** *P*

l. A pair of Doulton vases, each printed and painted with Arabs on camels, in green, yellow and orange, printed and painted marks, 20thC, 9½in (24cm) high.
£400–500 *S*

A Doulton jug, incised by Edgar Wilson, glazed in blue and green, impressed Lambeth mark, '270', incised artist's monogram, dated '1882', 9½in (24cm) high. **£700–900** *S*

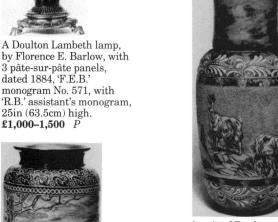

A pair of Doulton stoneware vases, by
Hannah Barlow, 1888, 7in (17.5cm) high.
£700–900   *DWB*

A Doulton Lambeth
stoneware three-handled
loving cup, by Florence
E. Barlow, decorated in
pâte-sur-pâte, with silver
rim, 'F.E.B.' monogram,
6½in (16cm) high.
£500–600   *P*

A Doulton Lambeth lamp,
by Florence E. Barlow, with
3 pâte-sur-pâte panels,
dated 1884, 'F.E.B.'
monogram No. 571, with
'R.B.' assistant's monogram,
25in (63.5cm) high.
£1,000–1,500   *P*

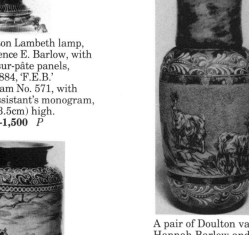

A pair of Doulton vases, decorated by
Hannah Barlow and Florence Roberts,
detailed in brown glaze against a
stippled buff ground between tube-
lined floral border glazed in brown,
pale green and blue, one cracked,
impressed Lambeth mark, incised
artists' monograms, No. 78 and
assistant's initials of Bessie Newbery,
c1890, 12½in (32cm) high.
£800–1,000   *S*

A pair of Doulton vases, incised by
Hannah Barlow and Florence Roberts,
glazed in brown, olive and blue, minor
restoration to one rim, impressed lion,
crown and circle, incised artists'
monograms and numerals, date code
for 1903, 11in (28cm) high.
£1,000–1,500   *S*

A Doulton oviform
vase, outlined in white
on a green ground, by
Hannah Barlow,
impressed 'Royal
Doulton England',
11½in (29cm) high.
£600–800   *CSK*

r. A Doulton pottery
baluster vase, painted
pâte-sur-pâte, on a blue
ground, by Florence Barlow,
impressed 'Royal Doulton',
12in (30.5cm) high.
£300–350   *CSK*

*Florence more frequently
painted in slip, and also
worked on Doulton other
than stoneware.*

l. A Doulton ewer, incised by
Hannah Barlow and Eliza
Simmance, glazed in shades of
green, brown and mauve,
impressed Lambeth mark,
incised artists' initials, 653 and
1000, dated 1877, minor chip to
foot, 14in (35.5cm) high.
£500–700   *S*

r. A Doulton jug, by
Hannah Barlow, incised
with a cat and 4 kittens,
in pale blue on a
stoneware ground, blue
and green foliage neck
and handle, impressed
'Doulton Lambeth' 1880,
9in (22.5cm) high.
£800–1,200   *CSK*

A Doulton Lambeth jug, by Arthur B. Barlow, glazed in shades of blue and brown, artist's monogram 'SG', No.777?, assistant's mark, dated '1873', 6½in (17cm) high.
£200–300 *P*

A Doulton Lambeth stoneware jug, decorated by Hannah Barlow, Florence Barlow and Mark V Marshall, glazed in greens, brown and beige, incised 'H.B.B.', monogram 'No. 214, F.E.B. No. 341, M.U.M. No. 3.', 9½in (24.5cm) high.
£1,000–1,200 *P*

A Doulton stoneware jardinière, in blues, browns and grey, incised 'H. Doulton Lambeth', 7½in (19cm) high.
£700–900 *C*

A Doulton stoneware jug, decorated by Hannah Barlow and probably Lucy Barlow, inscribed and printed marks, dated '1884', 9½in (23.5cm) high. **£400–500** *Bea*

l. A Doulton stoneware vase, designed by Frank Butler, impresssed Royal Doulton mark, incised artist's monogram 'F.A.B.', 18½in (47cm) high.
£2,000–2,500 *C*

A Doulton tapering mug, decorated by Hannah Barlow, impressed 'Doulton Lambeth', incised 'H.B.B., 209', dated '1874', 4in (10cm) high.
£350–450 *CEd*

A Doulton Lambeth faïence tile panel, printed on reverse, indistinct painted monogram on one, 'R' to bottom tile, 24⅛in (61.5cm) high.
£300–350 *P*

r. A Doulton Lambeth stoneware baluster vase, by Florence E Barlow and Frank A Butler, in rich blues, browns and greens, the neck rim carved as a row of scrolls, 'F.E.B.' and 'F.A.B.' monograms, numbered '345' and '385' respectively and 'RHM' monogram of assistant, 21in (53cm) high.
£1,500–2,000 *P*

A pair of Doulton Lambeth vases, by George Tinworth, in dark blue and with pale blue beadwork tendrils and flowerheads on an ochre coloured ground, both with incised monogram to body, 11in (28cm) high.
£600–800 *L*

r. A Doulton Lambeth siliconware vase, by Edith D. Lupton and Ada Dennis, in white, brown and blue, top reduced, 'E.D.L.' artist's monogram, numbered '378', 'AD' monogram, numbered '16', dated '1885', 8in (20.5cm) high.
£400–500 *P*

l. A Doulton Lambeth stoneware vase, by Mark V. Marshall, glazed in mottled brown, blue and cream, artist's monogram, No. 3 and assistant's mark, 10in (25cm) high.
£300–350 *P*

r. A Doulton Lambeth vase by Emily Stormer, glazed in blues, greens, white and brown, artist's monogram, numbered '825' and 'EM' for Emma Martin, dated '1877', 9½in (24.5cm) high.
£300–350 *P*

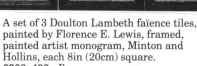

A set of 3 Doulton Lambeth faïence tiles, painted by Florence E. Lewis, framed, painted artist monogram, Minton and Hollins, each 8in (20cm) square.
£300–400 *P*

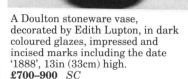

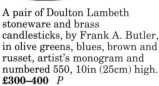

A pair of Doulton Lambeth stoneware and brass candlesticks, by Frank A. Butler, in olive greens, blues, brown and russet, artist's monogram and numbered 550, 10in (25cm) high.
£300–400 *P*

A Doulton stoneware vase, decorated by Edith Lupton, in dark coloured glazes, impressed and incised marks including the date '1888', 13in (33cm) high.
£700–900 *SC*

A pair of Doulton Lambeth stoneware jardinières, by Edith D. Lupton, incised with olive green foliate scrolls against deep blue, with artist's initials, numbered 512 and 513, and assistant's initials for Eliza J. Hubert, dated '1877' 8in (20cm) high.
£800–1,000 *P*

r. A Royal Doulton oviform stoneware vase, by Mark V. Marshall, incised with artist's initials, No. 685, assistant's mark for Emily Partington, date shield for 1907, 12in (30cm) high.
£400–500 *P*

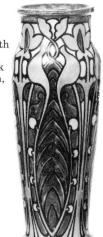

A Doulton Lambeth jug, by Mark V. Marshall, incised artist's initials, No. 105, assistant's initials 'MH' and 'JBH', 9in (22.5cm) high.
£2,500–3,000 *L*

Doulton Glazing Techniques

• 'Sung' and 'Chang' wares draw upon old Chinese glazes with their bright mottled colours against a flambé ground.
• 'Titanian' wares, introduced in 1915, required a fine porcelain body, often with artist's illustrations under a blend of metallic pigments to form a silvery-blue glaze.
• 'Kingsware', the distinctive treacle brown glaze often found on flasks and bottles made for Dewars' Whisky, was made with a transparent ivory glaze fired over coloured slips.

A Doulton cylindrical jug, by M. V. Marshall, modelled with a band of blue and brown foliage outlined in white on a stoneware ground, impressed Doulton Lambeth England mark, 10½in (26cm) high. **£300–400** *CSK*

A pair of Doulton stoneware vases, by Eliza Simmance, with stylised lily motifs on a streaked pale green ground, impressed mark, incised artist's initials, 1900s, 9in (23cm) high.
£700–900 *SS*

A Doulton Lambeth stoneware ewer, by Mark V. Marshall, in ochre, cobalt and green, shown at the 1893 Chicago Columbian World Fair, 72in (183cm) high.
£18,000–20,000 *Bon*

A pair of Royal Doulton vases, c1900, 11in (28cm) high.
£150–180 *HAE*

A pair of Doulton saltglazed stoneware vases, by Hannah B. Barlow, in green and brown with tube-lined Art Nouveau swirling motifs in a band above and below, large chip to rim of one, impressed factory marks, incised monogram 'BHB' and others of Assistants, c1885, 11in (28cm) high.
£900–1,200 *S(C)*

A Doulton group, 'The Love Letter', HN 2149.
£150–200 *Bea*

A Doulton brown and white model of a standing bulldog, HN 1045.
£350–400 *Bea*

A pair of Doulton flambé models of penguins, set in an alabaster ashtray with silver mounts, with assay mark for London 1919, 6½in (17cm) high.
£250–300 *Bea*

l. A Doulton coffee service, 'Reynard the Fox' with printed marks and pattern number H4927.
£300–400 *DN*

l. A large Doulton loving cup, produced to commemorate the Silver Jubilee of King George V and Queen Mary, no. 980 of a limited edition of 1,000.
£300–400 *Bea*

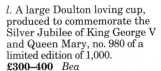

A white Doulton character jug, 'Simon the Cellarer', 3in (8cm) high.
£150–200 *DN*

A Doulton saltglazed metal mounted stoneware biscuit barrel, highlighted in blue, with impressed factory mark and date, and incised monogram 'Hannah B. Barlow', 1880, 7½in (19cm) high.
£450–550 *S(C)*

A Doulton porcelain vase, by Arthur Leslie, decorated with a maiden holding a white dove in a landscape, dated '5.11', 9in (23cm) high.
£400–450 *S(C)*

A Doulton pottery vase, the body decorated with a fox-hunting scene between bands of flowers, cracked, 22½in (57cm) high. **£200–300** *Bea*

A Royal Doulton Limited Edition loving cup to commemorate the reign of Edward VIII, modelled by H. Fenton, edition No. 699 of 2000, printed inscription and factory mark, and a certificate signed by Charles J. Noke, 10in (25cm) high.
£400–500 *TW*

A Royal Doulton pottery 'Nelson' loving cup, inscribed 'I Was In Trafalgar Bay' and 'England Expects', decorated in colours and incised 'Fenton', the base with printed inscription and mark in green, limited edition number 579 of 600, 10½in (27cm) high.
£700–900 *HSS*

A Royal Doulton character teapot and cover, 'Old Charley', date code for 1939, introduced 1939, withdrawn 1960, 7in (18cm) high.
£600–800 *P*

A Royal Doulton Golfing Series mug, decorated in relief with figures in period costume, glazed in colours, D5716, 6in (15cm) high.
£200–250 *P*

A Royal Doulton character jug, 'Mephistopheles', designed by C. J. Noke and H. Fenton, introduced 1937, withdrawn 1948, 6in (15cm) high.
£500–700 *P*

A Royal Doulton character teapot and cover, 'Sairey Gamp', date code for 1939, introduced 1939, withdrawn 1960, 7in (18cm) high.
£600–800 *P*

r. A Kingsware whisky flask and stopper, printed Royal Doulton, England marks, 8in (20cm) high.
£200–250 *CSK*

A Doulton flambé figure, by Noke, with pagoda-like red silk and cream braid shade with metal mounted faceted glass drops, printed mark and original printed label, c1930, 22½in (58cm) high.
£800–1,000 *C*

A pottery character jug modelled as Santa Claus, D6690, printed Royal Doulton England marks, 7½in (19cm) high.
£60–80 *CSK*

l. A Royal Doulton 'Bunnykins' candleholder with loop handle, 'Santa Claus' and 'Lambeth Walk', designed by Barbara Vernon, made between 1940 and 1949, 'Bunnykins' back stamp, 7in (18cm) high.
£100–200 *P*

Restored or not Restored?

In salesrooms or at fairs, some readers may have seen potential buyers biting into pieces of Doulton with their teeth. They haven't skipped lunch, they are testing for restoration. This can be detected as a soft putty on the surface of the glaze and hence will be soft to the teeth. A more hygenic method is to open a paper clip and first touch the surface of the piece – it will glide over the shiny glazed surface but stick into the restored area. Best of all, ask the seller to 'blue light' the piece for you; any restoration will show up under an ultra violet lamp.

A Royal Doulton figure, 'Smuts' designed by H. Fenton, 7in (17.5cm) high. **£500–600** *P*

A Royal Dulton figure, 'Dulcinea', designed by L. Harrdine, HN1419, introduced 1930, withdrawn 1938, 5½in (14cm) high. **£750–800** *LT*

A pottery character jug of 'Johnny Appleseed', printed Royal Doulton marks, D6372, 6½in (16.5cm) high. **£100–150** *CSK*

A Royal Doulton Kingsware Dewar's whisky flask, as a figure of 'George the Guard', printed marks, 8½in (21.5cm) high. **£120–150** *Bon*

A Royal Doulton figure, 'Marquise Silvestra', 9in (24cm), c1920. **£3,000–5,000** *Bon*

A Royal Doulton figure, 'The Lilac Shawl', after a model by C. J. Noke, printed mark and title, HN44, date code for 1918, 8½in (21.5cm) high **£800–1,200** *S*

A Royal Doulton Kingsware Dewar's whisky flask, decorated with a 16thC town-crier, printed marks, 9in (22.5cm) high. **£150–200** *Bon*

A Royal Doulton figure, 'Lady Ermine', green painted mark, HN54,. No. 15, incised date 2.18.1918, 8½in (22.5cm) high. **£1,000–1,500** *SC*

A Royal Doulton figure, 'Robert Burns', HN42, inscribed 'E. W. Light Sc.' and 'No 5', 14in (35.5cm) high. **£2,500–3,000** *P*

A Royal Doulton figure, 'Fruit Gathering', designed by L. Harradine, HN562, impressed date '9.23/8?', 8in (20cm) high. **£850–950** *P*

A Royal Doulton figure, 'Pretty Lady', HN70, date code for 1919, 9½in (24cm) high. **£500–600** *S*

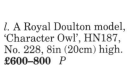

r. A Royal Doulton model of a fox, lying curled with its tail around its head, having dark and light marking, HN147, impressed date '2.1.36.', 3½in (9cm) wide. **£300–400** *P*

l. A Royal Doulton model, 'Character Owl', HN187, No. 228, 8in (20cm) high. **£600–800** *P*

r. A Royal Doulton figure, 'The Perfect Pair', designed by L. Harradine, HN 581, impressed date 10.26, 7in (18cm) high. **£300–400** *P*

A Doulton Slaters patent vase, decorated with panels of charcoal-grey and royal blue, painted 'M.L. X1974', 12in (30.5cm) high. **£150–200** *P*

l. A Doulton Lambeth saltglazed figure of a Boer War soldier, designed by John Broad, on a green and caramel base, impressed marks, 12ins (30.5cm.) high.
£400–600
c. A Doulton Burslem urn, painted by D. Dewsberry, on an ivory ground, bordered by gilt friezes, printed mark, 14in (36cm) high.
£200–400
r. A Royal Doulton 'Chinese jade' vase, covered with a green streaked glaze, printed mark, 6in (15cm) high.
£450–500 *Bon*

A Doulton jug, with brown glazed borders, the body printed in black with 'The Handyman', a sailor from *HMS Powerful*, flanked by bust portraits of Capt. H. Lambton and P. M. Scott, impressed 'Doulton Lambeth England', 8½in (21cm) high.
£150–200 *CSK*

A Royal Doulton 'Chang' vase, glazed in shades of crimson, blue and green and over-painted with brightly coloured butterflies, faintly impressed and painted 'Doulton' and numerals, 9½in (24.5cm) high.
£1,000–1,200 *S*

A Royal Doulton Flambé 'Sung' vase, with a mauve, amber and crimson ground, mottled brown glaze, printed lion, crown and circle, impressed 'Doulton' and numerals, painted Sung script mark, No. 2653E, dated '3–24', 8in (19.5cm) high. **£500–700** *S*

A limited edition Doulton jug, 'Regency Coach', decorated in low relief and colours with a coach drawing up outside an inn, printed and painted marks, No. 329, 10½in (26.5cm) high.
£400–500 *CSK*

A Doulton mug, decorated in 'Shakespeare's Knights' pattern, c1928, 5½in (14cm) high.
£40–50 *SN*

A set of 10 Doulton plates, decorated by Kelsall, painted in polychrome with gilt borders, chips to one plate, the majority with painted title on reverse and printed marks, 9in (23cm) diam.
£350–500 *CSK*

A two-handled loving cup, with King George VI and Elizabeth, 1937, limited edition no. 949/2000.
£400–500 *MGM*

r. A limited edition jug, 'Chart of Treasure Island', decorated in colours and relief with Treasure Island characters, cracks to base, printed and painted marks, no. 3, 7in (18vcm) high.
£300–500 *CSK*

A pair of Royal Dux porcelain figural vases, modelled with scrolling golden leaves and pink tinged flowers, raised pink triangle mark, 16½in (42cm) high
£250–300 *CSK*

A Rozenburg twin-handled pottery vase, by Jan van der Vet, printed crown and stork mark, artist's monogram, date code for 1902, 14in (35.5cm) high.
£400–600 *P*

A Villeroy and Boch 'Mettlach' wall plaque, in pale pink, matt red and petrol blue, with a gilded rim, impressed factory marks and number '2549', 18in (46cm) diam.
£300–500 *P*

l. A small Rozenburg 'egg-shell' vase, painted in greens, yellow, purple, black and orange, painted factory marks, numbered '1588' and date code for 1900, 5in (12.5cm) high.
£500–800 *P*

A Rozenburg dish, decorated with a Chinese dragon, the border with yellow geometrical pattern, marked 'Rozenburg Den Haag 758 NKx, 1896', repaired, 17½in (44cm) diam.
£500–800 *C(Am)*

A Royal Dux figure of a boy, picked out in pale colours and gilding, applied triangle mark and impressed '1810', c1900, 20½in (52.5cm) high.
£250–300 *SC*

A Royal Dux bowl, painted in muted enamel colours and gold, 11in (28cm) wide.
£300–500 *Bea*

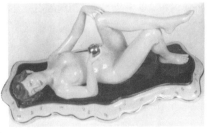

A Royal Dux porcelain figure, seated on a green rocky base, marked 'P. Aichele, No. 1379', 18½in (47cm) high.
£500–800 *DSH*

A pair of Royal Dux porcelain figural vases, with scrolling golden leaves and pink tinged flowers, raised pink triangle mark, 16½in (42cm) high. **£300–500** *CSK*

A Royal Dux figure, 'The Girl with the Golden Apple', c1920, 22in (55.5cm) wide.
£1,400–1,600 *BEV*

A pair of Martin Brothers stoneware panels, the arched forms impressed and incised with profile images of Cowper and Chaucer, each against a patterned background, covered in a salt glaze in shades of blue and brown, indistinct marks and date, 17in (43cm) long.
£500–700 *C*

A pair of Minton Art Pottery moon flasks, painted in blue with frogs and fish or birds and rabbits within chevron bands, the short cylindrical neck flanked by a pair of loop handles, impressed, printed and painted marks, c1870, 8½in (21.5cm) high.
£700–900 *S(S)*

A Martin Brothers jug, in a mottled blue-green on a brown ground, the neck with a band of vertical incised lines, incised 'Martin Bros., London & Southall, 2-1894', chip to spout, c1894, 8½in (21.5cm) high.
£300–500 *S(S)*

A Martin Brothers vase, painted with spiny fish and eels swimming among water weeks and aother aquatic life, in shades of grey and brown on a buff ground, incised 'Martin Bros., London & Southall, 10-1891', repaired, 7½in (19cm) high, and a miniature Martin ware vase.
£400–600 *CSK*

A Linthorpe vase, by Christopher Dresser, shape no. 24, 12½in (32cm) high.
£230–250 *NCA*

A Martin Brothers stoneware tobacco jar and cover, modelled as a comic bird with curly plumage, standing erect with eyes closed, glazed in shades of blue and buff, base incised 'Martin Bros. London & Southall', cover incised 'Martin 30.8.81 London & Southall', repaired, 12in (31cm) high.
£2,000–3,000 *CSK*

A Minton Art Pottery Studio moon flask, one side with painted head and shoulders portrait of a girl in the style of W. S. Coleman, framed by a band of holly, the reverse in dark blue, impressed 'Minton 1498', and printed mark 'Minton's Art Pottery Studio Kensington Gore', damaged, 14in (35cm) high.
£700–900 *P(S)*

A set of 20 Minton stoneware tiles, designed by A. W. N. Pugin, the ochre ground with brown and black glazed decoration of quatrefoil reserve with central flowerhead within foliate motifs, reverse with moulded marks 'Minton & Co., Stoke-upon-Trent, Patent', each tile 6in (15cm) square.
£600–800 *C*

A Brannam pottery slipware vase, the red body overlaid with white slip, decorated with 3 sgraffito panels of armorial style beasts and foliage, flanked by foliate and geometric panels and borders, beneath a honey glaze, signed 'C. Brannam, Barum, N. Devon' and dated '1991', 'R' on neck, 15in (13cm) high.
£600–800 *P*

A Bretby 'jewelware' vessel, 16in (41cm) high.
£150–200 *ZEI*

l. A pair of Ault brown and black earthenware vases, c1930, 10½in (26cm) high.
£60–80 *OCA*

A pair of Fenton Sutherland Art Ware vases, by Frank Beardmore & Co., with pink, green and yellow decoration, 12½in (31.5cm) high.
£500–800 *ASA*

A Watcombe Pottery terracotta tea set, designed by Christopher Dresser, with bands of ridged decoration, comprising: a teapot and cover, milk jug, sugar basin, cup with saucer and tray, with impressed 'W', teapot 3in (8cm) high.
£600–700 *C*

A stoneware jug, both sides modelled with the face of a mildly amused, overweight and ageing male, with strap handle, incised '10.12.1909 R.W. Martin & Brothers, London & Southall', 7in (18cm) high.
£800–1,200 *P*

An Austrian wall plaque by Boss, 6½in (16cm) high.
£100–200 *ASA*

A tapering jug, incised with a gentleman and companion in Medieval costume, flanked by flowers and leaves on a brown ground, incised mark, 'R.W. Martin, London and Southall', and dated '15th July 1881', 8½in (21cm) high.
£270–350 *DN*

A Hadcote vase, with raised slip design in turquoise, made for Liberty & Co., 7in (18cm) high.
£125–175 *ZEI*

A pair of Martin Brothers stoneware candelesticks, each on sloping footed square base, incised with panels of water birds, surmounted by twisted columns incised with foliage and the monogram 'PA', glazed in shades of green and blue, incised factory marks, damaged, 8in (20cm) high.
£250–350 *CSK*

A Martin Brothers stoneware double faced jug in buff coloured glaze, inscribed on base 'R. W. Martin Brothers, London & Southall, 2.2.1903', 7in (18cm). **£1,200–1,800** *Re*

A Martin Brothers stoneware spirit flask, with a grinning face, and a silver mounted stopper, inscribed on base 'R. W. Martin Brothers, London and Southall, 11.1901', 9½in (24cm) high. **£1,000–1,500** *Re*

A stoneware jug, with mottled blue ground, incised on base 'Martin Brothers, London & Southall June 1897', 10½in (26cm) high. **£800–1,000** *Re*

A stoneware vase, decorated with incised fish and water snakes among seaweed, in mottled brown glaze, incised 'R. W. Martin London & Southall 3.1891', 7in (18cm) high. **£500–600** *CSK*

A stoneware jug, with incised decoration of an underwater scene, with grotesque fish in shades of brown, green and blue on a cream coloured ground, inscribed 'Martin Bros. London & Southall, 1888', 9in (23cm) high. **£250–300** *CSK*

A Martin Brothers stoneware bottle vase, incised with 2 grotesque frogs painted in shades of green and brown against a light honey-coloured ground, incised 'Martin Bros. London & Southall 4.1913', 5in (12.5cm) high. **£500–600** *C*

A Martin Brothers stoneware bottle vase, incised with 2 frogs among grasses, painted in shades of green, brown and white, incised 'Martin Bros. London & Southall 4.1913', 4in (10cm) high. **£500–600** *C*

r. A Martin Brothers stoneware sundial, the base glazed in various shades of brown, green, blue and yellow, below a brass sundial, incised 'R. W. Martin Brothers, London & Southall 4–1888', 33in (84cm) high. **£3,000–4,000** *CSK*

A Martin ware stoneware vase, painted with orchids in shades of ochre and pale lilac on a brown ground, inscribed 'Martin Bros. London & Southall 3.1898', 13in (33cm) high. **£500–600** *CSK*

A Martin Brothers stoneware grotesque double faced jug, in pale grey glaze mottled with brown, the hair and handle in a darker brown, incised 'R. W. Martin & Bros. London and Southall', c1900, 6in (17cm) high.
£1,000–1,500 *C*

A Martin Brothers stoneware vase, signed 'Martin Bros., London and Southall' and dated '8–1894', 14in (34.50cm) high.
£700–900 *P*

A Martin ware imp musician 'Tambourine Player' modelled as a grotesque creature with exaggerated ears and grinning expression, signed on tambourine 'Martin Bros, London and Southall', 4½in (11.25cm) high.
£750–850 *P*

An early Martin ware jug, decorated in blues, brown and greens, signed 'R. W. Martin' and 'E9' 8½in (21.50cm) high.
£200–300 *P*
The form this decoration takes shows the obvious influence of the designs of Christopher Dresser, perhaps from The Art of Decorative Design *of 1862.*

A Martin ware pouring vessel, decorated with a sunburst centred with a grotesque face, all against a dark brown ground, signed 'Martin, London', 9in (23cm) high.
£600–900 *P*

A Martin Brothers fantastic animal, inscribed, damaged, 11in (28cm) high.
£4,000–6,000 *DWB*

A Martin ware vase, incised 'Martin Brothers, London, Southall', 7in (17.5cm) high.
£280–320 *CSK*

A Martin Bros. stoneware flower vase, with blue, grey and brown glazes on a pricked surface, incised marks, 12½in (31cm) high.
£300–400 *CSK*

A stoneware vase, incised 'Martin Bros. London & Southall 3–1894' 9½in (24cm) high.
£300–400 *C*

r. A stoneware jardinière, glazed in blues and greys on a stone coloured ground, incised 'Martin Brothers, London & Southall 10–1892', 11in (27cm) high.
£1,000–1,500 *C*

Ferdinand Preiss
(German, 1882–1943)

The Preiss-Kassler Foundry was formed in Berlin in 1906. Preiss himself designed most of the models produced by the firm, although by 1914 there were about six designers working for him.

Most figures by Preiss are made of chryselephantine, a combination of bronze and ivory. He also made a few ivory figures, often small classical female nudes. The quality of his carving was usually very high, and he specialised in sporting figures, based on real sportsmen and sportswomen, and also actresses. His figures usually bear the 'PK' monogram, for the Preiss-Kassler foundry, and the signature 'F. Preiss'. Copies do exist, often made from a softer type of stone which resembles onyx. Beware of any figures attributed to Preiss that have a very elaborate base. Most bases on Preiss figures are made of green, black, or a combination of green and black, Brazilian onyx, sometimes banded with black Belgian slate.

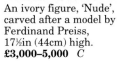

An ivory figure, 'Nude', carved after a model by Ferdinand Preiss, 17½in (44cm) high.
£3,000–5,000 C

An Art Deco jade, lapis lazuli and mother-of-pearl table clock, base repaired, signed by Cartier, No. 1216.
£11,000–15,000 CNY

Three gilt bronze and ivory figures, after models by A. Gory:

l. 'Exotic Dancer', inscribed in the bronze 'A. Gory', 15in (37.5cm) high.
£2,000–2,800

c. 'Flower Girl', inscribed 'A. Gory Salon des Beaux Arts, Paris', 14in (35cm) high.
£800–1,200

r. 'Flower Seller', inscribed 'A. Gory', 15in (38cm) high.
£1,000–1,500 C

Cartier

Cartier made a variety of timepieces, usually desk and carriage clocks, or wristwatches. The firm treated the clock almost as a sculpture, and it is not always immediately apparent what the piece's function is. Designs were often exotic or Oriental. Chinoiserie forms, and decorative motifs with a Chinese influence, are common. Semi-precious stones were often embellished with fine quality gems.

Clocks can be dated by their serial number, which can be checked with Cartier, who keep a record of everything they make. Pieces which come from Cartier in Paris carry more of a premium than those from Cartier in either New York or London.

A calendar table clock, with adjustabl day and date, marked 'Cartier', stand stamped 'Cartier 2324 Paris', 4½in (11cm) high.
£3,500–4,500 *C*

r. A Swiss lapis lazuli and jade table clock, face gilded, c1925, 10in (25cm) wide.
£4,000–5,000 *CNY*

A black lacquered metal, mother-of-pearl and glass table clock, inscribed 'Cartier No. 1074, Made in France', 5in (12.5cm) high, with original battery movement and fitted case.
£4,000–5,000 *CNY*

l. A cloisonné box, brass inlaid with a geometric design, incised 'Jean Goulden CVIII 30', and stamped 'J', 5in (12cm) wide.
£2,500–3,000 *C*

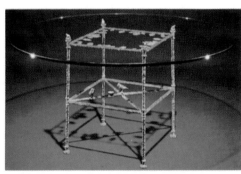

A bronze and glass dining table, by Diego Giacometti, the glass top with 4 frogs for attachment above a gilt leaf band, signed 'Diego', 60in (152cm) diam.
£90,000–100,000 *CNY*

Two bronze armchairs, by Diego Giacometti, the arms formed by the front leg rising to a button top, 32in (81cm) high.
£15,000–18,000 *CNY*

A black vase, 'Martins Pêcheurs', moulded with songbirds in flowering branches, with impressed signature 'R. Lalique', 9½in (23.5cm) high. **£6,000–7,000** *C*

An ebonised and rosewood cabinet, by Carlo Bugatti, with brass, pewter and ivory inlay, 35½in (30cm) wide. **£9,000–10,000** *C*

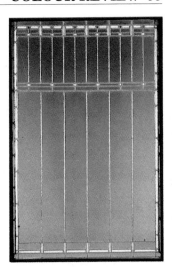

A leaded glass window, designed by Frank Lloyd Wright, c1900, 41½ by 27in (105 by 68cm). **£3,500–4,500** *CNY*

An oak dining table and 8 chairs, designed by Frank Lloyd Wright, c1903, table 54½in (138cm) wide. **£350,000+** *CNY*

A Daum pâte-de-verre figure, by Almaric Walter, moulded monogram 'AW', carved 'Daum Nancy', with Cross of Lorraine, 6½in (17cm). **£7,500–9,000** *C*

A cameo glass bowl, by Thos. Webb & Sons, with a silver rim, London 1901, 8in (20cm) diam. **£1,700–2,000** *SWO*

An oak side chair, by Charles Rohlfs, Buffalo N.Y., 1901, 47in (119cm) high. **£16,000–19,000** *CNY*

An oak side chair, designed by Frank Lloyd Wright, c1902. **£14,000–16,000** *CNY*

above right. A pâte-de-verre paperweight, designed by H. Bergé, with moulded signature 'A. Walter Nancy H. Bergé', 3in (7.5cm) high. **£10,000–12,000** *C*

r. A Favrile glass vase, by Tiffany Studios, inscribed 'L. C. Tiffany E136', c1896, 20in (50.5cm) high. **£4,000–5,000** *CNY*

A silver and ivory tea service, the hammered bodies raised on 4 short feet, impressed mark of Gorham and Martelé '9584 WDL', samovar with stand 13in (33cm) high, 218oz. **£11,000–13,000** *CNY*

Two earthenware vases, by Rookwood, c1910, 14in (35.5cm) high. *l.* Designed by Carl Schmidt. **£3,000–4,000** *r.* Designed by Edward Diers. **£600–800** *CNY*

l. and r. Two Guild of Handicraft mustard pots, one by C. R. Ashbee, stamped 'CRA', c1900, largest 3½in (9cm) high, 4oz 11dwt. **£1,000–1,200 each** *c.* A box and cover, designed by C. R. Ashbee, stamped 'G of H Ltd.', c1900, 8in (20cm) high, 16oz 15dwt. **£4,000–5,000** *C*

An enamelled three-piece demi-tasse service, by Tiffany & Co., New York, bearing touchmark of Pan-American Exposition in Buffalo, N.Y., 1901, marked on base, coffee pot 9in (23cm) high, 37oz 10dwt. **£17,000–19,000** *CNY*

A Liberty & Co. silver bowl with matching spoon, designed by Archibald Knox, stamped 'L & Co.', Cymric and Birmingham 1899, 4in (10cm) wide, 21oz. **£4,000–5,000** *C*

An earthenware vase, by Rookwood, designed by Carl Schmidt, 1900, impressed firm's mark, 8½in (21.5cm) high. **£4,500–5,500** *CNY*

A Doulton Lambeth faience tile panel, 'Sleeping Beauty – the Fairies at the Christening', painted by Margaret E. Thompson, signed, 41 by 55in (104 by 139.5cm). **£4,000–5,000** *P*

l. A Martin Brothers stoneware model of a grotesque bird, with removable head, signed on neck, rim and base 'R. W. Martin & Bros.', dated '12-1900', 15in (38cm) high. **£5,000–7,000** *P*

A silver sugar bowl and teapot, by Tiffany & Co., New York, with a green stone finial and applied with insects, 1877–91.
Sugar bowl: 3in (7.5cm) high, 13oz. **£7,000–8,000**
Teapot: 5in (13cm) high, 15oz. **£12,000–14,000** *CNY*

A G. Argy-Rousseau pâte-de-verre glass vase, marked, c1920, 4in (9.5cm) high. **£8,000–10,000** *S*

A clear and frosted Alexandrite vase, 'Tortues', intaglio moulded 'R. Lalique', 10½in (26cm) high. **£8,000–10,000** *Bon*

A Müller Frères cameo glass vase, cameo mark, 12in (30.5cm) high. **£1,600–2,000** *S*

An opalescent vase, 'Bacchantes', with engraved signature 'R. Lalique, France', 9½in (24cm) high. **£8,000–10,000** *C*

A glass and earthenware table lamp, shade by Tiffany, base by Ruth Erikson. **£6,750–10,000** *CNY*

A double overlaid and etched glass table lamp, cameo signature 'Müller Frères, Luneville', 21½in (54cm) high. **£6,000–7,500** *CNY*

l. A Gabriel Argy-Rousseau pâte-de-verre table lamp, marked on shade and base, 15½in (39.5cm) high. **£26,000–30,000** *C*

A glass scent flaçon, 'Bouchon Mûres', chip to underside, moulded 'R. Lalique', 4⅜in (11cm) high. **£12,000–15,000** *Bon*

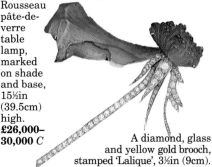

A diamond, glass and yellow gold brooch, stamped 'Lalique', 3½in (9cm). **£45,000–50,000** *CNY*

A French blue vase, 'Penthièvre', stencilled 'R. Lalique', 10in (25cm) high. **£5,000–6,000** *Bon*

A glass table, 'Cactus', by Lalique et Cie, engraved 'No. 37 le 3/12/82', 60in (152cm) diam. **£13,500–15,000** *CNY*

A Pilkington Royal Lancastrian lustre vase, decorated by Wm. S. Mycock, potted by E. T. Radford, marked, 1929, 15½in (39.5cm) high.
£800–1,200 *C*

A leaded glass and bronze table lamp, by Duffner & Kimberly, 29in (73.5cm) high.
£4,000–5,000 *CNY*

A majolica simulated basket jardinière, by Holdcroft, on a shaped stand, late 19thC, 11in (28cm) high.
£140–160 *PCh*

A Royal Doulton vase, with inscription 'Presented to Mr A. Baldwin by his colleagues at Royal Doulton Potteries on the occasion of his marriage, 2nd Sept. 1925', signed by his colleagues.
£180–200 *PCh*

A Martin Bros. stoneware bird, signed and dated '9-1898', 14½in (37cm) high.
£5,000–6,000 *P*

A daffodil leaded glass and bronze table lamp, impressed 'Tiffany Studios, New York, 25882', 22in (56cm) high.
£6,000–7,000 *CNY*

A Royal Doulton character jug, 'Paddy', with a musical box playing an Irish jig.
£400–450 *PCh*

An Art Deco glass table lamp, acid etched with geometric panels, signed 'Daum Nancy France' on base and shade.
£5,000–6,000 *P*

A stoneware Toby jug, signed 'Martin Bros. London & Southall', dated '11-1903', 10in (25cm) high.
£3,000–4,000 *P*

r. A Royal Doulton figure, 'Europa and the Bull', impressed 'H. Tittensor, Noke', and '203', 10½in (26cm) wide.
£2,000–3,000 *P*

A lacquered metal bowl, on a raised foot, with founded flaring body and everted rim, distressed gold body and coral red interior, signed in red lacquer 'Jean Dunand', c1925, 4in (10cm) high. **£800–1,200** *C*

An oviform ginger jar and cover, enriched with gilt decoration, printed marks 'Carlton Ware, Made in England, Trade Mark', 12in (30.5cm) high. **£1,500–2,000** *C*

A Clarice Cliff vase, hand painted marks 'Inspiration by Clarice Cliff Newport Pottery, Burslem England', signed, c1930, 16in (40.5cm) high. **£2,000–3,000** *C*

A pâte-de-verre vase, with stylised moulded decoration of fish swimming through waves, moulded signature 'G. Argy-Rousseau', c1925, 6in (15cm) high. **£2,500–3,000** *C*

A Lalique butterscotch glass statuette, 'Thais', inscribed 'R. Lalique', 9in (22.5cm) high. **£3,500–4,000** *CSK*

Three Fauré vases, silver and thick enamel, with geometric abstract designs, signed 'C. Fauré, Limoges', c1925. **£1,500–2,000** *C(Am)*

Two René Lalique drinking services:
l. 18 pieces, after 1934. **£1,000–1,200**
r. 29 pieces, after 1924. **£2,500–3,000** *S*

A René Lalique opalescent glass vase, 'Orleans', marked, 8in (20cm) high. **£800–1,000** *S*

An opalescent glass clock, 'Inseparables', by René Lalique, after 1926, 4⅛in (11.5cm) high. **£1,200–1,400** *S*

A Lalique moulded, frosted and enamelled glass vase, model introduced in 1926, inscribed 'R. Lalique', 7in (18cm) high. **£5,000–6,000** *S(NY)*

A René Lalique opalescent glass plate, 'Assiette Calypso', stencilled mark, after 1930. **£1,600–2,000** *S*

l. A Lalique glass vase, 'Tournesol', after 1927. **£800–1,000**
r. A Lalique perfume bottle. **£600–800** *S*

A René Lalique table decoration, 'Faisans', comprising: 2 glass candelabra and a serving dish, dish with engraved mark, chips to dish, after 1942. **£1,200–1,500** *S*

A René Lalique glass and nickel plated metal plaque, moulded mark, slightly polished, c1925, 16in (40cm) high. **£3,000–3,500** *S*

A Lalique moulded and frosted glass vase, 1914 model, moulded and inscribed. **£1,200–1,500** *S(NY)*

A René Lalique glass vase, 'Aras', moulded mark 'R. Lalique', after 1924, 9in (23cm) high. **£4,000–5,000** *S*

A Lalique moulded glass perfume bottle, 1926 model, 3in (7.5cm) high. **£1,600–2,200** *S(NY)*

A black enamelled clear glass vase, wheel cut 'R. Lalique', and engraved 'France No. 970'. 8in (20cm) high. **£1,600–2,000** *CNY*

l. A glass vase, designed by Koloman Moser, 7in (17cm) high.
£1,200–1,600
c. A glass vase, by Loetz, 8in (20cm) high.
£1,200–1,500
r. A Ferdinand Poschinger Glasshütten vase, engraved
signature and marked 'Bayern No. 189', 10in (25cm) high.
£1,200–1,500 *C*

A Daum cameo glass vase,
9in (23cm) high.
£1,200–1,500 *PSG*

A Gallé cameo glass vase,
10in (25cm) high.
£2,000–2,400 *PSG*

A Gallé cameo glass vase,
12in (30.5cm) high.
£1,200–1,500 *PSG*

A glass vase, overlaid on amber with a design of lilies and lotus rising from a pond, signed 'Gallé', c1900, 8½in (21.5cm) high.
£1,400–1,600 *PSG*

An elephant mould blown double overlay glass vase, with incised signature 'Emile Gallé', 15in (38cm) high.
£40,000–50,000 *CNY*

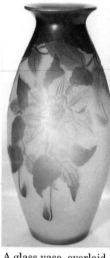

A glass vase, overlaid with a design of clemat signed 'Gallé', c1900, 12½in (32cm) high.
£1,800–2,000 *PSG*

A glass vase, engraved with silver scrolling flowers and foliage, inscribed 'Loetz, Austria', 9in (23cm) high.
£1,800–2,200 *Bea*

A glass vase, with red flowering creeper overlaid on amber, signed 'Gallé', c1900, 9in (23cm) diam.
£1,600–2,000 *PSG*

An wheel-carved cameo glass vase, signed 'Daum, Nancy', 8in (20cm) high.
£30,000–33,000 *P*

A wheel carved and enamelled cameo glass vase, by Daum, Nancy, c1900, 5in (12.5cm) high.
£2,800–3,200 *PSG*

An internally decorated glass vase, by Daum, Nancy, 14in (35.5cm) high.
£30,000–40,000 *C*

A wheel-carved cameo glass vase, 10in (25cm) high.
£14,000–16,000 *P*

Two glass vases, decorated with spring flowers, signed 'Gallé', c1900.
l. 14in (35.5cm) high. **£2,000–2,200**
r. 8in (20cm) high. **£1,200–1,500** *PSG*

A bronze mounted 'veilleuse', with 3 dragonflies forming the stand, with carved signature of 'Gallé', 7in (17.5cm) high. **£6,500–7,500** *C*

l. A plum mould blown triple overlay glass vase, by Emile Gallé, 13in (33cm) high. **£8,000–10,000**

r. An apple mould blown triple overlay glass vase, by Emile Gallé, 11½in (29.5cm) high. **£10,000–12,000** *CNY*

l. A vase, modelled as a Fu Dog, clear glass with blue and gilt enamelling, engraved with a grasshopper enriched with gilding, engraved 'EG' and Cross of Lorraine, c1875, 6in (15cm) high. **£8,000–10,000** *C*

A blow-out vase, with moulded decoration of clematis flowers, moulded 'Gallé' signature, 10in (25cm) high. **£6,000–7,500** *C*

Two cameo baluster vases, with carved 'Gallé' signatures, 23in (59cm) high. **£9,000–11,000 each** *C*

A cameo glass vase, overalid with amethyst tone acid etched flowers and leaves, signed in cameo form 'Gallé', 16in (40.5cm) high. **£2,000–2,400** *P*

An Art Nouveau leaded stained glass panel, signed 'Jacques Gruber', dated '04', 101in (256cm) high. **£10,000–12,000** *C*

Two Minton majolica cockerel and hen planters, designed by David Henck.
£1,600–2,000 *PCh*

A Gouda pottery charger, in 'Syncap' design, c1927, 12in (31cm) diam.
£150–200 *OO*

A Doulton Luscian ware vase, by H. Piper, c1895, 8in (20cm) high.
£250–350 *HER*

A Gouda pottery vase, marked 'Zuid (Holland)', c1920, 10in (25cm) high.
£250–350 *OO*

A Rosenthal porcelain ginger jar and cover, by Kurt Wendler, c1920.
£900–1,000 *S(NY)*

A Carlton Ware butter dish, c1940, 10½in (26cm) wide.
£800–950 *ARE*

Once part of the Elton John Collection.

A Doulton ball teapot, decorated with flowers and butterflies, c1916, 5½in (14cm) high.
£125–150 *HER*

A Gouda pottery vase, from the Goedewaagen factory, c1915, 4½in (11cm) high.
£80–120 *OO*

A Royal Dux Art Nouveau blue and gilt decorated figure of a ram, 7in (17.5cm) high.
£95–125 *PCh*

A selection of four Royal Doulton figures, 'Veronica', HN 1517, 8in (20cm) high, 'Aileen', HN 1645, 6in (15cm) high, 'Prue', HN 1996, 7in (17cm) high, and 'Easter Day', HN 2039, 7½in (18cm) high.
£100–150 each *CAG*

A Foley Intarsio clock, designed by Frederick Rhead, c1900, 9in (22.5cm) high.
£350–450 *AJ*

A Martin Brothers face jug, incised 'R. W. Martin and Brothers, London and Southall', marked '20 12 1898', 8½in (21cm) high. **£1,200–1,800** *DWB*

A Martin ware triple bird group, each with a removable head, signed on heads and base, 'R. W. Martin & Bros. Southall' and 'B–37', 7in (17.5cm) high. **£2,000–4,000** *P*
This piece is an example of the work produced by Clement Martin in collaboration with Captain H. Butterfield.

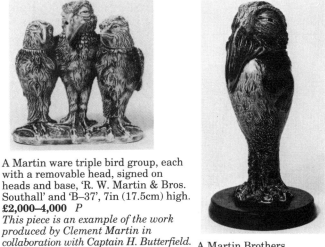

A Martin Brothers stoneware model of a grotesque bird, signed 'R. W. Martin & Bros. London & Southall', dated '5-1884', 13in (33cm) high. **£4,000–6,000** *P*

A Martin Brothers face jug, the eyes black and white against the buff glaze, incised marks and dated '8–(18)98', spout chipped, 8in (20cm) high. **£400–500** *SS*

A Martin Brothers stoneware vase, incised and glazed in shades of blue, on a pitted brown and biscuit ground, incised 'R. W. Martin & Bros. London & Southall 2–1892', 17½in (45cm) high. **£600–900** *CSK*

A Robert Wallace Martin & Brothers stoneware face jug, the 2 impish grinning faces covered in a matt ochre glaze, incised 'R. W. Martin & Bros. London & Southall, 1–1–1903', 6in (15cm) high. **£1,300–1,400** *CSK*

A Martin Brothers oviform pottery vase, incised 'R. W. Martin & Bros. London & Southall', '4–1887', 8in (20cm) high. **£500–800** *P*

A pair of stoneware slender baluster vases, by the Martin Brothers, incised and painted in shades of brown and green with exotic birds, incised 'Martin Bros. London & Southall 2–1897', 10in (26.5cm) high. **£600–900** *C*

r. A Martin Brothers pottery vase, incised 'Martin Bros. London & Southall, 10–1901', 18cm high. **£300–500** *P*

A stoneware face jug, incised 'R. W. Martin & Brothers, London & Southall 3-1-1903', 9in (23cm) high. **£1,200–1,800** *CSK*

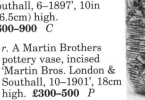

r. Two Martin Brothers ovoid vases incised 'Martin Bros. London & Southall, 10–1901', 7in (17.5cm) high. **£1,600–1,800** *DWB*

l. A Martin Brothers pottery vase, coloured in shades of brown against a buff ground, incised 'Martin Brothers London & Southall, 4–1890', 5in (13cm) high. **£300–500** *P*

A Martin Brothers vase, green, blue and brown on a buff ground, incised mark, dated '8-1885', minor chip, 7½in (19cm) high. **£300–500** S

A pair of Martin Brothers vases, with honey coloured glaze, incised marks and dated 6-1904, 10in (26.5cm) high. **£750–850** S

A Martin Brothers 'Gourd' vase, incised mark and dated 9-1899, 8½in (21.5cm) high. **£450–500** S

l. A Martin Brothers bowl, glazed in brown against a washed blue and green ground, incised mark, dated '7-1911', 9½in (24cm) diam. **£500–700** S

A De Morgan lustre dish, impressed '17', 1898–1907, 14½in (37cm) diam. **£800–1,200** S

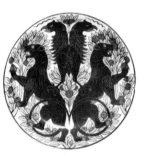

A Robert Wallace Martin Brothers stoneware jug, incised 'R. W. Martin & Bros, London & Southall 2-1887', 8½in (21cm) high. **£350–400** *CSK*

A De Morgan lustre dish, decorated in ruby, salmon-pink and buff, impressed numerals '24', 1898–1907, 14in (36cm) wide. **£500–800** S

A De Morgan lustre dish, impressed '17', painted 'EK' initials, late Fulham period, 14in (36cm) diam. **£800–1,200** S

An early Martin Brothers clock-case, incised 'R. W. Martin Fulham, 6', restored, c1874, 11in (28cm) high. **£1,000–1,500** S

Two De Morgan lustre dishes, one decorated in ruby lustre with a griffin, the other with an infant, the latter with painted 'ad infinitum' mark, 1898–1907, 12in (30.5cm) diam. **£300–500 each** S

A Martin ware tile picture, depicting grotesque fish, painted in muted enamel colours, each inscribed 'Martin Brothers London', some damage, 14½ by 17½in (37 by 44.5cm). **£1,000–1,500** *Bea*

A De Morgan lustre dish, ruby and salmon-pink, cracked, 1898–1907, 14in (35.5cm) diam. **£500–800** S

A stoneware double bird vase, one half of the vessel formed by the body of a bird with 'shifty' expression, the other squinting, their plumage picked out in browns, ochre, beige, blue and black, signed on base 'R. W. Martin & Brothers, London & Southall', dated '3-1892', 8½in (21cm) high.
£2,500–3,000 *P*

A stoneware bird, with removable head, resembling a duck with beak parted to reveal a tongue, the creature glazed dark brown and resting on a circular wooden base, signed on neck and near base 'Martin Brothers, London & Southall', indistinct date, 8in (20cm) high.
£1,000–1,500 *P*

A C. H. Brannam sgraffiato six-handled vase, fish motif with trailed organic Art Nouveau forms, 5in (13cm) high.
£200–250 *L&E*

Martin Brothers
The pottery firm owned by the Martin Brothers was active in London between 1873 and 1914. It was best known for its grey stoneware, often in grotesque shapes or with incised decoration.

l. A stoneware bird, with removable head, modelled with broad beak, heavy head plumage resembling eyebrows, in browns, ochre and beige with areas of pale blue, signed on neck and base 'R.W. Martin & Bros, London & Southall' dated '3-1901', 12in (31cm) high.
£5,500–6,000 *P*

A stoneware flask, finely incised on one side with an amusing face of the Sun, the reverse side showing a bearded Man in the Moon amid stars and comets signed 'Martin Bros, London & Southall', and dated '11-1891', 6½in (16.5cm) high.
£1,200–1,700 *P*

r. A C. H. Brannam vase, by F. Braddon, 1906, 11in (28cm) high.
£150–200 *ZEI*

A stoneware face jug, both sides of the jug modelled with a face of a grinning, chubby cheeked fellow, incised '3-1891, Martin Brothers, London & Southall', 7in (17.5cm) high.
£800–1,000 *P*

l. A Minton Secessionist jardinière and stand, tube-lined with stylised vertical floral banding in mauve and pale blue enhanced with sinuous green tendrils on a blue ground, marked 'Minton Ltd., No. 72' to each base, slight repair, 40in (102cm) high.
£900–1,200 *P*

A stoneware effigy, modelled as a young boy sleeping, in blue, brown and cream, incised 'He rests, He sleeps, nor dreams of any harm' Edwin Bruce Martin, R. Wallace, Martin S.C., original plaster cast, modelled in Wandsworth Road, about 1862.
£800–1,200 *Bon*

A Moorcroft MacIntyre 'Blue Poppy' design salad bowl and servers, c1902, 10in (25cm) diam. **£850–1,000** *LIO*

A Moorcroft two-handled 'Blue Pansy' design biscuit barrel, c1929, 7in (17.5cm) high. **£550–750** *LIO*

A biscuit tin, by W. R. Jacobs & Co., moulded in a Moorcroft shape and transfer decorated with the 'Pomegranate' design, 6in (16cm) high. **£50–50** *WIL*

r. A Moorcroft MacIntyre 'Yellow Cornflower' design tobacco jar, c1910, 6in (15cm) diam. **£600–700** *LIO*

r. A Moorcroft MacIntyre vase, heightened with ruby lustre against deep blue in panels, an olive green ground, MacIntyre mark, signed 'W. Moorcroft' and and 'M2980', repaired, 6in (15cm) high. **£250–300** *P*

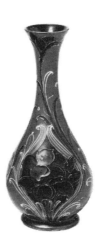

A Moorcroft Spanish pattern oviform vase, in reds, butterscotch and pale brown against a shaded beige/blue ground, signed 'W. Moorcroft and part of Liberty retail label, 10½in (27cm) high. **£700–900** *P*

A Moorcroft vase, in shades of deep rose, ochre, and olive against a mottled blue/green ground, impressed 'Moorcroft Burslem', painted signature in green, slight damage, c1910, 12½in (32cm) high. **£600–900** *S*

l. A pair of Moorcroft vases, painted in the 'Pomegranate' pattern in shades of pink, green and purple on an inky blue ground, impressed marks, signed in green, 15in (38cm) high. **£600–700** *CSK*

A Moorcroft exhibition 'Pomegranate' design ginger jar, 1927, 12in (31cm) diam. **£3,000–4,000** *LIO*

A Moorcroft MacIntyre blue teapot, 18thC design, c1906. **£450–550** *LIO*

A MacIntyre footed bowl, the exterior decorated with sprays of blue pansies on a green ground, impressed factory marks, signed in green, rim restored, 9in (22.5cm) diam. **£200–300** *CSK*

Three Moorcroft MacIntyre Florian ware vases.
£2,500–3,500 *SWO*

A Moorcroft vase with loop handles, with 'Poppy' design, c1925, 12in (30.5cm) high.
£900–1,100 *PGA*

A Moorcroft MacIntyre 'Peacock' pattern candlestick, c1900, 13½in (34.5cm) high.
£250–350 *PGA*

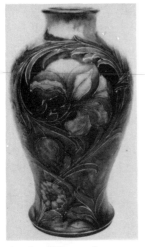

A pair of Moorcroft vases, trailed in white slip with scrolling flowers and foliage, picked out in dark glazes, green script signature, impressed Burslem mark, c1920, 12⅜in (31.5cm) high.
£1,100–1,300 *SC*

A Moorcroft vase, with the 'Claremont' design, on a mottled green ground, c1915, 9in (22.5cm) high.
£800–900 *PGA*

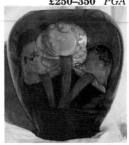

A Moorcroft vase, with toadstool design, under a brown lustre glaze, 8in (20cm) high. **£800–900** *PGA*

A Moorcroft jardinière, with the 'Claremont' toadstool design, with green signature, c1905, 7in (18cm) wide.
£850–950 *PGA*

A Moorcroft Tudric 'Hazeldene' bowl, decorated internally and externally with stylised trees in the 'Eventide' palette, raised on a Tudric pewter base, stamped 'Tudric Moorcroft 01311', 10⅜in (26.5cm) diam.
£600–900 *P*

A Moorcroft Burslem vase, with a flambé fish design on blue/lilac ground, c1910, 12⅜in (31.5cm) high.
£800–1,000 *PGA*

A Moorcroft Florian ware vase, painted in lilac pattern in shades of blue, printed marks and inscribed 'W.M.' 7in (17.5cm) high.
£300–500 *CSK*

A Moorcroft pottery vase, painted on a mottled blue/green ground, blue signature, impressed Royal marks, 7in (17.5cm) high.
£400–500 *P(Re)*

A Moorcroft vase, with a fish design, on a pale flambé ground, c1930, 12in (30.5cm) high.
£950–1,150 *PGA*

A Moorcroft vase, painted with a fish, in yellow and green on a green to blue ground, impressed marks, signed in green, 12in (30.5cm) high.
£600–900 *CSK*

A Moorcroft MacIntyre Florian ware vase, with slip-trailed decoration of dark blue flowers, green painted 'W. Moorcroft' signature, printed mark, c1900, 12½in (31.5cm) high.
£1,000–1,500 *C*

A MacIntyre Aurelian ware tazza and cover, attributed to William Moorcroft, dark blue ground, gilded panels with orange flowers and leaves, printed 'MacIntyre Burslem England', monogram, marked 'Made for Ward & Son, Doncaster', c1898, 12in (30.5cm) high.
£300–500 *C*

r. A Walter Moorcroft ginger jar and cover, with a turquoise and blue mottled ground, painted initials impressed facsimile signature, factory mark and potter to the Queen, c1945, 11in (28cm) high.
£400–600 *WIL*

A pair of MacIntyre Florian ware vases and covers, decorated by William Moorcroft and anemones in blue and green, on an ivory ground, one with slight hair crack, 8½in (21.5cm) high.
£700–800 *Bea*

A Moorcroft pottery vase, painted with green trees on a yellowy blue ground, green painted signature and printed 'Made for Liberty & Co.', mark to base, 9in (22.5cm) high.
£900–1,000 *BWe*

r. A Moorcroft vase, 10½in (26cm) high.
£350–400 *SBA*

A Moorcroft vase, c1912, 10in (25cm) high.
£300–350 *SBA*

A Moorcroft Florian ware vase, signed, c1895, 10in (25cm) high.
£450–550 *SBA*

A pair of Moorcroft MacIntyre vases, signed, cc1898, 10in (25cm) high.
£850–950 *SBA*

l. An early Moorcroft vase, with the 'Pomegranate' pattern, c1912, 10½in (26cm) high.
£300–350 *SBA*

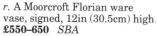

r. A Moorcroft Florian ware vase, signed, 12in (30.5cm) high.
£550–650 *SBA*

A Moorcroft pottery vase, decorated in the 'Claremont' pattern with toadstools in shades of red, yellow, green and blue, printed marks, signed in green, 6in (15cm) high. **£600–700** *CSK*

A Moorcroft pottery vase, decorated in the 'Hazeldene' pattern, in shades of yellow, green and blue, painted signature, c1915, 6in (15cm) high. **£600–800** *TW*

A Martin Bros. stoneware vase, brown and buff glazed, with decoration of flowering tendrils, mark to base 'R. W. Martin & Bros., London and Southall. 8/84'. **£200–300** *A*

A Moorcroft wheat ear motif vase, with green and purple tones on an off-white ground, blue signature, 13½in (34.5cm) high. **£800–1,200** *LE*

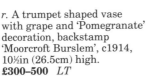

l. A Moorcroft vase, in the 'Dawn' pattern, painted in blue against a pale sky, impressed marks, 3½in (9cm) high. **£150–200** *CSK*

r. A trumpet shaped vase with grape and 'Pomegranate' decoration, backstamp 'Moorcroft Burslem', c1914, 10½in (26.5cm) high. **£300–500** *LT*

A Moorcroft 'Tudor Rose' pattern vase, decorated in white tube-lining, glazed in green, blue and heightened with red and reserved against a turquoise ground, signed 'W. Moorcroft des.', printed 'Made for Liberty & Co., Rd. no. 431157', 10in (25.5cm) high. **£400–600** *P*

A pair of MacIntyre plates, attributed to William Moorcroft, decorated in white slip trailing with blue irises and green leaves against an off-white ground, printed MacIntyre marks, Rd. No. 211991, 8in (20cm) diam. **£200–300 each** *P*

A William Moorcroft 'Claremont' pattern bowl, slip-trailed with red flushed toadstools on a mottled green/blue ground, facsimile signature, Liberty mark, early 20thC, 10½in (26cm) wide. **£400–450** *SS*

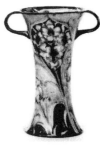

A Moorcroft Florian ware twin-handled vase, decorated in white, yellow, blue and pale green, reserved against a shaded blue ground, signed 'W. Moorcroft des.', printed mark, 8in (20cm) high. **£500–800** *P*

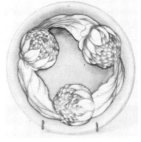

A Moorcroft 'Waratah' plate, decorated with 3 white and red flower blooms and green elaves against a green ground, impressed facsimile signature, 'Potter to H.M. The Queen, Made in England', 9in (22.5cm) diam. **£1,000–1,500** *P*

A Moorcroft 'Spanish' pattern pot pourri, with pierced cover, decorated with blue and green blooms on green scrolling stems, reserved against a pale green ground, signed 'W. Moorcroft 12/1911', impressed '189 W', 4in (10cm) high. **£300–500** *P*

A Moorcroft tobacco jar and cover, painted with the 'Cornflower' pattern, purple flowers amongst green scrolling foliage on a creamware ground, impressed mark and signed 'W. Moorcroft' in green, 5½in (13cm) high. **£400–600** *CSK*

A pair of Moorcroft Tudric vases, decorated with trees against a dark blue ground, with flared pewter bases, No. 01310, 9in (22.5cm) high. **£1,000–1,200** *HCC*

A Moorcroft vase, painted in shades of red, green, yellow, white and blue on a dark blue ground, impressed marks, 17in (43cm) high. **£800–850** *CSK*

A Moorcroft MacIntyre vase, painted with red and purple cornflowers with green foliage, MacIntyre trade mark on base, and green signatures, 10in (25cm) high. **£700–750** *P(M)*

A Moorcroft Eventide pottery vase, decorated with green and brown trees and green hills, against a flame coloured sky, stamped marks, signed in blue, 10in (25cm) high. **£800–1,200** *CSK*

A Moorcroft two-handled pottery vase, decorated in the 'Claremont' pattern, with toadstools under a deep flambé glaze, impressed marks, signed in green, 7in (18cm) high. **£1,200–1,500** *CSK*

A pair of Moorcroft pottery vases, decorated in the 'Hazeldene' pattern, with tall blue and green trees and hilly landscape, on a yellow/green ground, cracks to body of one, printed marks for Liberty & Co., signed in green 'W. Moorcroft des.', 9½in (24cm) high. **£650–700** *CSK*

A Moorcroft pottery vase, decorated with poppies on a dark blue ground, impressed marks 'Made in England, Potter to H. M. Queen', signed 'W. Moorcroft', factory paper label, 15in (37.5cm) high. **£300–500** *AGr*

A Moorcroft 'Eventide' pottery vase, decorated with green and brown trees and green hills against a flame coloured sky, impressed marks, signed in blue, 9½in (22.5cm) high. **£800–1,200** *CSK*

A deep flared bowl, by Moorcroft, painted in the 'Claremont' design with pink, yellow and blue toadstools on a mottled blueish green ground, the border inscribed 'Facta non verba vincit omnia veritas', impressed 'Moorcroft, Made in England', green painted signature, 14in (35.5cm) diam. **£800–1,200** *C*

Above left. A Moorcroft MacIntyre Florian Ware two-handled vase, decorated in the 'Peacock Feathers' pattern, the rim glazed in tones of blue, yellow, grey and green, printed mark, green painted initials 'W. M. des.', c1902, 5in (13cm) high.
£650–750

Above right. A Moorcroft MacIntyre vase, decorated in the 'Daisy' pattern, in tones of blue, green and white, green painted mark 'W. Moorcroft des.', c1900.
£1,500–2,000 *Bon*

A Moorcroft 'Moonlit Blue' vase, with flaring rim, tube-lined with a landscape in blue and green with a blue sky, impressed Royal Warrant, blue painted signature 'W. Moorcroft', c1925, 9½in (24cm) high.
£900–1,200 *S*

A Moorcroft 'Pomegranate' pattern vase, with white piped decoration, covered in a puce, green, red and blue glaze, green facsimile signature 'W. Moorcroft', 12½in (32cm) high.
£2,000–2,500 *C*

l. A Moorcroft Burslem candlestick, decorated in 'Cornflower' pattern, c1914, 9in (23cm) high.
£600–700 *Bon*

A Moorcroft Florian Ware jardinière.
£700–750 *DM*

A Moorcroft bottle vase, painted with the 'Pomegranate and Grape' pattern, impressed marks and painted signature, 10½in (26cm) high.
£350–450 *Bea*

A Bernard Moore lustre vase, painted with scrolling foliage beneath the glaze, 6in (15cm) high.
£150–200 *CDC*

A pair of William Moorcroft Florian ware candlesticks.
£400–450 *DM*

l. A Moorcroft Liberty pewter mounted 'Eventide' landscape vase, the cylindrical body tube-lined with tall trees in a hilly landscape, set against a red to orange-red ground, mounted in a flared beaten pewter base, restored, c1928, 7½in (19cm) high.
£250–350 *S(C)*

A Moorcroft earthenware bottle vase, painted after Christopher Dresser, facsimile signature, 29½in (75cm) high. **£400–450** *SS*

A Moorcroft floral jardinière, 5½in (14cm) high.
£100–150 *PCh*

A Moorcroft Flamminian ware dish, incised signature, 12in (30.5cm) diam.
£250–300 *CSK*

A Moorcroft Florian Ware 'Poppy' vase, in shades of blue, Florian stamp, signed 'W. Moorcroft', c1898, 11½in (29cm) high.
£500–700 *OBJ*

A Moorcroft Florian Ware jug, in shades of blue with silver plated lid, stamped, signed, c1898, 8in (20.5cm) high.
£400–500 *OBJ*

A Moorcroft 'Claremont' vase, decorated in green and red, made for Liberty, signed 'W. Moorcroft', c1903, 6in (15cm) high.
£800–1,000 *OBJ*

A Moorcroft pottery vase, painted with red, beige and purple cornflowers and green foliage, on a blue/green ground, green signature on base, 12in (30cm) high.
£750–800 *P(M)*

A Moorcroft plate, impressed and signed, 6in (15cm) high.
£30–50 *BRE*

A Moorcroft Florian Ware vase, with iris and forget-me-nots, stamped, signed, c1900, 6in (15cm) high.
£450–550 *OBJ*

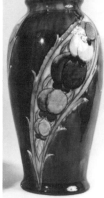

A Moorcroft vase, signed and dated 1929, 22in (56cm) high.
£1,200–1,500 *SWO*

l. A Moorcroft vase, with cornflowers in shades of blue, Florian Ware stamp, signed, c1900, 5in (12.5cm) high.
£200–300 *OBJ*

r. A Moorcroft MacIntyre Florian Ware vase, 10in (25.5cm) high.
£800–900 *PBJ*

A Moorcroft MacIntyre vase, with a design of pansies in bright translucent glazes, printed mark in sepia, full signature in green, dated '1912', 12in (30.5cm).
£500–800 *SC*

A pottery bowl, painted with the 'Pomegranate' pattern, on a blue-green ground, signed in green 'W. Moorcroft', 10in (25cm) diam.
£250–300 *CSK*

A fish vase, with ivory and grey coloured fish, on a grey/pale brown ground, impressed 'Moorcroft – Made in England' and signed 'WM', 7in (17.5cm) high. **£600–800** *P*

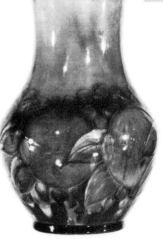

A Moorcroft vase, tube-lined in white, with green and blue, printed Liberty mark, signed in green, c1910, 10in (25cm) high.
£500–800 *S*

A Moorcroft MacIntyre vase, printed mark in sepia, full signature in green, dated '1912', 11in (28cm) high. **£300–500** *SC*

l. A pottery vase, by William Moorcroft, in shades of purple, pink and white on a merging green and turquoise ground, incised, impressed and painted marks, 14½in (37cm) high.
£200–400 *WHL*

A pair of Moorcroft vases, with 'Pomegranate' design in deep rose, green and mauve on a blue ground, slight damage, impressed 'Moorcroft, Burslem, England', painted signature in green, c1915, 9½in (24cm) high. **£600–900** *S*

A Moorcroft 'Hazeldene' vase, decorated in blue, impressed, signed and inscribed 'Garfield Set? Vase', dated '1920', 18½in (47cm) high.
£500–600 *P*

l. A Moorcroft vase, decorated with band of pink and green flowers on an inky-blue ground, impressed mark, painted signature and label, c1940, 3½in (9cm) high.
£80–100
r. A Moorcroft vase, in red-brown toning to dark blue, label covering impressed and painted marks, c1940, 3½in (9cm) high.
£80–100 *TW*

A Moorcroft vase, painted with the 'Pomegranate' pattern, orange and red fruits with ochre foliage on a cinnamon and blue ground, impressed 'Burslem' mark, signed 'W. Moorcroft' in green, 8½in high.
£300–500 *CSK*

A Florian style bulbous vase with daffodil motif, signed 'W. Moorcroft des', c1900, 6in (15.5cm) high.
£450–550 *LT*

A Moorcroft 'Yacht' design meat dish, c1934, 16⅓in (42cm) long.
£60–90 *LIO*

The 'Yacht' design was introduced by William Moorcroft in 1934, taken from an original sketch by his daughter, Beatrice Moorcroft.

A Moorcroft pottery jardinière, with Florian style daisy and poppy decoration in green, blue and yellow glazes, with two loop handles, impressed Cambridge factory mark, and green painted signature, c1916, 10in (25cm) wide.
£1,000–1,500 *AH*

A Moorcroft small 'Blue Pansy' design jardinière, c1928, 4in (10cm) high.
£200–300 *LIO*

A Walter Moorcroft 'Caribbean' design mug, c1962, 4⅓in (11cm) high.
£180–250 *LIO*

A Moorcroft MacIntyre Florian ware 'Blue Tulip' design jug, c1901, 12in (31cm) high.
£800–1,000 *LIO*

r. A Moorcroft 'Claremont Toadstool' design vase, decorated in shades of yellow, mauve and blue on a mottled green ground, signed in green, impressed 'Moorcroft, Burslem', 1914, 4½in (11cm) high.
£500–600 *WIL*

A Moorcroft MacIntyre 'Aurelian' design coffee pot, c1897, 7in (17.5cm) high.
£350–450 *LIO*

A Lisa B. Moorcroft 'Toadstool' design plaque, dated 1990, 16in (41cm) diam.
£250–350 *LIO*

Lisa B. Moorcroft is the daughter of Walter Moorcroft, who ran the factory from 1945–86 and the grand-daughter of the founder, William Moorcroft.

A Moorcroft 'Pink Flamminian' design teapot with cup, saucer and plate, c1914.
£250–350 *LIO*

A Moorcroft blue teapot, c1918, 6in (15cm) high.
£50–80 *LIO*

A William Moorcroft saltglaze vase, decorated with 'Orchid' design, c1930, 7in (18cm) high.
£400–500 *RUM*

A William Moorcroft 'Poppy' design clock case, with original movement, c1920, 5in (13cm) high.
£1,000–1,500 *RUM*

A Moorcroft MacIntyre teapot and stand, with 'Seaweed' design, c1902.
£700–900 *RUM*

A Walter Moorcroft 'Orchid' design cup and saucer, c1949.
£130–180 *RUM*

A Moorcroft MacIntyre 'Peacock' design vase, on a celadon ground, signed 'W.M. Des', c1900, 10in (25cm) high.
£1,800–2,300 *RUM*

A Moorcroft vase, tube-lined in white, coloured in shades of green, blue and yellow, printed 'Rd. no. 326689', painted 'W. Moorcroft des.' in green, c1910, 10in (25cm) high.
£500–800 *S*

A Moorcroft MacIntyre 'Florian Poppy' design vase, c1904, 3½in (9cm) high.
£300–400 *RUM*

A Moorcroft MacIntyre vase, coloured in shades of green, blue and yellow, printed MacIntyre mark, 7in (18cm) high. **£500–800** *S*

A Moorcroft MacIntyre tea kettle, decorated with 'Pomegranate' design, c1912.
£1,200–1,500 *RUM*

l. A Moorcroft MacIntyre blue Florian vase, highlighted with gilt, incised 'W. M. Des', c1898, 9in (22.5cm) high.
£1,000–1,500 *RUM*

A Moorcroft ovoid footed bowl with inverted rim, decorated with fish and water weeds, in shades of green, blue and yellow, impressed factory marks, signed in green, 6in (15cm) high.
£800–1,000 *CSK*

A Moorcroft MacIntyre Florian Ware 'Poppy' pattern jug, with simulated bamboo moulded handle, EPNS mount, hinged cover and thumbpiece, damaged, printed mark in brown, initialled 'WM' in green, early 20thC, 8½in (21.5cm) high.
£350–450 *HSS*

A MacIntyre 'Claremont' pattern bowl, designed by William Moorcroft, the green and blue streaked ground with decoration of crimson, blue and green mushrooms, printed marks 'Made for Liberty & Co.', registered no. 420081, signed 'W. Moorcroft', c1903, 8½in (21.5cm) high.
£1,000–1,500 *C*

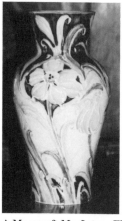

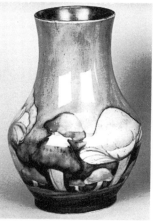

A Moorcroft MacIntyre Florian Ware vase, with blue and yellow flowers, c1903, 6in (15cm) high.
£750–950 *RUM*

A Moorcroft MacIntyre tobacco jar and cover, with a celadon ground and red flora, c1903, 5in (13cm) high. **£700–1,000** *RUM*

A Moorcroft 'Claremont' pattern vase, designed by William Moorcroft, the swollen cylindrical form with flared neck and everted rim, blue and green mottled with yellow, pink, green and blue mushrooms, restored, impressed 'Moorcroft, Made in England', and green signature 'W. Moorcroft', c1920, 6½in (17cm) high.
£350–450 *C*

l. A William Moorcroft saltglaze 'Fish' design vase, c1928, 9in (23cm) high.
£900–1,100 *RUM*

A William Moorcroft 'Pansy' design vase, on a blue ground, c1925, 9in (23cm) high.
£300–400 *RUM*

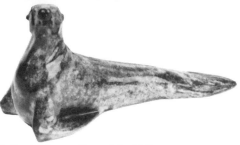

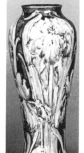

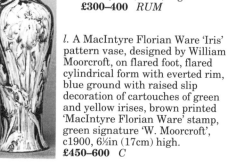

A flambé figure of a seal, by William Moorcroft, 8in (20cm) long.
£1,000–1,500 *LT*

l. A MacIntyre Florian Ware 'Iris' pattern vase, designed by William Moorcroft, on flared foot, flared cylindrical form with everted rim, blue ground with raised slip decoration of cartouches of green and yellow irises, brown printed 'MacIntyre Florian Ware' stamp, green signature 'W. Moorcroft', c1900, 6½in (17cm) high.
£450–600 *C*

A Moorcroft bowl, painted with red and green toadstools on a mottled green ground, printed marks and signed in green, 8in (20cm) diam.
£600–900 *CSK*

A pair of Moorcroft 'Dawn' pattern vases, painted in deep blue against a pale blue sky, between chevron borders of blue and cream, painted initials in blue, impressed 'Moorcroft, Made in England', 8in (20cm) high.
£600–800 *L*

A Moorcroft Florian Ware vase, with black stylised foliage on a white and black ground, printed marks, signed in green 12½in (32cm) high.
£400–600 *CSK*

A Moorcroft 'Brown Cornflower' vase, decorated in reds, dark blue and orange against a shaded beige-blue ground, impressed 'Moorcroft Burslem' and signed 'W. Moorcroft', 8in (20cm) high. **£200–300** *P*

A Moorcroft Macintyre, tobacco jar, decorated in reds, blues, browns, greens and apricot, Macintyre marks and signed 'WM', 4½in (11cm) high.
£500–800 *P*

A Moorcroft two-handled trumpet-shaped vase, with a matt blue ground, signed, c1898–1900, 10in (25cm) high.
£800–1,000 *LT*

A Moorcroft MacIntyre vase, with Florian style decoration, full signature, c1900, 7in (18cm) high.
£300–400 *LT*

William Moorcroft (1872–1945)

From 1898, Moorcroft headed the Art Pottery department of MacIntyre & Co., the Staffordshire pottery firm established in about 1847 at Burslem. His early designs, known as Aurelian wares, were generally printed in underglaze blue with overglaze iron-red and gilt, and decorated with designs reminiscent of the textiles of William Morris. His later work for MacIntyre, retailed as Florian ware, was possibly the foremost British contribution to Art Nouveau ceramics.

r. A Moorcroft 'Claremont' pattern vase, decorated on a greeny-blue ground, base chipped, impressed 'Moorcroft Burslem England 1440' and with green painted 'W. Moorcroft' signature, 8in (22cm) high.
£600–800 *C*

l. A Moorcroft MacIntyre baluster vase, decorated in blue-green and gold against olive green, MacIntyre marks signed 'W.M. des.' and Rd. No. '404017', 12½in (31cm) high.
£400–500 *P*

A Moorcroft pottery base, the body painted with the 'Anemone' pattern on a red ground, 6½in (17cm) high. **£260–300** *Bea*

A Moorcroft MacIntyre pottery baluster vase, with 2 loop handles, polychrome floral decoration on a white ground with gilt banding, 7½in (19cm) high. **£600–700** *AH*

A Moorcroft flambé 'Eventide' vase, tube-lined with trees in a hilly landscape and richly coloured in mauve, orange and red, minor chip restored on foot, impressed 'Moorcroft, Made in England' and signed in blue 'W. Moorcroft', 8in (20cm) high. **£2,000–2,500** *S*

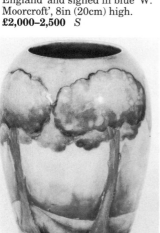

A Moorcroft 'Eventide' vase, decorated with green and brown trees and hills against a flame coloured sky, impressed mark, signature in green, 5½in (14cm) high. **£750–850** *AH*

A Moorcroft pottery vase, painted with the 'Hibiscus' design on a deep red ground, impressed marks and painted signature, 8½in (21cm) high. **£300–350** *Bea*

A Moorcroft pottery vase, painted with the 'Pomegranate and Grape' design on a deep blue ground, impressed marks and painted signature, 6½in (17cm). **£170–220** *Bea*

A Moorcroft 'Apple Blossom' bowl, tube-lined with branches of flowers and berries in tones of green, hair crack, impressed 'Moorcroft Burslem 1914', signed in green 'W. Moorcroft' and dated '1914', 10in (25cm) high. **£800–1,200** *S*

A Moorcroft Florian Ware bottle vase with fluted rim, decorated in blue and green with the 'Poppy' design on a white ground, pattern No. 401753, printed mark, signed, 6in (15cm) high. **£400–450** *Bea*

A Moorcroft Florian Ware vase, tube-lined with yellow and blue flowerheads and green foliage on a light and dark blue ground, printed Florian Ware mark and signed in green 'W. Moorcroft', c1902, 11½in (30cm) high. **£1,500–2,000** *S*

l. A Moorcroft MacIntyre Florian Ware blue 'Landscape' pattern vase, signed 'W. Moorcroft', c1903, 12in (30.5cm) high.
£1,500–2,00 *RUM*

l. A Moorcroft MacIntyre Florian Ware vase, tube lined in white, decorated in green and gilt on a blue ground, printed mark and pattern no. 'M2019', 9in (23cm) high.
£500–600 *DN*

A William Moorcroft Flambé 'Landscape' vase, c1928, 12in (30cm) high.
£3,000–4,000 *RUM*

A Walter Moorcroft 'Bougainvillea' design vase, on a green ground, c1955, 10in (25cm) high.
£450–550 *RUM*

l. A William Moorcroft 'Toadstool' design vase, 7in (18cm) high.
£350–450 *LT*

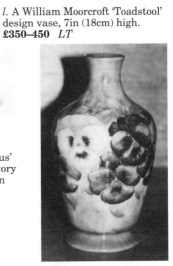

A Walter Moorcroft 'Bougainvillea' design vase, on a green ground, c1955, 10in (25cm) high.
£450–550 *RUM*

l. A Walter Moorcroft 'Hibiscus' design vase, on ivory ground, c1955, 8in (20cm) high.
£150–200 *RUM*

A William Moorcroft 'Pansy' design vase on pale green ground, impressed Burslem, signed in green, c1913, 5in (13cm) high.
£500–700 *RUM*

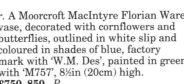

A Moorcroft 'Cornflower' vase, decorated with blue flowers and leaves, reserved against a very pale blue ground, impressed marks, signed in full in blue, with paper label, 12½in (31.5cm) high.
£650–750 *P*

A MacIntyre Florian 'Peacock' pattern vase, designed by William Moorcroft, blue ground with raised slip decoration of blue, green and yellow stylised peacock eyes, with brown printed MacIntyre Florian Ware stamp, Reg. No. 347807, green monogram 'W.M.', c1900, 3½in (9cm) high.
£600–700 *C*

r. A Moorcroft MacIntyre Florian Ware vase, decorated with cornflowers and butterflies, outlined in white slip and coloured in shades of blue, factory mark with 'W.M. Des', painted in green with 'M757', 8½in (20cm) high.
£750–850 *P*

A Linthorpe pottery bowl, designed by Christopher Dresser, with silver rim, impressed mark and signature, 10in (25cm) diam.
£200–250 *DN*

A Bretby figure of a fisher boy, standing on a rocky mound, c1895, 35in (89cm) high.
£500–600 *OCA*

A Linthorpe pottery ewer, designed by Christopher Dresser, the red body covered with a streaked milky green-brown glaze, facsimile Dresser signature 'HT' momogram for Henry Tooth and numbered '502', 8⅜in (21cm) high.
£500–600 *P*

A Gallé faience cat, painted with polychrome floral sprays on a yellow ground, wearing a pendant with dog medallion and grey and white floral scarf, green glass eyes, some damage, unmarked, 13in (33cm) high.
£1,500–2,000 *Bon*

l. An Austrian 'Femme Fleur' pottery vase, glazed in green and beige, impressed numbers and letters, 16½in (41.5cm) high.
£200–300 *P*

A Minton Secessionist jug, with green, yellow and grey glaze, 11½in (29cm) high.
£100–150 *ZEI*

A pair of Brannam pottery vases, by James Dewdney, decorated in sgraffito with oval panels of birds perched on flowering boughs, in red slip against stippled white beneath a blue translucent glaze, incised 'C.H. Brannam, Barum J.D. 1888', 'R' to necks 14½in (37cm) high.
£200–300 *P*

An Art Nouveau hanging plaque, 9in (23cm) diam.
£200–250 *ASA*

r. A Carlton Ware charger, 13in (33cm) diam.
£80–120 *ASA*

A Brannam pottery slipware vase, the red body overlaid with white slip, decorated with sgraffito panels of birds and flowering shrubbery, flanked by formal flower and leaf motifs, beneath a pale honey glaze, signed 'C. H. Brannam, Barum, N. Devon', dated '1881', 'R' on neck, 15in (38.5cm) high.
£700–800 *P*

l. A Continental green boat vase, 16in (41cm) wide. **£60–80** *THA*

A jug and basin, with green and pink embossed design, jug 12½in (32cm) high. **£120–140** *PAR*

A Foley plate, produced for the American market, signed 'F. Micklewright', c1893, 9in (23cm) diam. **£80–140** *AJ*

Two Foley Intarsio Toby jugs, John Bull and Scotsman, 7½in(19cm) high. **£250–300** *AJ*

An Eichwald tazza, c1920, 11in (28cm) high. **£180–200** *BEC*

r. Two early E. Radford Burslem vases, tallest 6½in (16cm) high. **£40–60 each**

A pair of Eichwald vases, 12in (31cm). **£90–120** *BEV*

An E. Radford jug, Anemone pattern, 6½in (16cm) high. **£40–50** *MA*

An E. Radford vase, Strawberry pattern, 9in (22cm) high. **£50–60** *MA*

An early E. Radford jug, Ranunculus pattern. **£90–120** *MA*

l. An early E. Radford vase, Anemone pattern. **£75–85** *MA*

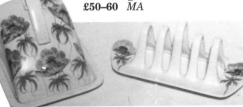

l. An E. Radford cheese dish and toast rack, Anemone pattern. **£10–15 each** *MA*

A Linthorpe pottery pouring vessel, designed by Christopher Dresser, the brown body streaked milky-green with yellow speckling, 'Linthorpe Chr. Dresser' mark, 'HT' for Henry Tooth and '267', 5½in (14cm) high.
£300–500 *P*

l. A pair of William de Morgan tiles, with Isnik style decoration of stylised flowerheads, on a pale green ground, framed together, 8in (20.5cm) square.
£200–400 *C*

A Pilkington 'Royal Lancastrian' oviform vase, by William Salter Mycock, painted in golden and ruby lustres against a shaded blue ground, impressed rosette mark, incised 'E.T.R.' for E T Radford the potter, artist's monogram and date code for 1933, 8½in (21cm) high.
£400–600 *P*

A Mintons Secessionist ware garden stool, decorated in raised outline against a printed ground of flowers and foliage, glazed in turquoise, green, brown and yellow against a cream ground, indistinct impressed marks, date code for 1908, 21in (54cm) high. **£400–450** *P*

Above. A Mintons Secessionist jardinière and stand, probably designed by John Wadsworth and Leon Solon, in pinks, reds and yellows against a ground of block-printed foliage in greens, the cylindrical stand similarly decorated, printed marks and date code for 1902 on stand, 42in (105cm) high overall.
£800–1,200 *P*

A Maw & Co. oviform vase, designed by Walter Crane, painted in olive green, signed on base, 13in (32.5cm) high.
£700–900 *P*

l. A Mintons Secessionist ware jardinière, decorated in green slip-trailing with cream-amber stylised buds on blue stems, reserved against a purple ground, stamped marks and printed mark 'NO.1', 10½in (26.5cm) high.
£350–400 *P*

A Mintons art studio pottery twin-handled moon flask, the design in the manner of Christopher Dresser, decorated in 2 tones of grey, white and gilt, on a chocolate-brown ground, circular 'Kensington Gore' marks, impressed 'Minton' with date code for 1872, printed marks 'S.122' and 'K92', 13in (33cm) high.
£200–250 *P*

Four William de Morgan tiles, ruby lustre on a cream ground, c1890, 6in (15cm) square.
£700–900 *C*

A William de Morgan ruby lustre charger, c1900, 14in (36cm) diam.
£800–1,200 *C*

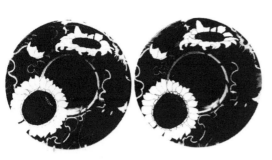

A pair of Foley Intarsio circular wall plates, designed by Frederick Rhead, printed factory marks and 'Rd Nos. 330399' for 1898–99, 12in (31cm) diam.
£700–800 *P*

A Gallé yellow ground cat, c1900, 13½in (33.5cm) high.
£1,500–2,000 *GCA*

A Gallé cat in tartan garb, c1900, 13in (33cm) high.
£1,500–2,000 *GCA*

l. A terracotta bust of a lady, signed 'Lefevre', c1900.
£300–500 *P*

An Ault pottery vase, designed by Christopher Dresser, the magnolia-coloured body painted possibly by Clarissa Ault, impressed facsimile signature and 'No. 247', 27½in (69.5cm) high.
£600–700 *P*

A Linthorpe pottery ewer, designed by Christopher Dresser, with linear decoration beneath a streaked honey, green, blue and grey glaze, factory marks, facsimile signature and 'HT' for Henry Tooth, 9in (22cm) high.
£200–400 *P*

A Christopher Dresser Linthorpe pottery pot pourri vase and cover, silver mounted with blue glazed underside, the pierced silver cover with fluted dome and ball finial, impressed marks and 'No. 277', c1900, 9½in (23.5cm) diam.
£400–450 *TW*

A Linthorpe pottery tobacco jar, the brown glazed body having electro-plated rim and swing handle, impressed mark, Henry Tooth monogram and shape 'No. 913', late 19thC, 5in (12.5cm) high.
£50–70 *TW*

l. A globular green glazed bowl, designed by Christopher Dresser, impressed with facsimile signature, 5½in (14.5cm) high.
£1,000–1,500 *C*

A Christopher Dresser Linthorpe vase, decorated in plum and green crackle effect glaze, impressed marks and shape 'No. 875', late 19thC, 12in (30cm) high.
£100–130 *TW*

Above left. A pottery plate, designed by Christopher Dresser, with a speckled jade green glaze, impressed 'Linthorpe', monogram 'HT' for Henry Tooth, and facsimile 'Dresser' signature, 11⅛in (29cm) diam.
£200–300 *P*

Above centre. A Della Robbia vase and cover, slip decorated in sgraffito against a shaded turquoise ground, Galleon mark, initials for George Seddon and painted by Liz Wilkins, no. '74A/74B', 11½in (29cm) high.
£250–350 *P*

Above right. A Pilkington Lancastrian circular wall plate, by William Salter Mycock, impressed Bees mark but later signed with 'WSM' monogram, dated '1919', 13in (33cm) diam.
£300–400 *P*

A Brannam/Barnstaple vase, incised signature and date '1916', 20in (50.5cm) high.
£250–350 *SC*

A Wedgwood vase, decorated by Alfred Powell, the body painted in shades of blue, green, brick-red and bronze-lustred mauve, impressed 'Wedgwood', incised 'P.21', painted monogram and '89', c1910, 15in (38cm) high. **£700–900** *S*

A Ruskin vase, turquoise and lavender, impressed oval mark, dated '1907', 8½in (21.5cm) high.
£300–400 *S*

A Louis Wain pottery figure of 'The Lucky Haw-Haw Cat', with an aperture in the back, possibly for a vase, 5in (12.5cm) high.
£250–350 *CSK*

r. A Burmantofts faïence Art Nouveau jardinière and stand, decorated in blue, yellow and turquoise, impressed marks and numbered '2273/4', 39in (99cm) high. **£300–400** *P*

r. A Louis Wain model of a pig, with green and lemon body, facsimile signature and 'Made in England', 4½in (12cm) high.
£300–400 *P*

Above left. A Minton's Art Pottery jardinière, c1890, 9½in (24cm) high.
£200–300
right. A Minton's Secessionist pottery jardinière, 1900–08, 10in (25cm) high.
£200–300 *CDC*

l. A Royal Copenhagen group, entitled 'The Rock and the Wave', depicting a man tethered to a rock and a woman rising from the waves, wave mark and 'ØF' in underglaze blue, incised '1132A.W.', incised monogram 'T.L.', dated '1897', 18½in (47cm) high.
£550–650 *SS*

A William de Morgan art pottery dish, decorated with a dragon in ruby copper lustre on a white ground, 14½in (36cm) diam. £600–900 *Bea*

A Goldscheider porcelain head of a woman, printed 'Goldscheider U.S.A.', 11½in (29cm) high. £300–400 *CSK*

A Mintons Secessionist jardinière and stand, with tube-lined decoration, printed and impressed marks 'Minton Ltd.', c1910, 41½in (103.5cm) high. £1,000–1,500 *C*

A Mintons Secessionist jardinière, the peacocks outlined in relief, green transfer and impressed mark to base, early 20thC, 17in (43cm) diam. £400–450 *WIL*

A Pilkington's Royal Lancastrian ware vase, in yellow, blue and ruby lustre, decorated by Gordon M. Forsyth for Pilkington's, impressed Bee mark, 'VIII, England 218', 8in (20cm) high. £400–600 *C*

A William de Morgan tile, impressed 'DM98' in circle, and a tile with stylised carnations and leaves, impressed 'Sand's End Pottery' mark, both 6¼in (15.5cm) square. £40–60 each *P*

A Pilkington's Royal Lancastrian vase, decorated by Gordon M. Forsyth, with lions in silver mottled lustre against a bright blue ground, printed marks, artist's monogram on base, c1905, 11½in (29cm) high. £600–800 *HSS*

A Pilkington's Royal Lancastrian highly decorated lustre bowl, by Mycock, c11900, 5in (13cm) diam. £200–300 *ASA*

l. A Pilkington's Royal Lancastrian wall plaque, possibly by Gwladys Rodgers, impressed 'Royal Lancastrian, Made in England', 10½in (26cm) diam. £200–400 *P*

A Minton's moon flask, painted by W. S. Coleman, signed neck damaged, 17in (42.5cm) high. £800–1,000 *PWC*

l. An Austrian vase, 12½in (32cm) high.
£100–200 *ASA*

A Royal Dux ceramic figure on a sea shell, 14in (36cm) high.
£350–500 *ASA*

A pair of German tiles, both depicting maidens with flowing hair, in coloured glazes, depicting the Muse of Dancing, and the Muse of Music playing a harp, 5in (14cm) wide.
£700–750 *P*

A terracotta lamp by Goldscheider, 28in (71.5cm) high.
£1,500–2,000 *ASA*

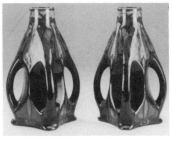

A pair of Zuid Holland vases, with 4 undercut edges and applied handles, painted with pendant stylised flowers on the neck, painted mark 'Made in Zuid, Holland, J.H.' and incised '213', 8½in (22cm) high.
£300–350 *S(S)*

A Reps and Trinte pottery clock case, the base supporting a female bust flanked by 2 floral buttresses beneath triangular face, impressed marks and incised 'Stellmacher', damaged, early 20thC, 21in (53cm) high.
£500–800 *S(S)*

A Clement Massier turquoise glazed earthenware jardinière and stand, moulded in relief with leaves, flowers and branches, the oviform bowl on cylindrical stand, impressed factory marks, 37in (94cm) high.
£1,000–1,500 *CSK*

A Rozenberg vase, painted in rich polychrome colours, black printed factory mark and year symbol of a flower, 'Rozenberg, den Haag', a cross in a square, '372', c1913, 6in (15.5cm) high.
£300–400 *S(S)*

A pair of Rozenberg vases, decorated in rich polychrome colours, black painted factory mark and year symbol of a flower, 'Rozenberg, den Haag', cross in a square, '472', c1913, 8½in (21.5cm) high.
£300–400 *S(S)*

An Elton ware jardinière, with triple loop handles, signed 'Elton', 10in (25.5cm) high.
£500–800 *HOD*

An Elton ware jug, with fruit design in shades of green and red, c1890, 6½in (16cm) high. **£200–300** *OBJ*

Elton, Sir Edmund Harry (1846–1920)

English art potter who, in 1883, succeeded to a baronetcy and inherited Clevedon Court in Somerset. There, with the aid of an assistant potter, G. Masters, he made earthenware vessels decorated with flower patterns in coloured slips (blue, red or green). His products, known as 'Elton ware', were shown at the Arts and Crafts Exhibition Society, of which he was a member.

An Elton ware pre-Columbian shaped jug, with floral decoration and butterflies in shades of green, c1885, 8½in (22cm) high.
£200–300 *OBJ*

r. An Elton ware vase in gold 'crackle' with black slip underneath, c1910, 5½in (14cm) high.
£400–500 *OBJ*

l. An Elton ware vase, decorated with sunflowers in shades of blue, c1900, 9in (20cm) high.
£200–300 *OBJ*

l. An Elton ware vase with daffodil design in shades of blue, green and brown, c1890, 7in (18cm) high.
£100–200 *OBJ*

An Elton ware jug, in green slip with gold crackle, c1910, 6½in (16cm) high.
£250–350 *OBJ*

An Elton ware trefoil shaped jug, in shades of purple and red, c1900, 6in (15cm).
£400–500 *OBJ*

l. An Elton ware 'crackle' jug, c1921, 7in (18cm).
£300–400 *OBJ*

This jug was made by his son after Elton had died, and is signed 'Elton' with a cross.

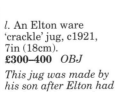

An Elton ware gourd shaped vase, with insects design in shades of purple and red, c1885, 9½in (24cm) high.
£200–300 *OBJ*

An Elton ware vase, with bird and leaf design in shades of green, blue and yellow, c1900, 10in (25.5cm) high.
£300–400 *OBJ*

A dish, with a figure of a lady in the centre, by Ernst Wahllis, Vienna, c1900, 8½in (21.5cm) high.
£500–700 *ASA*

A William de Morgan tile, painted in brown and yellow with a sailing boat, impressed Sand's End mark, mounted as a teapot stand, 7in (17.5cm) square.
£300–400 *P*

A William de Morgan tile, painted in red lustre with stylised carnations, with painted signature 'W. de Morgan & Co., Fulham, London', 8in (20cm) square.
£80–140 *C*

l. An Elton ware jug, with central gold lustre decoration of a fish and wings, base with monogram for George Masters, 7in (17.5cm) high.
£700–800 *HOD*

l. A lustre pottery vase, attributed to William de Morgan, painted by Frederick Passenger, in pink and ruby lustres on a white ground, blue painted initials 'FP' on base, 7in (17.5cm) high.
£300–500 *CSK*

A Bretby jardinière, decorated with fish.
£300–500 *ASA*

l. A Dutch jardinière and stand, decorated in batik style with flowers, foliage and trellis panels, supported on a broad cylindrical stand, signed 'Corona Holland', 39in (99cm) high.
£550–650 *P*

A Watcombe Pottery vase, decorated in green and red, 8in (20cm) high.
£80–120 *STU*

An Elton ware jar and cover, with floral design in shades of blue and green, c1890, 6½in (16.5cm) high.
£200–300 *OBJ*

A Linthorpe Pottery ewer, designed by Christopher Dresser, the reddish body streaked with milky-green and brown, marked 'Linthorpe HT', and facsimile signature, 9½in (24cm) high.
£200–300 *P*

A William de Morgan tile, painted in black with a stylised dodo, impressed Sand's End Pottery mark, mounted as a teapot stand, 7in (17.5cm) high.
£300–350 *P*

A Wade vase, with floral decoration, c1930, 9in (22.5cm) high.
£60–100 *STU*

A Burmantofts faïence plaque, painted by William Neatby, impressed 'Burmantofts Faïence', signed 'Wm. Neatby', dated '1887', 16in (40cm) diam.
£300–500 *P*

A French stoneware figural vase, by James Vibert, glazed shaded turquoise and brick red, signed 'J. Vibert' on the handle, 'E. Müller' as maker, 6½in (16.5cm) high.
£250–300 *P*

James Vibert was born in Switzerland in 1872, and in 1892 was employed in the workshops of Rodin.

A Riessner,Stellmacher and Kessel Art Nouveau porcelain vase, coloured in green, yellow and gilding against a shaded yellow and white ground, impressed crown mark, 'Amphora, Austria, 15024-46', 15in (38cm) high.
£100–150 *P*

An Austrian lustre glazed porcelain pitcher, by Ernst Wahliss, c1900.
£350–400 *VAS*

A Theodore Deck faïence circular wall plate, 'Phryne', impressed 'T. H. Deck', signed 'R. Collin' (?), 24½in (62cm) diam.
£600–900 *P*

A Pilkington Royal Lancastrian vase, painted by Richard Joyce, in golden lustre and red against a powder blue ground, impressed rosette mark and artist's monogram, 12in (30.5cm) high.
£600–800 *P*

A Della Robbia clock case, designed by Ruth Bare and decorated by Alice Jones, painted ship mark flanked by 'DR' above the artist's monogram 'LJ' and '57', c1904, 18in (45.5cm) high.
£800–1,200 *SC*

The inscription is linked with Ruth Bare's involvement with the Positivist Movement.

A Hancocks Morris Ware vase, by Hancock, designed by George Cartlidge. **£200–250** *THA*

A pair of Rozenburg pottery vases, on a green ground, painted marks with a date mark for 1898, 9½in (24cm) high.
£450–550 *C(Am)*

An early Rozenburg pottery wall plate, attributed to Th. A. C. Colenbrander, signed on base 'Rozenburg, den Haag', date letter for 1890, 15in (38cm) diam. **£500–700** *P*

l. A pair of Mettlach Villeroy and Boch vases, each incised and painted in ochre, red and green on a blue ground, rim chip to one, incised marks and '2416', 16in (40.5cm) high. **£300–500** *CEd*

An early Rozenburg pottery wall plate, attributed to Th. A. C. Colenbrander, probably painted by W. F.Abspoel, 'WG' mark for W. von Gudenberg, den Haag, date letter for 1888, and artist's device, 15in (38cm) diam. **£500–700** *P*

An Austrian porcelain coffee set, painted in mauve, green and yellow with delicate flowers, and further embellished with gilding, factory marks for Carl Knoll of Karlsbad, Austria. **£1,500–2,000** *P*

A Minton Art Studio jug, in turquoise and honey colours, restored, c1875, 8in (20cm) high. **£200–250** *CEd*

r. A vase, by Jessie Marion King, cracked, 'J.M.K.' marks, 6in (15cm) high. **£150–200** *CEd*

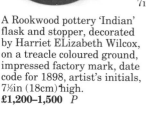

A William de Morgan red lustre tile panel, made from 2 large tiles, painted in red and pink lustres, framed. **£400–600** *P*

An Ault pottery vase, the base with raised 'Ault' mark, impressed 'C. W. Dresser', signature and 'No. 246', 7in (17.5cm) high. **£550–650** *HOD*

A Rookwood pottery 'Indian' flask and stopper, decorated by Harriet ELizabeth Wilcox, on a treacle coloured ground, impressed factory mark, date code for 1898, artist's initials, 7½in (18cm) high. **£1,200–1,500** *P*

An Ault pottery twin-handled vase, designed by Christopher Dresser, decorated in red, white and apple green, factory mark, No. 246, facsimile signature, 7in (17.5cm) high. **£700–800** *P*

An Ault pottery freeform vase, designed by Christopher Dresser, impressed facsimile signature, 12½in (32cm) high. **£300–350** *P*

An Elton ware vase, decorated with gold and platinum crackle glaze, base with signature, 21½in (54cm) high. **£800–900** *HOD*

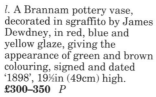

l. A Brannam pottery vase, decorated in sgraffito by James Dewdney, in red, blue and yellow glaze, giving the appearance of green and brown colouring, signed and dated '1898', 19½in (49cm) high. **£300–350** *P*

r. A Dalpayrat high fired porcelain vase, the white body glazed in shades of sang-de-boeuf, mauve, eau-de-nil, and blue, signed, numbered '12', 2in (5cm) high. **£150–200** *P*

A Foley china 'Harjian' vase, with 3 loop handles, decorated in brown, white, turquioise and green, with a frieze of dancing Negro figures, printed Foley Art China and rope mark and 'Harjian', 10½in (27cm) high.
£300–500 *P*

A Carlton Ware plaque painted in gilt, orange, blue, green and white, printed mark, design No. 7898, 3787, 15½in (39cm) diam.
£150–200 *CEd*

A ceramic câchepot by Max Lauger, the celadon ground decorated with green branches and black fruit, hairline crack, impressed mark on the base, 8in (20cm) high.
£500–800 *CG*

A Linthorpe earthenware jug, designed by Dr Christopher Dresser, covered in a streaked lustrous olive brown and turquioise glaze, impressed 'Linthorpe', with facsimile signature 'Chr. Dresser', 7½in (19.5cm) high.
£300–400 *C*

A William de Morgan deep bowl, decorated by Fred Passenger in copper, blue and silver lustre, the exterior in golden and ruby lustre with scroll motif, painted marks 'W. de Morgan Fulham FP', 16½in (41.5cm) wide.
£2,000–3,000 *C*

An Ernst Wahliss pottery wall plaque, in muted naturalistic colours, stamped 'Made in Austria, Ernst Wahliss, Turn-Wien', 20in (50.5cm) high.
£280–360 *P*

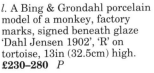

l. A Bing & Grondahl porcelain model of a monkey, factory marks, signed beneath glaze 'Dahl Jensen 1902', 'R' on tortoise, 13in (32.5cm) high.
£230–280 *P*

A Carlton Ware limited edition punch bowl, moulded in relief with a frieze of Henry VIII and his wives and children, glazed in bright colours and heightened with gilding, with full inscription on base, numbered 50 of an edition of 250, 8in (20cm) high.
£400–600 *P*

A Scottie Wilson ceramic plate, painted in colours, signed on the plate 'Scottie', 14in (35.5cm), mounted, framed and glazed.
£200–400 *P*

An Austrian 'tube line' decorated plant trough, 11in (28cm) wide.
£120–160 *ASA*

A Goldscheider pottery bust, impressed factory mark, 14½in (37cm) high.
£400–500 *P*

An E. Radford 'coaching' jug, 10½in (27cm) high. **£100–125** *MA*

l. Three pieces of Radford ware, 'Ranunculus' pattern. **£25–100 each** *MA*

An E. Radford moulded vase, 'Rose' pattern, 6in (15cm) high. **£50–70** *MA*

An early E. Radford, Burslem teapot, 5½in (14cm) high. **£80–100** *MA*

A large E. Radford moulded jug, 'Indian Tree' pattern, 8½in (21cm) high. **£60–80** *MA*

Two E. Radford vases, 'Anemone' pattern, 7½in (19cm) and 10in (25cm) high. **£40–60** each *MA*

An early E. Radford, Burslem, jug, 7in (17cm) high. **£70–90** *MA*

An E. Radford plate and vase, vase 8in (20cm) high. **£40–60 each** *MA*

Two E. Radford wall pockets, 'Anemone' pattern 4½in (11cm). **£40–60 each** *MA*

An early E. Radford, Burslem, table lamp base. **£70–80** *MA*

A Royal Doulton Art Nouveau miniature cup, impressed '7498', incised 'CA', 2in (5cm) high.
£20–30 *HM*

A blue and white faïence dish and cover, painted with a crest and 'Pour n'Oublié', marked 'Gallé Nancy St Clement', 1880s, 10in (25cm) wide.
£500–800 *SB*

A Zsolnay centrepiece, in green-blue and golden purple lustre glaze, moulded circular 'Zsolnay' mark, 21½in (54.5cm) high.
£1,500–2,000 *C*

A faïence seated cat, black glazed, painted with amber and gilt scroll motifs, one flank painted with a crest, slight damage, 13in (33cm) high.
£1,500–2,000 *C*

A French pottery bust of an Arthurian style lady, after Jacob, shaded in turquoise and rose, picked out in gold, impressed mark, (8in (20cm) high.
£200–300 *SBe*

A French pottery plate, with a design by Alphonse Mucha and painted in colours, marked 'Mucha 97', and on reverse 'Au Grand Depot, 21 rue Drouot, Paris', 12in (31.5cm) diam.
£600–900 *P*

A Koenig and Lengsfeld ceramic figure of a young woman, peeting into an oval mirror, in shades of grey and lavender, impressed 'Koenig & Lengsfeld, Koln Lindenthal 2687', 27½in (70cm) high.
£500–700 *C*

A Scottish painted low relief plaster panel, incised initials 'GAW', c1905, 12in (30.5cm) wide.
£150–200 *SB*

A Della Robbia earthenware cream glazed vase, decorated by Liza Wilkins, incised mark, painted initials, 10½in (27cm) high.
£200–300 *CSK*

An Arte Della earthenware vase, impressed and painted factory insignia, c1905, 13½in (34.5cm) high.
£500–700 *SB*

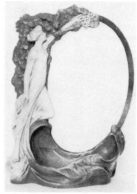

A Royal Dux earthenware mirror, impressed factory mark, numbered '1098', c1900, 21½in (54.5cm) high.
£800–1,000 *SB*

A Clement Massier lustre glazed earthenware vase, decorated with green, pink and peacock metallic lustre, painted mark 'M. C. Clement Massier Golfe Juan a.m.', c1900, 12in (30.5cm) high.
£600–900 *SB*

l. A Gallé faïence pot pourri and cover a copy of a Kutani koro and cover, painted in Japanese style in shades of blue and rust against a pale blue ground, detailed with gilding, enamelled mark 'Gallé Nancy editeur St Clement terre Lorraine', 1870s, 10in (25.5cm) high.
£800–1,200 *SB*

A Wedgwood Fairyland lustre 'Elves and Bell Branch' bowl, after a design by Daisy Makeig-Jones, decorated with elves and fairies dancing among tall grass against a black ground with a gilt spider's web, printed Portland vase mark, painted number 'Z4968', minor rubbing, c1920, 3in (7.5cm) high.
£700–900 *S(S)*

A pair of Shelley 'Intarsio' vases, after a design by Walter Slater, decorated with stylised pink flowerheads among foliage in green, brown, and blue, printed mark 'Late Foley, Shelley, England, Intarsio', and painted number '544 3617', c1915, 6½in (16.5cm) high.
£300–400 *S(S)*

A Rye Pottery vase, with flared neck, applied with daffodils and leaves, marked on base 'Sussex Ware Rye', 6in (15cm) high.
£120–170 *RAG*

A pair of Wedgwood Fairyland lustre vases, after a design by Daisy Makeig-Jones, each decorated with the 'Imps on a Bridge and Tree House' pattern, against a flame red ground, Portland vase mark 'Wedgwood, Made in England', and painted number 'Z5481', c1920, 10in (26cm) high.
£3,500–4,000 *S(S)*

A Pilkington's Royal Lancastrian lustre wall plaque, after a design by Walter Crane and painted by Charles E. Cundall, in copper lustre with red details on a mauve ground, the reverse with 4 copper lustre floral motifs, damaged, impressed factory 'P' and Bee mark, 'VII', and lustre monograms, c1907.
£600–700 *S(S)*

A Wileman & Co. 'Intarsio' jug, after a design by Frederick Rhead, modelled as the body of a bird with an Egyptian style head, in typical palette, raised on 3 feet, printed factory mark, registration No. 330274, painted number '3076', c1900, 5in (12.5cm) high.
£320–400 *S(S)*

A Rye Pottery bowl, the brown body profusely covered with applied green hops, the rim banded with leaves, marked on base 'Rye Sussex', dated '1919', 8in (20cm) diam.
£300–400 *RAG*

A Wedgwood Fairyland lustre 'Woodland Bridge' bowl, after a design by Daisy Makeig-Jones, decorated outside with orange, yellow, green and purple shrubs on a black ground, the interior with the 'Fairy with Large Hat' pattern, cobwebs in the trees, fairies and elves among the toadstools on the banks of a river, gilt printed factory mark and painted number 'Z4968', c1920, 6in (15cm) diam.
£2,000–2,500 *S(S)*

A tapering vase, applied with branches, acorns and oak leaves, marked on base 'S.R.W. Rye', 4in (10cm) high.
£70–90 *RAG*

r. A Wileman & Co. 'Intarsio' jardinière, after a design by Frederick Rhead, decorated with a frieze of geese between foliate bands, in typical colours printed factory mark, registration No. 330400, printed number '3143', c1900, 7in (18cm) high.
£500–600 *S(S)*

A vase by C. H. Brannam, c1885, 10in (25cm) high.
£160–170 *NCA*

A pair of spill vases, by C. H. Brannam, converting to candlesticks, 10in (25cm) high.
£300–350 *NCA*

A Bretby spill vase, decorated in yellow with a stork and bamboo, 12in (31cm) high.
£70–80 *NCA*

A blue frog, by C. H. Brannam, 3in (7.5cm) high.
£50–60 *NCA*

A Bretby 'copperette' jug, 12in (31cm) high.
£140–150 *NCA*

A Watcombe cheese dish, attributed to Christopher Dresser, 6½in (16.5cm) high.
£160–180 *NCA*

An early Burmantofts turquoise blue planter, No. 1082, 7in (18cm) high.
£150–200 *NCA*

A green vase, by C. H. Brannam, with 6 handles, 1903, 6.5in (16cm) high.
£70–100 *NCA*

A Burmantofts vase, decorated with dragons, by V. Kremer, 9½in (24cm) high.
£580–600 *NCA*

A figure of The Brighton Wet Nurse, with nodding head and suspended body, dressed in a cloak and gown baring a bosom to a babe in arms, standing on a circular base marked 'Rye B4', 6in (15cm) high.
£320–370 *RAG*

A collection of William de Morgan tiles, decorated with a parrot, flowers, guinea fowl, great curassow, pelican with fish, and ships, some lustre and some polychrome, various marks, two 8in (20cm) square, the others 6in (15cm) square.
£2,000–2,500 *CSK*

r. A Pilkington's vase, 6in (15cm) high.
£50–75 *AOS*

A Pilkington's Royal Lancastrian 'Vermillion' glaze vase, moulded with fish amongst waves on a green ground under a speckled orange glaze, impressed factory marks, c1920, 8in (20cm) high, and a similar vase, after a design by William S. Mycock and modelled by E. T. Radford, with a mottled green and speckled orange glaze, impressed factory marks 'E.T.R.', painted monogram and year cypher, c1929, 7in (18cm) high.
£200–250 *S(S)*

'Ruskin Pottery' high-fired stoneware lettering, the speckled green glaze with areas of cloudy blue, mounted on copper panels, c1905, each letter 7in (18cm) high.
£3,500–4,500 *C*

These are the original letters used at the Ruskin Pottery factory.

A Royal Lancastrian uranium glazed vase, by Richard Joyce, 5in (13cm) high.
£150–250 *NCA*

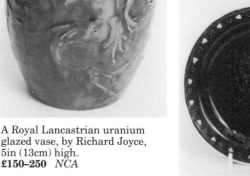

A Ruskin plate, with incised mark, 6in (15cm) diam.
£25–40 *AOS*

A Ruskin lustre vase, dated '1922', 8in (20cm) high.
£50–100 *AOS*

A Ruskin blue vase, c1930, 5½in (14cm) high.
£50–75 *AOS*

A Rye Pottery 'Sussex Pig', lead glazed mainly in blue, with a hook-on head, inscribed with the motto 'Wun't be druv', 4½in (11.5cm) long.
£200–240 *RAG*

A Mintons Secessionist jardinière, decorated in purple, turquoise and green, repeated around the body, impressed and printed factory marks 'Mintons, No. 72', c1910, 13in (32.5cm) high.
£300–500 S(S)

A Mintons stoneware bread plate, designed by A. W. N. Pugin, inscribed 'Waste Not, Want Not', with rust and blue encaustic glazes, stamped '430', 13in (33cm) diam.
£800–1,200 C

A William de Morgan two-tile panel of a manned galley within a classical harbour, with green, turquoise, amethyst and yellow glazes, c1880, 12in (31cm) long.
£900–1,200 C

A William de Morgan deep red lustre bowl, decorated by Fred Passenger, with decoration of an eagle attacking a grotesque lizard within a scrolling foliate border, painted 'FP' initials, c1890, 10in (25cm) diam.
£700–800 C

A Mintons Secessionist jardinière, after a design by Léon V. Solon and John W. Wadsworth, decorated in turquoise above printed scrolling green foliage, moulded 'Minton's, England', impressed factory marks and date cypher, damaged, 12⅝in (32cm) high.
£300–400 S(S)

A William de Morgan dish, painted by Frederick Passenger, in ruby lustres against white, signed 'F.P.', 14⅝in (37cm) diam.
£500–800 P

r. A William de Morgan four-tile panel of 2 snakes among flowering foliage against turquoise ground, with green, puce and amethyst glazes, chipped, each impressed 'WM', Merton Abbey seal, c1882, 16in (41cm) square.
£1,400–1,700 C

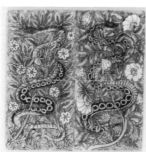

A Pilkington's red vase, 5½in (13.5cm) high.
£50–75 AOS

A Bernard Moore enamelled flambé plate, the centre painted and enamelled with the bust of a female figure, the face in profile, hands clasped in prayer, with an inscription in a halo, on a flambé ground, overpainted hands and face, painted monogram 'B.M.', circular frame, 10in (25.5cm) diam.
£700–800 C

A Pilkington's Royal Lancastrian lustre charger, by Mycock, inscribed on reverse, c1900, 11⅜in (29cm) diam.
£800–1,200 ASA

A Pilkington's Royal Lancastrian vase, signed, 6½in (16cm) high.
£75–100 AOS

An Ault vase, by Christopher Dresser, 12in (31cm) high. **£180–200** *NCA*

A pair of Bretby pottery vases, with applied horn and insect decoration, No. 1470, 14in (35.5cm) high. **£200–300** *NCA*

A Burmantofts pottery ewer, 10in (25cm) high. **£150–180** *NCA*

A Burmantofts green pottery vase, with Gothic decoration, 9½in (24cm) high. **£130–150** *NCA*

A vase by Thomas Forester, 8in (20cm) high. **£75–125** *AOS*

A Linthorpe pouring vessel, designed by Christopher Dresser, covered in a mottled and streaked green glaze, impressed Linthorpe, 312', facsimile signature 'Chr. Dresser' with Linthorpe Pottery seal, 6½in (16.5cm) high. **£800–1,000** *C*

A Linthorpe pottery vase, after a design by Christopher Dresser, in a streaked brown glaze, with a pierced flower and foliage in the centre in green, stamped 'Chr. Dresser, HT', c1880, 8½in (21.5cm) high. **£450–600** *S(S)*

A Minton porcelain vase, designed by Chrispher Dresser, painted in gold, green, yellow, blue, black and orange enamels, restored, 11½in (29cm) high. **£2,000–2,500** *C*

r. A Linthorpe vase, designed by Christopher Dresser, impressed with a spiralling feather design, covered in an olive green glaze, impressed 'Linthorpe' with facsimile signature 'Chr. Dresser, 298' and 'HT' monogram, 7½in (19cm) high. **£350–550** *C*

A Linthorpe vase, by Clara Pringle, 9½in (24cm) high. **£280–300** *NCA*

A Quimper cup and saucer,
c1905, saucer 7in (18cm) diam.
£40–60 *VH*

An Elton ware loving cup,
c1890, 8½in (21cm) high.
£300–375 *SAI*

A Brannam beaker/mug, part of a
lemonade set, with inscription.
£80–100 *BLO*

l. A Ruskin green cup and
saucer, 5½in (14cm) diam.
£70–90 *PC*

A Brannam blue Toby jug,
4in (10cm) high.
£30–50 *BLO*

A pair of Frederick Rhead Foley
Intarsio ewers, c1880, 11in
(28cm) high.
£800–900 *BEV*

A Brannam puffin jug, c1900,
8in (20cm) high.
£80–100 *BLO*

A Barum jug, inscribed 'The
Lundy Parrot', 5in (12.5cm)
high. **£70–90** *BLO*

l. A Ruskin dark green cup and
saucer, from the Ferneyhough
collection, saucer 6in (15cm)
diam. **£90–110** *PC*

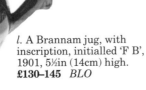

l. A Brannam jug, with
inscription, initialled 'F B',
1901, 5½in (14cm) high.
£130–145 *BLO*

A Barum blue puzzle jug,
with inscription, 5in (12.5cm)
high. **£35–40** *BLO*

A Sèvres Art Pottery bowl, in blue tones sponged with yellow, c1930, 11in (28cm) diam.
£50–100 *HOW*

A Sèvres Art Pottery dish in red, green and brown, 7in (17.5cm) diam.
£40–65 *HOW*

A Brannam pink dog with toothache, 6½in (16.5cm) high.
£55–60 *BLO*

A Brannam green owl jar with lid, made for Liberty, 5in (12.5cm) high.
£50–80 *BLO*

A Brannam cat, green with black markings, 11in (28.5cm) high.
£200–220 *BLO*

An Upchurch pottery bowl with three handles, in blue and grey, 7in (17.5cm) diam.
£50–70 *BLO*

A Brannam flower holder, initialled 'B W', c1900, 10in (25cm) wide.
£175–200 *BLO*

A Brannam blue frog, 2½in (6cm) high.
£60–80 *BLO*

A Brannam chamber stick, initialled 'S W', 4in (10cm) high.
£120–150 *BLO*

A Bretby apple vase, 3½in (9cm) high.
£30–45 *BLO*

l. A Ruskin green cup and saucer, with decoration, 3½in (9cm) diam.
£60–80 *PC*

r. A Brannam blue boot, 8½in (21cm) long
£130–150 *BLO*

A Bretby bowl, c1895, 8½in (21cm) diam.
£85–110 *BLO*

A Bretby jardinière, decorated with fish.
£300–500 *ASA*

A William de Morgan tile, painted in red lustre with stylised carnations, with painted signature 'W de Morgan & Co., Fulham, London', 8in (20cm) square.
£80–140 *C*

A Bretby earthenware 'bamboo' stick stand, with a seated monkey at the base, his arms wrapped around the stand, the monkey painted in naturalistic colours, the stand shading from yellow to amber and green, rim cracked, impressed mark, 23in (59cm) high.
£350–450 *Bon*

A William de Morgan red lustre vase and cover, the white ground decorated in red, cover restored, the base impressed 'W de Morgan, Sand Pottery', with Morris & Co. paper label, 13in (33cm) high.
£1,000–1,500 *C*

A pair of Bretby vases, c1885, 14in (36cm) high.
£500–600 *BLO*

A pair of Bretby vases, with grey metal finish, c1900, 8½in (22cm) high.
£40–50 *STU*

A William de Morgan jar, decorated in the Persian style, in turquoise, blue, dark purple and grey with stylised floral arabesques, 16in (41cm) high.
£2,000–3,000 *P*

l A Minton pottery plaque, painted by W. S. Coleman, in pastel colours, printed 'Minton Art Pottery Studio, Kensington Gore,' c1870, 18in (46cm) wide.
£1,500–2,000 *Bon*

A pair of steel candle sconces, attributed to Edward Spencer and the Artificers Guild, 12in (31cm) high.
£2,000–2,500 *P*

A Barum ware jardinière, green ground with fish decoration, some damage, late 19thC, 9in (22cm) high.
£70–100 *PCh*

A Della Robbia vase, marks include 'AB' and 'CEMB', 9in (22.5cm) high.
£170–190 *BLO*

A pair of Brannam vases, with sgraffito design in brown and blue on a cream ground, initialled 'WB' and dated 1889, 10in (25cm) high.
£400–600 *BLO*

A Gouda vase, c1925, 13in (33cm) high.
£150–200 *BEV*

A Gouda vase, c1920, 7½in (19cm) high.
£50–60 *BEV*

r. A Barum vase, decorated with a with lizard in relief, 7in (17.5cm) high.
£90–110 *BLO*

A Gouda vase, c1925, 10in (25cm) high.
£70–80 *BEV*

A Gouda vase, c1900, 14in (36cm) high.
£150–200 *BEV*

A Lauder vase, with sgraffito fish design, 6½in (16cm) high.
£80–90 *BLO*

A Bretby jug, with flowing glaze spout, copperette handle and body, 12in (30.5cm) high.
£140–160 *BLO*

A jug, by Louis Desmant, Normandy, with scenes from the Bayeux Tapestry, 5½in (14cm) high.
£40–60 *BLO*

A Lauder green jug, 8in (20cm) high.
£100–110 *BLO*

A Barum green frog candle holder, 6in (15cm) high.
£90–100 *BLO*

A Belgian pottery candle holder, 11½in (29cm) high.
£50–60 *BLO*

A Gouda ceramic candle holder, c1920, 8½in (21cm) high.
£70–80 *BEV*

A Ruskin candlestick, marbled grey with burgundy trim, marked, 3in (7.5cm) high.
£150–200 *PC*

A Wardle mauve candle holder, 9in (22.5cm) high.
£40–60 *BLO*

A Frederick Rhead candle holder, 15in (38cm) high.
£250–300 *BEV*

A Chameleon ware container with lid, 8½in (21cm) high.
£70–80 *BEV*

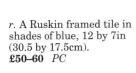

r. A Ruskin framed tile in shades of blue, 12 by 7in (30.5 by 17.5cm).
£50–60 *PC*

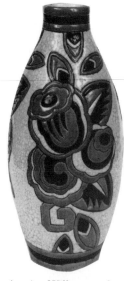

A pair of Villeroy and Boch vases, 10½in (26cm) high.
£300–350 *BEV*

A Boch blue and white vase, c1930, 12in (30.5cm) high.
£200–250 *BEV*

An E. B. Fisher vase, 8½in (21cm) high.
£80–40 *BLO*

A Maw's pink vase, c1900, 12½in (32cm) high.
£120–140 *THA*

An early Frederick Rhead vase, 10in (25cm) high.
£300–350 *BEV*

An Upchurch pottery vase, in pink/grey, 10in (25cm) high.
£70–80 *BLO*

l. A majolica vase, c1880, 6in (15cm) high.
£60–70 *HOW*

A pair of Ault vases with pansy decoration, one signed by William Ault, 9½in (24cm) high.
£80–100 *BLO*

A Bretby deep blue vase, 12in (30.5cm) high.
£70–90 *BLO*

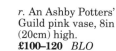

l. A pair of Bretby vases, painted with ships on a chocolate coloured field, 13½in (34cm) high.
£70–100 *BLO*

An Ault pottery vase, designed by Christopher Dresser, covered with liver-red glaze, impressed facsimile signature on base, 20in (50cm) high.
£550–600 *P*

r. An Ashby Potters' Guild pink vase, 8in (20cm) high.
£100–120 *BLO*

A Carlton Ware lustre pottery vase, painted with a bold chequered and geometric design in vivid orange, yellow, tan and black, printed mark, 10in (25cm) high. **£250–300** *CSK*

l. A Royal Dux tazza, pink triangle mark, 6½in (16.5cm) high.
£250–300 *P*
c. A Royal Dux candelabrum, with shaped framework outlined in green and pink, pink triangle mark, 14in (35.5cm) high.
£300–400 *P*
r. A Royal Dux figure of a girl, partially covering her body with a puce and green robe that her pet dog tries to remove, pink triangle mark, 14½in (37cm) high.
£400–500 *P*

A Royal Dux Art Deco part bisque figure, 10in (25cm) high. **£200–300** *CDC*

A Jean Mayodon Art Deco faïence vase, impressed monogram 'J.M.', c1925, 11in (28cm) high. **£100–125** *S*

A Hutschenreuther porcelain figure of Mephistopheles, by K. Tutler, factory marks, 11in (28.5cm) high. **£300–400** *P*

A Zsolnay lustre ewer, in the form of a bird, spires mark and 'Zsolnay Pecs', 13in (33cm) high. **£400–500** *P*

A Royal Dux figure of dancer, in a revealing blue dress, 12in (30.5cm) high. **£200–300** *Re*

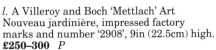

A Goldscheider figure of a dancer, impressed marks, 16½in (42cm) high. **£800–1,000** *N*

An Art Deco pottery vase, incised and painted in brown with stylised flamingoes on turquoise mounds, on a cream ground, inscribed 'Simone Liarrieu', 12in (30.5cm) high. **£300–400** *CSK*

An Art Deco Goldscheider pottery figure, by Claire Weiss, impressed marks, inscribed 'C. Weiss', 12½in (32cm) high. **£500–800** *CSK*

l. A Villeroy and Boch 'Mettlach' Art Nouveau jardinière, impressed factory marks and number '2908', 9in (22.5cm) high. **£250–300** *P*

A Shelley teaset, yellow and black on a white ground, comprising: a teapot, sugar bowl, milk jug, 2 square sandwich platters, 12 cups and saucers, 9 side plates, printed mar, Reg. No. 723404, c1930, teapot 5in (12.5cm) high.
£500–800 *C*

A Beswick teapot, in the form of a panda, c1930.
£70–100 *BRI*

A Goldscheider pottery head of a woman, 9½in (24cm) high.
£200–400 *CDC*

A Louis Wain model of a cat, with a lemon, green, yellow and red coloured body, printed and painted marks, 6½in (16cm) high.
£400–600 *CSK*

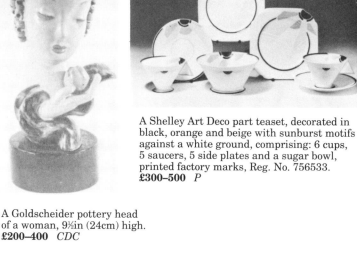

A Shelley Art Deco part teaset, decorated in black, orange and beige with sunburst motifs against a white ground, comprising: 6 cups, 5 saucers, 5 side plates and a sugar bowl, printed factory marks, Reg. No. 756533.
£300–500 *P*

A Shelley Mode teaset, decorated in grey and acid green on a white ground, comprising: a milk jug, sugar bowl, 6 cups and saucers, 6 side plates, printed 'Shelley England', Reg. No. 756533, c1930.
£700–900 *C*

A Shelley three-piece pottery nursery teaset, in bright colours on a white ground, designed by Mabel Lucie Attwell, painted artist's signature on each piece, c1925, largest 7½in (19cm) high.
£400–600 *C*

An Art Deco ceramic night light holder.
£30–50 *ASA*

An ashtray, formed of interlinked circles with a recess in the rim applied with a female head with orange curly hair on the edge, stamped 'Goldscheider Wien', c1925, 10in (25cm) wide.
£300–500 *S(S)*

A Shelley lustre ware bowl, signed by Walter Slater, c1920, 12in (30.5cm) diam.
£60–80 *AJ*

A Shelley Harmony ware strainer, c1930, 8in (20cm) diam.
£40–60 *AJ*

A Carlton Ware Apple Blossom breakfast set, c1930.
£300–350 *RO*

r. A Shelley 22-piece teaset, with orange, silver and black geometric decoration, comprising: teapot, milk jug, sugar basin, 6 cups, saucers and plates, and a cake plate.
£500–600 *TW*

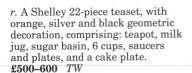

A wall mask, by Leonardi, with a mushroom coloured face and green scarf, Reg. No. 825795, c1930, 20½in (52cm) high.
£60–80 *AW*

A Shelley ginger jar, in orange and yellow, c1930, 8½in (22cm) high.
£100–150 *AJ*

A Quimper cup, Pêcheur pattern, signed, 2in (5cm) high.
£15–20 *VH*

A Robj earthenware bowl and cover, formed as a Red Indian's head, with dark red glazed feather headdress, with impressed mark 'Robj Paris, Made in France', 8in (20cm) high.
£400–500 *C*

A Lenci bust, by Essevi Samdo Vachetti, 8½in (21.5cm) high.
£300–400 *BEV*

A Lenci bust, Essevi Samdo Vachetti, c1938, 7in (17.5cm) high.
£300–400 *BEV*

A 55-piece Jean Luce dinner service.
£500–600 *C*

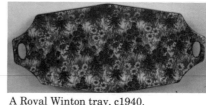

A Royal Winton tray, c1940.
£40–45 *CIR*

A stylised floral ceramic umbrella stand, probably French, c1920.
£100–120 *ST*

A Shelley plate, decorated with the 'Melody' pattern, 7in (19cm) diam.
£12–15 *CIR*

A Crown Ducal bowl, designed by Charlotte Rhead, decorated in the 'Manchu' pattern in green, blue, orange and gilding against a green ground, printed factory marks, signed 'C. Rhead', 10in (25cm) diam.
£150–250 *P*

A Shelley vase, 6in (15cm) high.
£30–35 *CIR*

A Gray's pottery plate, signed 'Nite', with clipper mark.
£90–110 *DEC*

A Gray's pottery plate, with clipper mark, 10⅓in (26.5cm) diam.
£55–65 *DEC*

l. A Myott hand-painted jardinière, 8in (20cm) diam.
£70–110 *DEC*

r. A Carlton Ware vase, with lid, chipped, 12in (31cm) high.
£60–80 *CIR*

A Pilkington's Lancastrian vase, with everted rim, decorated by Walter Crane in yellow lustre on a blue/green ground, impressed Bee mark, painted artist's monogram, wheat ear motif, 10½in (26.5cm) high.
£800–1,200 *C*

A Crown Devon porcelain bridge set, with black and gilt geometric decoration, comprising: 4 coffee cups and saucers, 2 ashtrays, and a card box, printed marks 'Crown Devon Fieldings, Made in England, 2714', in original box.
£200–400 *C*

A face mask, by
C. Copes & Co., c1930,
7in (17.5cm) high.
£50–100 *BEV*

A milk jug,
2½in (6.5cm) high.
£8–10 *BEV*

r. A Carlton Ware vase,
decorated on a mottled
purple and white ground,
enriched with gilding,
marked 'Carlton Ware, Made
in England, Trade Mark',
c1930, 10½in (27cm) high.
£300–400 *C*

A Gray's pottery jug,
A923, 7½in (19cm) high.
£30–50 *DEC*

A Japanese flask, entitled
'Just a Little Nip', c1900.
£40–60 *BEV*

A Susie Cooper coffee pot,
5in (13cm) high.
£30–35 *PC*

A Barker Bros.
hand painted jug,
6in (15cm) high.
£45–50 *DEC*

A Susie Cooper tea cup and coffee cup.
£10–15 *BEV*

A Hancock's ivory
ware jug, decorated in
blue, yellow and green,
8½in (21.5cm) high.
£25–30 *CIR*

A Susie Cooper coffee set, pot 8in (20cm) high.
£80–100 *CIR*

A Shelley 22-piece tea service, decorated with
yellow 'Phlox' pattern.
£150–180 *CIR*

A Carlton Ware bowl, and a drainer, with 'Water Lily' design, bowl 9½in wide.
£45–65 each *ADC*

A Burleigh jug, with 'Parrot' design, c1930, 8in (20cm) high.
£55–80 *AOS*

A Burleigh jug, with 'Kingfisher' pattern, c1930.
£50–75 *AOS*

A Royal Cauldron fruit bowl, c1935, 9in (23cm) diam.
£65–100 *AOS*

l. A Burleigh jug, decorated with a fox and stork, 8in (20cm) high.
£75–125 *AOS*

A Hancock vase, decorated with 'Autumn' design, 7in (18cm) high.
£100–150 *AOS*

A Charlotte Rhead Crown Ducal plaque, decorated in light and dark pink and grey on a cream background, no. 6778, 12½in (32cm) diam.
£220–300 *ADC*

A pair of banded Shelley vases, 8in (20cm) high.
£65–100 *AOS*

A Carlton Ware dish, with 'Pink Daisy' design, 4½in (11cm) wide.
£20–25 *ADC*

r. A Carlton Ware blue toilet jug and bowl set, with chinoiserie pattern, printed mark in blue.
£300–400 *HSS*

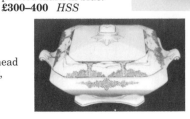

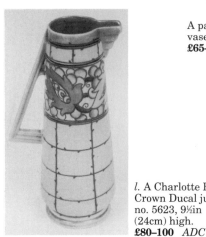

l. A Charlotte Rhead Crown Ducal jug, no. 5623, 9½in (24cm) high.
£80–100 *ADC*

l. A Crown Ducal vegetable dish, decorated in a red trees pattern, c1925.
£20–35 *AOS*

A pair of cantilever nickel plated steel, leather and glass armchairs, and a coffee table, by Josef Müller, Berlin, glass replaced, table 24in (61.5cm) diam. **£95,000–100,000** *S*

An Eavestaff 6-octave mini piano, in an Art Deco walnut case, 51in (129.5cm) wide, and a matching stool. **£400–600** *PCh*

A satinwood and walnut 'Stafford' wardrobe, by Gillow & Co., in 3 sections, stamped 'L5778', 87½in (222cm) high. **£5,000–6,000** *C*

An inlaid mahogany writing bureau, with metal attachments, c1903. **£6,000–7,000** *S*

A wrought iron and gilt bronze firescreen, by Edgar Brandt, c1925, 33in (84cm) high. **£9,000–10,000** *S(NY)*

A rosewood, parchment and marble dining room suite, by Gio Ponti, c1935, table 87½in (222cm) long. **£13,000–15,000** *S(NY)*

A firescreen, by Edgar Brandt. **£10,500–12,000** *S(NY)*

A wrought iron hall stand, attributed to Paul Kiss, c1925. **£7,250–8,500** *S(NY)*

A carved mahogany dining table, and 18 dining chairs with carved foliate frames and upholstered in tooled leather, c1910. **£12,000–15,000** *CNY*

A wrought iron firescreen, c1925, 31in (79cm) wide. **£3,000–4,000** *S*

A mahogany and stained glass cabinet, by George Ellwood, for J. S. Henry, c1900, 77½in (197cm) high.
£2,000–2,500 S

A pair of Art Deco stained oak bergères, re-upholstered, c1925, 33in (84cm) wide.
£3,500–4,000 S

An oak dresser, by Shapland and Petter, inlaid with pewter, mother-of-pearl and brass, possibly designed by Baillie-Scott, c1890.
£1,700–2,200 S

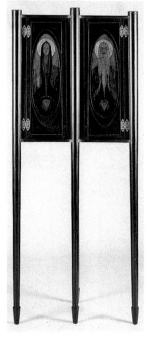

An ebonised and painted corner cabinet, designed by Charles Rennie Mackintosh, with painted panel by Margaret Macdonald Mackintosh, c1897, 72½in (183cm) high.
£20,000–30,000 C

An oak and brass cabinet, with double doors, attributed to Léon Jallot, c1907, 76in (193cm) high.
£2,000–3,000 S

A pair of Heal's oak and rush ladderback armchairs, c1905.
£2,200–2,500 S

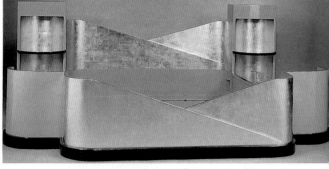

A lacquered, gilt and silvered wood double bed, by Paul Poiret, with nightstands and stools, c1929, 82in (208cm) long.
£4,500–6,000 S(NY)

A thuya wood side cabinet, c1870, 40in (101.5cm) high.
£2,000–2,500 S

An oak and rush high back armchair, c1907.
£2,500–3,000 S

An oak and brass buffet, attributed to Léon Jallot, c1907, 52in (132cm) high.
£2,000–3,000 S

An Aesthetic Movement ebony and lacquer cabinet, signed and stamped 'Gregory & Co.', 62in (158cm) wide.
£2,000–3,000 *C*

r. An American Arts & Crafts clock, with a brass face, c1910.
£600–800 *ST*

An ebonised, rosewood and vellum covered games table, by Carlo Bugatti, the top with 4 covered wells and inlaid with a pewter chessboard, inlaid signature, 31½in (79cm) wide.
£8,000–12,000 *C*

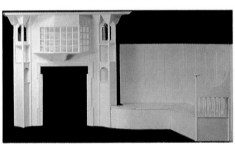

A white painted fire surround and inglenook, designed by M. H. Baillie-Scott, c1898, 83in (211cm) high.
£4,000–6,000 *C*

A walnut dining suite, with yew crossbanding, labels for Russell & Sons, Broadway, Worcs., c1920, table 66in (167cm) wide. **£12,000–15,000** *P*

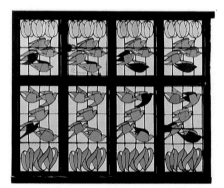

A lead and stained glass window, designed by M. H. Baillie-Scott, with a wooden frame, c1898, 70in (177.5cm) high.
£14,000–15,000 *C*

An ebonised and painted sideboard, the painting attributed to Henry Stacy Marks, 78in (198cm) wide.
£3,000–4,000 *P*

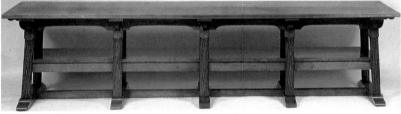

A Morris & Co. green stained oak centre table, the design attributed to Philip Webb with George Jack, 125in (320cm) wide.
£18,000–20,000 *P*

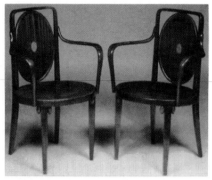

A pair of beechwood open armchairs, designed by
J. Hoffman, branded 'J & J Kohn, Wien, Austria'.
£4,000–5,000 *C*

A set of 6 dining chairs and 2 armchairs, by Asprey. **£28,000–30,000**
A glass and chromed metal dining table, by Asprey,
inlaid with panels by Lalique. **£100,000+** *C*

Josef Hoffmann (Austrian, 1870–1956)

Originally trained as an architect, Josef Hoffmann was influenced by Charles Rennie Mackintosh and the Glasgow School. In 1897 he founded the Vienna Secession, an association of artists and architects disillusioned with the work of the Viennese Society of Visual Artists. Inspired by the attempts of the Vienna Secessionists to bring more abstract and purer forms to design, in 1903 Hoffmann founded the Wiener Werkstätte, or Vienna Workshops. Associated designers included Josef Olbrich and Koloman Moser and, as well as buildings and furniture, the group designed silver, glass, ceramics and metalwork.

Hoffmann's furniture designs were mainly geometric in form, and were mostly executed by one of the largest Viennese furniture manufacturers, Jacob & Josef Kohn, together with another large Viennese firm, the Thonet Brothers.

l. The Gerrit Rietveld '1919 Red/Blue Chair', by G. A. van der Groenekan, in beech and plywood. **£3,000–4,000** *C*

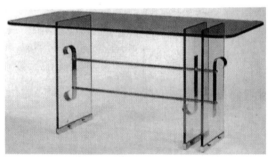

A Fontana Arte plate glass and chromium plated table, c1935, 67in (170cm) wide. **£4,000–5,000** *C*

A wrought iron and mahogany table, by Pierre Chareau, 19½in (49.5cm) wide. **£10,000–12,000** *CNY*

A bentwood salon suite, designed by Josef Hoffmann, made by J. & J. Kohn, c1905, settee 47½in (121cm) wide. **£7,000–8,000** *CNY*

A pair of Art Deco burr walnut bedside cabinets, by Mercier Frères, 23in (58.5cm) wide. **£3,500–4,000** *C*

An oak smoker's cabinet, by Gustav Stickley, c1903, 17in (43.5cm) wide. **£3,000–4,000** *CNY*

An oak sewing cabinet, by Gustav Stickley, with red decal, c1905, 20in (50.5cm) wide. **£2,800–3,200** *CNY*

A walnut, maple and chrome display cabinet, by Gordon Russell workshops, c1930. **£3,500–4,500** *S*

A mahogany and marquetry side cabinet, c1900, 55in (139.5cm) wide. **£3,000–4,000** *S*

A carved mahogany and marquetry cabinet, by Louis Majorelle, 25in (63.4cm) wide. **£30,000–35,000** *CNY*

An inlaid oak music cabinet, designed by Harvey Ellis for Gustav Stickley, c1903. **£4,000–4,500** *CNY*

A carved mahogany and marquetry cabinet, by Louis Majorelle, 68in (172.5cm) high. **£20,000–25,000** *CNY*

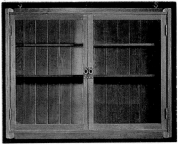

An oak hanging trophy case, by Gustav Stickley, c1904, 60½in (153.5cm) wide. **£4,500–5,500** *CNY*

An Art Deco three-piece bedroom suite, comprising: grand lit, and 2 bedside tables, branded 'Leleu'. **£6,000–7,000** *C*

A carved mahogany and marquetry cabinet, by Louis Majorelle, boldly carved and inlaid, 75in (190.5cm) high. **£28,000–32,000** *CNY*

An Art Deco Macassar ebony, and vellum daybed, 86in (218.5cm) long. **£5,500–6,500** *C*

r. A Guild of Handicraft oak cabinet, designed by C. R. Ashbee, with two drawers below a pair of doors inlaid in fruitwoods with stylised flowers, the inner face veneered in satinwood and painted and gilt with flowers, silver lamp fitting above, writing flap extending on to hinged supports, and a pair of doors enclosing a fitted shelf, the hinge and key plates pierced with stylised flowers, stamped 'The Guild of Handicraft Ltd., Essex House, Bow E.', c1900, 41½in (105cm) wide.
£25,000–35,000 *S*

r. A Gordon Russell walnut and mahogany writing cabinet, the panelled fall-front inlaid in ebony with fine stringing, enclosing a writing compartment, above three drawers edged with ebony stringing and with ebony knobs, on octagonal legs linked by cross-stretchers, paper label 'This piece of furniture design No. 570 was made throughout in The Russell Workshops Broadway, Worcestershire, Designer: Gordon Russell/Foreman: Edgar Turner/Cabinet Maker: T. Lees/Metal Worker: D. Keen/Timber used: English Walnut and White Mahogany/ Date: 15/2/27', 47in (120cm) wide.
£6,000–8,000 *S*

An oak director's table, by Gustav Stickley, with branded mark, c1912, 72in (182.5cm) wide.
£6,500–7,500 *CNY*

A walnut and marquetry étagère, by Louis Majorelle, 48½in (123cm) high.
£2,000–2,500 *C*

A two-tier table, marquetry inlaid with flowers and leaves, signed 'Gallé Nancy', 17in (43cm) wide.
£3,000–4,000 *CNY*

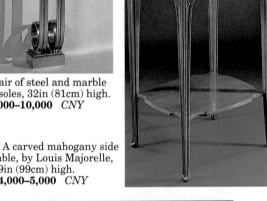

A burr walnut and marquetry centre table, designed by Oscar Kaufmann, two-tier table, 41⅛in (105cm) diam.
£4,000–5,000 *C*

A pair of steel and marble consoles, 32in (81cm) high.
£9,000–10,000 *CNY*

r. A carved mahogany side table, by Louis Majorelle, 39in (99cm) high.
£4,000–5,000 *CNY*

An oak library table, by Gustav Stickley, the 2 drawers with hand forged oval pulls, model No. 461, c1905, 54in (137cm) wide.
£500–1,000 *CNY*

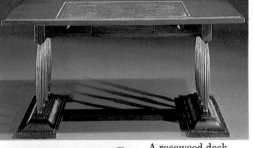

A rosewood desk, by Jacques-Emile Ruhlmann, the top inset with a leather panel, fitted with 2 drawers, branded, c1925, 60in (152cm) wide.
£120,000–150,000 *CNY*

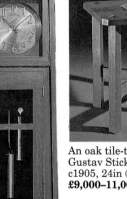

An oak tile-top table, by Gustav Stickley, labelled, c1905, 24in (61cm) wide.
£9,000–11,000 *CNY*

l. An oak and brass dinner gong, by Gustav Stickley, c1909, 24in (61cm) wide.
£4,500–6,500 *CNY*

l. A longcase clock, by Gustav Stickley, labelled, model No. 3, 72in (182.5cm) high.
£30,000–40,000 *CNY*

Two chairs by the Bookcase & Chair Co., Grand Rapids, under the label 'Lifetime', c1912.
£2,500–2,800 *ST*

A teak garden table and 4 chairs, from a design by Ambrose Heal. **£1,000–1,200** *ST*

An American Arts & Crafts Movement extending oak dining table.
£2,000–3,000 *ST*

An oak dining table, probably by Liberty & Co., c1885.
£1,400–1,700 *ST*

l. An American Arts & Crafts Movement oak display cabinet, c1905.
£1,000–1,200 *ST*

r. An American Arts & Crafts Movement telephone table and window seat, c1900.
£250–350 each *ST*

An oak chair, by Stickley Bros., Grand Rapids, c1910.
£300–350 *ST*

l. An American Arts & Crafts Movement oak chair, by Morris & Co., c1905. **£1,000–1,500** *ST*

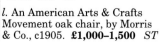

Two American oak stands, and a footstool, c1905.
£150–300 each *ST*

A French Art Nouveau
armoire, c1900, 105in
(266.5cm) high.
£5,000–6,000 *S(NY)*

Art Nouveau Furniture

The French were the foremost exponents of the
Art Nouveau style, and adapted the organic
elements of Arts & Crafts to sculptural Art
Nouveau forms, rather than use the strict
carpentry forms of the English. There were two
distinct schools of French Art Nouveau, one
based in Paris, the other in Nancy. The Nancy
School, epitomised by the work of Emile Gallé
and Louis Majorelle, was more prolific and
consequently seen to be more readily synonymous
with Art Nouveau design. It was this school
that first used marquetry panels, often created
from local woods and depicting flora and fauna.

A mirrored, bronze and
painted wood wardrobe,
and a pair of nightstands,
by Archibald Taylor, c1940.
£4,000–5,000 *S(NY)*

A Scottish mahogany,
hammered copper and
leaded glass
firescreen, c1900.
£2,000–2,500 *S(NY)*

A mahogany and marquetry
inlaid bed, and a pair of nightstands, by Louis Majorelle, c1900.
£16,000–20,000 *S(NY)*

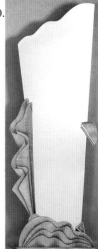

A mirror, by
John Cederquist.
£3,000–3,500
S(NY)

An Austrian
Biedermeier
style painted
wood corner
étagère, c1920.
£3,000–3,500
S(NY)

A Marsh & Jones
inlaid linen press,
attributed to
Charles Bevan,
89½in (227cm) high.
£2,500–3,500 *C*

An Art Nouveau mahogany, fruitwood
marquetry and mother-of-pearl inlaid
cabinet, School of Nancy, c1900.
£11,000–13,000 *S(NY)*

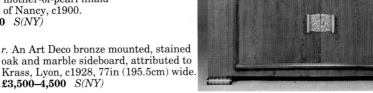

r. An Art Deco bronze mounted, stained
oak and marble sideboard, attributed to
Krass, Lyon, c1928, 77in (195.5cm) wide.
£3,500–4,500 *S(NY)*

A set of 8 Everaut pressed metal stacking chairs, c1930.
£4,000–5,000 *S*

A pair of Apelli and Varesio side chairs, by Carlo Mollino, c1945.
£5,500–6,500 *C*

A 'Cloud' suite of leather furniture, comprising: a three-seater settee and 2 armchairs, c1930.
£2,500–3,500 *S*

Frank Lloyd Wright (American, 1867–1959)

Frank Lloyd Wright was the foremost exponent of the Prairie School, an American Modernist movement in domestic architecture established c1895, and his furniture shows an architectural influence. His pieces were usually made from oak, and often hand-made. Shapes and motifs are commonly cubistic or angular, many reflecting a Mayan, Aztec or Japanese influence.

An aluminium chair, designed by Frank Lloyd Wright for the H. C. Price Company tower.
£9,000–10,000 *CNY*

A 'Kota' chair, by Sue Golden, made from fibreboard and steel.
£800–1,200 *C*

An Art Deco leather upholstered 'Cloud' three-piece suite.
£4,000–5,000 *C*

A Cassina chaise longue.
£1,200–1,500 *S*

An inlaid oak side chair, designed by Harvey Ellis, made by Gustav Stickley, model No. 338, c1904.
£2,200–3,000 *CNY*

An Irish pearwood Art Nouveau three-piece suite, by James Hayes, upholstered in brown leather, labelled 'Millar and Beatty Ltd.', c1902.
£6,000–7,000 *C*

A Carlo Bugatti painted vellum ebonised and inlaid side chair, seat restored, painted signature.
£4,000–5,000 *C*

A pair of Liberty and Co. oak armchairs, leather upholstered, labelled.
£2,500–3,000 *C*

A set of 6 dining chairs, designed by Harvey Ellis, produced by Gustav Stickley, model nos. 353 and 353A, c1910.
£2,500–3,500 *CNY*

An oak wardrobe, by
Peter Waals.
£2,500–3,500 *C*

A Carlo Bugatti
inlaid chair, and
a hanging shelf.
**£4,000–5,000
each** *CNY*

'Metropole', a Memphis
clock, designed by
George J. Sowden,
made in Italy.
£1,500–2,000 *C*

An oak dressing table
mirror, 1906, 23in (58cm)
wide. **£5,000–6,000** *S*

An oak blanket chest, by Gordon
Russell, dated '20.6.27', 65in
(166cm) wide. **£4,500–6,000** *C*

An oak sideboard, by Gustav Stickley, model no. 804, with
firm's branded mark, 54in (137cm) wide. **£8,000–10,000** *CNY*

A Carlo Bugatti
ebonised pedestal,
51in (130cm) high.
£3,000–4,000 *C*

A Liberty & Co. oak
revolving bookcase, c1900.
£6,000–7,000 *S*

A black lacquered dining table,
the top with curved corners, on
a U-shaped base, c1930, 66in
(168cm) wide. **£2,000–3,000** *S*

Carlo Bugatti
(Italian, 1855–1940)

Bugatti's designs looked back
to 13th and 14thC Moorish
Spain and North Africa for
inspiration, and his decorative
approach was highly original.

An oak serving table, by
Gustav Stickley, with the
firm's branded mark, c1912.
£2,500–3,500 *CNY*

A spruce coffee table, designed by
Frank Lloyd Wright, c1950, 74in
(188cm) wide. **£8,500–9,500** *CNY*

A carved mahogany and
marquetry cupboard, by
Louis Majorelle, 46in
(117cm) wide.
£6,000–7,000 *CNY*

l. A Shapland and Petter oak
sideboard, the central reserve
decorated with a copper relief
panel of stylised flowers, 90in
(228cm) wide.
£5,000–6,000 *C*

A carved mahogany and marquetry
sideboard, by Louis Majorelle,
signed. **£8,000–10,000** *CNY*

Louis Majorelle
(French, 1859–1926)

Majorelle was a member of the
Nancy School, and was
influenced by Gallé. His
individual, elegant designs were
either architectural in form, with
inlaid decoration, or sculptural,
with mainly carved decoration.

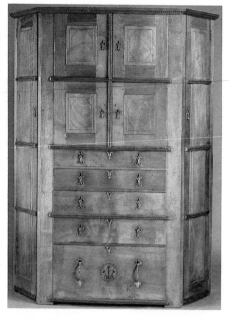

A walnut fishing tackle cabinet, by Ernest Gimson, with barber's pole inlay, the brass mounts by Alfred Bucknell, the bottom drawer inlaid with fruitwoods, dated '1913', 79in (200.5cm) high.
£15,000–20,000 *C*

An inlaid oak piano and bench, designed by Harvey Ellis, executed by Gustav Stickley, with stylised brass and wood inlay, unsigned, c1904, 62½in (159cm) wide.
£10,000–12,000 *CNY*

An oak and leather hexagonal table, Model No. 624, by Gustav Stickley, with original finish, leather and tacks, part of craftsman's paper label, c1910, 48in (122cm) wide.
£12,000–15,000 *CNY*

A walnut bureau cabinet-on-stand, by Ernest Gimson, with fitted interior, the frieze drawer with barber's pole inlay, on a black painted stand, c1906, 39in (99cm) wide.
£15,000–18,000 *C*

A walnut bookcase, by Sidney Barnsley, with 2 glazed doors edged with rosewood, above 2 panelled doors with rosewood handles, 42in (106.5cm) wide.
£10,000–15,000 *C*

Two oak high spindle back chairs, designed by Frank Lloyd Wright, probably executed by Neidecken-Wallbridge Co., for Ray Evans House, Chicago, Illinois, c1908, 45in (114cm) high.
£25,000–30,000 each *CNY*

A set of 7 high backed dining chairs, by L. & J. G. Stickley, Model Nos. 814 and 812, including one carver, with original finish and original leather drop-in seats, c1910, 45½in (115cm) high.
£12,000–15,000 *CNY*

A Carlton Ware dish, designed as pear fruit, flowers and leaves, c1935, 4½in (11.5cm) high.
£30–60 *BRI*

A 15-piece Carlton Ware coffee service, with gilt interiors and highlights, all painted and gilded in bright colours with exotic birds and stylised clouds. **£200–250** *P(Re)*

A Carlton Ware cream jug, decorated with anemones in relief on a yellow ground, c1930, 3in (7.5cm) high.
£40–70 *BRI*

l. A Carlton Ware oviform vase, the dark and pale blue ground with purple, lavender and green zig-zag motif outlined with gilt decoration, printed marks 'Carlton Ware, Made in England, Handcraft 8490', 10½in (27cm) high. **£200–300** *C*

r. A Carlton Ware lustre jug, with gilt loop handle, the body painted and gilded with stylised floral and fan decoration, 5in (13cm) high.
£140–170 *P(Re)*

A large Goldscheider wall mask of a lady holding beads, various makers' marks, Austria, c1930.
£350–550 *ASA*

A Swedish pottery Modernist bust, modelled as a girl with green curly hair, orange lips and an orange necklace, covered in a speckled green glaze, impressed 'b' within a crowned shield, 12in (30.5cm) high.
£600–700 *P*

A toast rack by Shorter, decorated with purple anemones, on a green base, c1930, 6in (15cm) long.
£25–35 *BRI*

A Carlton Ware dish with clematis on a green ground, c1930, 7in (18cm) diam.
£40–60 *BRI*

A Carlton Ware sugar sifter with flower and leaves in relief, c1930, 5in (13cm) high.
£50–70 *BRI*

A Carlton Ware beaker with a design of anemones on a yellow ground, c1930, 4in (10cm) high.
£30–70 *BRI*

A Czechoslovakian coffee service,
decorated in yellow, silver gilt and black.
£80–120 *CIR*

A Burleigh ware coffee set, decorated with
the 'Dawn' pattern.
£120–150 *DEC*

A Carlton Ware tea set for
2 people, with fin handles.
£300–350 *BEV*

A Shelley vase,
6½in (16cm) high.
£30–35 *CIR*

A Crown Derby vase,
decorated in autumn
colours, 6in (15cm) high.
£40–45 *CIR*

A Grays pottery jug, A.2447,
5in (13cm) high.
£40–60 *DEC*

A Shelley jug,
in shades of green,
9½in (24cm) high.
£50–55 *CIR*

A Falcon Ware jug,
7in (18cm) high.
£60–65 *CIR*

A Crown Devon dark red jug,
with gilt trim, 5in (13cm) high.
£45–50 *CIR*

A Gray's pottery flower trough,
9in (23cm) wide.
£60–100 *BEV*

A Crown Devon Lotus type
jug, c1930, 13in (33cm) high.
£200–225 *CIR*

l. A Shelley milk jug,
3½in (9cm) high.
£20–30 *CIR*

A Shelley tea set for two, Oxford shape, with green leaf motif, No. 12387, c1935.
£125–175 *AOS*

A Shelley banded jam pot, 4½in (11cm) high.
£20–30 *AOS*

A Poole Pottery teapot stand, c1930.
£20–30 *AOS*

A Radford ware jug and vase, c1930.
£30–45 *AOS*

A Wedgwood 44 piece dinner service, 'Travel', designed by Eric Ravilious, grey ground transfer printed in black and heightened in blue enamel, printed marks 'Travel, designed by Ravilious, Wedgwood of Etruria & Barlaston, Made in England', c1953, dinner plate 10in (25cm) diam.
£2,500–3,000 *C*

A Shelley nursery plate, with Mabel Lucie Attwell design, printed in colours with a little girl standing with her doll beneath an umbrella, watching a parade of pixies, with inscription 'Fairy folk with tiny wings flying all over my plates and things', printed factory marks, 8in (20cm) diam.
£80–120 *CSK*

A Staffordshire model of a cat, after a design by Louis Wain, in green, yellow, red, blue and black, slight rubbing, impressed and overpainted facsimile signature on the back, stamped 'Made in England' and impressed registration mark, 1920s, 5in (13cm) high.
£400–500 *S(S)*

A Czechoslovakian vase, 8in (20cm) high.
£45–75 *AOS*

A W. H. Grindley coffee service, comprising 15 pieces.
£75–125 *AOS*

A Carlton Ware teapot, milk jug and sugar bowl, in 'Water Lily' pattern, c1930.
£100–150 *AOS*

A Carlton Ware blue coffee service, decorated in jewelled enamels and gilt with exotic birds and with wisteria, with gilt interiors, comprising: coffee pot and cover, two-handled sucrier and cover, cream jug and 6 coffee cups and saucers, printed mark in black.
£200–300 *ASA*

Three Gray's Paris jugs, with geometric design by Susie Cooper.
£250–300 each *CAR*

A Hancock part coffee service.
£125–175 *AOS*

l. A Gray's pottery plate and bowl, by Susie Cooper, bowl 5in (13cm) wide, **£250–300**, plate **£150–180** *CAR*

A Carlton Ware tête-a-tête, each piece with a speckled pale blue ground heightened with gilding, applied with solid gilt ribbed handles, comprising: teapot and cover, 2 cups and saucers, jug, sugar bowl, jam pot and cover, plate, and biscuit barrel and cover, printed marks, 1930s.
£450–550 *S(S)*

A pair of Compton Pottery stoneware bookends, each trefoil form with relief decoration of a butterfly, on a semi-circular base, covered in a matt green glaze with black, ochre and yellow painted decoration, impressed seal 'Compton Pottery, Guildford', c1945, 5in (12cm) high.
£150–300 *C*

A Susie Cooper cased part coffee set, each piece painted with wash and solid bands in mixed grey, brown and blue, comprising: 6 coffee cans, saucers and electroplated shell moulded spoons with blue bead ends, in a fitted case, printed factory marks 'A Susie Cooper Production, Crown Works, Burslem, England', coffee cans 2in (5.5in) high.
£100–150 *S(S)*

A Maling ware fruit bowl, 8½in (21.5cm) diam.
£95–145 *AOS*

A Maling ware oval dish in the 'Stork' design, decorated by Janet Taylor, c1932, 10in (25cm) wide. **£120–140** *IS*

A Hancock bowl, decorated with 'Pomegranate' pattern, 9in (23cm) diam. **£85–125** *AOS*

A pair of Hancock vases, in 'Cremorne' pattern, 11in (28cm) high. **£175–275** *AOS*

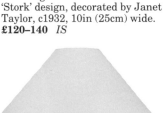

A Gray's pottery lamp base, painted with golfers, c1930, 6in (16cm) high. **£750–800** *CAR*

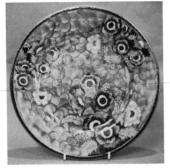

A Maling ware wall plaque, decorated in the 'Anemone' pattern, c1936, 11in (28cm) diam. **£180–220** *IS*

A Gray's pottery teapot, with Cubist face design, decorated with orange and yellow enamel, 4½in (12cm) high. **£200–250** *CAR*

A Maling ware ginger jar, c1950, 8in (20cm) high. **£45–85** *AOS*

A Hancock bowl, decorated with 'Water Lily' pattern, 9in (23cm) diam. **£85–125** *AOS*

A Poole Pottery jug, with geometric design, 6in (15cm) high. **£55–85** *AOS*

A Maling ware wall pocket in the 'Michaelmas Daisy' pattern, c1938, 9in (23cm) high. **£180–200** *IS*

A Maling ware oval bread basket decorated in the 'Gladioli' pattern, c1936, 11in (28cm) wide. **£150–180** *IS*

A Poole Pottery bowl, 1960s. **£8–12** *AOS*

A Radford ware vase, with 'Tree' design, c1930, 10in (25cm) high. **£65–95** *AOS*

A Gouda vase, 'Rembrandt' design, c1927, 6½in (16cm) high. **£100–110** *OO*

A Poole Pottery tin glazed doorstop, designed by Harold Stabler, modelled as a galleon in full sail, blue, green, yellow and white, 21in (53cm) high. **£500–800** *CSK*

A Dutch Arnhem Factory vase, 'Isolda design', green background, c1920, 14in (36cm) high. **£180–200** *OO*

A Charlotte Rhead dressing table set, decorated in the Trellis pattern, in shades of orange, yellow, green and coffee lustre on a cream ground, comprising: a tray, powder bowl and cover, 2 squat candlesticks, and 4 other items, printed factory marks. **£250–300** *CSK*

A Shelley Art Deco coffee service, decorated in orange and black, comprising: a coffee pot, sugar bowl, cream jug, 6 cups and saucers, pattern no. 11792, coffee pot 7½in (19cm) high. **£350–400** *AG*

A Shelley China Mode shaped part tea service, lightly printed in black and overpainted in bright blue, green, black and orange, comprising: 4 tea cups and saucers, 6 tea plates, sugar basin and milk jug, printed mark in green, registered No. 756533, pattern No. 11755, inscribed in burnt orange. **£250–300** *HSS*

A Gouda vase, 'Bochara' design, c1920, 9in (22cm) high. **£150–170** *OO*

A Gouda vase, 'Kalman' design, c1929, 8in (20cm) high. **£80–90** *OO*

Locate the Source

The source of each illustration in *Miller's Art Nouveau and Art Deco Buyer's Guide* can be found by checking the code letters below each caption with the Key to Illustrations.

A Poole Pottery fruit bowl, with fruit design, in brown and coral, impressed mark, c1926, 13in (33cm) diam.
£45–55 *OCA*

A Gouda jardinière, 'Marga' design, c1921, 6½in (16.5cm) high.
£160–180 *OO*

A French porcelain golfing flask and stopper, signed 'E. Marquis', and 'P. Bastard, Editeur, Paris, France', on base, 11in (27.5cm) high.
£200–250 *P*

A Poole Pottery historic plaque, entitled 'Poole Whaler, 1783', inscribed on reverse 'This dish was made and painted at the Poole Pottery in the year 1932, ship drawn by Arthur Bradbury, painted by Margaret Holder', 14½in (37cm) diam.
£300–350 *MSL*

A Poole Pottery 'Festival of Britain 1951' presentation bowl, with broad everted rim painted with rose, shamrock, thistle and daffodil symbolising unity in the British Isles during Festival year, the centre with Poole's coat-of-arms in red, green, mauve, blue and yellow, 17in (43.5cm) diam.
£450–550 *P*

Probably designed by Claude Smale, this piece would have been part of the small output of presentation pieces granted to the pottery under licence during Festival year, and is possibly unique in representing the town of Poole itself.

A Carlton Ware Rouge Royale ginger jar and cover, with domed cover, mottled maroon glaze with gilt and polychrome enamel decoration of pagodas and scenes of Oriental life, printed factory marks, 10½in (26.5cm) high.
£350–550 *C*

A Carlton Ware ginger jar and cover, decorated with coloured enamels in a chinoiserie pattern featuring a repeating scene of an Oriental couple in traditional costume amid pagodas, birds and trees, in orange, blue, green, mauve and yellow against a brown ground heightened with gilt, marked 'W.& R Carlton Ware' on base, 12in (31cm) high.
£350–450 *P*

A French Art Deco crackle glazed ceramic group, modelled as a lady wearing a full ball gown of cream and gold, with Harlequin standing behind her in black, silver and cream, marked 'C.H. France,' and 'G. Deblaze', 14in (36cm) high.
£200–300 *P*

A Poole Pottery historic plaque, entitled 'Waterwitch, built by Meadus, Poole 1871, 207 tons, Master Captain C.H. Deacon, drawn by Arthur Bradbury, 1932', painted by Ruth Paveley, 14½in (37cm) diam.
£200–250 *MSL*

l. A Robj Art Deco porcelain figural lamp, modelled as a woman with gold bobbed hair, standing swathed in a long white robe and holding a large bunch of flowers, with a depression for aromatic oils, with flowers at her feet, painted with gilt highlights, printed 'Robj, Paris, Made in France', 13in (33cm) high. **£400–500** *P*

A Carlton Ware pottery Glamour tea set for two. **£150–200** *W*

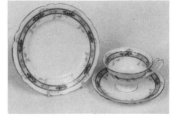

A Shelley Gainsborough Trio, decorated in 'Classical' design, c1918. **£25–45** *AJ*

A Shelley Regent Trio, decorated in 'Yellow Phlox' design, c1933. **£25–35** *AJ*

A Poole Pottery cream vase, c1925. **£30–45** *OCA*

A Poole Pottery blue and white geometric vase, 10in (25cm) high. **£500–550** *CHa*

r. A Shelley Vincent Trio, decorated with Dorothy Perkins (yellow rose) pattern, no. 1168/2, c1920. **£25–45** *A*

l. A Shelley lustre vase, by Walter Slater, painted in colours and gilt on a petrol blue ground with a Japanese beauty carrying a lantern, walking beside a river bank flanked by willows, a bridge in the distance, beneath a moonlit sky, printed factory marks and facsimile signature, 15½in (39.5cm) high. **£400–500** *CSK*

A Royal Dux figural vase, the twin-handled vessel formed as a tree trunk with green leaf and mistletoe embellishment, supporting to one side the standing figure of an Art Nouveau maiden in long flowing green dress, pink triangular mark to base, 26in (65.5cm) high. **£700–800** *P*

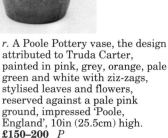

r. A Poole Pottery vase, the design attributed to Truda Carter, painted in pink, grey, orange, pale green and white with ziz-zags, stylised leaves and flowers, reserved against a pale pink ground, impressed 'Poole, England', 10in (25.5cm) high. **£150–200** *P*

A Radford ware dish,
11in (28cm) diam.
£25–45 *AOS*

A Radford ware jug, decorated with
carrots, c1930, 6⅜in (16cm) high.
£35–45 *AOS*

A Charlotte Rhead jug,
6in (15cm) high.
£45–65 *AOS*

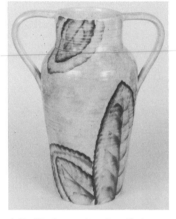

A Radford ware two-handled
vase, 10in (25cm) high.
£50–75 *AOS*

A Charlotte Rhead Crown Ducal
vase, No. 5623, 7in (18cm) high.
£95–135 *ADC*

A pair of Charlotte Rhead vases,
7in (18cm) high.
£400–500 *HEW*

A Rosenthal porcelain figure, naturalistically modelled and coloured as a female nude reclining on a rock, green printed and painted marks, c1934, 16in (41cm) wide.
£900–1,200 *S(S)*

A Saint Clement Ged Condé polar bear, c1920, 11in (28cm) wide.
£240–265 *POW*

A Saint Clément Ged Condé fish, with white crackle glaze, c1920, 10½in (26cm) wide.
£170–185 *POW*

A Royal Dux porcelain group, in dark blue with gilt detailing, raised on a scallop edged circular base, applied pink triangular mark, stamped 'Made in Czechoslovakia, 2993 4', c1930, 12in (31cm) high.
£450–550 *S(S)*

A Rosenthal porcelain figure of Pierrot, 12in (31cm) wide.
£800–1,200 *ASA*

r. A Boch Frères Keramis Ch. Catteau figure of 'The Skaters', 13in (33cm) high.
£250–285 *POW*

A French white porcelain figure, signed, 13in (33cm) high. **£350–450** *ASA*

A Lenci earthenware group, modelled as a naked adolescent girl seated at the foot of a kneeling woman wearing a flowing blue robe and cream scarf spangled with gilt stars, minor glaze chips, painted factory mark, 1938, 16in (41cm) high.
£400–450 *CSK*

A Goebels Pottery set of ashtrays and a jockey cigarette box, decorated in orange and black, box 6in (15cm) high.
£20–40 each *ASA*

r. A Goldscheider Butterfly model of a figure, after a design by Lorenzl, incised marks 'Goldscheider, Wien, Lorenzl, 5917 515, 4', facsimile signature on the base, 1930s, 10in (25cm) high.
£800–1,000 *S(S)*

A Gouda jug, 'Peter' design, c1923, 11in (28cm) high.
£120–130 *OO*

A Gouda vase, 'Westland' design, c1927, 12in (30.5cm) high.
£160–180 *OO*

A Gouda vase, 'Ali' design, c1924, 6 ½in (16cm) high.
£100–120 *OO*

r. A Carter Stabler Adams Poole Pottery dish, a variation on Truda Carter's spotted deer, the centre painted in colours with a spotted deer amid flowering branches, impressed pottery marks, 15in (37.5cm) diam.
£320–400 *P*

A Gouda wall vase, 'Paula' design, c1920, 6in (15cm) high. **£100–110** *OO*

An Art Deco pottery flat backed bust of a sailor, advertising Senior Service cigarettes, 14in (35cm) high.
£65–85 *GAK*

A Gouda jug, 'Costia' design, c1926, 7½in (18cm) high.
£40–50 *OO*

l. A Gouda bowl, Collier design, c1922, 8in (20cm) diam.
£140–150 *OO*

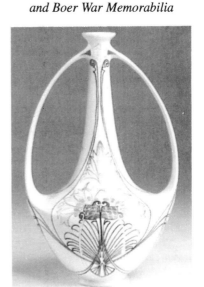

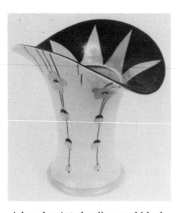

A hand painted yellow and black vase, by Myott & Son, 8½in (21cm) high. **£55–85** *LB*

A Beswick wall mask, with brown hair, wearing a green and yellow necklace, with blue and yellow petalled flowers behind, impressed 'Beswick, Made in England, 436', late 1930s, 12in (31cm) high. **£200–300** *S(C)*

A Pilkington's Royal Lancastrian lapis-ware wall plate, decorated by W. S. Mycock, grey on an orange ground, with impressed Pilkington mark and artist's monogram, 12½in (32cm) diam. **£100–150** *C*

A Charlotte Rhead Burslem jug, c1920, 9in (23cm) high. **£65–70** *SCO*

A Pilkington's Royal Lancastrian vase, by Mycock, 8½in (21cm) high. **£600–800** *ASA*

A Shelley Regent shape coffee service, transfer printed with a Lakeland scene, comprising coffee pot and cover, milk jug, sugar basin, 6 cups and 6 saucers, c1935, printed factory mark 'Shelley, England', registration number '781613', painted number '12336'. **£250–350** *S(C)*

A Pilkington's Royal Lancastrian vase, by Mycock, 8½in (21cm) high. **£400–600** *ASA*

A Shelley porcelain tea service, each piece decorated with irises and stylised flowers on a pink and white ground, comprising: a teapot and cover, hot water jug, sugar basin, milk jug, 2 bread and butter plates, 12 tea plates, teacups and saucers, slight damage to sugar basin. **£400–600** *Bea*

l. A Pilkington's Royal Lancastrian vase, by Cundall, 9in (23cm). **£500–700** *ASA*

r. A Shelley 20 piece tea service, with abstract black pattern, slight damage, no. 756533. **£350–450** *IM*

A Goldscheider model of a dancing girl, by Lorenzl, with a mauve, blue and black skirt, the cylindrical column on a circular base, signed 'Lorenzl', painted factory marks and impressed '5581828', 9½in (24cm) high.
£650–850 *P*

A Goldscheider figure of an Eastern dancer, by Kostial, with mauve pantaloons and flared skirt, artist's signature, factory marks, impressed '5549 48 8' to base, 17½in (44.5cm) high.
£1,200–1,500 *P*

A Goldscheider figure of a dancing girl, after Lorenzl, with a peacock design dress in mottled blue and green glazes, on a domed circular base, transfer printed and impressed marks, 15in (38cm) high.
£650–800 *W*

l. A Carlton Ware 'Egyptianesque' ginger jar and cover, decorated in colours and gilding, against a powder blue ground, factory marks on base, 15½in (39cm) high.
£2,000–2,200 *P*

r. A pottery bowl, by Susie Cooper, by Crown Works, Burslem, 9½in (24cm) diam.
£80–120 *HM*

An Art Deco pottery ornament, depicting a leapint ibis, by Vago-Weiss, 18in (46cm) wide.
£80–100 *GAK*

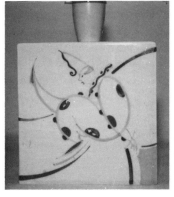

l. A Susie Cooper Art Deco table lamp base, 5in (12.5cm) high.
£850–900 *LT*

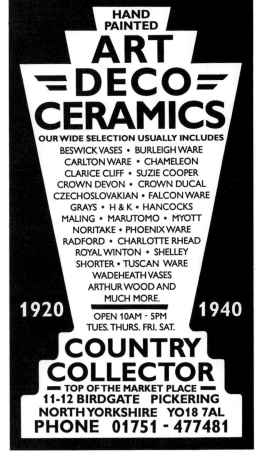

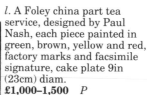

l. A Foley china part tea service, designed by Paul Nash, each piece painted in green, brown, yellow and red, factory marks and facsimile signature, cake plate 9in (23cm) diam. **£1,000–1,500** *P*

A Foley Intarsio character teapot, designed by Frederick Rhead, No. 3359, late Foley mark, Rd. No. '363131', 4½in (11.5cm) high. **£650–750** *P*

A Foley Intarsio vase, designed by Frederick Rhead, in brown, with 4 yellow 'scaled' panels with mauve irises below against a green ground, factory marks and numbered '3003', 8½in (21.5cm) high. **£300–400** *P*

A Foley Art China coffee set, designed by George Logan, comprising: 6 cups and saucers, 6 side plates and a sandwich platter, in green and lilac on white ground, printed mark 'Foley Art China Peacock Pottery'. **£500–700** *C*

A Foley china 'Dainty White' shape part teaset, comprising: 12 cups and saucers, 12 plates, 2 cake plates, milk jug and slop bowl, each piece decorated in pink, red, green, blue and butterscotch with a white ground, printed factory marks, Rd. No. 272101, 1896. **£200–250** *P*

A Foley Intarsio vase, decorated in blue, white, pink, green and brown, printed factory marks, No. 3469, 9in (23cm) high. **£250–350** *P*

A Shelley 23 piece tea service, 1930s. **£150–200** *Re*

l. A Shelley Mode shape 'Sunray' pattern coffee set, each piece decorated in beige, yellow and black against a white ground, printed factory marks, Rd. No. 76533. **£500–700** *P*

r. A Foley Intarsio tapering cylindrical vase, printed marks, 8½in (21.5cm) high. **£300–500** *CSK*

A Shelley Mode shape 'Butterfly Wing' pattern part teaset, comprising: 6 cups and saucers, 6 plates, a cake plate, milk jug and sugar bowl, each piece decorated in green, black and grey against a white ground, printed factory marks, Rd. No. 756533. **£700–900** *P*

A Carlton Ware coffee service, glazed in pale primrose, comprising: coffee pot, cream jug, covered sugar bowl and 6 cups and saucers, printed marks. **£250–350** *Bon*

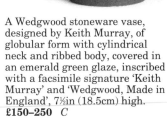

A Shelley 22 piece tea service with teapot, 'English Cottage' design, low Queen Anne shape.
£150–180 *AJ*

A Shelley 22-piece tea service, with green and silver pattern, c1933.
£200–300 *AJ*

A Wedgwood stoneware vase, designed by Keith Murray, of globular form with cylindrical neck and ribbed body, covered in an emerald green glaze, inscribed with a facsimile signature 'Keith Murray' and 'Wedgwood, Made in England', 7½in (18.5cm) high.
£150–250 *C*

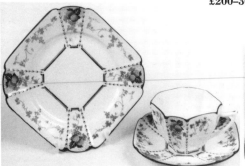

l. A pair of Wedgwood bookends, designed by Keith Murray, each of right angle form, covered in a green glaze, and with fluted decoration, stamped 'Wedgwood', 5½in (14.5cm) high.
£100–150 *C*

A Shelley 21-piece tea service, including teapot, low Queen Anne shape, with peaches and grapes design, c1920.
£150–180 *AJ*

l. A Shelley tea service, decorated with 'Apple Blossom' pattern, comprising: 12 teacups, 12 saucers, 12 square tea plates, a pair of bread plates, teapot, hot water jug, cream jug, sugar bowl and a circular teapot stand, pattern no. 12287, Reg. No. 756533.
£400–600 *AG*

A Shelley 21-piece tea service, 'Sunburst' pattern, c1931.
£600–800 *RO*

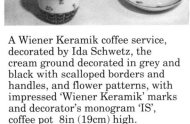

A Wiener Keramik coffee service, decorated by Ida Schwetz, the cream ground decorated in grey and black with scalloped borders and handles, and flower patterns, with impressed 'Wiener Keramik' marks and decorator's monogram 'IS', coffee pot 8in (19cm) high.
£450–650 *C*

r. A Linthorpe vase, designed by Christopher Dresser, decorated with 4 grotesque heads, each forming a handle, covered in a streaky green glaze, running and pooling, impressed facsimile signature 'Chr Dresser 254', 9in (23cm) high.
£1,000–1,500 *C*

A Linthorpe jug, by Christopher Dresser, shape no. 346, 10in (25cm) high.
£600–700 *BLO*

A Shelley whte porcelain coffee set, painted in orange, black and silver, comprising: coffee pot, 6 cups with solid triangular handles, 6 saucers, cream jug and sugar bowl, printed marks.
£500–600 *CSK*

A Goldscheider ceramic wall head, c1930.
£800–1,000 *ASA*

A Carlton Ware figure, 'Mrs Bun', designed by John Hassell.
£300–350 *BEV*

A Brannam egg separator, c1910.
£100–150 *BLO*

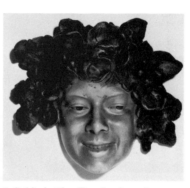

A Goldscheider 'Bacchus' mask, signed 'Lorenzac'.
£200–250 *CS*

A Rosenthal figure, by Boehs, c1920, 9in (23cm) high.
£400–500 *BEV*

A Rosenthal figure of a child with a bird, by Liebermann, c1920, 9in (23cm) high. **£400–450** *BEV*

l. A Goldscheider earthenware figure of a woman, wearing a pink and grey skirt, the rose bodice with pink halter neck, restored, printed factory mark, 'Made in Austria', signautre and impressed number '6126 42 6', 15in (39cm) high.
£300–350 *HSS*

Three figures, 'Egg Men', by John Hassell, modelled as a boy scout, a country yokel and a policeman, all with painted marks 'J. Hassell', 6in (15cm) high.
£300–400 each *CSK*

r. An Imperial amphora bowl, designed by Louis Wain, modelled as a stylised seated cat of cubist inspiration, in orange, purple, black and blue on an acid green ground, printed mark 'Imperial Amphora', and painted facsimile mark 'Louis Wain', 6in (15cm) high.
£1,500–2,000 *C*

A Lenci centrepiece, modelled as a young naked girl, inscribed 'Lenci Made in Italy Torino', 18in (46cm) high. **£1,500–2,000** *C*

A Goldscheider figure, from a model by Lorenzl, printed marks, column inscribed 'Lorenzl', 13in (33cm) high. **£500–800** *CSK*

A Goldscheider pottery figure of a dancing girl designed by Lorenzl, base impressed 'Lorenzl', printed marks, 16in (40.5cm) high. **£750–850** *CSK*

A Lenci figure, modelled as a naked girl, 'Lenci, Made in Italy' and printed paper label, 12in (30.5cm) wide. **£1,500–2,000** *C*

A Berlin white porcelain figure of a nymph with a deer, designed by Gerhard Schliepstein, inscribed 'G. Schliepstein', underglaze blue sceptre mark and impressed 'MZ 12050', 8in (20.5cm) high. **£300–500** *C*

A porcelain Katshutte figure, marked, 20½in (52cm) high. **£450–600** *ASA*

An Italian china 'Gallé' figure of a kneeling semi-clad female figure, 1950s, 18in (45.5cm) high. **£600–700** *Re*

A Royal Dux figure of Gandhi, c1930, 12in (30.5cm) high. **£220–280** *CS*

l. A Wiener Keramik polychrome figure by Gudrun Baudisch, some damage, impressed 'WW' monogram and artist's monogram 'GB', 7½in (19.5cm) high. **£900–1,000** *C*

A Royal Dux pottery group, raised triangular mark, 13⅜in (35cm) high. **£300–350** *CSK*

A Torquay pottery jug, 5in (13cm).
£30–35 *CIR*

A green teapot in the form of a
car, c1930. **£30–50** *CIR*

A Grays Pottery dish, 14in
(35cm) wide. **£80–100** *DEC*

A Lingardware teapot in yellow, 7½in
(19cm) high. **£30–50** *HOW*

An orange cube teapot by G. Clews
Ltd., c1930, 4in (10cm) high.
£20–25 *CIR*

A Simple Simon teapot.
£65–75 *BEV*

A Carlton Ware grey teapot, c1950, 9½in
(24cm) wide. **£30–35** *CIR*

A Burleigh ware biscuit barrel
with the Susie Cooper pattern,
plated lid and handle, 7½in
(19cm) high. **£60–100** *DEC*

A Myott biscuit barrel, 7½in
(19cm) high. **£40–60** *DEC*

A Shelley tea cup, saucer and plate.
£30–40 *CIR*

A Burleigh ware plaque in the form
of a galleon, with matt green glaze,
13in (33cm) diam.
£30–60 *CDC*

A Gray's Pottery jam pot, with
Pharaoh's mark, 4½in (12cm) high.
£30–25 *DEC*

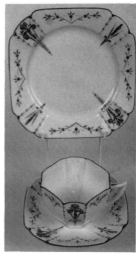

A Shelley tea cup, saucer
and plate, in the 'Blue Iris'
design. **£20–30** *CIR*

r. A Ruskin high-fired transmutation glaze vase and matching circular stepped stand, with cloudy deep purple glaze with green mottling and speckling over a mottled pale grey ground, vase and stand impressed 'Ruskin England', c1930, 14½in (36cm), including stand.
£800–1,200 *C*

l. A KPM white porcelain mask, by Hubatsch, blue printed 'KPM' device and moulded signature 'Hubatsch 1930', 9½in (25cm) high.
£400–600 *C*

A Sèvres porcelain lantern, with bronze tassel, designed by Henri Rapin, glazed in dark celadon and amber on a cream ground and embellished with gilding, circular red printed 'Manufacture Nationale Décoré a Sevre 1923', and black rectangular 'S 1923DN' marks, 20in (51.5cm) high.
£500–800 *C*

A Berlin KPM porcelain box and cover, in colours and gilding, with oval intaglio panels of birds and flowers, sceptre mark and 'KPM' and orb inside cover, 'SR' on base, 8⅛in (22.5cm) high.
£250–350 *P*

A Rosenthal ginger jar designed by Kurt Wendler, with abstract design in blues, red and green heightened with gilding on a white ground, printed 'Rosenthal Selb Bavaria' mark and artist's signature, 'Kurt Wendler', c1925, 8½in (21cm) high.
£320–400 *C(Am)*

An Amphora vase, polychrome on a white porcelain ground, enriched with gilding, impressed 'Amphora' and printed 'Turn Teplitz R. St.K.' with maker's device and 'D.464', c1930, 7½in (18.5cm) high.
£1,000–1,200 *C*

r. A Brannam green glazed model of a dragon, with yellow and blue markings, incised marks, 8in (20cm) high.
£100–200 *CSK*

A Limoges porcelain box and cover designed by Sandoz, with white and yellow plumage and blue beak, 6⅓in (16cm) high, and another similar, 2in (5cm) high, both with printed marks, signed 'Sandoz'.
£200–300 *CSK*

A Fornasetti porcelain circular rack plate, printed in black against white, 'eye' mark, 'Tema E. Variazioni, Fornasetti-Milano, Made in Italy', numbered '94', 10½in (26.5cm) high.
£100–200 *P*

A Fraureuth porcelain box and cover, blue and white with black and gilt stylised foliate hand-painted decoration, printed mark 'Fraureuth Kunstabteilung', c1920, 8½in (21cm) high.
£100–150 *C*

A Limoges Art Deco coffee set, marked with a cockerel and 'T.L.B.' for Touze, Lemaitre Frères and Blancher, pot 9in (22.5cm) high. **£200–300** *P*

A Carlton Ware vase, with stylised flowerheads in polychrome enamels, c1930, 9in (23cm) high. **£300–350** *CAR*

A porcelain lamp, modelled as a girl standing beside a porcelain and brass lamp post supporting a fabric 'umbrella' shade, printed factory marks, 'Fraureuth Künstableitung', 20in (51cm) high. **£150–200** *P*

A Royal Dux figure by Schaff, the girl wearing blue and gilt trousers, signed 'Schaff', pink triangle mark, printed 'Made in Czechoslovakia, 3101', 17½in (44.5cm) wide. **£300–400** *P*

A Royal Dux figure, hollowed for use as a vase, covered with foliage, pink triangle mark, '440', 15in (38.5cm) high. **£250–350** *P*

A Boulogne pottery figure, 'La Soie', designed by Marcel Renard, the crackled glazed body partially clad in a gilt and mauve mottled robe, impressed factory marks, signed in gilt 'Marcel Renard', 19in (48.5cm) high. **£500–800** *P*

A Goldscheider earthenware mask, printed factory mark, no. '7888', c1920, 12in (30.5cm) high. **£300–400** *SB*

l. An earthenware teapot, in the form of an aeroplane, yellow crackled glazed with silver details, impressed 'T. Plane Made in England', 1930s, 9½in (24cm) long. **£150–200** *S*

A Goldscheider 'Bat Girl', the blue wings veined with yellow, inscribed 'Lorenzl', impressed 5230/422/16, printed factory mark, 18½in (47cm) high. **£1,000–1,500** *CSK*

A pottery wall mask, moulded as a girl's head with a pink sun-bonnet, marked 'Royal Doulton', c1930, 8in (20cm) high. **£200–300** *EEW*

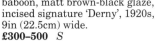

A Derny earthenware figure of a baboon, matt brown-black glaze, incised signature 'Derny', 1920s, 9in (22.5cm) wide. **£300–500** *S*

l. A Goldscheider porcelain head of a young woman, in 1940s style, stamped, circular mark, impressed '507', 11½in 29.5cm) high. **£300–400** *C*

FURNITURE

One of the biggest influences on people buying furniture is the architectural style of their homes. They may be attracted to a certain maker, or to the workmanship and quality, but very few buy furniture in the way that others collect Royal Doulton or wine glasses. The basic criteria may be the same (authenticity and condition) but with one additional factor: does it fit?

The slowness of the housing market over the last few years has had an effect on the sale of furniture recently, as people are not so readily changing either their home or their furniture! This may well not be the case in the very top echelons where items will always change hands for many thousands of pounds, but it does apply to that middle range of selective buying. Prices have not changed as dramatically in the last few years as they did from 1979 to 1989 when the job and housing markets seemed more secure, and the notion of collecting antiques was taken up by a wider audience.

In the middle of the last century, John Ruskin and William Morris bemoaned the lack of style and taste of applied arts in this country, and so began the 'alternative' to mainstream Victorian art and artefacts. The Gothic revival was inspired by what was considered the last great age of British architecture namely medieval; the Aesthetic Movement was influenced by Oriental design with the opening up of Japan in the 1860s; and the Arts & Crafts movement grew out of Morris's teachings of simplicity and integrity: 'fitness for purpose'. These 'movements' did not remain static, they took from each other, grew and were adapted. Out of them came Art Nouveau, the designs of Mackintosh and the Vienna Secession, which in turn became Art Deco and Modernism. The latter could not have evolved from mainstream Victorian Art.

What seems striking now, in retrospect, is that here began the age of the 'designer'. Most of the prominent creative figures in these movements were architects or artists, but now they were interested in interior aesthetics as well as buildings or pictures. The work of these leading designers is also the most sought after today: names such as Burgess, Godwin, Talbert, Morris, Voysey, Gallé, Mackintosh, Hoffmann, Moser, Ruhlmann, Lloyd Wright, Breuer, Aalto and many others – all these will make a great deal of difference to the price you may have to pay for a piece of furniture.

Apart from the name of the designer or maker and the condition of a piece, the factors that will make the most difference to the price will be the quality and style. Style is particularly important when considering the age in which it was made. Not all furniture made in the 1920s or 1930s is 'Art Deco' or 'Modern'; some will be reproductions of earlier styles, other pieces may reflect the period but will be tame and bland in design. Art Deco, for example, is collected because it is different to any other style, as is Art Nouveau, and the closer an item is to the epitome of the style at its best, the more collectable the piece becomes.

However desirable a piece of furniture, before making your final commitment to buy because of its aesthetic appeal, make certain of the item's condition and authenticity. The auction house or dealer should be happy to give condition reports, answer any questions, and give the assurances you need. But it is always good to look oneself.

When assessing the item's condition ask yourself, 'what is it made of, how is it constructed and what could go wrong?' If it is wood it could split, be scratched or stained, or have woodworm, and the joints could be loose. If they are, is it just a question of the restorer re-glueing them or are they actually broken? Does it have sturdy legs? If a piece is veneered, is the veneer intact? A little piece missing on an edge may not be a big problem, but damage to larger areas can be more serious and may prove costly because of the difficulty in matching the veneer.

If it is a glazed cabinet, are all the panes present and intact? What type of glass is it, would it be difficult to match? For furniture made from laminated woods look carefully at the structure. Is it still strong and flexible? Look out for splits and 'tiredness'. If an item has metal in it, be it wrought iron or steel, with or without nickel or chromium plating, again think about the material and what could go wrong with it. Is it split, badly dented, rusted or the plate flaking? Generally, when considering restoration, bear in mind how extensive it needs to be to restore the item to its former glory, and how this will affect its authenticity and perhaps its selling price later on.

One of the advantages of buying items of antique or 'old' furniture is that they generally maintain their value better than brand new 'department store' pieces. Usually one can trade them in more easily for different or more valuable items – this is not only an enjoyable way of working to enhance your home but, in this world of diminishing resources and materials, a very 'green' approach.

Fiona Baker

An ebonised side cabinet, in Arts & Crafts style, inset with blue and cream glazed pottery tiles, 37in (93cm) wide.
£600–700 *HSS*

A glazed cabinet, c1910, 63in (160cm) wide. **£1,100–1,300** *SV*

An Edwardian mahogany display cabinet, inlaid with a stylised peacock in various woods, 48in (120cm) wide.
£800–1,200 *TW*

An Aesthetic Movement mahogany corner desk, 30in (75cm) wide. **£300-400** *P*

An Aesthetic Movement simulated satinwood bedroom suite, by Gillows & Co., with wardrobe, dressing table, washstand and bedside cabinet, stamped on door stiles 'Gillow & Co.'.. **£600–800** *MSh*

A late Victorian Arts & Crafts ebonised and pollard oak sideboard, 90in (229cm) wide.
£500–800 *CDC*

A late Victorian Arts & Crafts oak kneehole pedestal desk, 57½in (144cm) wide.
£1,300–1,500 *CSK*

An Arts & Crafts oak desk, attributed to the workshops of L. & J. G. Stickley, 38½in (96cm) wide.
£500–800 *P*

An Aesthetic Movement ebonised occasional table, after a design by E. W. Godwin, 26½in (66.5cm) wide.
£180–220 *P*

A Gallé two-tiered marquetry tea table, the satinwood top inlaid with fruitwoods, bronze handles, 31in (79cm) wide.
£1,500–2,000 *P*

A mahogany armchair, 48in (122cm) high.
£350–400 *OB*

An oak and copper hall seat and chest, embellished in copper with plant form panels and studded edging, 30½in (76cm) wide.
£300–400 *P*

A set of 6 Arts & Crafts teak chairs, c1900.
£1,000–1,200 *ST*

An oak bookcase, with copper handles, by the Sickley brothers, Grand Rapids, Michigan, c1910.
£900–1,000 *ST*

A wrought iron and glass side table, 22½in (63cm) high.
£1,600–2,000 *C*

A beech armchair, by Liberty & Co., with label.
£450–500 *P*

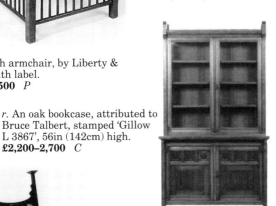

An Arts & Crafts oak hall stand, with copper fittings, c1905, 78in (198cm) high.
£1,000–1,500 *ST*

r. An oak bookcase, attributed to Bruce Talbert, stamped 'Gillow L 3867', 56in (142cm) high.
£2,200–2,700 *C*

A set of 6 teak dining chairs, in the style of A. W. Simpson.
£1,000–1,500 *ST*

A mahogany, ebonised and marquetry jardinière, in the style of Charles Bevan, with 9 marquetry panels inlaid with various fruitwoods, with zinc liner and later burr walnut chamfered cover, 29in (73.5cm) wide.
£2,800–3,200 *C*

A mahogany open armchair, inlaid with marquetry and white metal. **£500–650** *LRG*

An Arts & Crafts coal scuttle. **£150–200** *ST*

l. A mirror, attributed to Bugatti, decorated with beaten copperwork and copper and pewter inlay, c1900, 26in (66cm) high.
£2,000–3,000 *C*

l. An Arts & Crafts desk, by Shapland & Petter of Barnstaple, c1905. **£900–1,000** *ST*

A limed oak dining room suite, by Heal's, comprising: dining table, sideboard, 6 chairs, including one armchair, and a serving trolley, with inset manufacturer's label, c1935. **£2,500–3,000** *C*

An Arts & Crafts armchair, c1900. **£800–900** *ST*

A Gallé walnut and marquetry side table, the top inlaid with fruitwood, inlaid signature 'Gallé', 21in (53cm) wide. **£800–1,200** *C*

An American Arts & Crafts mahogany occasional table, c1910. **£300–400** *ST*

A Victorian Aesthetic Movement ebonised chair, similar to a Fred Maddox design for Floris & Co. **£400–500** *ST*

An Arts & Crafts oak chair, Glasgow School, c1900. **£700–800** *ST*

l. An oak revolving bookcase, the design attributed to Richard Norman Shaw, the top with carved inscription 'The Tabard Inn, the true university of these days is a collection of books', 73in (186cm) high. **£1,200–1,600** *C*

r. A pair of Liberty & Co. oak side chairs, designed by Archibald Knox, engraved plaques 'Liberty & Co. Ltd., London W.' **£450–500** *C*

l. A George Walton oak armchair, the tapering back splat with heart-shaped piercing, the out curving arms and rush seat on square section legs joined by plain stretchers. **£1,500–1,800** *C*

A pair of limed oak chairs, by Heal's, c1908. **£450–500** *ST*

far left. An oak tabouret, by the Grand Rapids Bookcase and Chair Co., c1910. **£200–300** *ST*
left. An oak tabouret, by Stickley Brothers, Grand Rapids, c1905. **£300–400** *ST*

A set of 6 Finmar stained birch chairs, designed by Alvar Aalto, with Finmar Ltd. label.
£200–300 *P*

A walnut side cabinet, with a grey slate top, 4 cupboard doors, inlaid with slate panels, 1900–20, 58in (147cm) wide.
£600–800 *S*

The small plate panels are replacements, presumably instead of the original pietra dura panels.

A pair of 'Fledermaus' side chairs, designed by Josef Hoffmann, with J. & J. Kohn label beneath upholstery, c1907.
£600–800 *S*

A French oak dining chair, designed by Charles Plumet and Anthony Selmersheim. **£400–500** *P*

An oak settle, by Walter Cave, designed by C. F. Voysey, c1900, 54in (137cm) wide. **£1,000–1,500** *S*

A satinwood inlaid stand, and a pair of chairs. **£400–500** *LRG*

An oak chair, by Wylie and Lochhead, the design attributed to E. A. Taylor.
£350–450 *C*

A corner chair, by Bugatti, the sides slung with beaten copper and kid drums, inlaid with pewter and ivory.
£1,500–2,000 *CSK*

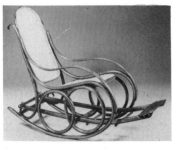

A bentwood rocking chair, by Thonet, c1904.
£300–400 *CNY*

l. A mahogany and marquetry settle, the top and frieze inlaid with various fruitwoods, c1890, 73in (185cm) wide.
£1,100–1,300 *C*

An oak 'Granville' chair, by Edward Pugin, stamped 'P.O.D.R.', mark for 1870.
£1,000–1,200 *S*

An Arts & Crafts oak smoking cupboard with coppered hinges, marked 'Rd 39192', c1885, 12in (30.5cm) wide.
£40–50 *ROW*

A mahogany gateleg table, by Kenton & Co., designed by Ernest Gimson, the sides with rose and briar palmwood inlay, c1891, 32in (81.5cm) wide extended.
£3,500–4,000 *C*

An oak writing desk, designed by George Walton, the rectangular top above 3 drawers, on square tapering supports, c1900, 37in (94cm) high.
£800–1,000 *C(S)*

A Thebes mahogany stool, 17in (43cm) square.
£350–450 *APO*

r. An Arts & Crafts ebonised card table, 36in (91.5cm) wide.
£450–500 *APO*

A pair of highback ash armchairs, by Clisset, designed by Ernest Gimson, with ladderbacks above rush seats, on turned tapering legs joined with turned stretchers.
£1,000–1,200 *C*

An oak side table, designed by Gordon Russell, 33½in (85cm) wide.
£400–500 *C*

An Arts & Crafts hall table/bureau, in the manner of Gustav Stickley, the 2 drawers with copper handles, 49in (124.5cm) wide.
£600–700 *APO*

A mahogany and cane newspaper basket, designed by Sir Edwin Lutyens, with carved 'rope' decoration and cane panels, the rectangular basket on 4 square section legs, each pair joined with single plain stretcher, on casters, 32in (81cm) wide.
£4,500–5,000 *C*

This newspaper basket was designed Sir Edwin Lutyens for his own use, certainly at 13 Mansfield Street, where he lived from September 1919. However, it may have been designed earlier while he was living in Bedford Square. His daughter, Mary Lutyens, remembers the piece being in constant use.

l. An oak chequered inlaid wardrobe, possibly designed by M. H. Baillie-Scott, 85in (216cm) wide, and a matching chest with 2 hinged lids above a pair of doors and 3 drawers, on octagonal supports, 55in (139.5cm) high, both with copper curved handles.
£1,800–2,200 *C(S)*

A mahogany and satinwood breakfront cabinet, the design attributed to Thomas E. Collcutt, the marquetry to Stephen Webb, with original red velvet interior, stamped 'Collinson & Lock, 900', c1885, 65in (165cm) wide.
£2,000–2,500 *C*

A corner cabinet, by Heal & Son, on a plinth base, 21½in (54cm) wide. **£400–500** *C*

Four dining chairs and one carver, by George Walton, 40in (101.5cm) high.
£250–300 *APO*

An Arts & Crafts dark oak high backed elbow chair, with solid seat.
£100–120 *LF*

A pair of oak side chairs, designed by J. P. Seddon, the moulded arched backs with carved leaf motifs, upholstered backs and seats, stamped 'Seddon, New Bond Street, 9969'.
£2,000–2,500 *C*

An oak low chair, by Arthur Simpson of Kendal, the curving arched back with pierced motif, with similarly curved seat on square section arched legs, damaged.
£500–600 *C*

A set of 7 Arts & Crafts oak dining chairs, including an open armchair.
£1,000–1,200 *CSK*

A set of 6 oak side chairs, designed by A. W. N. Pugin, on turned and chamfered legs joined by chamfered stretchers, upholstered in brown hide, with casters on front legs.
£1,500–2,000 *C*

An oak tea table, inlaid with ebony, with 4 fold-down shelves. **£400–500** *ST*

A Gustav Stickley oak armchair, c1903. **£600–700** *ST*

A Gustav Stickley oak settee, c1903. **£1,700–2,500** *ST*

r. A stained beech table, with pegged construction, by Liberty's, c1905. **£275–325** *ST*

An Arts & Crafts mahogany armchair, c1900. **£400–500** *ST*

A set of 5 Gordon Russell oak dining chairs and an armchair, with drop-in seats, on tapering square section legs jointed by plain stretchers. **£1,800–2,000** *C*

An American Arts & Crafts oak magazine/book rack, by the Lake Craft Shops, Sheboygan, Wisconsin, c1905. **£800–1,200** *ST*

An oak occasional table, by Heal's. **£300–400** *ST*

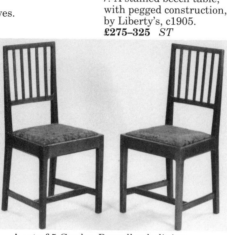

An oak sofa/table, the table top swivels down to reveal settee, c1910. **£900–1,000** *ST*

l. An inlaid mahogany writing desk, the single frieze drawer with brass drop handles, leather top, 33in (84cm) wide. **£500–550** *IM*

An oak plant stand, with copper banding, c1900, 36in (91.5cm) high. **£200–250** *ST*

An Arts & Crafts oak bookcase, with unusual copper metal work and leaded light panels in the doors, probably Liberty's, c1900, 85½in (217cm) wide.
£1,800–2,500 *ST*

An Arts & Crafts Movement oak sideboard, by Liberty's, probably designed by Leonard Wyburd, with geometric leaded glass and copper strapwork handles, c1895, 94in (238cm) wide.
£4,000–6,000 *ST*

A walnut cabinet, 66in (167.5cm) high.
£1,500–2,000 *RG*

A mahogany display cabinet, 48in (122cm) wide.
£1,400–1,600 *CEd*

An inlaid mahogany display cabinet, with enclosed shelves, inlaid in fruitwoods with Art Nouveau foliage and flowers.
£1000–1,400 *P*

r. A mahogany display cabinet, 54½in (138cm) wide.
£2,000–2,500 *CEd*

r. An Arts & Crafts ebonised oak book cabinet, the top with brass panel inscribed 'Studies Serve for Delight', 50in (127cm) wide.
£500–550 *P*

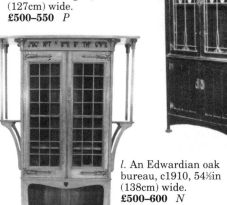

l. An Edwardian oak bureau, c1910, 54½in (138cm) wide.
£500–600 *N*

r. An Arts & Crafts style mahogany display cabinet, the back with design registration mark '634145768', 53in (134.5cm) wide.
£600–800 *P(CW)*

An Arts & Crafts
tub chair.
£250–300 *ARF*

Two Arts & Crafts armchairs
with 4 matching side chairs.
£950–1,200 *ARF*

An Arts & Crafts
carver chair.
£150–200 *ARF*

A set of 8 Arts & Crafts
rush seated chairs,
including 2 carvers.
£800–1,200 *ARF*

A set of 6 Arts &
Crafts chairs.
£700–800 *ARF*

A Gothic chair.
£130–150 *ARF*

A set of 4 Arts & Crafts
chairs. **£400–450** *ARF*

A set of 8 Arts &
Crafts chairs, by
William Birch.
£1,000–1,200 *ARF*

An Arts & Crafts
pot cupboard, 32½in
(82cm) high.
£150–200 *ARF*

A Gothic style bedroom suite
comprising: pot cupboard,
wardrobe and dressing table.
£2,500–3,000 *ARF*

A pair of Arts & Crafts
adjustable book shelves,
36in (92cm) high.
£250–350 each *ARF*

A pair of Gothic oak
pillars, with painted
decoration, 49in
(124.5cm) high.
£650–750 *ARF*

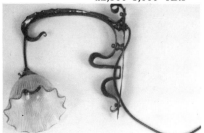

An Arts & Crafts copper wall light.
£60–70 *ARF*

A Newlyn copper repoussé tray, 17½in (44.5cm).
£150–180 *BLO*

A pair of Arts & Crafts oak reclining chairs, c1920.
£630–650 *OCA*

An Arts & Crafts oak armchair, attributed to William Birch.
£350–450 *P*

A William Birch oak armchair, attributed to E. Punnett, the back inset with 2 rush panels, above a rush seat and 4 rectangular section legs with an H-shaped stretcher.
£500–700 *C*

A pair of oak reclining chairs, with 2 cushions, c1920.
£230–260 *OCA*

An Arts & Crafts oak chest, attributed to Heals, with 3 long drawers beneath an enclosed cupboard, the doors set with fielded chestnut panels, with exposed joints throughout.
£1,500–1,700 *P*

An Arts & Crafts oak reclining armchair, attributed to William Birch, the ladder back with turned uprights, having an adjustable rod support, shaped armrests, turned front and square back supports united with stretchers, with William Morris fabric cushions.
£700–800 *P*

An Arts & Crafts mahogany display cabinet, in the style of J. S. Henry, the angled glazed doors separated and bounded by planks inlaid with stylised floral patterns in fruitwood, supported above a pointed pedestal base by 3 groups of 2 frontal columns and a solid back.
£800–1,000 *P*

A Fradgley Arts & Crafts three-piece salon suite, comprising: a two-seater settee and a pair of armchairs, inlaid with ebony stringing and a fruitwood stylised floral inlay.
£1,700–2,000 *P*

r. An Arts & Crafts oak dining table, the top made from 3 pieces of wood, 84½in (214cm) long.
£800–1,200 *P*

A Gothic style oak side table, in the manner of Pugin, 42½in (107cm).
£550–650 *P*

An Arts & Crafts oak sideboard by Stanley Davis of Windermere, marked under top with maker's monogram SDW 1927, and 'J.E.O'. monogram, 54in (137cm) wide. **£800–900** *P*

A mahogany escritoire, with a marquetry panel, by Shapland & Petter of Barnstaple, c1905.
£1,500–1,800 *ST*

An Austrian mahogany kneehole desk, attributed to Otto Wagner, the top inset with green leather, with brass gallery, on flared brass feet, 47½in (121cm), and a matching mahogany chair, with drop-in seat, revolving action, on similar brass supports.
£2,500–3,000 *P*

An Aesthetic Movement walnut hanging cabinet, with hand painted panel, c1875.
£350–380 *P(Re)*

r. An Aesthetic Movement corner cupboard, the bow fronted doors enclosing 3 shelves and painted in colours, one door unfinished, on a three-legged base with a single drawer and undertier, 27in (69cm) wide.
£300–400 *P*

A mahogany and marquetry buffet, attributed to Louis Majorelle, with bronze mounts and marble tops, the gallery with a narrow shelf at the top, 56in (143cm) wide.
£900–1,000 *C(Am)*

A Dutch Arts & Crafts tea buffet, designed by Jac. van den Bosch for 'het Binnenhuis', with a metal tag 't Binnenhuis Raadhuisstraat, Amsterdam', and with branded monogram 'J.v.d. Bosch' and the numbers '848', 61½in (156cm) high.
£1,300–1,500 *C(Am)*

An Amsterdam School sideboard, rosewood bordered in coromandel, 65in (165cm) wide.
£350–450 *C(Am)*

An Arts & Crafts pollard oak bedroom suite of 8 pieces, in the manner of C. F. A. Voysey.
£2,000–2,500 *P(Re)*

r. An Arts & Crafts oak dresser, with brass hinges, 50in (127cm).
£1,100–1,500 *RG*

A tubular chromium plated chaise longue, designed by Le Corbusier and Charlotte Perriand, upholstered in ponyskin, on a black painted steel base.
£2,500–3,000 *C*

A burr maple sideboard, the design attributed to Ray Hille, 54in (137cm) wide.
£700–900 *C*

A walnut cabinet, by A. J. Rowley, the stepped top above 3 mirrored compartments, the central ne inset with carved panel, on silvered plinth base, with printed label 'Rowley, Church Street, Kensington, Est. 1898', 35in (89cm) wide.
£2,000–2,500 *C*

A mahogany dressing table, 51½in (130cm) wide.
£650–800 *P*

A French daybed, with mattress covered in black and white zebra skin, with a matching cylindrical cushion, on 4 tapering fluted legs, 1930s, 74in (188cm) long.
£1,500–1,800 *C*

l. A six-piece cloud-back suite, veneered in walnut and re-upholstered in cream leather, c1930, settee 65in (165cm) wide.
£3,000–4,000 *ST*

An occasional table, designed and labelled by Waring and Gillow, 21in (53cm) high.
£200–250 *ARF*

An Art Deco nest of tables, 30in (76cm) diam.
£250–350 *ARF*

An Art Deco circular table, 36in (91.5cm) diam.
£800–900 *ARF*

r. An Art Deco glass and walnut coffee table, 21in (53cm) high.
£150–200 *ARF*

A Modernist chrome and glass coffee table, 1930s, 24in (61.5cm) diam. **£400–500** *S*

A Barcelona chair and stool, by Mies van der Rohe, designed 1929, 28½in (73cm) high. **£400–600** *S*

A pair of cantilever Modernist armchairs, 1930s, 30in (77.5cm) high. **£600–800** *S*

A Modernist chromed tubular steel sofa, 1930s, 63½in (161cm) wide. **£700–1,000** *S*

A pair of French Art Deco armchairs, c1920, 28½in (73cm) wide. **£700–1,000** *S*

A coffee table in pale burrwood, 1930s, 40in (101cm). **£400–600** *S*

A Bauhaus bedroom suite comprising: cabinet, chair, dressing table, 2 single bed-ends, 2 bedside tables, 1930s, tables 23in (58.5cm) high. **£1,000–1,500** *S*

l. An Art Deco grand lit en lac d'or, 71in (180cm) wide. **£1,000–1,300** *C*

Three Modernist side tables, 1930s, 23½in (60cm) diam. **£700–800** *S*

An Art Deco dressing table, veneered with Macassar ebony, 1930's, 47½in (120.5cm) wide. **£800–1,200** *S*

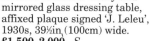

A Leleu Macassar ebony and mirrored glass dressing table, affixed plaque signed 'J. Leleu', 1930s, 39½in (100cm) wide. **£1,500–2,000** *S*

A Finmar Ltd plywood armchair, designed by Alvar Aalto, Finmar label, 1930s, 23½in (60.5cm) high. **£100–140** *S*

A set of 6 Finmar Ltd. plywood dining chairs, designed by Alvar Aalto, Finmar labels, stamped 'Aalto Design Made in Finland', 31½in (80cm) high. **£400–500** *S*

An Art Deco cabinet,
24in (61.5cm) wide.
£150–200 *ARF*

A dressing table from an Art Deco
bedroom suite, comprising: a dressing
table, bedside cupboard and large
cupboard in oyster maple, 48in
(122cm) wide. **£800–1,000** *ARF*

A chestnut wardrobe, the top
with chamfered finials above
2 panelled cupboard doors, on
octagonal section legs, with
printed paper label 'Design
No. 101/1283, Designer
Gordon Russell, Date
27.11.30', stamped 'E.A.
Dorley', 76in (193.5cm) high.
£1,000–1,500 *C*

r. A Rowley bedroom suite,
comprising: a dressing table,
stool, chest and bedhead, with
illuminated side panels,
dressing table 34in (86cm) wide.
£600–800 *ARF*

A chrome bar
stool made by
PEL, c1930,
30in (76cm) high.
£60–80 *ARF*

An Art Deco
chrome stool,
37in (94cm) high.
£40–50 *ARF*

An Art Deco chrome and
maroon glass cocktail trolley,
25½in (65cm) high.
£125–185 *ARF*

A Robert Thompson
'Mouseman' oak wardrobe,
with beaten iron fittings, on
short square section legs, with
mouse signature carved in
intaglio, 48in (122cm) wide.
£2,500–3,000 *C*

A Rowley Gallery corner unit, with
inset picture of lion killing a deer,
44in (111.5cm) wide.
£200–300 *ARF*

An occasional table designed by
Piero Fornasetti, with wooden
top covered in black lacquer
printed sun and ray motif, on
tripod steel legs modelled with
nodules, with printed paper
label, 29½in (75cm) high.
£900–1,200 *C*

An Art Deco French table,
c1930, 24in (61.5cm) high.
£150–200 *ARF*

An Art Deco rosewood, burr-
maple and walnut centre table,
in the style of Emile Ruhlmann,
inlaid with ivory lattice stringing
above plain frieze and chamfered
legs, 33in (84cm).
£1,000–1,500 *C*

An Art Deco mantel clock, the French movement in a copper and brass case, 10½in wide.
£60–80 *HM*

A silver mounted mantel clock, the face set in an engine turned surround, on a glass base, decorated with cutting and black enamel, maker's mark 'S. & M. Birmingham 1935', 45cm (11.5cm) high.
£100–150 *SBe*

An Art Deco table, 32in (81.5cm) diam.
£500–600 *ARF*

A French Art Deco bureau de dame, decorated in a matt crackled polish and painted in relief, with a fitted interior, 47in (120cm) high.
£800–1200 *C*

An Edward Barnsley walnut breakfront bookcase, made by Charles Bray, 1932, 89in (226cm) wide.
£6,000–8,000 *SB*

An Art Deco blond wood bookshelf/display cabinet, 1930s, 31½in (80cm) high.
£600–700 *SB*

An oak chair, with label 'Designed by Frank Brangwyn R.A., Manufactured by E. Pollard & Co. Ltd.', monogram 'FB', c1930, 42in (106cm) wide.
£500–600 *SB*

A pair of tub-shaped easy chairs, attributed to Mercier Frères, c1928, 28½in (73cm) high.
£800–1,200 *SS*

An Art Deco maple shagreen and ivory cocktail cabinet, panelled in a pale green shagreen, twin doors below, the top opening out, 1930s, 22in (56cm) wide.
£1,500–2,000 *SB*

An oak chest of drawers, designed by Robert Thompson, the 'Mouseman', c1930, (91.5cm) wide.
£600–800 *SB*

A black leather covered desk, early 1930's, 57in (145cm) wide.
£600–800 *SB*

A Strohmenger small grand piano, the sycamore casing with double satinwood banding, numbered 'S 16413', 1930's.
£5,000–7,000 *SB*

A Gordon Russell oak bedroom cabinet, with moulded walnut knob handles, 73in (185cm).
£2000–3000 *C*

An Epstein & Goldbart mahogany cocktail cabinet, veneered in sycamore, with a fitted interior, 60½in (153cm) high.
£550–650 *CSK*

A white painted side chair by Edmund Moiret, with triple bar stretcher, c1907.
£1,500–2,000 *C*

Edmund Moiret, 1883–1967, was born in Budapest and became a leading member of the Hungarian Secession Movement. He began his studies at the Academy of Art in Budapest but went on to study in Vienna and Brussels. He was awarded a major prize at the Budapest Winter Salon in 1910 and settled in Hungary where he taught sculpture from 1911 at the Budapest Technische Hochschule. He later lived and worked in Vienna. In 1985 a commemorative exhibition was held at the Osterreichisches Museum für Angewandte Kunst.

A sycamore kneehole desk, with 2 slide pulls, 7 drawers and one false drawer, inset with a circular printed ivory label, 'Tottenham Court Road, HEAL'S, London W.1', 28in (71cm) high.
£1,100–1,300 *C*

A set of 4 walnut side chairs.
£1,200–1,500 *C*

A set of 8 dining chairs.
£1,100–1,300 *C*

A Robert Thompson, 'Mouseman', oak writing desk, signed with a carved mouse, 72in (182cm).
£450–650 *C*

A Heal's oak writing desk, designed by Ambrose Heal, with fall flaps at each end and enclosing 6 file trays, inlaid with printed ivory label 'Heal and Son Ltd London N.W', 60in (152cm).
£3,000–3,500 *C*

A Peter Waals walnut dressing table, 46in (116cm).
£1,200–1,500 *C*

A coffee table with a parquetry top, on 4 scrolling wrought iron legs, 31½in (79.5cm) diam.
£500–600 *C*

A French rosewood dining table, c1928, 63in (160cm) wide.
£3,000–3,500 *CNY*

An occasional table, veneered and inlaid with ebony, boxwood, satinwood and oysterwood, 25in (63.5cm) high.
£500–700 *ASA*

r. A bird's-eye maple dining suite, comprising: a table, serving table, sideboard, and 10 chairs upholstered in green leather, 1930s, 120in (305cm).
£3,000–3,500 *CSK*

A quartered oak dining table, designed by Gordon Russell, made by G. Cooke, with label to underside, c1923, 66in (167cm) wide.
£2,500–3,000 *HCH*

A drinks cabinet, veneered in burr walnut, with 4 cupboards and a slide, 42in (106cm) wide.
£700–800 *P(Ch)*

A walnut veneered circular display cabinet, 45in (114cm) diam.
£260–300 *P*

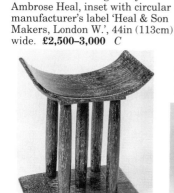

A gilt salon chair, attributed to Jules Leleu, upholstered in beige fabric.
£1,700–2,000 *C*

An Austrian Secessionist painted writing table and chair, 23in (58cm) high. **£2,500–3,000** *C*

An oak cabinet designed by Ambrose Heal, inset with circular manufacturer's label 'Heal & Son Makers, London W.', 44in (113cm) wide. **£2,500–3,000** *C*

A walnut dining table, with walnut veneer, 71in (179cm) long.
£700–900 *C*

A maple veneered side table, 40in (100cm) wide.
£600–700 *P*

l. An oak and chestnut sideboard, by Gordon Russell, cabinet maker P. J. Wade, c1927, 52½in (136cm) wide. **£2,000–2,500** *HCH*

A limed oak Ashanti-style stool, stained black, 20½in (52cm) high.
£250–300 *P*

A walnut centre table, 31in (78.5cm) high.
£700–800 *C*

An Egyptian style bed, the headboard with a beaten copper panel, 42in (108cm) wide.
£600–700 *C*

A set of 4 chairs, designed by Ludwig Mies van der Rohe.
£1,000–1,200 *C*

An Art Deco three-piece red leather upholstered cloud suite, comprising a sofa a 2 armchairs each with scallop shaped backs and curved sides, sofa 66in (167.5cm) wide.
£1,500–2,000 *CSK*

A French Art Deco calamander table, part veneered, the oval top supported on 4 stocky legs with a cross stretcher between, the legs and feet carved with Oriental scrolls, 59in (150cm) long.
£650–850 *P*

An Art Deco burr walnut cocktail cabinet, the central cupboard with twin fluted doors enclosing shelves, flanked by stepped side cupboards enclosing shelves, on arched supports on a solid ebonised base, 47½in (119.5cm) wide.
£1,600–2,000 *P*

An Art Deco cocktail cabinet, in veneered light walnut, the 2 panelled doors enclosing fitted pink mirrored interior, on slender carved floral and acanthus supports, by Epstein, 46in (116.5cm) wide.
£600–700 *MSL*

An Art Deco inlaid walnut fire screen, 34½in (87cm) wide.
£135–165 *OCA*

l. An Art Deco D-shaped console table, in wrought iron with a partly painted marble top, in the manner of Edgar Brandt, 42in (106.5cm) wide, and a matching overmantel.
£700–800 *CSK*

r. An Art Deco bird'seye maple dining room table, with a glass cover, on 2 U-shaped supports on solid feet, united by a stretcher, 78in (198cm) long.
£1,000–1,500 *P*

A French Art Deco console, in wrought iron, marble and wood mirrored console, in the style of Paul Kiss, the rectangular mirror plate within a simple hammered framework, with lower D-shaped black marble shelf with a single support composed of stylised floral devices, raised on a moulded wooden plinth, c1925, 72in (183cm) high.
£3,800–4,800 *S(NY)*

l. An Art Deco style gilt metal and glass dining table, the inset square top, the frieze cast with Greek key motifs, raised on 4 curved legs similarly cast conjoined to a stepped square base, raised on 4 feet, 48in (123cm) square.
£3,500–4,500 *S(NY)*

An Art Deco cherry wood framed sofa,
with carved back rail and cornucopia
arm supports, in original patterned
silk cover.
£600–700 *LRG*

An Art Deco Hille birch veneer
sofa and chair, upholstered in
muted pink fabric with small
dots, together with a chair,
66½in (171cm) wide.
£3,500–4,000 *P*

An Art Deco Macassar ebony
bedroom suite, comprising: a
double bed, 63in (160cm) wide,
bedside cabinets, 20in (50cm)
wide, and a large wardrobe,
75in (109cm) high.
£1,500–2,000 *C*

An Art Deco gilded armchair
and stool, in the manner of
Maurice Dufrène, upholstered in
green velvet dralon, with a
matching footstool and cushions.
£1,000–1,200 *P*

An Art Deco three-piece cloud
back suite, upholstered in cream
coloured leather, on casters.
£2,000–2,500 *P*

r. A pair of Art Deco armchairs, the
reclining back and seat upholstered
in original beige/brown fabric, each
arm enclosing a magazine rack and
bookshelves with diamond motif
frieze at the front, stamped at the
back 'W. Hudson 2842'.
£300–400 *P*

An Art Deco three-piece suite,
possible designed by Paul
Follot, in walnut, comprising: a
canapé and 2 bergères, with
yellow gold patterned velvet
upholstery, each piece with a
shaped upholstered cushion.
£4,000–5,000 *P*

An Arts & Crafts mahogany secrétaire, the fall flap enclosing a central cupboard with mother-of-pearl inlay, 48in (122cm) wide. **£1,000–1,500** *P*

A walnut and marquetry bookcase, the top inlaid in fruitwoods with swallows and a gothic pinnacle, on a later revolving base, inlaid 'Gallé signature, 20in (51cm) wide. **£7,000–9,000** *C*

A three-fold wood framed and leather covered screen, decorated across the top with a tooled and gilded frieze of seagulls, with sailing boats below, the lower frieze depicting fish, crabs and shells, 70in (177.5cm) high. **£1,000–1,500** *P*

An Austrian mahogany kneehole desk, and a chair, attributed to Otto Wagner, with ivory inlay, satinwood stringing and bronze plaques, 48in (122cm) wide. **£2,500–3,000** *P*

Two jade table screens, carved in relief with birds in landscapes, Immortals gathered in groves and flowering peonies, cracks to wood, 19thC, 7in (17.5cm) high. **£18,000–20,000** *CHK*

An oak bookcase, designed by Harvey Ellis, Model No. 700, made by Gustav Stickley, c1903, 36in (91.5cm) wide. **£6,000–9,000** *CNY*

r. An ebonised and rosewood lady's writing desk, by Carlo Bugatti, with pewter and ivory inlay, signed 'Ricardo Telligrini 1897', 30in (76cm) wide. **£5,000–7,000** *C*

A mahogany display cabinet, designed by
Carl Davis Richter, 65in (165cm) wide.
£3,000–4,000 *C*

An Ernest Gimson bureau, with an elaborately
fitted interior, barber's pole inlay, made by
Sidney Barnsley, 33in (83.5cm) wide.
£10,000–12,000 *C*

l. A Sidney Barnsley walnut
dresser, with diamond pattern
moulding, 75in (190.5cm) wide.
£6,000–8,000 *C*

r. An oak daybed, by
Charles Eastlake, with
panelled sides, the
headrest carved with
daisies, with a gothic
roundel, upholstered in
green velvet, on turned
legs, 73in (185cm) long.
£4,000–5,000 *C*

A Gustav Siegel leather upholstered stained bentwood and brass seating group, made by J. & J. Kohn, c1905, settee 48in (122cm) wide.
£7,000–8,500 *S(NY)*

An Austrian burr maple settee, upholstered in khaki twill, c1920, 55in (139.5cm) wide.
£4,250–5,000 *S(NY)*

A French Art Deco parcel gilt mahogany five-piece salon suite, upholstered in silk moiré, c1925, settee 50in (127cm) wide.
£5,000–6,000 *S(NY)*

A pair of Jacques Adnet black lacquered wood 'cube' club chairs, upholstered in beige canvas, c1930.
£9,000–11,000 *S(NY)*

A Josef Hoffmann leather upholstered bentwood 'Buenos Aires' three-piece seating group, made by J. & J. Kohn, c1904, settee 52in (132cm) wide.
£10,500–11,500 *S(NY)*

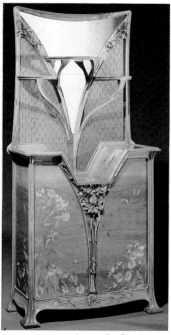

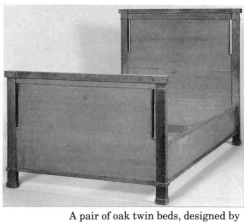

A pair of oak twin beds, designed by Frank Lloyd Wright, probably by Niedecken-Walbridge Co. for Ray Evans House, Chicago, c1909, 47in (119cm) wide. **£6,000–7,000** *CNY*

A marquetry cabinet, by Louis Majorelle, inlaid with flowers and butterflies, the upper section with a mirror, 39½in (100cm) wide. **£15,000–18,000** *CNY*

r. A marquetry cabinet, 'Aux Grenouilles', with carved frog feet, inlaid panels with dragonflies and mushrooms, marquetry 'Gallé' signature, 26in (66cm) wide. **£15,000–18,000** *CNY*

A carved and marquetry vitrine, branded 'L. Majorelle, Nancy', 31in (78.5cm) wide. **£8,000–10,000** *CNY*

An upholstered mahogany three-piece salon suite, carved with ferns and 2 snails, by Louis Majorelle, settee 54½in (138cm) wide. **£5,000–6,000** *CNY*

A marquetry umbrella stand, with original tin liner, marquetry 'Gallé' signature, 21in (53cm) wide. **£18,000–20,000** *CNY*

Two inlaid oak armchairs, designed by Harvey Ellis, made by Gustav Stickley, c1904, 47in (119cm) high. **£9,000–10,000 each** *CNY*

A pair of French mahogany upholstered club chairs, c1935.
£2,500–3,500 *S(NY)*

A Bruno Paul maple armchair, restored, manufacturer's monogram, Munich, 1901.
£14,000–17,000 *S(NY)*

A pair of Josef Hoffmann stained bentwood and brass side chairs, by J. & J. Kohn, Austria, c1901.
£5,500–7,500 *S(NY)*

The Aesthetic Movement

The 1870s and 1880s saw a growth in the Aesthetic Movement in Britain, with designers producing ebonised furniture in simple forms, and decoration restricted to confined areas rather than applied all over. Unnecessary ornament was rejected as vulgar. William Morris and his company were the most important retail outlet for Aesthetic-style furniture, while the Japanese influence was particularly evident in the work of Edward Godwin. The Aesthetic style was especially popular in the United States, where it was adopted with great success by the Herter Brothers.

An Aesthetic Movement ebonised and inlaid open armchair, c1870.
£2,000–2,500 *C*

A painted deal 'Berlin' chair, designed by Gerrit Rietveld in 1923, branded label, made by Gerard van de Groenekan, c1960.
£7,000–11,000 *S(NY)*

A Josef Hoffmann bentwood 670 'Sitzmachine', manufactured by J. & J. Kohn, c1905.
£22,000–28,000 *S(NY)*

A pair of French upholstered club chairs, attributed to André Arbus, c1945.
£3,500–4,500 *S(NY)*

A 'Red/Blue' chair, in beech and deal, by Gerrit Rietveld, designed in 1918, executed in 1919.
£26,000–30,000 *S(NY)*

A Le Corbusier, Pierre Jeanneret and Charlotte Perriand white painted metal and canvas chaise longue, manufactured by Thonet, designed c1928, 63in (160cm) wide.
£35,000–40,000 *S(NY)*

A painted steel and leather side chair, by Frank Lloyd Wright, c1904.
£3,500–4,000 *S(NY)*

Henri van de Velde (Belgian, 1863–1957)

Henri Clemens van de Velde trained as a painter, architect and graphic designer in Antwerp and Paris, and was instrumental in the evolution of the Belgian Art Nouveau style. He designed all manner of items, incuding whole interiors, but was particularly influential in the fields of furniture, ceramics, jewellery and metalwork. His furniture often combines innovative elements with tradition. It tends to be substantial, concentrating on restrained, sculptural, well balanced forms for interest, rather than the applied decoration and inlay commonly used by adherents of the Nancy School.

A pair of oak side chairs, with rush seats, designed by Peter Behrens.
£3,500–4,000 *C*

A stained mahogany side chair, by Richard Riemerschmid, manufactured by B. Kohlbecker & Sohn, Munich, 1903.
£1,500–2,500 *S(NY)*

A mahogany and leather armchair, by Henry van de Velde designed for the Haby Salon, Berlin, 1901.
£8,500–10,500 *S(NY)*

A pair of French palmwood upholstered side chairs, c1930.
£2,500–3,500 *S(NY)*

*l.*An ash and painted canvas armchair, by Wharton Esberick, signed 'Hedgerow/to Jasper MCMXXXVII Wharton'.
£7,000–8,000 *S(NY)*

A black metal and ponyskin chaise longu by Le Corbusier, Pierre Jeanneret and Charlotte Perriand, manufactured by Embru Corporation, Switzerland, c1932.
£7,000–9,000 *S(NY)*

A copper and mica table lamp, the base of trumpet form, stamped 'Dirk van Erp', c1915, 22in (56cm) high. **£12,000–15,000** *CNY*

A cameo glass table lamp, the conical shade acid etched with pendant branches of honeysuckle, shade and base signed in cameo 'Gallé', 8½in (21cm) high. **£6,000–7,500** *P*

An earthenware and glass table lamp, by Fulper, the shade of mirrored black glaze over green flambé inset with leaded glass, base and shade marked, 15¼in (39cm) high. **£9,000–12,000** *CNY*

A 'Woodbine' leaded glass chandelier, impressed 'Tiffany Studios New York 2-609', 27in (68cm) diam. **£23,500–33,500** *CNY*

A 'Trumpet Vine' double overlay and etched glass table lamp, with cameo signature 'Gallé', 26½in (67cm) high. **£14,000–17,000** *CNY*

A 'Hanging Head Dragonfly' leaded glass and bronze table lamp, shade and base impressed 'Tiffany Studios New York, 1507', and '7984', 32½in (82cm) high. **£25,000–40,000** *CNY*

An 'Oriental Poppy' glass and bronze floor lamp, impressed 'Tiffany Studios New York 2404 and 378', 76in (193cm) high. **£117,000–133,000** *CNY*

l. A 'Woodbine' leaded glass and bronze table lamp, the shade and base stamped 'Tiffany Studios New York', 21in (53cm) high. **£17,000–23,500** *CNY*

A copper and mica table lamp, stamped 'Dirk van Erp', c1910, 25½in (65cm) high. **£40,000–43,000** *CNY*

A 'Turtleback' tiled, leaded glass and bronze table lamp, stamped 'Tiffany', 22in (56cm) high. **£8,000–10,000** *CNY*

A 'Laburnum' leaded glass and bronze table lamp, stamped 'Tiffany Studios New York, 397', 27in (68.5cm) high. **£40,000–50,000** *CNY*

A 'Daffodil' leaded glass and bronze table lamp, stamped 'Tiffany Studios', 22in (56cm) high. **£9,500–12,000** *Bon*

A Favrile glass and bronze table lamp, small repair, stamped 'Tiffany Studios D856', 25in (63.5cm) high. **£8,000–12,000** *CNY*

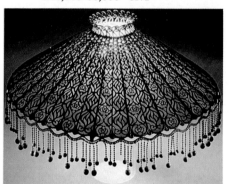

A leaded glass and filigree bronze lamp shade, by Tiffany Studios, 19in (48cm) diam. **£2,000–2,500** *CNY*

A Tiffany Favrile 'Lily' glass and bronze 12-light table lamp, 19½in (49cm) high. **£13,500–17,000** *CNY*

r. A Tiffany 'Turtleback' tile and bronze chandelier, 27in (68.5cm) diam. **£8,000–10,000** *CNY*

A 'Wisteria' leaded glass and bronze table lamp, stamped 'Tiffany Studios New York, 7806', 27½in (70cm) high. **£85,000–100,000** *CNY*

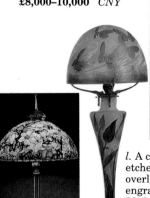

r. A 'Magnolia' leaded glass and bronze floor lamp, stamped 'Tiffany Studios', 77½in (196cm) high. **£200,000–250,000** *CNY*

l. A carved and acid etched triple overlay table lamp, engraved 'Gallé', 23½in (60cm) high. **£10,000–15,000** *C*

r. An applied, carved and etched glass table lamp, carved 'Daum Nancy' on shade, 14in (35.5cm) high. **£16,000–20,000** *Bon*

A 'Peacock' table lamp, the base impressed 'Tiffany Studios New York 23923', 26in (65cm) high.
£70,000–90,000 *CNY*

A 'Magnolia' leaded glass and bronze floor lamp, the shade impressed 'Tiffany Studios New York 1599', the base cast with a band of leaves and impressed, numbered '379', 80in (203cm) high.
£150,000–185,000 *CNY*

A 'Peony' leaded glass and bronze table lamp, by Tiffany & Co., the shade and base impressed with maker's marks and numbered '1505' and '550' respectively, 31in (79cm) high.
£65,000–75,000 *CNY*

l. An 'Apple Blossom' leaded glass and bronze table lamp, by Tiffany & Co., shade and base impressed with maker's marks, base numbered '7806', 26in (66cm) high.
£40,000–55,000 *CNY*

A 'Dragonfly' leaded glass and gilt bronze table lamp, stamped 'Tiffany Studios New York', 23in (58.5cm) high. **£17,000–20,000** *CNY*

A Handel reverse painted glass and cold painted metal lamp, c1920. **£9,500–11,000** *S(NY)*

A Handel reverse painted glass and patinated metal lamp, c1915. **£3,500–4,500** *S(NY)*

A leaded glass and bronze floor lamp, by Tiffany Studios. **£5,500–7,000** *CNY*

A leaded glass and bronze table lamp, 'Favrile Fabrique', by Tiffany Studios. **£5,500–7,000** *CNY*

A Tiffany Favrile glass and bronze 'Peony' lamp, c1910, 23in (58cm) high. **£20,000–22,000** *S(NY)*

A Tiffany Favrile and bronze 'Poinsettia' border lamp shade and base, c1910. **£15,000–17,000** *S(NY)*

A Tiffany Favrile glass and gilt bronze 'Poppy' filigree lamp, c1920. **£20,000–22,000** *S(NY)*

A Handel reverse painted glass and patinated metal lamp, c1920. **£9,000–10,000** *S(NY)*

l. A Pairpoint reverse painted glass 'Scenic Seagull' lamp, c1915, 25in (64cm). **£3,500–5,000** *S(NY)*

A Gallé carved and acid etched double overlay table lamp, carved signature, 25½in (65cm) high.
£12,000–15,000 *C*

A Gallé carved, acid etched and fire polished double overlay table lamp, 23in (59cm) high.
£22,000–26,000 *C*

A double overlay and etched glass table lamp and shade, both parts signed 'Gallé' in the overlay, 10½in (27cm) high.
£10,000–12,000 *HFG*

A double overlay and etched glass table lamp, cameo signature 'Gallé', 22in (56cm) high.
£12,000–15,000 *CNY*

An overlaid and etched glass table lamp, cameo signature 'Gallé' on shade and base, 20in (51cm) high.
£12,000–15,000 *CNY*

A double overlaid and etched glass table lamp, with original bronze mounts, cameo signature 'Gallé' on shade and base, 30in (77cm) high.
£80,000–100,000 *CNY*

A 'Dragonfly' leaded glass and bronze table lamp, both shade and base stamped 'Tiffany Studios', 18in (46cm) high.
£30,000–50,000 *CNY*

A 'Geranium' leaded glass and bronze table lamp, stamped 'Tiffany Studios New York', 16½in (42cm) high.
£30,000–50,000 *CNY*

r. A leaded glass and bronze table lamp, by Tiffany Studios, 15½in (40cm) high.
£3,000–4,500 *CNY*

A Favrile glass and metal table lamp, stamped under fuel canister 'Tiffany Studios', 20½in (52cm) high.
£9,000–10,000 *CNY*

r. An 'Autumn Leaf' leaded glass and bronze table lamp, by Tiffany Studios, 31in (79cm) high.
£35,000–40,000 *CNY*

A Daum etched glass and copper lamp, shade and base, engraved 'Daum Nancy France', 1920s, 16⅜in (42cm) high. **£3,500–4,000** *S*

A pâte-de-verre and wrought iron lamp, by G. Argy-Rousseau base and shade, signed, 1926, 14⅝in (37cm) high. **£12,000–15,000** *S(NY)*

A Favrile 'Lily' ten-light glass and bronze table lamp, by Tiffany Studios. **£10,500–13,500** *CNY*

A Daum etched and enamelled glass table lamp, signed on base, 12⅝in (32cm) high. **£6,500–9,000** *CNY*

A Tiffany Studios 'Lotus' leaded glass and bronze table lamp, base stamped 'Tiffany Studios New York 6874', 18in (46cm) high. **£13,500–20,000** *CNY*

A Le Verre Français cameo glass and wrought iron mushroom lamp, 1920s. **£1,600–2,000** *S*

A Daum etched glass and wrought iron chevron lamp, shade and base, with engraved mark 'Daum Nancy France', 1920s, 12in (31cm) high. **£3,000–3,500** *S*

A pair of Albert Cheuret gilt bronze and alabaster tulip lamps, each inscribed, c1925. **£6,500–7,500** *S(NY)*

A Pairpoint reverse painted blown out and patinated metal boudoir lamp, c1920. **£2,500–3,500** *S(NY)*

A Daum etched, applied and wheel carved 'snail' vase, 10⅛in (26cm) high. **£10,000–12,000** *CNY*

LOUIS COMFORT TIFFANY & TIFFANY STUDIOS

Associated mostly with his leaded glass table lamps and windows, Louis Comfort Tiffany's talent and restless energies led him into numerous disciplines within the decorative arts, including windows, lamps, vases, enamels, ceramics, bronzes, fancy goods, art jewellery, paintings and mosaics. Objects manufactured at Tiffany Studios were of the highest artistic and technical level and were produced in a variety of shapes and designs, incorporating a mixture of materials such as bronze, mosaics, enamel and glass.

For twenty years, prices for Tiffany Studios objects have continued to strengthen in the art market, mostly thanks to the auction house which has played an integral role in establishing prices. Auctions, traditionally the market place for dealers, began to attract private collectors from the mid-1970s. The booming economy of the late 1980s, which generated such high spirits and spending on Wall Street, exploded into the art world and sent auction salesrooms into a frenzy. Spectacular prices for Tiffany lamps, generated in part by overseas purchasers, were evident both in auction rooms and through dealers. Enormous interest from Japanese buyers pushed prices for Tiffany lamps to levels never before imagined. Although the market saw a rapid decline in late 1990 as prices tumbled as quickly as they had risen, it stabilised within two years.

In 1992, Sotheby's New York sold a Tiffany leaded glass and mosaic 'Spider' lamp for $770,000 (£513,300), which established a new world record at auction. That record was broken in April of 1995, when a unique model, a 'Virginia Creeper' table lamp, sold at Sotheby's New York for $1.1 million, (£733,300), the first lamp to break the million dollar barrier at public auction. A highly important 'Cobweb' table lamp in the same sale realised $783,500, (£522,300), making it the second highest price paid at auction for a Tiffany lamp.

Collectors continue to favour the highly colourful floral lamp shades, such as the peony, poppy or dogwood models, although Arts & Crafts enthusiasts have created a solid market for the geometric and turtle-back models which complement the simplistic proportions of the styles' interiors. Some of the most desirable lamps, including the magnolia, wisteria, laburnum, Oriental poppy and elaborate peony models, rarely decrease in value, and important examples of these models steadily continue to escalate in price.

Prices for Tiffany objects no longer categorise them as the bargains that they were thirty years ago, but there is still the opportunity to build good collections. Although availability of high quality lamps and windows does make this increasingly difficult, the firm produced such a broad selection of high quality items, including glassware, candlesticks, and desk sets, that such objects can still be purchased at affordable prices.

Fakes and Reproductions

The problem of mis-attribution is a common event for the collector and the issue of evaluating a Tiffany work of art for authenticity poses a constant concern in a market that has its fair share of fakes and forgeries. Fraudulent lamps (or 'fakes') are becoming more evident, no doubt because prices have been increasing steadily for the last twenty years. While imitation is a recognised form of flattery, Mr. Tiffany would no doubt find these imitation lamps – many bearing his trademark signature – a serious form of deception. Before purchasing a Tiffany Studios lamp (or any object that the firm produced) a wise collector must consider several points. Issues such as age, condition, material and provenance are serious factors to address when examining an object.

One must examine the glass quite carefully as no one yet, despite many attempts, has been able to achieve quite the qualities that Tiffany perfected in this medium. Condition is also an important factor when considering a lamp. Due to their age and fragile composition, many shades have cracks in the glass. While minor cracks do not effect a lamp's value, a shade which has numerous cracks throughout the design can decrease its worth. However, a lamp that has no cracks nor dirt nor any sign of age whatsoever could possibly reveal that it is a reproduction, as Tiffany lamps should show some signs of age. Also, beware of lamps which are sold at prices which seem too good to be true. With the widely recorded prices for lamps today, it is very difficult (if not impossible) to find a real bargain. If one is offered a lamp for $5,000 (£3,000), when a similar one sells at auction for $20,000, (£13,000), be wary.

It is always a good idea to ask questions about the history of an object. The better the provenance, the better off one is. If it was bought through auction, ask to see the catalogue. If the lamp has ever been appraised or insured, ask to review the documentation. Knowledge and curiosity are the best tools in becoming a wise collector. Try to see as many authentic works as possible: museums, auction houses, and reputable dealers continue to serve as good sources of study. The more lamps one sees and examines, the more one learns about the medium and the marketplace. There have been numerous books written on Louis Comfort Tiffany and Tiffany Studios which prove to be valuable references in learning about the objects the firm produced and the techniques which were used to make them. It is always a good idea prior to acquiring any antique of value, to seek the professional advice of a recognised authority who knows the market and can offer a valuable knowledge in his/her area of expertise.

MaryBeth McCaffrey

A Daum winter landscape glass table lamp, the mottled orange and yellow body acid etched, signed on underside of base 'Daum Nancy', 16in (41cm) high.
£8,000–10,000 *P*

A Müller Frères glass and gilt bronze chandelier, the central domed glass shade of mottled pink, green, blue and white tone, supported by foliate bronze mounts, each shade marked 'Müller Frères, Lunéville', 27½in (70cm) high.
£1,200–1,400 *P*

A Daum cameo glass table lamp, the predominantly yellow body shading to amethyst at the edges and overlaid with streaked red, greyish white and deep blue, signed in cameo on shade and base 'Daum Nancy', and monogram, 26in (66cm) high.
£12,000–15,000 *P*

l. A Daum glass table lamp, the white flecked body shading to amethyst, acid etched and painted in natural colours with violet and leaves, signed on base 'Daum Nancy', 14½in (37cm) high.
£12,000–15,000 *P*

A Gallé cameo 'Magnolia' table lamp, the amber tinted body overlaid with 2 tones of rich ruby glass acid etched with branches of magnolia, signed in cameo on base and shade 'Gallé', 23in (28.5cm) high.
£18,000–22,000 *P*

r. A reproduction glass and bronze floor lamp, in the manner of Edgar Brandt and Daum, cast as a cobra rising from a basketwork base, its neck coiled around a mottled, frosted orange glass shade with wide everted rim, 64in (162cm) high.
£2,000–2,500 *Bon*

A Müller Frères cameo glass table lamp, the glass yellow tone streaked with colours, overlaid with red and brown glass acid etched with anemones, signed in cameo 'Müller Frères, Lunéville', 29in (73.5cm) high.
£10,000–12,000 *P*

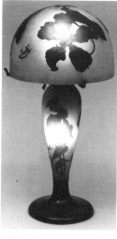

A Gallé cameo glass table lamp and shade, in purple glass on a yellow stained and frosted ground, each piece signed 'Gallé', 13in (33cm) high.
£5,000–6,000 *HAM*

A leaded glass lampshade, unmarked, but attributed to Tiffany, 12in (30.5cm) diam. **£1,200–1,500** *P*

An Almeric Walter pâte-de-verre panel, mounted as a table lamp, amber glass tinged with amethyst, moulded decoration of fish and seaweed, fitted for electricity, moulded signature 'A. Walter Nancy', 8½in (21.5cm) high.
£2,800–3,200 *C*

A Tiffany Studios bronze table lamp, and a glass shade in semi-opaque glass of yellow tones against a variegated green ground, stamped and applied marks, c1900, 21½in (55cm) high.
£9,500–12,000 *SS*

An Art Nouveau Tiffany style pewter table lamp, stamped on base 'C.I.D.', 26in (66cm) high.
£600–700 *MPHS*

A Tiffany Studio bronze and leaded glass table lamp, with 'Dogwood' border, the shade with green, pink, mauve and blue glass panels, shade stamped 'Tiffany Studios, New York', stand unmarked, some damage, 22in (56cm) high.
£6,500–10,000 *SBe*

A gilt bronze lamp base, probably French, fitted for electricity, 13½in (35cm).
£300–350 *SBe*

An acorn leaded glass and bronze table lamp, by Tiffany Studios, the shade with segments of green and amber, impressed 'Tiffany Studios, New York', 18½in (47cm) high.
£4,500–6,000 *C*

A French iron and glass lamp, with a mottled orange glass centre, signed 'Roby, Paris', c1900, 23½in (60cm) high.
£200–250 *SSS*

A patinated metal and glass table lamp, the shade with panels of cream and orange marbled glass, 25½in (56cm) high.
£400–450 *SBe*

An electroplated table lamp, modelled in the form of a young woman, fitted for electricity, 18½in (47cm) high.
£250–300 *SBe*

A cut glass biscuitière, with electroplated mount and cover, 8½in (47cm) high.
£250–300 *SBe*

A bronze table lamp with a leaded glass shade, with streaked white/beige glass, the rim with a frieze of pink flowers amidst green foliage, c1900, 23in (58.5cm) high.
£1,700–2,000 *SB*

An etched glass and wrought iron table lamp, with mottled orange glass shade, the shade etched 'Daum Nancy, France', base stamped 'Katona', 12in (30.5cm) high.
£3,500–4,000 *Bon*

An American Arts & Crafts Prairie School wall lantern, c1900. **£350–400** *ST*

A Lallemant vase mounted as a table lamp, with polychrome painted decoration, illustrating a nursery rhyme, with painted signature 'T. R. Lallemant, France', 9½in (24cm) high.
£350–400 *C*

A green patinated, bronzed metal figural lamp, on a veined marble base, inscribed 'Guerbe', stamped 'Le Verrier Paris', shade etched 'Daum Nancy, France', 15in (38cm) high.
£750–850 *Bon*

A Limousin spelter Art Deco table lamp, 16½in (42cm) high.
£150–200 *CDC*

A 'Le Verre Français' cameo glass and wrought iron table lamp, designed by Schneider, the pale green ground overlaid and etched with thorny berry-laden branches, striped cane signature on base, 15½in (39.5cm) high.
£2,500–3,000 *C*

A Tiffany bronze table lamp base, with pineapple decoration with brown patina, stamped 'Tiffany Studios New York 366', 23½in (60cm) high.
£3,000–3,500 *CNY*

An American copper table lamp, in the form of a Doric column, with 2 lamp holders, the shade in leaded green glass, the stepped base marked 'Gorham Co., Q497', and trademark, 19in (48cm) high.
£550–600 *P(S)*

An Austrian bronze lamp, the shade set with coloured stones, c1900, 20in (51cm) high.
£500–800 *ASA*

A glass and bronze desk lamp, by Tiffany Studios, the shade in iridescent peacock blue glass with radiating bands of silver dots, inscribed 'L.C.T. Favrile', the base impressed 'Tiffany Studios, New York 327 11413', 15in (38cm) high.
£950–1,100 *CNY*

A German silvered pewter and nautilus shell desk lamp, designed as either a wall or table lamp, monogram 'MH', and maker's symbol, c1900, 11in (28cm) high.
£1,500–1,700 *C*

A Laburnum leaded glass and bronze floor lamp, by Tiffany Studios, with yellow flower clusters amongst green leaves on a sky blue ground, impressed 'Tiffany Studios New York', 63in (160cm) high.
£20,000–25,000 *CNY*

An Agate Favrile glass and bronze table lamp, by Tiffany Studios, the deep amber baluster body banded with blue and ochre shading, between opalescent ribs, impressed 'Tiffany Studios New York', 14½in (37cm) high.
£900–1,000 *CNY*

l. A decorative gilt metal table lamp, modelled as a maiden, on a marble base, 29in (73.5cm) high.
£600–800 *P*

A gilt bronze table lamp, inscribed 'Raoul Larche', and impressed with the Siot Deceaville foundry seal, cast from a model by Raoul François Larche, wired for electricity, early 20thC, 17in (43cm) high.
£9,000–10,000 *CNY*

This is one of several models by Raoul Larche of 'La Loie' which were wired as table lamps. Known for her dramatic use of lighting and swirling scarves in her stage performances, Loie Fuller (1862–1928) was a great inspiration to artists in all media at the turn of the century.

An alabaster lamp, c1900, 36in (91.5cm) high.
£450–500 *SS*

A spelter figure, Libellule, designed as a lamp cast after a model by Auguste Moreau, printed metal tag 'Libellule par Aug. Moreau', c1900, 46in (116.5cm) high.
£1,600–2,000 *C*

A Sabino glass wall light, moulded mark internally 'Sabino No. 4684 Paris Déposé, c1930, 10in (25cm) high. **£700–900** *SB*

A glass hanging shade, with 6 pointed shades attached to a central hexagonal body, stencilled mark 'R. Lalique', 1920s, 31in (78.5cm) wide. **£2,600–3,000** *SB*

An iridescent glass shade, with feathered panels of blue and gold lustre against a white lustre ground, engraved mark 'Quezal', c1910, 6in (15cm) high. **£200–250** *SB*

An Art Deco lamp, partly gilded, with a spelter figure, 1930s, 24in (61cm) high. **£175–200** *F*

An Arts & Crafts copper hanging lantern, by the March brothers, 15in (38cm) high. **£75–150** *P*

An Art Deco brass and ivory lampstand, 1930s, 23½in (60cm) high. **£880–1,000** *SKC*

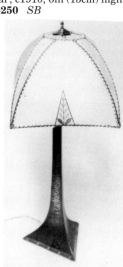

An Art Deco lamp, with pewter base and hessian shade covered in plastic, 24in (61cm) high. **£65–85** *LEX*

A decorative bronze table lamp, with a beaten copper shade, c1900, 23in (58.5cm) high. **£400–460** *SB*

An Art Deco alabaster, marble and spelter lamp, 1930s, 15in (38cm) high. **£95–105** *F*

A bronze and glass lamp, the shade signed 'Arsoli', the bronze signed 'Zach', fitted for electricity, c1910, 30in (76cm) high. **£800–1,200** *SB*

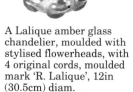

A Lalique amber glass chandelier, moulded with stylised flowerheads, with 4 original cords, moulded mark 'R. Lalique', 12in (30.5cm) diam. **£1,600–2,000** *CSK*

An Art Nouveau bronze lamp, c1900, 19in (48cm) high. **£1,200–1,500** *SB*

A Maignan gilt bronze lamp, signed in the maquette, foundry mark 'Eug. Blot Paris', c1900, 13½in (34cm) high. **£420–500** *SB*

DECORATIVE GLASS

The last ten years have been something of a roller coaster ride in terms of keeping in touch with Art Nouveau and Art Deco glass. Rapidly rising prices, followed by the big splash of the recession when prices dropped alarmingly, have recently been followed by a steady haul back to a more level and stable situation.

Until 1985, the market leaders – Gallé, Daum, Lalique and Argy-Rousseau were a firmly established collecting area – their pieces already relatively highly priced. A steady year-by-year increase in both demand and value was noticeable. It was a healthy situation, so it was not entirely welcome when the second half of the eighties saw prices accelerating so strongly that by 1989/90 it was almost a monthly occurrence. During this period, those of us actively buying and selling glass had to contend with a situation where it was never possible to replace stocks with similar pieces at similar prices. Wherever good examples were available, the prices had always increased.

It did not take long to realise what was happening. Along with other areas of art and antiques, Art Nouveau and Art Deco glass had become a 'commodity', another form of investment. This became clear to see when dark-suited gentlemen, previously unknown to the Decorative Arts market, appeared and bought very determinedly over a short period of time, then disappeared. I shall always remember a conversation with one such gentleman when meeting him for the first time. His interest lay with Argy-Rousseau glass and he let it be known he had 'a little over 500 pieces'! Thinking he must have been collecting for a considerable time, I was dumbstruck to learn that he had, in fact, only been buying for just over a year. An amazing example, his investment in Argy-Rousseau would have been at least £1million, possibly a great deal more!

Another significant factor in this phenomenon was the spectacular auction in 1988 in London of the Elton John collection of Art Nouveau and Art Deco, which included many fine examples of glass. Buyers flew in from all over the world – thus promoting very high prices. The down side to this situation was that prices really were rising too fast and, with hindsight, one can see that even if the recession had not brought everything to a halt, the market would inevitably have crashed through its own momentum. Towards the end of 1990 this is exactly what happened.

At this time good middle-range items in the £2,000–£20,000 price bracket dropped to around 45%–50% of the 1990 highs, the lowest point being reached in 1992. However, making price comparisons can only be a generalisation in such a diverse and varied field, and there are many exceptions.

Least affected by the recession are the very rare pieces which exhibit important techniques or designs. For example, the 'Rose de France' vase by Gallé which incorporates the marqueterie-sur-verre technique, together with applied and carved work in high relief, an example of which recently sold for £135,000. Such rare and important items may actually have increased in value through better appreciation as a result of the middle-range items no longer being over-valued.

Conversely, examples of Gallé's 'Rhododendron' lamp, which reached an astonishing £250,000, have recently sold for between £60,000 and £70,000! It will always be a very beautiful lamp, but for an item produced nearly 20 years after Gallé's death (d1904), an Art Nouveau 'stray' in the Art Deco period, its 1990 price was perhaps somewhat unrealistic. It may be that a finer discernment has come into play in addition to the effects of the recession.

Not until the end of 1993 could one feel with any confidence that the worst was over and that prices had, at last, 'bottomed out'. It is now evident that that has happened, as once again it has become possible to anticipate the prices at which items will sell and that confirms that the market has stabilised – albeit at the new lower level of prices. Today, middle-range items are probably up to 50%–60% of 1990 values. The well-known 'Snail' vases by Daum, for example, now sell at £8,000–£12,000 as against £16,000–£20,000 in 1990.

These same prices can also be applied to Lalique's popular Bacchantes vase and Suzanne figure (in opalescent glass). Glass by Argy-Rousseau was less affected due to its extra rarity and prices are probably around 70% of 1990 levels. Also, less affected are those items in the £500–£1,500 range, probably due to the greater numbers of buyers in this area.

Interestingly, there are even some areas where prices are now obviously strengthening: iridescent glass by Loetz being a notable example. This bodes well for the market as a whole, and for those collectors who stopped buying when prices rose strongly in the '80s prospects are now much more inviting.

The new, lower, perhaps more realistic, level of prices is also an encouragement to new buyers who, understandably, may have been intimidated by the high figures of the late eighties. Now, a beautiful example of Gallé or Lalique at, say, £1,500, that has been impossible to acquire for almost twice that amount, should be a very pleasing prospect to a serious collector.

Patrick Gould

A Lalique frosted and clear glass oval dish, etched 'R. Lalique', etched script mark 'France', slight reduction at rim, 17in (43cm) wide.
£400–800 *Bon*

A Lalique black glass box and cover, 'Pommier du Japon', moulded on the top with branches of prunus bossom, the sides finely ribbed, mouled on the base 'R. Lalique and Arys', 3⅓in (8.5cm) diam.
£1,000–1,500 *P*

A Lalique frosted and blue-stained nightlight, 'Hygenie', No. 10, with original bronze base, 6⅓in (16cm) high.
£700–900 *Bon*

A Lalique frosted glass clock, electric movement by ATO, enamelled chapter ring, marked 'No. 3' with 'France', 7in (18cm) high. **£1,000–1,200** *Bon*

A Lalique black glass ring, 'Fleurs', with solid domed top and intaglio moulded with florets and stems picked out with white enamelling, unsigned.
£400–600 *P*

A Lalique car mascot, 'Levrier', clear and satin finished glass moulded in intaglio, moulded signature 'R. Lalique, France', 2⅓in (7.5cm) high.
£1,600–2,000 *C*

A Lalique frosted and clear glass clock, the electric movement marked 'ATO', No. 10, without 'R', 4⅓in (11cm) high. **£800–1,000** *Bon*

A Lalique box and cover, 'Enfants', moulded with a band of naked children holding weights above their heads on a blue stained ground, the lid moulded with 5 tiers of rose bands similarly coloured, stencilled mark 'R. Lalique, France', c1930 3in (7.5cm) high. **£400–500** *S(S)*

A Lalique frosted glass ceiling dome, 'Charmille', minor chips and a small hole, 13⅓in (34cm) diam.
£1,000–1,200 *Bon*

r. A Lalique clock, the circular dial with black enamelled chapters, engraed 'R. Lalique, France', with chrome base enclosing light fitting, 7in (18cm) high.
£1,000–1,500 *C(S)*

A Lalique frosted glass clock, electric movement marked 'ATO', No. 3, with 'France', 8⅓in (22cm) wide.
£1,000–1,200 *Bon*

l. A Lalique frosted glass oviform vase, 'Archers', moulded with naked male archers aiming their bows at birds overhead, etched 'R. Lalique, France', 10½in (26.5cm) high.
£1,600–2,000 *P*

A Lalique enamelled globular vase, 'Baies', moulded overall in shallow relief with thorny branches and berries interwoven and heightened with black enamel, moulded 'R. Lalique' on base, 10½in (27cm).
£6,000–8,000 *P*

A Lalique blue opalescent 'Ceylan' vase, with raised budgerigar decoration, engraved 'R. Lalique, France', 9½in (23.5cm) high.
£1,800–2,200 *AG*

A Lalique smokey-grey glass vase, 'Archers', moulded with naked male archers aiming their bows at birds overhead, moulded 'R. Lalique', 10½in (26.5cm) high.
£1,800–2,200 *P*

r. A Lalique 'Avallon' vase, moulded with 6 birds perched among berry-laden branches, incised 'R. Lalique, No. 986, France' 5½in (14.5cm) high.
£1,000–1,200 *C(S)*

A Lalique frosted glass vase, in the form of two doves, signed 'Lalique, France', 1930s, 9½in (24cm) high.
£300–500 *N*

A Lalique green glass globular vase, 'Druides', signed 'R. Lalique France', and 'No. 937', 7in (18cm) high.
£650–800 *P*

A Lalique amber glass 'Chasseurs' vase impressed mark 'R. Lalique', 10½in 26.5cm) high.
£900–1,000 *SB*

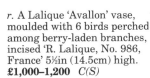

Six Lalique sherry glasses, 3¼in (8cm) high. **£60–80** *CSK*

l. Three Lalique perfume bottles, for Worth, deep blue, glear glass and star moulded, with moulded marks 'R. Lalique', 5, 3 and 4in (13, 8 and 10cm) high. **£200–300** *S*

Two Lalique glass perfume bottles, both heightened with blue, one of lozenge section, the other swollen cylindrical, engraved 'R. Lalique', and 'R. Lalique No. 478', 4 and 5in (10 and 12.5cm) high.
£250–350 *S*

A Lalique frosted and clear glass vase, 'Pierrefonds', one handle slightly ground on top, Mk. No. 3, 6in (15cm) high. **£1,500–2,000** *Bon*

A Lalique frosted glass vase and stopper, '12 Figurines avec Bouchon', Mk. No. 2, with 'France' in script, 11½in (29.5cm) high. **£2,200–2,600** *Bon*

A Lalique frosted glass statuette, 'Source de la Fontaine', heightened with siena stain, Mk. No. 3, with 'France', 28in (71cm) high. **£4,000–6,000** *Bon*

A Lalique frosted and clear glass vase, 'Bellecour', slight damage, Mk. No. 2, indistinctly marked 'France No. 9**', 11in (28cm) high. **£2,800–3,200** *Bon*

A Lalique frosted and black stained glass 'Peacock' lamp, Mk. No. 10, 16in (40.5cm) high. **£10,000–12,000** *Bon*

A Lalique frosted and clear glass bowl, moulded in relief with a design of hounds, Mk. No. 12 with 'France', 9½in (24cm) diam. **£350–400** *Bon*

A Lalique grey frosted glass vase and cover, 'Tourterelles', Mk. No. 2, 11½in (29cm) high. **£2,600–3,000** *Bon*

A Lalique opalescent deep bowl, 'Ondine Ouverte', moulded with a frieze of sirens, acid etched 'R. Lalique, France', 12in (30.5cm) diam. **£800–1,200** *CSK*

A Lalique frosted, opalescent and turquoise stained vase, 'Ceylan', Mk. No. 3, and a period lamp fitting with clear celluloid shade painted with similar parakeets, 18½in (47cm) high. **£1,800–2,200** *Bon*

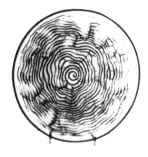

l. A Lalique opalescent glass bowl, Mk. No. 3, marked 'France', 11in (28cm) diam. **£400–500** *Bon*

A Lalique car mascot, 'Longchamps', in clear and satin finished glass, moulded signature 'R. Lalique', France, 5in (13cm) high.
£4,000–5,000 *C*

A Lalique car mascot, 'Archer', in clear and satin finished glass, etched 'R. Lalique France', 4½in (12cm) high.
£600–750 *C*

A Lalique plafonnier, in clear and satin finished glass, acid stamped signature 'R. Lalique, France', 14½in (37cm) diam.
£1,800–2,200 *C*

A pair of Lalique opalescent glass plafonniers, each bowl with acid signature 'R. Lalique France', 16½in (41cm) diam.
£1,800–2,200 *C*

A Lalique amber plafonnier, 'Saint Vincent', moulded signature 'R. Lalique', inscribed 'France', 13½in (24.5cm) wide.
£800–1,000 *C*

A Lalique plafonnier, the yellow frosted glass moulded with peaches and leaves, moulded 'R. Lalique, France', 15in (38cm) wide.
£1,200–1,500 *C*

A Lalique car mascot, 'Perche', in clear and satin finished glass engraved 'Lalique France', 3½in (9.5cm) wide.
£800–1,100 *C*

A St Christopher car mascot, by Lalique.
£400–500 *AAA*

René Lalique

The work of René Lalique spans both the Art Nouveau and Art Deco periods. He began his career as a designer of jewellery and was an innovator among goldsmiths in the 1890s, being more concerned with the craftsmanship and decorative elements of the work than its intrinsic value. His pieces at this time are recognised as the finest examples of Art Nouveau jewellery. By the 1900 Paris Exposition - 'the triumph of Art Nouveau' - the movement was actually on the wane. This, combined with the fact that he had more commissions than he could cope with and that numerous imitations of his work were appearing, made him turn elsewhere for inspiration. He found it in glass and exhibited some pieces at the Salon in 1902. In the same year he designed a new studio and set up a workshop where his most notable cire-perdue and glass panels were produced.

He was introduced to commercial glass production around 1907 when François Coty asked him to design labels for perfume bottles. In fact, Lalique designed the bottles as well. These were manufactured by Legras et Cie, until he opened his own small glassworks at Combs in 1909 to cope with the demands of this and other work. After WWI he opened a larger glassworks from which the bulk of his output was produced.

Just as Lalique had triumphed at the 1900 Paris Exposition with his Art Nouveau jewellery, so he dominated the 1925 Exposition, establishing himself as the leading exponent of mass-produced glassware. His designs by now were in the Art Deco style, but the earlier Art Nouveau influence was still apparent in some of the decorative elements. He was very much concerned with the commercial mass-production of his designs and he should be remembered as much as a pioneer of mass-produced art glass as for his earlier imaginative jewellery.

Beware of full crystal items produced during 1950s, all have intaglio moulded signature. Pre-WWII examples in demi crystal are not as white.

l. A Lalique opalescent globular vase 'Formose', moulded signature 'R. Lalique' 6½in (17cm) high. **£500–600** *C*

A Lalique brown stained vase, 'Milan', engraved signature 'R. Lalique, France, No. 1025', 11in (28cm) high.
£1,500–2,000 *C*

A Lalique amber glass vase, 'Avalon', moulded with birds among fruiting branches, incised 'R. Lalique, France', and '986', c1930, 5½in (14.5cm) high.
£1,600–2,000 *SBe*

A Lalique cobalt blue glass oval pendant, inscribed 'R. Lalique, France', 2in (5.5cm) wide.
£600–750 *C*

l. A pair of Lalique glass knife rests, moulded in intaglio with a dragonfly, heightened with deep blue staining, each engraved 'R. Lalique', c1920, 4in (10cm) wide.
£300–400 *S*

A Lalique amber glass vase, 'Formose', impressed 'R. Lalique', c1920, 7in (17.5cm) high.
£1,600–2,000 *SB*

A Lalique glass three-piece panel, c1920, each panel 11⅛in (27.5cm) high.
£1,800–2,200 *SB*

A Lalique vase, 'Oran', engraved 'R. Lalique, France', c1930, 10in (25cm) high.
£8,000–10,000 *SS*

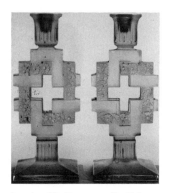

A pair of Lalique candlesticks, damaged, 9in (23cm) high.
£1,000–1,500 *C*

A Lalique opalescent glass vase, 'Paeon', the milky body heightened with blue staining, marked 'R. Lalique, France, No. 1017', c1925, 9½in (23.5cm)
£3,000–3,500 *SB*

l. A Lalique opalescent glass inkwell with cover, moulded 'Lalique', 6⅓in (16cm) diam.
£600–750 *SB*

A Lalique vase, 'Marisa', with graduated bands of fish, damaged, engraved signature 'R. Lalique, France, No. 1002', 9in (23cm) high. **£2,600–3,000** *C*

A Lalique glass statue, 'Source de la Fontaine', wheelcut 'R. Lalique France', mounted on a polished stone plinth, 22in (55cm) high.
£4,000–5,000 *Bon*

A Lalique 'Filix' glass bowl, the deep well moulded outside with a band of large fern leaves picked out with frosting, wheel engraved ' R. Lalique, France', c1927, 13in (33cm) diam.
£500–600 *S(S)*

A Lalique 'Roger' box and cover, moulded with long-tailed exotic birds perched in branches amongst cleart glass discs, engraved 'Lalique, France', c1927, 5in (12.5cm) diam.
£300–400 *S(S)*

A Lalique frosted and clear glass vase, 'Danaides', 7in (17.5cm) high.
£800–1,200 *Bon*

A Lalique moulded glass vase, 'Bacchantes', in satin finished glass with blue staining, incised signature 'R. Lalique France', c1930, 10in (25cm) high.
£2,500–3,500 *C*

A monumental mould blown vase, of frosted appearance, 'Palestre', with a continuous frieze of naked Olympian, 'Les Amis', engraved block capital mark 'R. Lalique', 17in (43cm) high.
£14,000–16,000 *Bon*

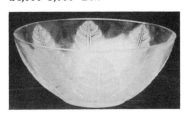

An amber glass shallow bowl, 'Martigues', marked 'R. Lalique', and wheel cut 'France', 14½in (36.5cm) high. **£1,800–2,200** *Bon*

A Lalique glass bowl, decorated with 5 opalescent milky swirling mermaids, marked 'R. Lalique France', 12in (30cm) high.
£1,800–2,200 *GC*

A Lalique opalescent glass box and cover, 'Deux Sirènes', engraved 'France No. 43', 10½in (26cm) diam.
£1,600–2,000 *Bon*

A frosted glass vase, 'Bacchantes', engraved mark in script 'Lalique', c1950, 10in (25cm) high.
£1,000–1,200 *Bon*

A frosted glass box, 'Paon', with a peacock perched on a bough, heightened with blue, engraved 'R. Lalique', 5in (12cm) diam. **£400–500** *Bon*

A glass box and cover, 'Libellules', moulded 'R. Lalique', 7in (17cm) wide. **£700–900** *Bon*

r. An opalescent bowl with beads graduating inside and forming a swirling pattern, with 'R. Lalique' in upper case, 8in (20cm) high. **£300–400** *P(M)*

A Lalique frosted glass vase, moulded with ibex, marked on the base 'R. Lalique, France', 8in (20cm) high. **£260–360** *P*

A Lalique blue tinted opalescent glass bowl, moulded with fishes. **£300–400** *GIL*

A frosted desk clock, 'Roitelets', the glass face surrounded by a band of wrens in flight, with Omega timepiece, stencilled 'R. Lalique France', 8in (20cm) high. **£2,600–3,000** *Bon*

l. A Lalique opalescent table clock, 'Inseparables No. 765', slight damage, 4⅛in (12cm) high. **£1,200–1,400** *Bea*

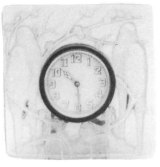

A Lalique hanging lamp in the form of a stylised globe artichoke, with blue enamelled detailing, marked on bottom 'R. Lalique France', with metal rosettes, hooks and cords for suspension, 9in (22.5cm) high. **£150–200** *P*

l. A Lalique opalescent bowl, 'Vase Coquilles', 9½in (24cm) diam. **£350–400** *Bea*

A clear and green stained bowl, 'Coupe Filix', moulded on the underside with broad leaves, wheel cut mark 'R. Lalique France', 13in (33cm) diam. **£500–600** *Bon*

A heavy Lalique glass vase, stencilled mark 'R. Lalique', 6½in (17cm) high. **£300–350** *S*

An opalescent and sienna stained dish, 'Anges', moulded in intaglio with facing pairs of kneeling angels, wheel cut 'R. Lalique France', 14½in (37cm) diam. **£1,600–2,000** *Bon*

A Lalique opalescent dish, decorated with birds, 8in (20cm) diam. **£200–250** *ASA*

A Nemours Lalique blue stained bowl, moulded 'R. Lalique France', 10in (25cm) high. **£400–500** *CSK*

A frosted glass powder box, 'Degas', engraved mark in script 'R. Lalique France No. 66', and moulded 'Lalique' on cover, 2½in (6.5cm) diam. **£500–600** *Bon*

A clear and frosted glass car mascot, 'Archer', intaglio moulded 'R. Lalique France', 5in (12.5cm) high. **£500–600** *Bon*

A Lalique car mascot, in clear and satin finished glass, moulded signature 'R. Lalique France', c1930, 6in (15.5cm) wide. **£800–1,000** *C*

A glass car mascot, 'Hirondelle', with pale amethyst tint, relief moulded mark 'R. Lalique France', rim chip base underside, 6in (14.5cm) high. **£1,200–1,500** *Bon*

A frosted and polished glass car mascot, 'Tête d'Aigle', relief moulded 'R. Lalique', circular base offset polished, 4½in (11.5cm) high. **£1000–1,200**

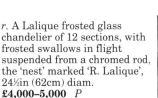

A Lalique frosted glass car mascot, 'Longchamps', moulded 'R. Lalique France', 5in (12.5cm) high. **£2,000–3,000** *P*

r. A Lalique frosted glass chandelier of 12 sections, with frosted swallows in flight suspended from a chromed rod, the 'nest' marked 'R. Lalique', 24½in (62cm) diam. **£4,000–5,000** *P*

A Lalique frosted glass car mascot, 'Vitesse', moulded 'R. Lalique France', and having original Breves Galleries, Knightsbridge chromed mount with coloured filter, 7in (17.5cm) high. **£2,600–3,000** *P*

l. A Lalique 'Epis No. 1' stained glass plate, the border moulded and stained in blue with a repeated band of wheatears, with a fluted radiating centre, moulded 'R. Lalique', engraved 'France', c1922, 12½in (31.5cm) diam. **£100–120** *ASA*

A Lalique frosted glass car mascot, 'Petite Libellule', with moulded veining, moulded 'Lalique France', and engraved 'R. Lalique France', 6½in (16cm) high. **£1,200–1,500** *P*

A Lalique blue opalescent glass vase, 'Soucis', in clear and satin finished glass, acid stamped signature 'R. Lalique', 6⅛in 17cm) high.
£1,200–1,500 *C*

A Lalique glass vase, 'Coqs et Plumes', heightened with blue staining, signed 'R. Lalique, France', 6in (15.5cm) high.
£500–600 *P*

A Lalique vase, 'Gui', the clear satin finished glass with turquoise staining, engraved signature 'Lalique', rim slightly ground, 7in (17cm) high.
£500–600 *C*

A Lalique frosted glass vase, 'Camargue', acid stamped 'R. Lalique, France', 11in (28.5cm) high.
£2,000–2,400 *C*

A Lalique amber glass vase of almost globular form moulded in high relief with spiralling motifs, 'Tourbillon', 8in (20cm) high, signed 'R. Lalique, France' and 'No. 973'.
£5000–6000

A Lalique blue opalescent cylindrical vase, 'Alicante', satin finished glass, engraved 'R Lalique', France, 9½in (24.5cm) high.
£3,500–4,000 *C*

A Lalique blue opalescent cylindrical vase, 'Danaides', in clear and blue satin finished glass, engraved 'R. Lalique, France, No. 972', 7in (18cm) high.
£1,600–2,000 *CEd*

A Lalique opalescent vase, 'Six Figurines et Masques', moulded and etched 'R. Lalique, France', with lamp fitting, 10in (25cm).
£2,500–3,000 *C*

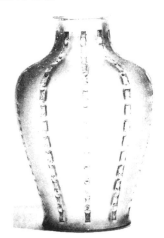

A Lalique opalescent glass ashtray, with beetle design, 5½in (14cm) diam.
£300-400 *ASA*

A Lalique baluster vase, the satin finished glass with blue staining, moulded signature 'R. Lalique', 9½in (23.5cm) high.
£500–600 *C*

A clear, frosted and stained table lamp, stencilled mark 'R. Lalique France', c1931, 13in (32cm) high.
£6,000–7,000 *Bon*

A clear frosted and blue stained vase, 'Bordures Epines', with everted rim moulded with trailing thorned branches, wheel cut mark 'R. Lalique', 8in (20cm) high.
£550–700 *Bon*

A Lalique glass vase of trumpet shape, the sides moulded with ears of barley, with pale brown staining, marked on base 'R. Lalique, France', 6½in (16.5cm) high.
£450–550 *P*

A Lalique opalescent glass vase, 'Chardons', heightened with blue staining, marked 'R. Lalique France' on base, 7½in (18.5cm) high.
£700–750 *P*

A blue stained frosted glass vase, the ground detailed with vertical ribbing, stencilled 'R. Lalique, France', 6½in (16cm) high.
£500–700 *Bon*

A clear and frosted glass vase, 'Yvelines', the handles moulded with deer amidst leaves spreading on to the vase, etched 'R. Lalique, France', 8in (20cm) high. **£750–800** *Bon*

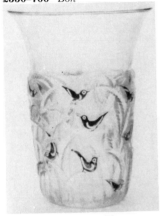

A clear, frosted and blue enamelled vase, 'Bornes', wheel cut mark 'R. Lalique, France', 9in (23cm) high.
£3,300–3,600 *Bon*

A smoked glass vase, 'Béliers', moulded at the rim with a pair of stylised rams, wheel cut 'R. Lalique', 7½in (19cm) high.
£1,500–2,000 *Bon*

A frosted, clear and green stained vase, 'Camees', relief moulded mark 'R. Lalique', 10in (25.5cm) high. **£2,000–3,000** *Bon*

A Lalique opalescent glass vase, 'St. François', with frosted surface, etched 'R. Lalique' on base, 7in (18cm) high. **£800–1,200** *P*

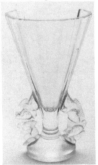

A clear and satin vase, 'Roitelets', stencilled 'R. Lalique, France', 11½in (29cm) high.
£1,000–1,200 *Bon*

A satin opalescent vase, 'Ronsard', the 2 handles moulded as semi-circular garlands of flowers, each enclosing a seated nude female figure, fracture to one arm, stencilled 'R. Lalique', engraved 'France', 8½in (21cm) high.
£1,500–2,000 *Bon*

A Lalique glass vase, heightened with blue staining, signed on base 'R. Lalique', 9in (23cm) high. **£950–1,100** *P*

A Lalique opalescent glass vase, engraved mark 'R. Lalique France', c1920.
£600–750 *SB*

A Lalique opalescent glass vase, 'Poissons', detailed with green stain, moulded mark 'R. Lalique', c1920, 9½in (24cm) high.
£1,800–2,200 *SB*

A Lalique frosted glass dahlia perfume bottle, c1930, 7in (17.5cm) high.
£450–550 *MT*

r. A Lalique frosted inkwell and cover, 'Trois Papillons', moulded 'R. Lalique', 3½in (9cm) wide.
£700–900 *Bon*

A set of 6 clear glass footed beakers, moulded with bands of leaping fish stained in blue, stencilled 'R. Lalique', 3½in (9cm) high.
£500–600 *CSK*

A drinking set, 'Hespérides', with electroplated carrying basket, the glass with acid-stamped signature 'R. Lalique', jug 8½in (22cm) high.
£1,000–1,200 *C*

l. A clear and sepia-stained claret jug and stopper, the handle moulded as a satyr mask with horns, etched script mark 'R. Lalique pour Cusenier', 9½in (24cm) high.
£800–1,000 *Bon*

A 17-piece drinking set, with moulded motif incorporating 2 male nudes, with acid-stamped and engraved signatures 'R. Lalique, France, No. 5084'.
£2,000–2,500 *C*

r. A plafonnier with gilt-metal mounts and suspension chains, damaged, moulded signature 'R. Lalique', 20½in (52cm) diam.
£2,200–2,400 *C*

A grey-stained frosted glass vase, 'Esterel', wheel engraved 'R. Lalique, France', 6in (15cm) high.
£150–200 *C*

A frosted and opalescent bowl, signed on base 'R. Lalique, France', c1930, 3½in (9cm) diam.
£400–500 *GH*

A grey stained opalescent vase, 'Oléron', moulded with a shoal of leaping fish, etched script mark 'R. Lalique, France, No. 1008'.
£600–750 *Bon*

An opalescent and clear vase, moulded in relief beneath the rim with poppy flowerheads, stencilled mark 'R. Lalique, France', 5½in (14cm) high.
£800–1,000 *Bon*

A Lalique opalescent vase, in milky glass with turquoise staining, engraved mark 'Lalique', 1920s, 9in (23cm) high.
£250–300 *SB*

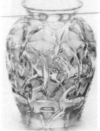

A blue stained clear and frosted vase, 'Chamois', moulded with panels of chamois antelope, stencilled 'R. Lalique, France', 5½in (14cm) high.
£800–1000 *Bon*

A frosted and opalescent vase, 'Pinson', moulded with sparrows among berried branches, all above a narrow foot, stencilled mark 'R. Lalique', 7in (18cm) high.
£1,200–1,800 *Bon*

A blue stained opalescent vase, 'Tournai', moulded with vertical panels of leafy branches, stencilled 'R. Lalique, France,' 5in (13cm) high.
£600–700 *Bon*

A Lalique table lamp, the clear satin finished glass with amber staining, etched and engraved signature 'R. Lalique', 10½in (26cm) high.
£5,000–6,000 *C*

l. A frosted, clear and amethyst stained vase, 'Charmille', moulded with overlapping beech leaves, intaglio moulded 'R. Lalique', 14in (33.5cm) high.
£1,600–2,000 *Bon*

A red-amber vase, 'Aras', moulded on the body with crested parakeets among berried branches, intaglio moulded 'R. Lalique', 9in (23cm) high.
£2,600–3,000 *Bon*

A Lalique frosted glass bottle and domed stopper, 'Enfants', base rim ground and polished, Mk. No.1, 4in (9cm) high. **£250–350** *Bon*

A Lalique frosted clear and black enamelled box, 'Roger'. **£500–600** *Bon*

A Lalique frosted glass mistletoe vase, c1930, 7in (17.5cm) high. **£300–400** *MT*

l. A Lalique clear scent bottle, 'Imprudence', designed for Worth, formed as a series of graduated discs, including the stopper, Mk. No. 1 with 'France', base with paper label printed with 'Fatice', 3in (7.5cm) high. **£200–300** *Bon*

This bottle contains its original contents, and is sealed.

r. A Lalique opalescent 'Bruce' parfum bottle, 'Papillons', Mk. No. 10, 7½in(19cm) high. **£1,200–1,500** *Bon*

A Lalique spherical frosted glass scent bottle and stopper, 'Dans la Nuit', moulded in relief with stars. the reverse stained blue, in original box, moulded 'R. Lalique', 3in (8cm) high. **£250–300** *CSK*

A set of 3 Lalique scent bottles, made for D'Orsay, heightened with brown staining, each moulded 'R Lalique', having paper labels for 'Fleurs de France', 'Charme D'Orsay' and 'La Flambe-D'Orsay', original fitted case, each bottle 3½in (9cm) high. **£400–500** *P*

A stylish frosted and enamelled scent bottle, designed for Lucien Lelong, heightened with black enamel, Mk. No. 10 with 'France', original chromed and enamelled metal case, echoing the design of the bottle, the base with 'Lucien Lelong' in stylish script, and 'VDSA 11876 1931', 4½in (11.5cm) overall. **£1,200–1,500** *Bon*

A Lalique opalescent and frosted glass encrier, '4 Sirènes', heightened with turquoise stain, Mk. No. 6, 6½in (16cm) diam. **£1,000–1,200** *Bon*

A Lalique opalescent jade green glass vase, 'Ormeaux', of spherical form with narrow neck and everted rim, moulded in relief with overlapping leaves, chips to rim and pontil, etched 'R. Lalique', No. 985, 6½in (16cm) high. **£1,200–1,700** *CSK*

r. A Lalique perfume bottle and stopper, 'Althea', base moulded, with rare 'RL' mark and 'Brevète', 4in (10cm) high. **£900–1,100** *Bon*

A Lalique glass vase, engraved signature, c1930, 8in (20cm) diam. £500–600 *SS*

A Lalique glass bowl and cover, heightened with pink-brown staining, engraved mark 'R. Lalique France No. 614', c1920, 6in (15cm) high. £1,000–1,200 *S*

A Lalique globular glass vase, 'Sauterelles', moulded with green stained grasshoppers on a matt blue stained ground, engraved in block letters 'R. Lalique', 11in (28cm) high. £1,000–1,200 *P*

Three Lalique glass perfume bottles, one for 'Jasmine' by Coty, with green staining, one moulded as a dahlia, green enamel details, one moulded with beaded swags, moulded 'R. Lalique', c1920, 5½in (14cm) high. £200–400 each *S*

A Lalique blue opalescent glass bowl, moulded with budgerigars, etched 'R. Lalique France', 9in (23cm) diam. £1,000–1,200 *CSK*

A Lalique frosted and polished glass vase, 'Martin Pêcheurs', with green and grey staining, damaged, moulded 'R. Lalique', 9½in (24.5cm) high. £1,500–2,000 *Bon*

A Lalique opalescent blue-stained vase, 'Tournesol', etched script 'R. Lalique, France', 4½in (11.5cm) high. £600–650 *Bon*

A Lalique cockerel mascot, engraved, c1920, 8in (20cm) high. £800–1,000 *S*

r. A Lalique car mascot, 'Victoire', moulded signature, minor chips, c1930, 10in (25cm) high. £1,000–1,500 *SS*

A Lalique glass scent bottle, 'Origan', made for D'Héraud, moulded on one side with the face of a girl with goat's horns, heightened with brown staining, with original box, 2½in (6.5cm) high. £600–700 *P*

A Lalique smoked glass two-handled vase, the handle moulded with flowerheads and foliage, moulded Lalique mark, 5⅓in (14cm) diam.
£400–600 *WW*

A Cristal Lalique glass paperweight, 'Perche', moulded as a fish resting on its dorsal fins, moulded on edge R. Lalique, and signed on base Lalique France, 4in (10cm) high.
£150–300 *P*

A set of 6 Lalique glasses, heightened with silver grey staining, signed in script 'R. Lalique France', 4in (10cm) high, in original Lalique fitted case for '24 Place Vendôme, Paris'.
£1,600–2,000 *P*

r. A Lalique blue stained scent bottle and stopper, catalogued 'Amphitrite', inscribed 'R. Lalique, France', 4in (10cm) high.
£1,600–2,000 *Bea*

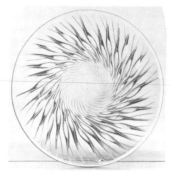

A Lalique opalscent glass shallow dish, etched mark, 14in (35.5cm) high. **£500–600** *WW*

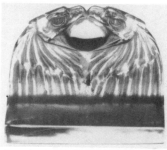

A sepia stained, clear and frosted presse-papiers, 'Deux Aigles', moulded as 2 eagle heads, jointly gripping a sphere in their beaks, moulded in intaglio R. Lalique, 3in (8cm) high.
£400–500 *Bon*

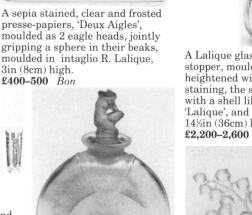

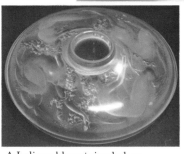

A Lalique blue stained glass inkwell, moulded with 4 mermaids, moulded 'Lalique' signature, 6in (15cm) diam.
£800–1,000 *P(Re)*

A grey stained clear glass cendrier, 'Archers', the everted rim moulded with panels of kneeling archers, moulded 'R. Lalique', 4½in (11.5cm) diam.
£400–500 *Bon*

A Lalique glass carafe and stopper, moulded in high relief, heightened with silver grey staining, the stopper moulded with a shell like spiral, moulded 'Lalique', and engraved 'France', 14½in (36cm) high.
£2,200–2,600 *P*

A frosted and clear glass scent bottle, 'Claire Fontaine', the stopper moulded as a spray of lily of the valley, etched 'Lalique, France', with 'Made in France' and 'Cristal Lalique' stickers, c1950, 4⅓in (12cm) high.
£100–150 *Bon*

r. A Lalique clock, with Swiss 8-day movement set in a milky blue panel with naked female figures, in an onyx and malachite frame, marked 'Lalique' in capitals, 5in (12.5cm) high.
£1,500–2,000 *GSP*

A Lalique amethyst and clear glass scent bottle, 'Flacon Muguet', the stopper formed as a spray of lily of the valley in frosted and polished glass, unmarked, 4in (10cm) high.
£3,000–3,500 *Bon*

A Lalique glass perfume bottle and stopper, moulded 'R. Lalique', 1920s, 5in (12.5cm) high. **£500–600** *SB*

r. A Lalique frosted glass statuette, 'Source de la Fontaine', on a wooden base, incorporating lamp fitment, 21in (53cm) high. **£2,000–2,500** *P*

An opalescent and frosted glass figure of a nude female dancer, 'Thais', her right hand slightly reduced, etched script mark 'R. Lalique, France', 8½in (21.5cm) high. **£2,500–3,000** *Bea*

l. An electric blue glass vase, 'Epines', intaglio moulded 'R. Lalique', 9½in (23cm) high. **£800–1,000** *Bon*

A Lalique frosted glass vase, 'Nefliers', moulded in relief with slender leaves and blossom of a medlar tree, heightened with pale mauve staining, signed on base 'R. Lalique, 5½in (14cm) high. **£300–500** *P*

r. A frosted glass figurine of a naked young woman, 'Grande Nue, Longs Cheveux', etched script mark 'R. Lalique, France, No. 836', 16in (40.5cm) high. **£7,500–8,500** *Bon*

A Lalique frosted glass vase, moulded with a thistle design and stained in light blue, signed ' R. Lalique, France, No. 979,' 8½in (21.5cm) high. **£600–700** *Bea*

Above left. A Lalique 'Alicante' vase, blue tinted with moulded budgerigar heads and wheat ears, etched signature 'R. Lalique, France', with removable fittings for use as a table lamp, 10in (25.5cm) high. **£1,000–1,500**
r. A Lalique 'Laurier' vase, in blued opalescent glass, incised mark and 'No. 947', 7in (18cm) high. **£400–600** *DN*

A Lalique pale brown opaque glass vase, 'Six Figurines et Masques', signed on base, 9½in (24cm) high. **£1,500–2,000** *P(Re)*

A large Lalique frosted glass vase, 'Penthièvre', signed on base 'R. Lalique France No. 1011', 10½in (25.5cm) high. **£2,500–3,000** *P*

An opalescent vase, 'Dordogne', intaglio moulded and engraved script mark 'R. Lalique, France', 7in (18cm) high. **£1,200–1,500** *Bon*

r. A blue stained opalescent vase, 'Coquilles', etched script mark 'R. Lalique, France', 7½in (18.5cm) high. **£700–800** *Bon*

An electric-blue frosted and polished vase, 'Perruches', moulded with billing parakeets on prunus boughs, traces of white satin, etched script mark 'R. Lalique, France, No. 876', 10in (25.5cm) high.
£6,000–7,500 *Bon*

A glass vase, moulded with a frieze of stylised antelopes, heightened with blue staining, stencilled mark 'R. Lalique France', 5in (12.5cm) high.
£700–900 *Bon*

An opalescent frosted and blue stained glass vase, stencilled 'R. Lalique, 9in (22cm) high.
£1,400–1,700 *Bon*

A frosted, clear and blue stained vase, 'Aigrettes', moulded with egrets in flight, chips to footrim, wheel cut mark, 'R. Lalique, France', 10in (25cm) high.
£2,600–3,000 *Bon*

A Lalique opalescent glass vase, 'Salmonides', heightened with matt blue staining, impressed 'R. Lalique, France, No. 1015', 11½in (29cm) high.
£6,000–7,500 *P*

An early, bluish-grey stained frosted vase, 'Ceylan', moulded with facing pairs of budgerigars perched on budding branches, minute chips to rim, unsigned, 13⅓in (34cm). **£3,500–4,000** *Bon*

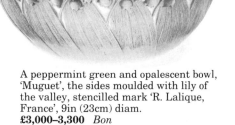

A Lalique frosted glass bowl, heightened with blue staining, marked on base 'R. Lalique, France', 9½in (24cm) diam.
£500–600 *P*

A frosted, clear and sepia stained surtout, 'Faisan', moulded with 4 panels each with an Oriental pheasant and serpentine garland interspersed by slender panels with candle scone surmounts, the base with stepped form, engraved script mark 'Lalique, France', 5in (14cm) high.
£750–1,000 *Bon*

r. A Lalique opalescent glass bowl, 'Coupe Calypso', marked on base in block 'R. Lalique France', 12in (30cm) high.
£2,500–3,000 *P*

A peppermint green and opalescent bowl, 'Muguet', the sides moulded with lily of the valley, stencilled mark 'R. Lalique, France', 9in (23cm) diam.
£3,000–3,300 *Bon*

A clear and satin polished mascot, 'Longchamps', damaged, moulded 'R. Lalique, France', 5in (12.5cm). **£6,000–6,500** *Bon*

A clear and frosted table clock, 'Pierrots', stencilled 'R. Lalique, France', 5in (12.5cm). **£900–1,000** *Bon*

A Lalique opalescent statuette, 'Moyenne Voilée', engraved 'R. Lalique, France', 5½in (14cm) high. **£1,000–1,500** *Bon*

A Lalique vase, in clear and satin finished glass, decorated with swallows in flight, moulded Lalique signature and engraved 'France', c1939, 9½in (24cm) high. **£1,000–1,200** *C*

l. A Lalique cockerel mascot, signed, 8in (20cm) high. **£800–1,000** *ASA*

An amethyst tinted polished car mascot, 'Têtes d'Eperviers', with chromium plated base, damaged, moulded 'Lalique, France', 2½in (6.5cm) high. **£1,200–1,500** *Bon*

A clear, frosted and sienna stained chalice, damaged, engraved 'Lalique', 7in (18cm) high. **£1,500–2,000** *Bon*

l. A set of 8 wine glasses, stem moulded with bunches of grapes, with engraved signature 'R. Lalique, France', 5in (13cm) high. **£900–1,200** *C*

r. An opalescent and frosted glass hanging shade with gilt metal suspension cords, wheel-cut 'R. Lalique, France', and engraved 'No. 385' in script, 12in (30cm) diam. **£600–750** *CSK*

A lamp base, 'Marisa', the milky-white glass moulded with fish, engraved signature 'R. Lalique, France', 9in (23cm) high.
£2,000–2,600 *C*

A plafonnier, moulded and engraved signature 'R. Lalique', 12½in (32cm) diam.
£1,000–1,200 *C*

l. An amber pendant, with the head of a young woman, etched 'Lalique', 1½in (4cm) high.
£400–500 *Bon*

l. An opalescent pendant, with a spray of lily of the valley, moulded 'Lalique', 1½in (4cm) long.
£450–500 *Bon*

r. A glass pendant, moulded with a woman and a dove, engraved signature 'R. Lalique, France'. **£400–500** *C*

A frosted glass hanging shade, 'Acanthus', inscribed 'R. Lalique, France', 18in (45cm) diam.
£900–1,200 *CSK*

l. A clear and frosted scent bottle, 'Tulipes', with traces of sienna staining, moulded 'R. Lalique, France', 3in (7.5cm) high.
£300–350 *Bon*

A blue-stained, frosted and clear decanter, 'Carafe Coquilles', engraved R. Lalique, France, with applied retailer's label, 13½in (34cm) high.
£800–1,000 *Bon*

l. A frosted pendant, in the form of a perfume amphora, engraved 'R. Lalique', 1½in (4cm) high.
£1,200–1,400 *Bon*

A mirror-pendant, the white metal mounted glass with a sea-sprite, the reverse with bevelled edged mirror, the frame stamped 'Lalique', 3½in (9cm) long.
£500–600 *C*

A frosted glass atomiser with gilt metal collar and plunger, marked 'Lalique, France', in block capitals, 3½in (9.5cm) wide.
£500–600 *P*

r. An amber-stained scent bottle and stopper, 'Pan', with moulded signature 'R. Lalique' and inscribed 'Lalique', 5in (13cm) high.
£500–600 *C*

l. A frosted glass atomiser, enamelled in orange, moulded 'R. Lalique, France', mounts stamped 'Le Parisien', 5½in (13.5cm) high.
£400–500 *CSK*

An amber glass pendant, engraved 'R. Lalique', 2½in (6cm) high.
£550–650 *Bon*

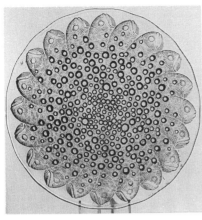

A clear blue stained dish, 'Roscoff', the underside moulded with radiating fish, the centre with a myriad of bubbles, engraved 'R. Lalique France', 14in (36cm) diam.
£800–1,000 *Bon*

A glass pendant, in white metal frame, the foil backed and black stained glass with relief decoration of a nymph in a wooded landscape, the reverse with mirror, with engraved signature 'R. Lalique France', 3in (8cm) long.
£600–750 *C*

A dark blue frosted dish, 'Phalènes', moulded to the underside with a stylised flower, the flat rim moulded in intaglio with moths, slight reduction to rim, wheel-cut 'R. Lalique France', 15in (38cm) diam. **£3,000–3,500** *Bon*

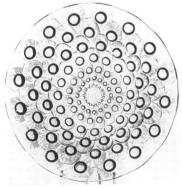

An opalescent dish, moulded on the underside with a peacock feather motif, engraved 'R. Lalique France', 12in (30.5cm) high.
£300–350 *Bon*

A glass pendant in white metal frame, the gold foil backed and black stained glass, with relief decoration of a maiden's face framed with flowers, the reverse with mirror, the frame stamped 'Lalique', 3in (8cm) long.
£600–750 *C*

A green glass broch, 'Sauterelles', signed 'LALIQUE', 3in (8cm) long.
£1,600–2,000 *CNY*

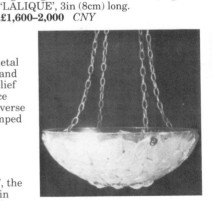

A frosted glass plafonnier of hemispherical form, 'Charmes', moulded in relief with overlapping beach leaves, with suspension chain and ceiling rose, moulded 'R. Lalique', 13½in (35cm) diam.
£650–850 *CSK*

l. An amber glass plafonnier, 'Soleil', the exterior moulded in relief with stylised sunburst motifs, small chip to rim moulded 'R Lalique', 12in (30.5cm) diam.
£1,200–1,700 *CSK*

r. A frosted glass plaffonier, 'Stalactites', moulded as pendant icicles, minor chips, wheel-cut 'R. Lalique', 10½in (26cm) diam.
£1,500–2,000 *CSK*

A black opaque pendant, moulded with 2 panels of wasps, heads facing inwards and with down-curved bodies, pierced at the top and base for supension cord and tassel, engraved 'R. Lalique', 2in (5cm) long.
£800–1,000 *Bon*

A clear and frosted glass chandelier, 'Charmes', moulded twice 'R Lalique', 14in (36cm) diam. **£1,500–2,500** *CNY*

A black glass scent bottle and stopper, moulded at each corner with a woman in long dress, moulded mark 'Lalique, AmbrE d'Orsay', original box, 5in (13cm) high. **£1,000–1,200** *CSK*

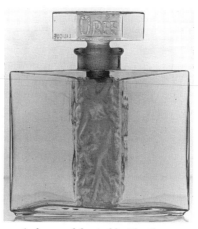

A clear and frosted bottle, the stopper moulded with the words 'Orée, Claire Paris', engraved 'Lalique' on stopper, 3in (8cm) high. **£1,400–1,700** *Bon*

A black glass bottle, with a central panel moulded with 'Le Parfum NN Forvil', and 'R. Lalique', 3½in (9cm) high. **£3,000–4000** *Bon*

A clear and frosted glass scent bottle and stopper, 'Amphyrite', traces of brown staining, moulded marks 'Lalique', 4in (10cm) high. **£1,400–1,700** *CSK*

A clear and russet-stained bottle, 'La Belle Saison', for Houbigant, moulded 'R. Lalique', 5½in (14.5cm) high. **£1,000–1,500** *Bon*

A clear glass scent bottle for Molinard, 'Le Baiser du Faune', outer ring for scent, intaglio moulded 'R. Lalique', 6in (15cm) high. **£1,600–2,000** *Bon*

A clear glass scent bottle, 'Paquerettes', with tiara stopper, for Roger et Gallet, stopper moulded 'Lalique', 3in (8cm) high. **£3,000–3,500** *Bon*

r. A glass perfume bottle, the stopper moulded as the figure of a maiden, moulded 'Lalique', with extended 'L', 4in (10cm) high. **£800–1,000** *P*

r. A cologne bottle 'Fleurettes', the stopper decorated with blue stained flower border, damaged, moulded signature 'Lalique', 8in (20cm) high. **£400–500** *C*

r. A frosted glass seal, 'Souris', damaged, engraved 'R. Lalique, France, No. 185', 4½in (11cm) high. **£1,200–1,500** *Bon*

A Lalique hanging light, 'Boule de Gui', composed of 2 hemispherical and 8 rectangular glass panels, linked by metal rings to form a globe, moulded with mistletoe, wired for electricity, 17½in (45cm) high.
£5,000–7,000 *C*

A frosted plafonnier, 'Deux Sirènes', moulded with 2 swimming water nymphs, their hair forming streams of bubbles, with matching ceiling rose, moulded 'R. Lalique', 15½in (39cm) diam.
£3,500–4,500 *Bon*

An opalescent glass and chromium plated metal table lamp, 'Coquilles', moulded with 4 clam shells, suspended from a C-shaped mount on stepped circular base, wheel-cut 'R. Lalique France', 12in (31cm) high.
£800–1,000 *Bon*

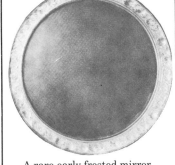

l. A frosted glass vase, 'Druids', moulded with entwined sprigs of mistletoe with polished clusters of berries in relief, moulded to base 'R. Lalique', 7in (18cm) high.
£500–700 *P*

A rare early frosted mirror, 'Anemones', moulded with flowerheads, with metal easel support, impressed 'Lalique', 15in (38cm) diam.
£4,000–5,000 *Bon*

A vase, 'Laurier', with raised leaves and berries in blue, etched near the base 'R. Lalique', 7in (17cm) high.
£700–900 *P(M)*

A clear glass vase, 'Paquerettes', moulded in relief with stylised daisy-like blooms against a heavily textured ground heightened with black staining, etched 'R. Lalique France', 7½in (19cm) high. **£700–900** *P*

A clear and frosted vase, 'Annecy', moulded with alternating waved and serrated horizontal bands, stencilled 'R. Lalique France', 6in (15cm). **£600–700** *Bon*

A turquoise stained vase, 'Oursin', the clear and satin finished glass moulded with protruding bubbles, with acid stamped signature 'R. Lalique France', 7½in (19cm) high.
£600–700 *C*

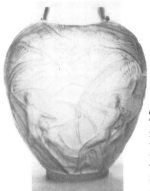

l. A grey stained vase, 'Archers', the satin finished glass moulded with archers and eagles, with engraved signature 'R. Lalique France No. 893', 10½in (26cm) high.
£1,600–2,000 *C*

r. An opalescent, clear and blue stained ashtray, 'Cendrier Statuette', in the centre a miniature 'Source de la Fontaine' figure, holding a lotus, etched 'R. Lalique', 4½in (12cm) high.
£500–600 *Bon*

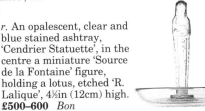

A Lalique black glass seal, 'Bleuet', on solid base and moulded with cornflowers, heightened with green staining, with metal base engraved with monogram, signed on edge 'R. Lalique', 2in (5cm) high.
£250–350 *P*

A Lalique opalescent glass plafonnier, 'Deux Sirènes', converted into a table lamp, comprising an oval marble base of 4 chrome bun feet, surmounted by semi-circular shade in chrome metal mount, minor chips, 15½in (39.5cm) high.
£700–800 *CSK*

A Lalique opalescent glass vase, 'Ceylan', moulded in relief, with 4 pairs of lovebirds perched amid prunus blossom, heightened with blue staining, etched 'R. Lalique France,' complete with original mica shade of octagonal outline painted with lovebirds amid berried boughs, and with detachable electrical mount, 20in (50.5cm) high.
£1,800–2,200 *P*

A set of 6 Lalique conical wine glasses, 'Strasbourg' the stems moulded in relief with 2 naked figures gripping hands, stencil etched 'R. Lalique', 6in (15cm) high.
£450–550 *CSK*

A Lalique vase, 'Aigrettes', chipped, 10in (25cm) high.
£400–600 *SS*

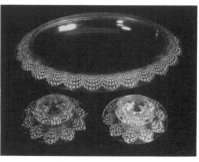

A Lalique clear glass oval fruit dish, 'Saint Gall', with folded over rim, the underside moulded in relief with swags of bubbles, and 4 matching candlesticks with detachable nozzles, acid stamped 'R. Lalique', damaged.
£400–600 *CSK*

l. A Lalique hand mirror, 'Narcisse Couché, moulded with panel depicting narcissus gazing into a pool, with foliate panels forming the surround later, signed 'R. Lalique', 11½in (29.5cm) long.
£1,200–1,500 *P*

A Lalique glass vase, 'Ricquewihr', of broad cylindrical shape, in clear glass decorated with horizontal banding moulded with grapes and vines, heightened with brown staining, marked Lalique in block letters, 5in (12.5cm) high.
£300–400 *P*

r. A pair of misty grey opaque vases, with high relief of birds of paradise, inscribed 'R. Lalique France, No. 988', 10in (25cm) high.
£1,200–1,400 *BA*

A set of 4 Lalique glass menu holders, in blue, green, amber and frosted glass, moulded 'Lalique', and hallmarks for Birmingham, 1924, 2in (5cm) high. **£400–500** *P*

A pair of brass table mirrors, in the manner of R. Lalique, 20in (50cm) high. **£2,000–2,400** *P*

l. A frosted seal, 'Figurine Mains Jointes',etched 'R. Lalique', 3½in (9.5cm) high. **£500–600** *Bon*

A Lalique clear glass scent bottle, for Worth, 'Requête', the stopper moulded with 'W', moulded 'Lalique, France', 3 1/2 in (9cm) high. **£300–400** *Bon*

A set of 6 knife rests, each with a satin-finished dragonfly, damaged, engraved signature 'R. Lalique', 4in (10cm) long. **£800–1,000** *C*

A glass and metal hand mirror, stamped on metal 'Lalique', 12in (30cm) long, in original case. **£2,000–2,400** *P*

A black polished glass seal, 'Tête d'Aigle', engraved 'R. Lalique, France No. 175', 3in (8cm) high. **£800–900** *Bon*

A clear and frosted paperweight, 'Taureau', stencilled 'R. Lalique, France', 3½in (8.5cm) high. **£450–550** *Bon*

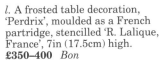

l. A frosted table decoration, 'Perdrix', moulded as a French partridge, stencilled 'R. Lalique, France', 7in (17.5cm) high. **£350–400** *Bon*

A clear and frosted vase, 'Faune', the stem moulded as the head of Bacchus, 2 exaggerated horns forming curved handles, stencilled 'R. Lalique, France', 12½in (32cm) high. **£1,700–2,000** *Bon*

A Gallé bottle and stopper, enamelled with small polychrome flowers on gilt stems, repeated on the button stopper, crack to neck, painted mark 'Emile Gallé', c1900, 4in (10cm) high. **£500–600** *S(S)*

A Gallé carved, acid etched and enamelled cameo vase, the pale amber glass with polychrome striations, overlaid with dark amber vines, with green enamel decoration, carved signature 'Gallé', 9in (24cm) high.

A Gallé cameo glass vase, yellow tinted grey glass body overlaid in shades of sealing wax red, cameo mark 'Gallé', c1900, 9in (23cm) high. **£650–850** *S*

l. A Gallé vase, overlaid in green and brown and etched with seed pods and leaves, cameo signature, c1900, 5in (13cm) high. **£300–500** *S(S)*

A pair of Gallé cameo glass vases, with brown foliage on an amber ground, signed, 20½in (52cm) high. **£1,000–1,200** *SWO*

A Gallé cameo vase, overlaid in red on a yellow ground, signed, 7in (18cm) high. **£650–700** *SWO*

A Gallé cameo glass vase, in pink tinted glass, overlaid in pale purple and green, cameo mark 'Gallé' with a star, c1904, 10½in (26.5cm) high. **£900–1,100** *SB*

r. A Gallé cameo glass vase, grey with blood red, overlaid with purple etched with anemones, cameo mark 'Gallé', c1900, 14½in (37cm) high. **£1,200–1,500** *S*

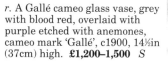

A Gallé cameo glass vase, in grey glass tinted with pink, dark red-brown and blue, incised mark 'Gallé', c1900, 7½in (19cm) high. **£1,000–1,200** *S*

A Gallé etched and enamelled green glass bottle vase, pink, mauve and white, marked 10½in (26.5cm) high. **£800–1,000** *CSK*

A Gallé cameo glass oviform vase, signed in cameo 'Gallé, 10in (25cm) high.
£1,200–1,500 *P*

A Gallé triple overlay mould-blown glass vase, of flared baluster form, the translucent yellow ground overlaid in red, chestnut and burgundy etched with cala lilies, with cameo signature 'Gallé', 14½in (36.5cm) high.
£40,000–50,000 *CNY*

A Gallé marine cameo glass vase, the lemon-tinted body having inky blue striations and overlaid with orange glass acid-etched with seaweeds and a snail, signed in cameo 'Gallé', 9½in (24cm) high. **£2,600–3,200** *P*

A Gallé double overlay etched glass vase, the transparent ground overlaid inpink and green etched with umbelliferous plants, intaglio signature 'Gallé', 7½in (19cm) wide.
£1,300–1,500 *CNY*

l. A Gallé cameo glass vase, of pale yellow metal cased in deep blue and carved with bleeding hearts, cameo signature and retailer's label, c1900, 5½in (14cm) high.
£800–1,000 *SS*

A Gallé cameo glass landscape dish, the amber tinted grey glass overlaid with deep blue, cameo mark 'Gallé', c1900, 5½in (14cm) high.
£1,600–2,000 *S*

A Gallé cameo glass dish, the body with deep inky turquoise-blue overlaid in bright pink and green, cameo mark 'Gallé', with a star, c1905, 7in (17.5cm) wide.
700–900 *S*

A Gallé cameo glass vase, green tinted and overlaid with orange and brown, signed in cameo 'Gallé, 6in (15cm) high.
£700–900 *P*

A Gallé cameo glass lamp base, etched with wild grass, cameo mark 'Gallé', c1900, 16½in (42cm) high.
£350–400 *S*

A Gallé glass perfume bottle and stopper, smoky-brown, enamelled and gilt, marked 'E. Gallé à Nancy', 1880s, 4in (10cm) high.
£600–650 *S*

A Gallé cameo vase, coral and green overlaid in green and brown, etched with trees, cameo mark, 8in (20cm) high.
£600–750 *CSK*

A Gallé fire polished cameo glass vase, the caramel ground shading to turquoise, overlaid and etched, cameo mark Gallé, 9in (22.5cm) high.
£1,200–1,500 *CSK*

A Gallé enamelled glass vase in twisted and ribbed smoked glass, decorated in pink, green, red and black enamel, heightened with gilding, enamelled mark 'Emile Gallé à Nancy', 1890s, 10in (25cm) high.
£1,800–2,200 *S*

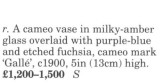

l. A Gallé cameo glass vase, the pink body overlaid with orange, mauve and green glass acid-etched with nasturtiums, signed in cameo 'Gallé', 7½in (18.5cm) high. **£700–800** *P*

r. A cameo vase in milky-amber glass overlaid with purple-blue and etched fuchsia, cameo mark 'Gallé', c1900, 5in (13cm) high.
£1,200–1,500 *S*

A Gallé double overlay glass vase, the grey ground overlaid with blue, green and amethyst, cameo mark, 8in (20cm) high.
£500–600 *CSK*

A Gallé cameo glass vase, in
grey glass tinted pink,
overlaid in white, deep purple
and dark green, cameo mark
'Gallé' with a star, after 1904,
10in (25.5cm) high.
£800–1,000 *SB*

A three colour layer cameo
glass vase, by Galle, c1900,
11¾in (30cm) high.
£800–1,000 *G*

A Gallé cameo glass vase, in
pink-tinted grey glass overlaid
with purple, cameo mark 'Gallé',
c1900, 23½in (60cm) high.
£2,000–2,400 *SB*

An overlaid spill vase, on
yellow oil ground with
mauve rose decoration, by
Gallé, 15in high.
£2,000–2,400 *Lan*

A two colour layer cameo
glass vase, by Gallé, c1900,
9½in (24cm) high.
£700–900 *G*

A Galle cameo landscape glass
vase, overlaid with brown and
lilac glass and acid etched,
signed in cameo Galle, 12in
(30cm) high.
£1,200–1,500 *P*

A fine two colour layer
cameo glass vase, by
Gallé, c1900, 11½in
(30.5cm) high.
£1,000–1,200 *G*

A Gallé cameo glass vase in
pinkish-grey glass, overlaid with
clear amber-green, incised mark
'Gallé', c1900, 13½in (35cm) high.
£1,000–1,400 *SB*

A Galle cameo glass vase, the
greyish body overlaid with
orange and deep ruby glass, acid
etched and polished, signed
'E. Gallé', 17½in (45cm) high.
£2,000–2,400 *P*

r. A three colour layer cameo
glass vase by Gallé, c1900,
10in (25cm) high.
£2,000–2,500 *G*

A Gallé carved cameo glass vase,
in opaque milky-green glass,
underside with impressed mark,
'Gallé modèle et décors déposés',
c1900, 7½in (19.5cm) high.
£800–1,200 *SB*

An early Gallé enamelled glass
vase, with inscription in gilt
'Lien d'Amour', signed in relief
'Galle', 6½in (16.5cm) high.
£1,000–1,200 *P*

A three-colour layer cameo glass vase, by Gallé, 9in (22.5cm) high.
£,5200–1,500 *G*

A Gallé cameo vase, in grey glass tinted pink at the base, overlaid in white lilac and green, cameo mark 'Gallé', c1900, 10½in (27cm) high.
£800–1000 *SB*

A three colour layer cameo glass vase by Gallé, c1900, 8½in (21.5cm) high.
£1,000–1,200 *G*

A three-colour layer mould blown 'Souffle' vase, of Japanese inspiration, by Gallé, c1900, 9½in (24cm) high.
£6,000–7,500 *G*

l. A Gallé two-handled bowl, the green tinted glass with polychrome enamelled floral spray, dragonfly and water lily decoration, with gilt and enamel borders, signed E. Gallé Nancy Déposé, 9½in (24cm) diam.
£1,600–2,000 *C*

A Gallé cameo glass vase, in grey glass tinted pink, overlaid in white and green, cameo mark 'Gallé', c1900, 12in (30.5cm) high.
£1,000–1,200 *SB*

A Gallé etched and enamelled vase, in pale green glass overlaid in milky-green glass, heightened with gilding, cameo mark, 'Gallé', c1900, 3½in (9cm) high.
£1,000–1,200 *SB*

A cameo glass flask, the greyish body overlaid with orange and ruby glass, stopper missing, signed 'Gallé' on a four-leafed clover, 5in (12.5cm) high.
£600–750 *P*

A three-colour layer cameo glass vase, by Gallé, 5in (12cm) high.
£1,200–1,500 *G*

l. A three-colour cameo glass vase, designed with Japanese inspiration, by Gallé, c1900, 10½in (26.5cm) diam.
£2,700–3,200 *G*

r. A Gallé purple glass flask, streaked internally with yellow/grey body, with incised signature, 'Gallé', c1900, 5in (13cm) high.
£1,000–1,200 *SB*

Two Gallé cameo glass vases, with signatures, 7in (23cm).
£800–1,000 *DSH*

A triple overlay etched glass vase, by Emile Gallé, of flattened, tapered cylindrical form with peaked rim, the translucent yellow ground overlaid in white, lime green and brown etched with a lake scene, a row of cottages in the background, with cameo signature 'Gallé', 14in (35.5cm) high.
£1,600–2,000 *CNY*

A Gallé cameo vase, the slim body overlaid in brown and green and carved with trees in a lakeland setting against a frosted pink tinged ground, signed, 8in (20.5cm) high.
£800–1,000 *Bea*

r. An etched and double overlay glass vase, the light amber ground overlaid in green and brown, etched, 'Gallé', 5in (12.5cm) high.
£600–800 *CG*

A tall Gallé cameo glass vase, the greyish body with evidence of slight vertical ribbing overlaid with ruby glass acid-etched with waterlily blooms, tendrils and leaves, fire-polished, etched on leaf with vertical signature 'Gallé', applied with brass rim to base, repaired, 22½in (57cm) high.
£1,000–1,500 *P*

A cameo double overlay glass perfume bottle, by Emile Gallé, in frosted white glass overlaid with sapphire blue and puce, with cameo signature, the matching stopper etched with a dragonfly, 4in (10cm) high. **£1,200–1,500** *CNY*

r. A vase, by Emile Gallé, the green and yellow ground etched, enamelled and gilded with a medallion, inscribed 'Cristallierie Emile Gallé à Nancy', 7in (17.5cm) high.
£6,000–7,000 *CNY*

l. A Gallé vase, the pale amber glass wit gold foil inclusions overlaid with white and blue, base engraved 'Gallé', 7½in (18.5cm) high.
£2,500–3,000 *C*

A plum triple overlay mould-brown glass vase, by Emile Gallé, the translucent yellow ground overlaid with sapphire, purple and chestnut brown, cameo signature, 15½in (39cm) high.
£7,000–9,000 *CNY*

r. A Gallé cameo glass vase, with mountainscape in blue and brown overlaid on amber, with a trefoil shaped rim, signed in cameo 'Gallé', 8½in (21.5cm) high.
£1,600–2,000 *PSG*

A Gallé flask-shaped scent bottle, enamelled with stylised flowers, branches and dragonflies in yellow and green against green tinted glass, enamelled signature 'E. Gallé Nancy déposé', rim chip, 5in (12.5cm) high.
£700–900 *C*

An enamelled glass jug with stopper by Gallé, enamelled signature on the bottom, 'E. Gallé a Nancy', chips on handle and rim, 8in (20cm).
£450–550 *C*

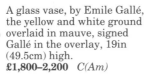

A baluster-shaped overlay vase, by Emile Gallé, minor chip to base, signed 'E. Gallé' on a leaf, c1900, 16½in (42.5cm) high.
£2,600–3,000 *C(Am)*

A Gallé cameo glass vase, tinted amber and overlaid with blue and amethyst glass acid etched with fir trees and mountains, signed 'Gallé' in cameo, 5½in (14cm) high.
£1,000–1,200 *P*

A Gallé clear glass jug, enamelled in colours, base enamelled 'Emile Gallé déposé', 9½in (24cm) high.
£700–900 *CSK*

A glass vase, by Emile Gallé, the yellow and white ground overlaid in mauve, signed Gallé in the overlay, 19in (49.5cm) high.
£1,800–2,200 *C(Am)*

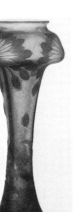

l. A Gallé cameo glass vase, the greyish body overlaid with pale green and brown, signed in cameo 'Gallé' with star, 13½in (34cm) high.
£1,000–1,200 *P*

A triple overlay glass vase, by Emile Gallé, the matt ground overlaid in white, ochre and green, signed 'Gallé' in the overlay, c1900, 16½in (42cm) high.
£1,600–2,000 *C(Am)*

An Art Nouveau marbled frosted glass vase, signed Gallé, 10in (25cm) high.
£1,000–1,200 *DSH*

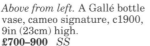

Above from left. A Gallé bottle vase, cameo signature, c1900, 9in (23cm) high.
£700–900 *SS*

A Gallé bottle vase, with purple wisteria on yellow ground, cameo signature, c1900, 6in (15cm) high.
£500–650 *SS*

A Gallé cameo glass vase, acid etched through violet overlay, cameo signature, c1900, 4½in (11.5cm) high.
£500–650 *SS*

A Gallé bottle vase, yellow metal cased in lavender blue, cameo signature, c1900, 9½in (24cm) high.
£700–900 *SS*

l. A Gallé cameo glass vase, the amber-tinted body overlaid with pale blue and amethyst acid-etched, signed in cameo 'Gallé', 10in (25cm) high.
£1,200–1,500 *P*

A Gallé cameo glass vase, the greyish body tinted amber in places, overlaid with amethyst glass, signed in cameo 'Gallé' with star preceeding, 16in (40.5cm) high.
£1,600–2,000 *P*

The star preceeding the signature was included after Gallé's death in 1903 as a tribute to him, and was used for a short time.

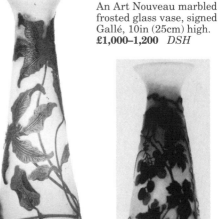

A Gallé cameo glass vase, cameo mark 'Gallé', c1900, 17½in (45cm) high.
£1,800–2,200 *S*

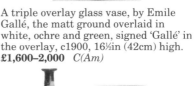

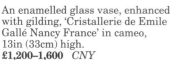

A Gallé glass vase, overlaid in pink and green, etched signature in the Chinese manner 'Gallé', 6in (15cm) high.
£700–900 *CNY*

An enamelled glass vase, enhanced with gilding, 'Cristallerie de Emile Gallé Nancy France' in cameo, 13in (33cm) high.
£1,200–1,600 *CNY*

A Gallé four-layer cameo glass vase, signed in cameo, 14½in (37cm) high. **£2,000–2,400** *PSG*

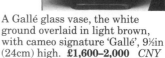

A Gallé glass vase, the white ground overlaid in light brown, with cameo signature 'Gallé', 9½in (24cm) high. **£1,600–2,000** *CNY*

A Gallé glass lamp base, the blue and white ground overlaid in olive green and brown, with cameo signature 'Gallé', 4in (10cm) high. **£500–600** *CNY*

A Gallé vase, the frosted and cream coloured ground overlaid with purple, with cameo signature 'Gallé', 5½in (14cm) high. **£1,500–2,000** *CNY*

A Gallé glass vase, the cream coloured ground overlaid in red, with cameo signature 'Gallé', 5in (13cm) high.
£600–750 *CNY*

A Gallé vase, ovelaid in deep brown, with cameo signature 'Gallé', 5½in (14cm) high.
£700–950 *CNY*

A Gallé 4 layer cameo glass vase, decorated with flowering clematis, signed in cameo, 6½in (17cm) high. **£2.500–3,000** *PSG*

A Gallé 4 layer cameo glass vase, decorated with chrysanthemum, signed in cameo, 6in (15cm) high.
£1,600–2,000 *PSG*

r. A Gallé cameo glass vase, in shades of purple, brown, blue and cream, 8in (20cm) high.
£900–1,200 *Bea*

l. A Gallé two-layer cameo glass solifleur vase, decorated with wild flowers, signed in cameo, 7in (17cm) high.
£600–750 *PSG*

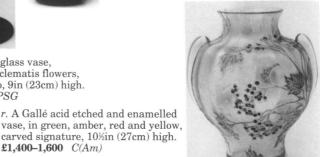

A Gallé 4 layer glass vase, decorated with clematis flowers, signed in cameo, 9in (23cm) high.
£1,000–1,200 *PSG*

r. A Gallé acid etched and enamelled vase, in green, amber, red and yellow, carved signature, 10½in (27cm) high.
£1,400–1,600 *C(Am)*

A Gallé 4 layer cameo glass vase, decorated with flowers and leaves, signed in cameo, 9½in (24cm) high.
£2,000–2,400 *PSG*

A Gallé cameo vase, decorated with a riverside landscape, in brown and ochre on a peach ground, 3½in (9cm) high.
£400–500 *HCH*

A Gallé plum overlay and mould-blown glass vase, the amber ground with purple pendant branches, cameo signature, 12½in (32cm) high.
£8,000–10,000 *C*

A Légras cameo vase, milky opaque amber body overlaid in mottled pink/brown glass with light iridescent sheen, cameo mark 'Légras', c1910, 20½in (52cm) high. **£1,000–1,200** *S*

A Gallé cameo glass 'acorn' vase, in deep green mottled internally with streaks of blue/brown and bubbling, overlaid in clear brown and etched, cameo mark 'Gallé', c1900 9½in (24cm) high.
£1,200–1,500 *S*

A Lalique glass box and cover, 'Meudon', heightened with pale blue staining, impressed on base 'R. Lalique', engraved 'France', 3½in (9cm) diam.
£250–300 *P*

An etched and overlay glass vase, by Charles Schneider, the milky white and pink mottled glass overlaid in claret and orange, etched 'Le Verre Français', 14in (35.5cm) high.
£500–700 *CG*

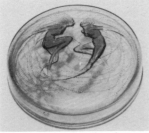

A Lalique circular glass box and cover, 'Deux Sirènes', of amber colour, moulded on cover 'R. Lalique', 10in (25cm) diam.
£1,800–2,300 *P*

A Lalique brooch, frosted glass over blue metallic foil, gilt-metal backing, stamped 'Lalique', c1910, 1in (3cm) diam. **£600–750** *S*

l. A Légras cameo glass vase, in green glass overlaid in grey and green, the mouth and neck streaked in amber, cameo mark 'Légras', c1910, 7½in (19cm) high.
£600–750 *S*

r. A Gallé cameo glass vase, the lemon coloured body overlaid and acid etched with violets on leafy stems, etched 'Gallé', 6½in (16.5cm) high.
£800–1,000 *P*

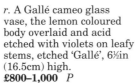

A Lalique circular glass box and cover, 'Rambouillet', heightened with blue/grey staining, moulded on cover 'R. Lalique', engraved on edge 'R. Lalique No. 60', 3½in (9cm) diam.
£300–350 *P*

l. A Daum vase, signed in gilt 'Daum/Nancy' with Croix de Lorraine, 4in (10cm) high.
£400–500 *Bon*

A d'Argental cameo glass vase, with deep turquoise sides overlaid in navy, signed in cameo 'd'Argental', 6in (15cm) high.
£500–600 *Bon*

A Gallé green glass jug, enamelled in white, blue and red, inscribed 'E. Gallé Nancy', 8½in (21.5cm) high.
£700–900 *CSK*

A Daum cameo glass vase, the matt streaked yellow ground overlaid in shades of purple, cameo signature 'Daum Nancy France', retailer's paper label, 19in (48cm) high.
£1,800–2,200 *C(Am)*

A cameo vase, 'Chestnuts', by Légras, 20in (50.5cm) high.
£1,000–1,200 *AA*

A Gallé enamelled and green glass jardinière, marked on base with acid etched mushroom and signed 'Emile Gallé delt, Serie C, ft', and 'déposé' in fine red script, 13in (33cm) wide.
£1,300–1,600 *P*

A De Latte cameo vase, overlaid in amber with orchids against a mottled ground, signed 'De Latte Nancy', 19½in (50cm) high.
£700–900 *C*

A Gallé oviform vase, overlaid and etched in amber, red and green with daffodils among grasses, cameo signature 'Gallé', bearing label, 13in (33cm) high.
£1,200–1,500 *C(Am)*

A Gallé cameo glass vase, tinged with yellow and pink overlaid in deep amber and decorated with acid etched and carved decoration of anemones, cameo signed 'Gallé', c1905, 10in (25cm) high.
£1,200–1,500 *C(Am)*

l. A Gallé cameo glass vase, the frosted white and lemon sides overlaid with deep purple, signed in cameo 'Gallé', 7½in (19cm) high.
£700–900 *Bon*

r. A cameo glass vase, by Gallé, with rich brown ochre overlaid on an amber ground with a design of tiger lilies, signed 'Gallé', 8in (20cm) high.
£1,800–2,200 *PSG*

A Loetz iridescent glass bowl, designed by Michael Powolny, with ruby tones and internal crackled silver iridescence, a pale green rim, supported on 3 black glass ball feet, 10½in (26.5cm) diam.
£700–950 *PC*

An iridescent glass vase, attributed to Loetz, covered with an all-over pulled thread design in a silvery yellow and blue, 7⅛in (18cm) high.
£1,200–1,500 *CSK*

A Loetz glass vase, the shape designed by Josef Hoffman, the red glass vessel having a black glass rim, 9in (22.5cm) high.
£500–600 *P*

A Loetz iridescent glass vase, deep ruby and peacock blue, 7in (17.5cm) high.
£1,200–1,500 *P*

An iridescent glass vase, attributed to Loetz, in deep blue decorated with splashed peacock lustre, c1900, 10⅛in (26cm) high.
£300–400 *S*

A Loetz iridescent glass vase, decorated with fine blue meandering bands and having random pale peacock blue/violet splashes overall, 8½in (21.5cm) high.
£600–650 *P*

An iridescent glass vase, attributed to Loetz, white glass decorated at the base with dappled pink/peacock lustre and pots of bright green with tiny metallic inclusions, the neck in dappled gold lustre, underside with faintly enamelled mark '2/219n787', 17in (43cm) high.
£200–250 *S*

A Loetz cameo glass vase, the pale lemon body overlaid with pale brown, apple green and red, signed in cameo 'Loetz', 6in (15cm) high.
£600–750 *P*

An Loetz iridescent glass shell vase, the shell splashed with a gold/green lustre, mottled surface, 9in (22.5cm) high.
£800–1,000 *Bon*

A Loetz iridescent glass vase, pale amber with internal pale peacock lustre, iridescent engraved crossed arrows mark, c1900, 12½in (32cm) high.
£800–1,000 *S*

A Loetz iridescent glass vase, the aubergine glass decorated with iridescent feather design, signed 'Loetz Austria, c1900, 5½in (14.5cm) high.
£700–900 *C(Am)*

l. A Loetz iridescent vase, designed in the manner of Josef Hoffmann, the body of yellow tone covered with marbled silver blue iridescence, 9¾in (24.5cm) high.
£700–900 *P*

A Gallé etched and enamelled casket, in clear amber glass, detailed in naturalistic enamels and gilding, c1890, 6in (15.5cm) wide.
£2,800–3,200 *SB*

A Lalique glass powder box and cover, with traces of green staining, moulded mark 'R. Lalique, Made in France', 1920s.
£400–500 *SB*

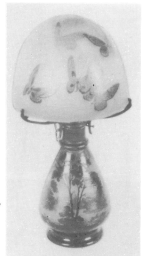

A Gallé acid etched table lamp and shade, signed, mounted in bronze, with electric light fittings, 16in (40.5cm) high.
£5,000–6,000 *HSS*

An Art Deco wall mirror, flanked by 2 Lalique panels, each well moulded with a jackdaw, 36in (91.5cm) wide.
£2,600–3,000 *P*

A Lalique glass inkwell, 'Mures', moulded on the underside with fruiting brambles, engraved 'R. Lalique France No. 431', 1920s, 6½in (16.5cm) diam.
£500–600 *SB*

A Daum etched glass vase, pale blue glass etched with horizontal bands, against a frosted ground, faint stencilled mark 'Daum Nancy', c1930, 9in (22.5cm) high.
£700–900 *S*

A Lalique smoky grey glass ashtray, 'Souris', centred with a model of a crouching mouse, signed 'R. Lalique France', 3in (7.5cm) high.
£200–250 *P*

l. A French Art Deco table lamp and shade, with landscape decoration, by Légras, 15in (38cm) high.
£1,000–1,200 *Lan*

A Daum green tinted etched glass vase, acid etched with stippled banding, incised 'Daum Nancy France', 1930s, 13in (33cm) high. **£800–1,000** *S*

An Etling opalescent glass figure, moulded 'Etling France 141', 13in (33cm) high.
£500–650 *P*

Above left and right: A pair of green Art glass cylindrical vases, signed 'Daum Nancy', 11in (28cm) high. **£1,200–1,500**
Centre left: A green Art glass conical shaped vase, signed 'Daum Nancy', 8½in (21.5cm) wide. **£500–600**
Centre right: A green Art glass three-tier shaped vase, signed 'Daum, Nancy', 13in (33cm) high. **£800–1,000** *DSH*

l. A Gallé cameo footed glass vase, the frosted white and light green sides overlaid with deep purple, signed in cameo 'Gallé', 4in (10cm) high.
£400–500 *Bon*

r. A Gallé cameo glass vase, overlaid in deep mauve with sprays of laburnum, cameo mark 'Gallé', c1900, 12½in (32cm) high.
£800–1,000 *L*

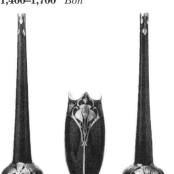

l. A Gallé enamelled glass vase, the clear sepia glass enamelled in tones of mustard, pink, turquoise and grey, details highlighted in gilt, etched 'Gallé, c1885, 11½in (29.5cm) high.
£1,400–1,700 *Bon*

A Gallé cameo glass vase, the frosted white sides overlaid in lime green, signed in cameo 'Gallé, 3½in (9cm) high.
£300–350 *Bon*

A Légras glass garniture, the 2 oviform vases with tall extended necks, all of white glass cased in a rich red glass and decorated with gilded stylised bell-shaped flowers, gilt mark 'L & Cie St. Denis - Paris', tallest 18in (45.5cm) high.
£700–900 *P*

l. A Gallé cameo glass vase, with cameo signature 'Gallé', 14in (35.5cm) high.
£900–1,100 *C*

A Gallé glass vase, with overlaid ruby decoration of flowers, signed, 5in (12.5cm) high.
£400–500 *CW*

A Gallé green ground overlay vase, with brown floral decoration, with a verse: 'Béni soit le coin sombre où s'isolent nos coeurs', by the French Symbolist poet, Marceline Desbordes-Valmore.
£3,500–4,000 *Wor*

A Gallé cameo glass vase, with amber tinted body overlaid with 2 tones of ruby glass, signed in cameo 'Gallé, 5½in (14cm) high.
£600–700 *P*

A Müller Frères cameo glass landscape vase, pale green overlaid in amber and blue, cameo mark 'Müller Frères, Lunéville', 1900, 8½in (21.5cm) high.
£800–1,000 *S*

A Loetz vase in iridescent pink and gold glass, c1900, 6in (15cm) high.
£600–750 *C(Am)*

A Müller Frères cameo glass vase, with mottled orange, ochre and deep violet sides overlaid with turquoise, signed in relief 'Müller Fres/Lunéville', 5in (12.5cm) high.
£1,000–1,200 *Bon*

Three Clutha glass vases, 2 in green glass with internal bubbling and coppery inclusions with white streaks, the third in opaque amber glass swirling with white, 1880s, largest 5in (12.5cm) high.
£300–400 each *S*

A green glass goblet, probably Clutha, with coppery internal streaks and profuse bubbling, c1880, 11in (28cm) high.
£700–900 *S*

A Daum cameo glass landscape vase, enamelled in shades of green and blue, the base inscribed 'Daum Nancy', 15½in (39.5cm) high.
£2,600–3,000 *WW*

A Daum silver-mounted, etched and enamelled glass bowl, the clear body overlaid in brilliant clear emerald green and etched, stencilled mark 'Daum Nancy', c1900, 10in (25cm) diam. **£1,600–2,000** *S*

A Daum cameo glass vase, the pale orange and yellow body overlaid with brown and green, signed in cameo 'Daum Nancy', 10in (25cm) high. **£800–1,000** *P*

A cameo glass vase, in amber glass overlaid with red and etched with fuschias, cameo mark 'd'Argental', c1900, 9½in (24cm) high. **£600–750** *S*

A Daum cameo glass vase, the dappled body overlaid with orange and brown glass, signed in cameo 'Daum Nancy, France', 10in (25cm) high. **£1,200–1,500** *P*

A Gallé cameo glass vase, the greyish body overlaid with rich amethyst glass, engraved signature 'Gallé', 8in (20cm) high. **£1,600–2,000** *P*

l. A Gallé cameo vase, in white, amethyst and green, signed, 23½in (60cm) high. **£2,200–2,600** *P*

A Gallé cameo 'vase parlant', with deep blue and rust-red inclusions, overlaid with brown glass, with a verse by Rollinat, signed in cameo 'Gallé', 14in (35.5cm) high. **£2,500–3,000** *P*

A Gallé cameo glass landscape vase, the greyish body tinted amber at the top, overlaid with apple green and ruby glass, signed 'Gallé', 19½in (49.5cm) high. **£3,500–4,000** *P*

l. A Gallé cameo glass vase, the greyish body amber tinted, overlaid with green and brown glass, signed in cameo 'Gallé', 9in (23cm) high. **£700–900** *P*

A Gallé cameo glass landscape vase, the amber tinted body overlaid with pale blue and amethyst showing as brown, intaglio signature 'Gallé', 13½in (35cm) high. **£3,500–4,000** *P*

A French cameo glass vase, signed 'Le Verre Français', c1900, 12in (30.5cm) high.
£600–750 *ASA*

A glass vase by Loetz, with all-over silvery iridescence, inscribed 'Loetz Austria', 6in (15cm) high.
£1,800–2,000 *CNY*

r. A Loetz glass vase, with random splashes of golden iridescence shading through pale turquoise and violet, and applied with a silver coloured metal collar, 13in (33cm).
£400–500 *P*

An overlaid and carved glass vase, inscribed 'D. Christian Meisenthal', 3½in (9cm) high.
£1,000–1,300 *CNY*

A glass vase, overlaid in green and aubergine, with finely etched leaves, vines and blossoms depicting passion flowers, inscribed 'D. Christian Meisenthal Loth', 7in (18cm) high.
£1,000–1,200 *CNY.*

A Favrile blue iridescent glass vase, inscribed 'X182, L. C. Tiffany Favrile', 9in (23cm) high.
£800–1,000 *CNY*

A double overlay and carved glass vase, by Eugène Michel, in green and white, and finely carved to depict water lilies in blossom, the interior with iridescence, 5in (13cm) high.
£2,500–3,000 *CNY*

A Favrile glass paperweight vase, with many stylised morning glory blossoms amidst streamers encased in the clear glass, the interior with iridescence, crack to foot, engraved 'U4113 Louis C. Tiffany', c1904, 7½in (19cm) high.
£500–550 *CNY*

A Favrile iridescent glass comport, inscribed 'L. C. Tiffany Inc. Favrile W41N', 3in (7.5cm) high.
£600–800 *CNY*

A Favrile iridescent glass comport, in all-over blue and purple iridescence on a short stem and circular foot, inscribed '1531 2104 L.L.C.T. Tiffany Favrile', 6½in (16.5cm) high.
£600–800 *CNY*

r. A Favrile iridescent gold glass flower bowl, with central detachable flower frog, both incised 'L. C. Tiffany Favrile 5344K', 14⅛in (36cm) diam.
£1,200–1,500 *CNY*

A Favrile glass centrepiece, the ribbed body with all-over blue iridescence, inscribed 'L. C. Tiffany Favrile, 8412K', 10in (26.5cm) diam.
£700–900 *CNY*

A Müller vase, in clear and frosted glass, signed 'Müller Lunéville France', c1930, 8in (20cm) high. **£500–650** *C*

An amethyst glass table lamp base, moulded 'A. Hunibelle, Modèle Dep de R. Cogneville, Made in France', 11in (28cm) high. **£300–400** *P*

A French geometric enamel and glass decanter, with black and red decoration, 12in (30.5cm) high. **£200–300** *ASA*

An Art Deco glass decanter, of Lalique style, and 6 glasses. **£299–259** *CDC*

An Art Deco glass decanter, black enamelled with geometric and starburst designs, 5 tots ensuite, 10in (25cm) high. **£250–300** *CSK*

An Orrefors grey tinted vase, designed by Simon Gate, engraved 'Orrefors S. Gate 234.27 A.D.', c1930, 9½in (24cm) high. **£1,600–2,000** *C*

A moulded glass vase, moulded signature 'A. Verlys France', c1930, 11½in (28.5cm) high. **£400–500** *C*

A cut glass decanter and stoppper, modelled with geometric patterns in black and frosted glass, 7½in (19cm) high, and 6 liqueur glasses en suite, 2½in (6cm) high. **£300-400** *CSK*

r. A pale amber coloured moulded glass vase, moulded signature 'Verlys France', c1930, 9in (22.5cm) high. **£250–300** *C*

A set of 6 Art Deco glass goblets, enamelled with peacocks in green and blue, and female figures, against a black enamelled ground, some signed 'Vedar', one chipped, 8in (20cm) high. **£700–900** *GSP*

An Etling opalescent glass figure, moulded 'Etling France 50', 8in (20cm) high.
£1,000–1,200 *P*

Seven glass goblets, and 8 finger bowls, signed 'Verdar'.
£1,200–1,500 *M*

A glass decanter set, decorated with panels of black enamel, and frosted and engraved linear decoration.
£350–400 *P*

A gilt metal mounted deeply engraved and clear glass octagonal lamp, 13½in (34.5cm) high.
£600–750 *CSK*

A decanter and glasses, in clear glass faceted with square panels and alternately flashed with amber, one chipped.
£200–250 *P*

An Austrian blue glass jar and cover, attributed to Moser of Karlsbad, in the manner of Josef Hoffman 6in (15cm) high.
£250–300 *P*

A Décorchement pâte-de-verre bowl, in green and brown marbled glass, with impressed mark, c1940, 10in (25cm) wide.
£2,600–3,000 *C*

A Moser blue glass vase, heightened with gilding, marked on base 'Moser', and 'L.K.M.' linked for Ludwig Moser Karlsbad, 13½in (34.5cm) high.
£200–300 *P*

A Venini patchwork vase, the clear glass internally decorated in red, green and blue, acid stamped 'Venini Murano Italia', 4½in (11.5cm) high.
£1,200–1,500 *C(Am)*

A Sabino opalescent glass lamp, signed 'Sabino France', 13½in (34.5cm) high, in a chromed base incorporating lamp fitments.
£700–800 *P*

A Sabino opalescent glass figure, 'Suzanne', unsigned, 9in (22.5cm) high, with wooden mount, incorporating fitments for use as a lamp.
£1,800–2,000 *P*

Identification checklist for buying Tiffany Lamps

- Does the shade or base bear a signature and model number?
- Is the shade made of leaded glass that looks as if it could be around 90 years old?
- Is the base made of bronze, with a century-old patina, and is the socket and cord old?
- Is the condition of the lamp good, with few cracks, and little replaced glass or hardware?
- Is there a good provenance (history) on the lamp?
- Is the price expensive, but not exceptionally high?
- Is the seller prepared to take the lamp back and provide a full refund if a mutually agreed expert will not authenticate the lamp?

A 'Cypriot' glass hanging lantern, by Tiffany Studios, 18in (46cm) high. **£8,000–10,000** *CNY*

r. A French lamp, 'L'Orchidée', from a model by Louis Chalon, early 20thC, 29in (74cm) high. **£4,500–5,500** *CNY*

l. A geometric leaded glass and metal chandelier, by Tiffany Studios, the shade suspended from 6 link chains, 14in (36cm) high. **£10,000–11,000** *CNY*

A geometric leaded glass and bronze lamp shade, by Tiffany Studios, 12½in (32cm) high. **£5,500–6,500** *CNY*

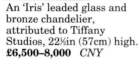

A 'Clematis' leaded glass shade, by Tiffany Studios, 18in (46cm) diam. **£25,000–30,000** *CNY*

A stained and leaded glass dome light shade, decorated with grapes and leaves, 28in (71cm) diam. **£600–700** *JL*

An 'Iris' leaded glass and bronze chandelier, attributed to Tiffany Studios, 22⅛in (57cm) high. **£6,500–8,000** *CNY*

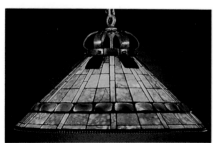

A geometric 'Turtleback' chandelier, by Tiffany Studios, 22in (56cm) high. **£7,000–10,000** *CNY*

r. A 'Turtleback' tile and leaded glass hanging lantern, by Tiffany Studios. **£17,000–20,000** *CNY*

An iridescent glass and brass chandelier, attributed to Koloman Moser, c1902, 25in (64cm) high. **£5,000–7,500** *CNY*

A paperweight glass bowl, by Tiffany Studios, inscribed '1333E L.C. Tiffany-Favrile', 8in (20cm) diam.
£4,500–5,000 *CNY*

A Le Verre Français cameo glass bowl, signed, 9in (22.5cm) high.
£900–1,000 *MAG*

A Favrile glass plaque, by Tiffany Studios, inscribed 'L.C.T.', 19in (48cm) high.
£4,000–6,000 *CNY*

An internally decorated and engraved glass coupe, 'La Vague', engraved 'Daum Nancy', 6⅛in (16cm) high.
£20,000–25,000 *HFG*

A mould blown, overlaid and etched glass bowl, signed 'Gallé', 12½in (32cm) diam.
£10,000–12,000 *HFG*

A 'Grand Vase de Tristesse', by Gallé, for the Paris Exposition, 1889, base cracked, signed, 14in (36cm) high.
£5,500–7,500 *CNY*

A glass vase, decorated with violets, signed 'Daum'.
£5,000–6,500 *CNY*

A triple overlaid and etched glass vase, cameo signature 'Gallé', 28½in (72cm) high.
£5,000–6,500 *CNY*

A double overlaid and etched glass vase, cameo signature 'Gallé', 26in (66cm) high.
£6,000–7,500 *CNY*

An overlaid and etched glass vase, cameo signature 'Gallé', rim damaged, 15½in (40cm) high.
£5,500–7,500 *CNY*

A cameo glass vase, signed 'Le Verre Français'.
£800–1,000 *MAG*

l. A cameo glass vase, signed 'Le Verre Français', 19in (48cm) high.
£50,000–60,000 *MAG*

A cameo glass vase, signed 'Le Verre Français. **£800–1,000** *MAG*

r. An internally decorated glass vase, marked 'Gallé'.
£40,000–50,000 *HFG*

A Monart blue and ochre vase, with whorls, 9in (23cm) high.
£200–230 *FA*

A Monart vase, the surface decorated in yellow and lustred white stripes, c1925, 8in (20cm) high.
£1,000–2,000 *FA*

A Gallé carved, acid etched and partially fire polished vase.
£6,000–6,500 *C*

A Gallé carved and acid etched double overlay vase, with carved signature, 12½in (32cm) high.
£2,800–3,200 *C*

A Daum martelé acid textured and carved vase.
£5,000–6,000 *C*

A Daum two coloured glass vase.
£10,000–12,000 *C*

A frosted glass vase, 'Perruches', by René Lalique et Cie, on a bronze stand, 10½in (26cm) high.
£3,500–4,000 *CNY*

An amber glass vase, 'Serpent', by René Lalique et Cie, 10in (25cm) high.
£6,000–7,500 *CNY*

l. A frosted amber glass vase, 'Languedoc', by René Lalique et Cie.
£9,000–10,000 *CNY*

r. A Favrile glass paperweight vase, by Tiffany Studios, 6in (15cm) high.
£9,000–10,000 *CNY*

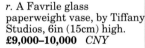

A Müller glass vase, c1900, 11in (28cm) high. **£1,600–2,000** *ABS*

l. An overlaid and etched glass vase, by Daum, 15in (38cm) high.
£4,000–6,000 *CNY*

r. A gold Favrile 'Jack-in-the-Pulpit' vase, by Tiffany Studios, 20in (51cm) high.
£9,500–11,000 *CNY*

A Tiffany Favrile lava glass vase, inscribed 'L. C. Tiffany/Favrile/ Exposition/Special, 6354N', 7in (17cm) high.
£18,500–20,000 *S(NY)*

A carved, enamelled and gilded vase, with gilt signature 'Emile Gallé', c1890, 8½in (21.5cm) high.
£2,000–2,400 *PSG*

A cameo glass vase, signed 'Daum Nancy', c1900, 13in (33cm) high.
£2,000–2,500 *PSG*

A marquetrie sur verre wheel carved cameo glass vase, by Emile Gallé, c1900, 9in (23cm) high.
£14,000–17,000 *S(NY)*

A glass vase, by Daum, with an etched and enamelled winter landscape, c1900, 5in (12cm) high.
£1,500–1,800 *PSG*

l. A four-layer cameo glass charger, signed 'Gallé', c1900, 14½in (37cm) diam.
£6,000–7,000 *PSG*

A cameo vase, decorated internally, signed 'Gallé', c1890, 9½in (24cm) high.
£4,000–5,000 *PSG*

A cameo glass table lamp, signed on base and shade 'Gallé', with star preceding, 24in (62cm) high.
£12,000–15,000 *P*

A Daum cameo glass vase, internally decorated, signed, c1900, 10½in (26cm) high.
£4,000–5,000 *PSG*

An enamelled cameo glass vase, signed 'Daum/Nancy', c1910, 20in (51cm) high.
£3,500–5,000 *S(NY)*

A Gallé four-layer cameo glass vase, signed, c1900, 7in (17cm) high.
£1,400–1,700 *PSG*

Four Daum glass vases.
£2,500–4,500 each *C*

A Daum internally
decorated glass lamp,
17in (43cm) high.
£3,500–4,000 *CNY*

A Daum cameo
glass and wheel
carved vase, signed
in intaglio, c1900,
7½in (18cm) high.
£1,600–1,900 *PSG*

A Daum
enamelled vase,
enamelled mark
'Daum Nancy',
c1900, 13in
(33cm) high.
£6,000–7,500 *S*

A Daum overlaid and
etched glass lamp,
18in (45.5cm) high.
£10,000–12,000 *CNY*

Three Daum carved, enamelled
and painted vases, painted
signatures and Cross of Lorraine.
£2,500–4,500 each *C*

A Daum carved
cameo and
marqueterie sur
verre glass vase,
engraved 'Daum
Nancy', c1900,
8in (20cm) high.
£5,000–8,000 *S*

A Daum enamelled glass
lamp, with mark 'Daum
Nancy', c1900, 24½in
(62cm) high.
£16,000–20,000 *S*

A Daum etched and
enamelled cameo glass
vase, signed, c1900,
7½in (18cm) high.
£1,800–2,200 *PSG*

An etched, enamelled and
applied snail vase, Daum
Nancy, 8in (20cm) high.
£10,000–15,000 *CNY*

Two carved and acid etched
lamps, carved signatures
'Daum Nancy', 14in (35cm)
high. **£3,000–4,000 each** *C*

l. A carved,
acid etched
vase, with
signature
'Daum Nancy',
with Cross of
Lorraine,
12½in (31cm)
high.
£3,500–4,000
C

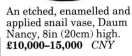

A Daum carved and
acid etched overlay
vase, 9in (23cm) high.
£15,000–18,000 *C*

A wrought iron lamp,
by Edgar Brandt, c1925.
£6,500–7,500 *S*

A double overlay and etched glass vase, signed 'Gallé', 22½in (57cm) high.
£8,000–10,000 *HFG*

A double overlay glass vase, by Emile Gallé, 8in (20cm) high.
£10,000–12,000 *HFG*

A Tiffany Favrile glass vase, engraved signature 'L. C. Tiffany Favrile', 12½in (32.5cm) high.
£2,000–2,500 *C*

A cameo glass vase, engraved 'Gallé', 16in (41cm) high.
£3,000–3,500 *PSG*

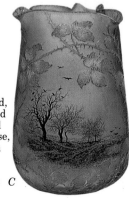

A cameo glass vase, amethyst overlaid on amber, signed 'Gallé', 8in (20cm) high.
£2,600–3,000 *PSG*

A cameo glass vase, signed 'Gallé', 6½in (16.5cm) high.
£1,400–1,700 *PSG*

An etched and enamelled cameo glass vase, by Daum, with enamelled signature, 9in (23cm) high.
£2,000–2,400 *PSG*

A cameo glass landscape vase, by Daum, enamelled signature, 5in (12.5cm) high.
£1,200–1,500 *PSG*

A Monart vase, in red, black and gold, 5½in (14cm) high.
£400–450 *FA*

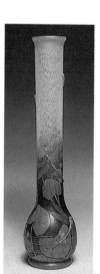

r. Two Lalique vases, 'Sophora' and 'Vases Davos', both signed, largest 11½in (29cm) high.
l. **£3,000–3,500**
r. **£2,600–3,000** *C*

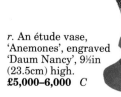

A cameo glass vase, probably by Thomas Webb, 6in (15cm) high.
£550–600 *SWO*

A 'Grand Vase Libellules', carved, acid etched and applied, carved signature 'Daum Nancy', 23½in (60cm) high.
£30,000–35,000 *C*

r. An étude vase, 'Anemones', engraved 'Daum Nancy', 9½in (23.5cm) high.
£5,000–6,000 *C*

r. An acid etched, carved, enamelled and gilt decorated landscape vase, signed 'Daum Nancy', 11in (28cm) high.
£3,000–3,500 *C*

A frosted glass vase,
'Lutteurs', relief moulded
'R. Lalique', engraved 'France',
5in (12.5cm) high.
£1,500–2,000 *CNY*

A cire perdue glass vase,
wheel cut 'R. Lalique, France',
c1924, 9in (23cm) high.
£30,000–40,000 *CNY*

Two Daum cameo glass vases,
cameo mark 'Daum Nancy', 16½
and 21½in (42 and 54cm) high.
l. **£1,800–2,000**
r. **£2,600–3,000** *Bon*

> ## Use the Index!
> *Because certain items
> might fit easily into any
> number of categories, the
> quickest and surest
> method of locating any
> entry is by reference to
> the index at the back of
> the book.*
>
> *This index has been fully
> cross-referenced for
> absolute simplicity.*

An etched and enamelled
coupe, signed 'Daum Nancy',
9in (23cm) high.
£1,600–2,000 *PSG*

An etched and
enamelled vase,
signed 'Daum Nancy',
10½in (26.5cm) high.
£2,000–2,500 *PSG*

A double overlay and
wheel carved martelé
vase, engraved signature
'Daum Nancy', with the
Cross of Lorraine, 15½in
(40cm) high.
£3,500–4,500 *C*

A Daum vase, with
overlaid enamel
painted Alpine scene,
enamelled signature
'Daum Nancy', with
the Cross of Lorraine,
11½in (29cm) high.
£2,600–3,000 *C*

An enamelled glass vase, 'Tourbillons',
wheel cut 'R. Lalique, France', engraved
'No. 973', 8in (20cm) high.
£12,000–14,000 *CNY*

r. A Daum vase, the frosted ground
overlaid with clear glass, gilt
signature 'Daum Nancy', with the
Cross of Lorraine, 23½in (60cm) high.
£2,500–3,000 *C*

A Gallé intrecalaire, intaglio carved 'verrerie parlante' vase, signed, 4⅓in (11cm) high.
£14,000–18,000 *C*

A Gallé glass vase, the frosted ground overlaid and etched to depict wisteria, cameo signature, 24⅛in (62cm) high.
£30,000–35,000 *CNY*

A Gallé vase, signed in cameo, 12in (30.5cm) high.
£2,800–3,200 *ABS*

A Gallé carved and acid etched double overlay landscape vase, carved signature, 33in (83cm) high.
£28,000–32,000 *C*

A Gallé cameo glass vase, signed, c1900, 8½in (21cm) high. **£4,500–5,000** *PSG*

A Gallé decorated martelé enamel vase, 12in (30.5cm) high.
£7,500–8,500 *C*

A Gallé 'Soufflé' vase, signed, 6½in (16.5cm) high.
£2,800–3,200 *C*

A Gallé triple overlaid and etched glass table lamp base, cameo signature, 15in (38cm) high, with metal mount.
£3,500–4,500 *CNY*

A Gallé cameo glass 'Iris' vase, cameo mark, c1900, 20⅛in (52cm) high.
£10,000–12,000 *S*

A Gallé glass vase, c1900, 14in (35.5cm) high.
£3,000–3,500 *S*

A Gallé internally decorated carved cameo vase, c1900.
£12,000–15,000 *S*

A Gallé vase, signed, 17in (43cm) high.
£8,000–10,000 *CNY*

r. A Gallé carved and acid etched vase, cameo signature, 17½in (44cm) high.
£16,000–20,000 *C*

A glass vase, overlaid with a design of spring flowers, signed 'Gallé', c1900, 9in (23cm) diam.
£2,300–2,600 *PSG*

l. A poppy triple overlay cameo glass vase, by Emile Gallé, with cameo signature, 24in (61cm) high.
£9,000–11,000 *CNY*

r. A glass vase, 'Les Sept Princesses', by Emile Gallé, inscribed 'Exposit', 1900, 9in (23cm) high.
£18,000–20,000 *CNY*

A glass vase, with a design of clematis, signed 'Gallé', 13in (33cm) high.
£2,000–2,300 *PSG*

A vase overlaid on amber, with a design of chrysanthemums, signed 'Gallé', 12½in (31.5cm) high.
£3,000–3,500 *PSG*

A glass vase, with a design of anemones, signed 'Gallé', c1900, 8in (20cm) high.
£2,500–3,000 *PSG*

A Gallé overlay glass vase, 'Roses de France', engraved Gallé, 7½in (19cm) high.
£60,000–75,000 *C*

A vase overlaid on apricot with a design of nasturtiums, signed 'Gallé', 9in (23cm) high.
£2,800–3,200 *PSG*

An etched and double overlay glass vase, signed 'Gallé', 8in (20cm) high.
£8,000–10,000 *C*

A double overlay and etched glass charger, with cameo signature 'Gallé', 15½in (39cm) diam.
£5,000–6,000 *CNY*

A carved acid etched triple overlay landscape vase, with carved signature 'Gallé', 20in (50cm) high.
£5,000–6,000 *C*

A blue lily triple overlay mould blown glass vase, cameo signature 'Gallé', 14in (35cm) high.
£50,000–60,000 *CNY*

An acid etched and enamelled vase, engraved 'Cristallerie d'Emile Gallé, Nancy', 28in (71cm) high. **£2,600–3,000** *C(Am)*

A bronze mounted vase, with engraved signature 'Gallé ft. 1891–93', bronze foot signed with 'EG' monogram, 11½in (28.5cm) high.
£16,000–20,000 *C*

A mould blown vase, carved and acid etched with rhododendrons, carved 'Gallé', 10in (25cm) high.
£7,000–9,000 *C*

A double overlay vase, by Gallé, repaired, 9in (23cm) high.
£1,200–1,500 *EG*

A triple overlay carved and acid etched vase, carved signature 'Gallé', 9in (23cm) diam.
£5,500–6,500 *C*

l. A triple overlay vase, 'Premier Gel d'Automne', carved signature 'Gallé', 13in (33cm) high.
£20,000–24,000 *C*

r. A pâte-de-verre vase, moulded signature 'G. Argy Rousseau' and 'France', 3½in (9cm) wide.
£8,000–10,000 *C*

Make the Most of Miller's

Condition is absolutely vital when assessing the value of an antique. Items in good condition are more likely to appreciate than less perfect examples. Rare, desirable items may command higher prices even when in need of restoration.

A bronze and ivory figure, 'Danseuse de Thebes', inscribed 'Cl. J. R. Colinet, 10in (25cm) high.
£6,000–9,000 *C*

l. A bronze and ivory figure, 'Mandolin Player', signed 'F. Preiss' in marble, 23½in (31.5cm) high.
£8,000–12,000
r. A bronze and ivory figure, 'Flute Player', from a model by F. Preiss, 19in (48cm) high.
£7,000–11,000 *C*

A bronze and ivory figure, 'Towards the Unknown', signed 'Cl. J. R. Colinet', 18½in (47cm) high.
£5,000–6,000 *C*

A French cold painted, damascened and silvered bronze and ivory group of a cabaret act, 'Two Girls', inscribed 'Laurent Hely' and 'Bronze', early 20thC, 21in (53cm) high.
£12,000–15,000 *CNY*

A Belgian cold painted, gilt bronze and white marble group of a snake charmer, 'Dance of Carthage', inscribed 'Cl. J. R. Colinet', early 20thC, 22in (55.5cm) high.
£9,000–11,000 *CNY*

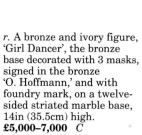

r. A bronze and ivory figure, 'Girl Dancer', the bronze base decorated with 3 masks, signed in the bronze 'O. Hoffmann,' and with foundry mark, on a twelve-sided striated marble base, 14in (35.5cm) high.
£5,000–7,000 *C*

A patinated bronze and ivory figural group, 'The Girls', by Demêtre H. Chiparus, mounted on an onyx base, minor losses, inscribed, 20½in (51cm) high. **£80,000–100,000** *S(NY)*

A patinated bronze and ivory figure, 'Ankara Dancer', by C. J. R. Colinet, c1925, 25in (63cm) high. **£31,000–35,000** *S(NY)*

A bronze and ivory figure, 'Hindu Dancer' by Demêtre Chiparus, c1925. **£8,000–12,000** *S(NY)*

Three bronze and ivory figures of female athletes, by Ferdinand Preiss, c1925: *l.* 'Oars Woman' *c.* 'Javelin Thrower' *r.* 'Skater', 12½in (32cm) high. **£4,000–6,000 each** *S(NY)*

A painted bronze and ivory figural group, 'The Sisters', by Demêtre H. Chiparus, c1925, mounted on a brown onyx base, 29in (74cm) high. **£30,000–50,000** *S(NY)*

A carved bronze and ivory figure, 'Cleopatra', by Bruno Zach, 14in (35.5cm) high. **£4,000–6,000** *ASA*

A cold painted bronze and ivory figural group, 'Finale', by Demêtre H. Chiparus, c1925, 16½in (41cm) high. **£20,000–30,000** *S(NY)*

Demêtre Chiparus (Romanian)

Although born in Romania, Chiparus worked in Paris. He was the chief exponent of chryselephantine, a combination of bronze and ivory, and specialised in depicting exotic women, many inspired by the Ballet Russes. He nearly always signed his work on the base.

A gilt and silvered bronze and ivory figure, 'Semiramis', by Demêtre Chiparus, c1925, 26½in (67cm) high. **£30,000–50,000** *S(NY)*

Two silver patinated bronze figures, 'Ball Player' and 'Stella', by M. Guiraud Rivière and Etling, Paris, largest 25½in (65cm) high.
£2,500–3,500 each *C*

A bronze and ivory figure, 'The Archer', on green onyx base, signed F. Preiss, 8½in (22cm) high.
£5,000–6,000 *C*

A bronze and ivory figure, 'Autumn Dancer', signed with F. Preiss monogram, 14½in (37.5cm) high.
£20,000–25,000 *C*

A bronze and ivory figure, 'Starlight', signed 'D. H. Chiparus', on a marble base, 23½in (58.5cm) high.
£12,000–15,000 *C*

A bronze and ivory figure, 'Charm of the Orient', signed 'A. Godard', on a marble base, 19½in (49cm) high.
£6,000–9,000 *C*

A bronze and ivory group, 'High Priestess', on a white marble plinth, signed on the base 'A. Bouraine', 24½in (62cm) high.
£10,000–15,000 *C*

A gold patinated bronze and ivory figure, 'Exotic Dancer', signed 'Gerdago', on an onyx base, 12in (30.5cm) high.
£10,000–15,000 *C*

A bronze and ivory table lamp, 'Batwoman', with a waxed cotton shade, signed in the bronze 'Roland Paris', 37in (94cm) high.
£7,000–9,000 *C*

A gilt bronze and silver patinated figure, the bronze base signed 'E. Barrias', 17in (43cm) high.
£7,000–9,000 *C*

r. A bronze statuette of the 'Spirit of Ecstasy', by Charles Sykes, 23½in (60cm) high.
£6,000–8,000 *C*

A bronze and ivory figure, marked 'Bruno Zach', 15in (38.5cm) high.
£2,000–2,500 *S*

A bronze figure, by Bruno Zach, c1930.
£2,000–2,800 *CNY*

A gold and enamel buckle, now fitted with a watch, stamped 'Vever Paris', c1900, 3in (7.5cm) high.
£9,000–10,000 *S*

A parcel gilt cold painted bronze figure, 23½in (60cm) high.
£6,500–7,500 *CNY*

A gilt and enamelled bronze figure of a snake dancer, by Otto Poertzel, c1930, 20½in (52cm) high.
£5,000–8,000 *ASA*

A bronze and ivory group, by Otto Poertzel, 16½in (41.5cm) high.
£9,500–11,000 *C*

A bronze and ivory figure, by Philippe, 14in (35cm) high.
£5,000–7,000 *ASA*

A parcel silvered bronze and ivory figure of an archer, by Pierre le Faguays, early 20thC, 17in (43cm) wide.
£2,000–3,000 *CNY*

An ivory figure, 'Ecstasy', by Ferdinand Preiss, 17in (43cm) high.
£5,000–6,000 *CNY*

A cold painted bronze and ivory female figure, by Ferdinand Preiss, early 20thC, 9in (23cm) wide. **£5,000–7,000** *CNY*

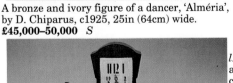

A bronze and ivory figure of a dancer, 'Alméria', by D. Chiparus, c1925, 25in (64cm) wide.
£45,000–50,000 *S*

l. A bronze and enamel clock, with enamelled dial, on a marble base, marked 'Maple & Cie, Paris', c1920, 10½in (27cm) wide.
£8,000–9,000 *S*

An Art Deco bronze and ivory figure, by Demêtre Chiparus, 21in (54cm) wide.
£40,000–60,000 *P*

A silvered, cold painted bronze, ivory, marble and onyx figure, 'Antinea', by Chiparus, c1925. **£40,000–50,000** *S*

A cold painted bronze, tinted ivory, marble and onyx figure, 'Ecstasy', by F. Preiss, c1930, 22in (56cm) high. **£4,600–6,000** *S*

A cold painted bronze and marble figure, 'Dancer with Thyrsus', by Pierre Le Faguays, 1920s, 22in (56cm) high. **£3,000–4,000** *S*

A cold painted bronze, ivory and onyx figure, by Ferdinand Preiss, 1930s. **£1,800–2,000** *S*

A bronze and ivory figure, 'Pierrot', by Chiparus, 1920s. **£3,000–5,000** *S(S)*

A bronze figure of a dancer, by Morante, 16in (41cm) high. **£1,000–1,500** *ASA*

A cold painted bronze, ivory and onyx figure, 'Dancer', c1925, 10in (25cm) high. **£700–1,000** *S*

A bronze and ivory figure, by Joe Descamp, 15in (38cm) high. **£4,000–5,500** *ASA*

'Daphne', silvered bronze and marble, by Fredy Stoll, c1925. **£10,000–12,000** *S*

A bronze figure, 'Bacchante', by Pierre Le Faguays. **£7,000–9,000** *C*

r. A bronze and ivory figure, 'Autumn Dancer', by Ferdinand Preiss. **£8,000–10,000** *C*

r. A cold painted bronze and ivory figure, 'Grecian with Torch', by Ferdinand Preiss. **£1,200–1,800** *S*

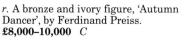

BRONZE & IVORY FIGURES

A freedom of expression hitherto unknown was demanded by the sculptors of the last decade of the 19th century. Previously the route to artistic acclaim required that they follow a rigid classical tradition. Young artists, desperately needing government patronage, had continued to interpret the Old Masters in a classical idiom because only by so doing could they hope to have work accepted for public display at the prestigious annual Salon exhibitions.

Gradually, demand from the public for private ownership of sculpture for the home was increasing. This was recognised by the bronze founders who exploited this new market by making use of a new invention called a pantograph – a type of tracing machine, use of which enabled them to accurately reproduce scaled down models of large marble sculpture to domestic proportions. The model, cut from a soft plaster blank, could then be cast in bronze. The Barbedienne founders made substantial profits by producing limited editions of bronzes from classical marble statuary.

Thankfully, they also recognised and catered for the growing demand for Romantic sculpture, thus providing a forum for those artists whose work had been previously eschewed by the Salons. The artists in turn could depend less on commissions for unique pieces and rely more on the royalties accruing from the multiple production of their work.

The beginning of the 20th century saw the burgeoning of Art Nouveau design. One of the more obvious images was the portrayal of 'woman'. Freed from the constraints of a 19th century literary tradition, which portrayed her as stiflingly respectable, and liberated physically from her rigid corsets, she now danced with gay abandon. The fluid sensual sculptures of Agathon Leonard, the mysterious 'Le Secret' by Maurice Bouval, and the oft-repeated image of the American dancer, Loïe Fuller, most notably portrayed by Raoul Larche, are among the more typical and desirable examples of Art Nouveau sculpture.

The electric light bulb was still a novelty and many artists engaged its properties. It

A typical example of a bronze and ivory female figure, 'Cabaret Girl', by Ferdinand Preiss, on a marble base, 15in (38cm) high.
£8,000–10,000 ASA

was to be found concealed within the scarf held above the head of Loïe Fuller as she danced, illuminating 'The Milky Way', a blue and opal glass globe, clutched by the pensive female sculpted by Leo Laporte Blairsy, secreted into nautilus shells held aloft by a mermaid, or often replacing stamen in the flowerheads of a myriad of lamps which combined the images of women and plant forms.

By the 1920s life had changed markedly. The rigours of war, the birth of the Machine Age, and the discovery of Tutenkhamen's tomb in 1921, were among the influences reflected in the work of the Art Deco artists and sculptors. The woman they portrayed was bolder, stylish and more self-assured.

Bruno Zach's ladies were often erotic, scantily clad and provocative. They were modelled in their underwear, holding whips or dressed in trousers and smoking cigarettes. 'Airwoman' by Ferdinand Preiss was almost certainly modelled on Amy Johnson and was undoubtedly a celebration of her achievements. The image, cast in bronze, her hands plunged deep into the pockets of her cold painted red flying suit, and her neat facial features captured in carved ivory, indicate the changing status of women. Whilst never portrayed covered in the mud of the trenches, artists such as Pierre le Faguays and Marcel Bouraine did cast some females symbolically in the role of noble warriors. Though still scantily clad, they could be seen throwing spears or dancing in victory, whilst waving daggers and shield. Lorenzl, meanwhile, was busy modelling females in a highly stylised and elongated fashion. His ladies were long and lithe, young and flawless. They danced, largely naked, but often waving scarves, or balancing hoops on their exaggerated outstretched limbs.

Theatrical images inspired by the birth of Hollywood pervaded the sculpture of the period. 'Lighter than Air', by Preiss, was modelled on Miss Ada May, who appeared in the 1930 C. B. Cochran review. Much of the later works of Demêtre H. Chiparus were based on the theatre and ballet. The Ballet Russe inspired many of his works, in particular 'Russian Dancers', which depicted Nijinsky and Ida Rubinstein in their roles in Scheherazade. The opening of the Pharaoh's tomb in the early 1920s was a terrific source of inspiration for Chiparus. He modelled Egyptian dancers in bronze and bronze and ivory, embellishing the bronze of their costumes and headdresses with beaded and jewelled decorative detail which was then highlighted in the cold painting process, with appropriately vivid colours.

Casting in bronze has always been expensive, whether the process of lost wax or sand casting is employed. Extensive highly skilled and labour intensive techniques are required to ensure a fine quality end result.

The stages of production begin once the sculptor has made a model of the subject, usually in clay or terracotta, which he takes along to a founder. In the 1920s, those founders known to produce the finest quality work allied themselves to the leading sculptors of the day. On Art Deco figures particularly, a founder's seal, together with an artist's signature, usually denotes work of a high standard.

When casting figures, it was not unusual for separate moulds to be made for the limbs, head and torso. A more complicated model requires more pieces to be cast separately and assembled later. The bronze that is removed from the moulds has quite a rough surface and lacks much of the finer detail of the original model. Following preparatory retouching it is the task of the chaser, using an engraving tool called a burin to carefully and painstakingly recreate that lost detail. This process is one the sculptor may choose to oversee.

Finally, the required finish or patina is applied. On many Art Nouveau sculptures this finish was achieved by painting a solution of mineral salts and acids on to the surface and applying heat with a torch to accelerate the chemical reaction. Most were applied with colours ranging from verdigris to rich chocolate, although it is not unusual to see gilding. The sculptors of the Art Deco period experimented much more with their finishes. Electroplating, cold painting, gilding and enamelling were used in various combination to create their exciting and colourful images.

Where ivory was used for the head and exposed limbs of a figure, these of course had to be carved and fitted to the bronze. Much of this was individually hand carved. Even when the preliminary carving was done by machine, the fine detailing of the final stages would be hand crafted.

Sadly, relatively few artists today work in bronze. Given the procedures outlined above, it is not difficult to see that the costs of the processes involved are now prohibitive.

Bronze sculpture from the first half of the 20th century has a unique flavour. It is dramatic and totally evocative of the age. The charm and spirit it exudes, together with the exquisite quality and craftsmanship it often displays have ensured increasing attention from a growing body of discerning collectors. Despite the high prices commanded for the most desirable pieces, in terms relative to the cost of current production, many are still affordable.

However, the supply is finite. The short lived Art Nouveau movement managed only to span two decades at the turn of the century. Its romantic, languid images could hardly survive once the nation's thoughts had turned to war. The Art Deco movement emerged after WWI, but a considerable amount of the artistic output and records relating to it were lost or destroyed during the devastation of European cities in WWII.

Art Deco style has grown so much in popularity over the last couple of decades that today the immense appeal of its instantly recognisable forms can be seen reproduced on a mass scale. The market for original pieces is stronger than ever, and the escalation in price is correspondingly impressive. Apart from a short time at the end of 1987 and during 1988, when prices surged wildly and then fell back, growth has been constant. Twelve years ago it was possible to buy medium sized Art Deco bronze figures by one of the more popular and prolific artists such as Lorenzl for between £100 and £200. Collectors can now expect to pay in the region of between £800 and £1,200 for a similar piece. Fine and highly stylised examples of bronze and ivory figures by Collinet, Phillipe, Chiparus, Preiss, Descomps, Zach and others command prices showing up to a tenfold increase.

A bronze figure, by Bruno Zach, 1920s, on a marble base, 28in (71cm) high.
£8,000–10,000 *ASA*

Those Art Deco figures made in the 1930s from less expensive materials such as spelter, (a metal containing zinc and lead, plated to resemble antique bronze or silver), and manufactured using simpler and cheaper processes, have seen some increase in price, but these have been less marked. A pair of spelter figure book-ends which sold in 1983 for between £60 and £90 would cost £150 to £175 today. Large spelter groups, depicting women and birds or small animals and mouted on marble bases, were made in abundance during the 1930s to satiate demand for the style at all social levels. The market value of such pieces in 1983 would have been in the order of £125 to £250. The most shining examples can still be found today at around £400 to £500.

Collectors should always endeavour to buy bronzes which display the talent of the artist and the skill of the founder. Discerning buyers will always seek out the finer pieces. As seen above, time does not improve the quality or desirability of poor examples. It has never been my policy to market bronzes based on their investment potential, but it is comforting and not at all surprising to see that, long term, they have proved to be more than competitive and a whole lot more attractive to look at than a bank book.

Audrey Sternshine.

A bronze bust, 'Dalila', cast from a model by E. Villanis, signed in the bronze and with 'Société des Bronzes de Paris' foundry mark, 17½in (44.5cm) high.
£1,000–1,500 *C*

A bronze figure of a pierrot, by L. Alliott, 13½in (34cm) high.
£900–1,200 *ASA*

A bronze figure cast from a model by Marius Vallet, on marble base, signed 'Mars Vallet, Siot Decauville Fondeur Paris', 12in (30.5cm) high.
£2,000–3,000 *P*

A gilt bronze figure of a dancer, cast from a model by Agathon Leonard, inscribed 'A. Leonard Sclp' and stamped with founder's seal, 'Susse Frères Editeurs, Paris, M', 19½in (49.5cm) high.
£6,000–9,000 *C*

A Lorenzl bronze figure of a dancer, signed, on an onyx base, 9in (23cm) high.
£500–800 *ASA*

A silvered bronze group, 'Carthage', cast after a model by Théodore Rivière, signed, marks for 'Susse Frères Editeurs, Paris', 22in (56cm) high.
£2,000–3,000 *P*

A French bronze figure of the Pied Piper playing a flute, with ivory face and hands, signed 'E. Barillot', on a slate socle, 10in (25cm) high.
£500–800 *GSP*

A bronze and ivory figure, cast and carved from a model by A. Brandel, on a shaped re-painted base, indistinctly signed 'A. Brandel', 10½in (26.5cm) high.
£500–800 *C*

A bronze bust, 'La Sibylle', cast from a model by E. Villanis, signed 'E. Villanis' and with 'Société des Bronzes de Paris' foundry mark, 28½in (72.5cm) high.
£2,600–3,000 *C*

A bronze sitting figure, by
Lorenzl, 4in (10cm) high.
£200–300 *ASA*

A bronze and ivory figure,
cold painted in rose pink,
marked on base 'F. Preiss',
1930s, 8in (20cm) high.
£350–550 *SB*

A bronze figure of a mummy
and sarcophagos, by
Bergman, 6in (15cm) high.
£400–600 *ASA*

A bronze figure,
'Dagger Dancer',
by Marquet, c1930,
19in (48cm) high.
£1,000–1,500 *ASA*

A French spelter figure,
'L'Inspiration', after T. H.
Somme, early 20thC, 22½in
(57cm) high, on a marble base.
£350–400 *GAK*

A bronze figure, by
Fesler Felix, signed,
14½in (37cm) high.
£280–360 *P*

A pair of spelter figures,
by Auguste Moreau,
c1900, 30in (76cm) high.
£1,500–1,800 *ASA*

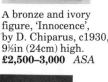

A bronze and ivory
figure, 'Innocence',
by D. Chiparus, c1930,
9½in (24cm) high.
£2,500–3,000 *ASA*

A green patinated bronze figure, etched on
base 'D. H. Chiparus', 29in (73.5cm) wide.
£300–400 *CSK*

l. A carved ivory
figure of a dancing
girl, by F. Preiss,
signed, 7in
(17.5cm) high,
on an onyx base.
£2,000–2,500 *P*

A bronze bust, signed in the
maquette 'H. Müller, c1900,
5in (12.5cm) high.
£400–700 *SB*

A painted bronze and ivory figure
of a young girl in a pleated dress
with a ruff collar, and a red
conical hat, cast and carved
from a model by Ferdinand
Preiss, signed, on a marble base,
6in (15cm) high. **£450–650** *P*

A gilt bronze and ivory figure of a dancing girl, signed 'Joe Descamps', on a marble socle, 1920s, 16½in (42cm) high.
£2,000–2,500 *SB*

A painted bronze and ivory figure, modelled as an Oriental maiden wearing a pale green kimono, signed 'Harders R.u.M.', 16½in (42cm) high.
£1,200–1,800 *P*

An Art Deco ivory and bronze figure, by Lorenzl, c1920, 11in (28cm) high.
£600–900 *LEX*

A painted bronze and ivory figure of a girl, wearing a silvered brown dress, on an onyx base, inscribed 'Lorenzl', 13½in (34.5cm) high.
£700–1,000 *P*

A painted bronze and ivory figure of a lady, wearing a green skirt with a gilt tunic, on an onyx base, inscribed 'Lorenzl', 13⅓in (34cm) high.
£1,200–1,600 *P*

A bronze group, on a mottled grey marble base, engraved mark 'Kelety', 1920s, 15½in (40cm) high.
£2,000–2,500 *SB*

A painted bronze and ivory figure, modelled as a girl wearing a pink tinted tunic, signed 'P. Philippe R.u.M.'
£3,000–3,800 *P*

A pair of silvered and gilt painted bronze figures, by Lorenzl, on an orange veined green onyx base, signed, 10½in (27cm) high.
£1,200–1,800 *CSK*

A painted bronze and ivory figure, 'The Hoop Girl', by F. Preiss, on a brown onyx base, 8½in (21cm) high.
£600–900 *P*

A bronze and ivory figure of a maiden wearing a gilt and green dress, inscribed F. Preiss, 7in (17.5cm) high.
£900–1,200 *P*

A pair of bronze and ivory figures, 6in (15cm) high.
£1,500–2,000 *ASA*

A bronze and ivory figure of a dancer, by Lorenzl, 15in (38cm) high.
£1,800–2,600 *ASA*

A figure of a bronze and ivory dancer, on a large onyx dish, 8in (20cm) high.
£800–1,200 *ASA*

l. A carved ivory figure of a young girl with a skipping rope, on an onyx base, signed 'F. Preiss', 6in (15cm) high.
£600–800 *P*

A gilded bronze and ivory figure of a dancing girl, on a green onyx pedestal, signed in the bronze 'H. Fugière', the base plate stamped 'Fabrication Française Paris - G.M.', little finger of right hand missing, 19in (48cm) high.
£1,000–1,500 *MAT*

A cold painted bronze and ivory figure, 'The Respectful Splits', cast from a model by Paul Philippe, signed 'P. Philippe', 7in (17.5cm) high, on a green onyx base.
£2,500–3,000 *Bon*

A bronze and ivory figure, by Claire J. Colinet, 12in (30.5cm) high.
£4,000–5,000 *ASA*

A bronze figure of a girl, by S. Molselsio, signed and dated 'S. Molselsio, 1919', 12½in (31.5cm) high.
£280–340 *P*

A bronze and ivory figure, by Montini of Henry Fielding playing Dante, one thumb missing, 1930s, 16in (41cm) high overall.
£900–1,100 *HCH*

An ivory figure, by F. Preiss, signed, on an onyx base, 7in (17.5cm) high.
£260–300 *SS*

A gilt bronze and ivory figure, 'Priestess', cast and carved from a model by Demêtre Chiparus, with enamelled blue and green sumulated jewellery, inscribed 'Chiparus', 17in (43cm) high.
£3,000–4,000 *C*

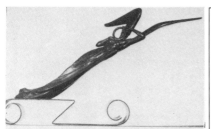

A bronze figure of a winged female, cast from a model by Charles Sykes, inscribed 'Chas. Sykes', 14in (35.5cm) high.
£650–700 *CSK*

A green patinated bronze figure, 'Boy with Frog', by William Reid-Dick, signed and dated 'Reid Dick 1931', 26½in (68cm) high.
£3,000–4,000 *P*

There is a similar figure in the Queen's Garden, Regent's Park, London, resulting from Queen Mary having seen this piece. The owner, instead of giving it to the Queen, gave her the name and address of the sculptor.

A French Art Deco polychrome bronze statuette of a woman dancer, cast from a model by A. Gory, surface rubbed in areas, on a mottled marble base, 20in (51cm) high.
£1,500–2,500 *C*

A green painted bronze figure, cast from a model by Fayral, inscribed, 20½in (52cm) high. **£800–1,200** *CSK*

A pair of cast bronze bookends, inscribed 'Raoul Benard', early 20thC, 9½in (24cm) high.
£300–500 *LBP*

A gold cold painted bronze figure, the flowers and bowl in painted plastic, on a mottled stepped brown marble base, engraved 'Duverand', 1930s, 12in (30.5cm) high.
£800–1,200 *S*

A gilt bronze figure, 'Juggler', cast from a model by Claire J. R. Colinet, on a buff onyx base, inscribed 'Cl. J. R. Colinet', 7in (17.5cm) high.
£600–900 *CSK*

A bronze group of 2 dancing Bacchantes, marble engraved 'Cl. J. R. Colinet', 1930s, 22in (56cm) high. **£2,000–2,800** *S*

l. An Art Deco bronze figure, by Lorenzl, c1920.
£1,200–1,800 *ASA*

A patinated bronze figure of a dancer with a hoop, by A. Bouraine, on a marble socle, 18in (45.5cm) high. **£1,000–1,500** *EH*

A French cold painted silvered bronze and marble bust of a lady in a turban, cast and carved from a model by A. Gory, inscribed 'A. Gory', early 20thC, 15in (38cm) high, on a white alabaster base.
£2,000–2,500 *CNY*

A bronze and ivory figure, 'Beach Ball Girl', inscribed 'F. Preiss', 15in (38cm) high.
£3,000–5,000 *CSK*

A gilded bronze and ivory figure of a girl on stepping stones, by F. H. Monginot, signed, 8in (20cm) high.
£500–800 *M*

A figure of a naked boy, seated on a tree stump, removing a splinter from his foot, raised on a tapered onyx base with malachite edge, inscribed 'F. Preiss', 4½in (11.5cm) high.
£300–500 *HSS*

An Austrian bronze draped female, by J. Benk, 1907, 11in (28cm) high.
£1,000–1,300 *ASA*

l. An Austrian gilt bronze and ivory figure, signed 'Brandel Wien', 19in (48cm) high.
£2,000–2,600 *P*

A bronze and ivory figure of an elegantly dressed young lady, cast after the model by Quenard, signed 'Quenard', 13in (33cm) high, on a marble base.
£800–1,200 *CSK*

A French part gilded bronze and ivory figure of a lady playing a harp, signed 'Gregoire', fitted for electric light, original shade, 13½in 34.5cm) high.
£1,000–1,500 *PWC*

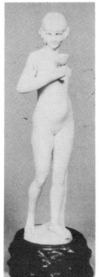

l. An ivory figure of a naked girl, slight damage, 20thC, 6in (15cm) high.
£800–1,200 *SC*

r. A bronze and ivory figure, 'Girl with a Cigarette', cast and carved after a model by Bruno Zack, ivory cracked at face, small piece missing from cigarette butt, signed in the bronze 'Bruno Zack', and monogram within a square, c1925, 29in (73.5cm) high.
£6,000–8,000 *C*

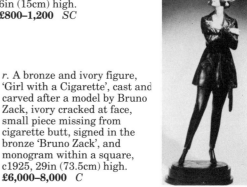

A bronze and ivory figure, by Gerdago, with coloured enamel decoration, c1920.
£2,000–2,500 *ASA*

A bronze figure of a girl, by Bruno Zach, with rich light brown patination, on a marble column, 18in (45.5cm) high overall.
£1,200–1,400 *S*

An Art Deco electroplated figure, by G. H. Gantchell, on a black marble base, 11in (28cm) high.
£100–150 *CDC*

A bronze figure, cast from a model by Lorenzl, inscribed, on a green onyx pedestal. **£600–700** *CSK*

A cold painted metal figure of a kneeling huntress, by D. H. Chiparus, 1930s, 23½in (60cm) wide. **£900–1,000** *S*

A bronze bust of a man's head, 'Energie', signed 'Kélety', bronze stamped '255', rich rubbed green patination, on a marble base with presentation plaque, early 20thC, 14½in (37cm) high.
£500–600 *SS*

r. A silvered bronze figure, 'Goat Charmer', signed by H. Fugère, 19½in (48cm) wide.
£800–1,200 *ASA*

l. A bronze and ivory figure of a young concertina player, signed 'D. H. Chiparus', early 20thC, 10in (25cm) high.
£500–550 *SC*

A bronze and ivory figure, 'Oriental Water Carrier', from a model by Dominque Alonzo, inscribed 'D. Alonzo, Etling Paris', 13½in (34cm) high.
£650–750 *CSK*

r. A bronze group of a woman and 2 greyhounds, signed in the maquette 'Cl. J. R. Colinet', 1920s, 17½in (44.5cm) wide. **£1,100–1,500** *S*

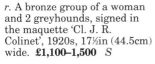

An Art Deco gilded bronze and ivory group of 2 children as flower and fruit sellers, by Joseph d'Aste, signed, 9in (22.5cm) high. **£500–600** *M*

A patinated bronze and ivory figure, 'Pierrot', inscribed 'D. H. Chiparus', 12in (30.5cm) high.
£1,300–1,500 *CSK*

An Art Deco bronzed spelter and simulated ivory figure, by Menneville, depicting a seated girl reclining on an an onyx veneered vase, 13in (33cm) wide.
£850–950 *S(S)*

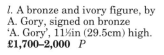

A bronze bust, inscribed Raoul Larche, founder's seal 'Silot Decauville Paris', serial No. 973K, 17½in (44.5cm) high, on a giltwood plinth.
£1,800–2,600 *C*

l. A bronze and ivory figure, by A. Gory, signed on bronze 'A. Gory', 11½in (29.5cm) high.
£1,700–2,000 *P*

A bronze and ivory figure, 'Dancing Girl', carved and cast from a model by Bruno Zach, signed, mounted on a black marble base, 15in (38cm) high.
£3,000–3.500 *C*

A bronze and ivory figure, 'Little Chilly One', cast and carved from a model by D.H. Chiparus, signed on marble base, 9in (22.5cm) high.
£800–1,000 *P*

An Art Deco bronze and ivory figure of a Dutch boy, by J. Bertrand, in the style of L. Sosson, 5½in (14.5cm) high, on a plinth, with incised signature.
£200–250 *HSS*

A gilded bronze and ivory figure of a girl feeding poultry, by D. Alonzo, signed, 9½in (24cm) high.
£700–800 *M*

r. A gilt bronze and ivory group, by D. H. Chiparus, signed, on an onyx plinth, 6in (15cm) high.
£950–1,000 *L*

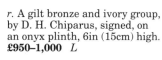

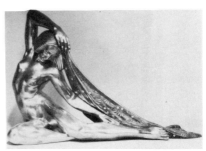

A parcel gilt bronze and ivory group, 'Morning Walk', cast and carved after a model by A. Becquerel, cold painted in red, on a marble base, inscribed 'Becquerel', 10½in (27cm) high.
£1,500–2,000 *C*

A damascened, silvered and gilt bronze figure of a scarf dancer, cast from a model by Raymond Guerbe, inscribed '42, Raymond Guerbe', early 20thC, 30½in (77.5cm) high.
£3,500–4,500 *CNY*

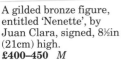

A gilded bronze figure, entitled 'Nenette', by Juan Clara, signed, 8½in (21cm) high.
£400–450 *M*

A German bronze group by Jager, signed 'Jager', 13½in (34cm) high.
£300–350 *P*

A bronze and alabaster lamp, cast after a model by A. Kélety, signed in the bronze 'A. Kélety', c1925, 22in (55cm) high.
£3,000–3,500 *C*

A bronze and gilt bronze figure, cast from a model by A. Gory, signed 'A. Gory', c1920, 21in (52cm) high.
£1,300–1,500 *C*

A bronze group of 2 men, by Nepa, on a marble base, 27½in (70cm) wide.
£450–500 *CSK*

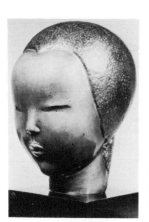

A painted bronze and ivory figure, by Lorenzl, signed on reverse 'Lorenzl', on 13in (33cm) high, a green onyx base.
£750–850 *P*

A bronze head of a young Oriental girl, cast after a model by I. Codreano, signed in the bronze 'I. Codreano 1927', 13in (33cm) high.
£1,000–1,200 *C*

r. A bronze figure, by Prof. Poertzel, 13in (33cm) high.
£2,200–2,600 *JJIL*

A Preiss bronze and ivory
figure of 'Vanity', 8½in (22cm).
£3,500–4,500 *ASA*

A painted bronze and ivory lamp,
'Oriental Waiter', cast and carved
from a model by Ferdinand Preiss,
signed on base, 19in (48cm) high.
£2,200–2,600 *P*

A bronze figure of a reclining
greyhound, cast from a model by Daniel
Bartelletti, base inscribed 'Bartelletti',
20in (50.5cm) long.
£300–400 *CSK*

An Art Deco figure group 'Friends', by
Demêtre Chiparus, on a shaped
brown onyx base, signed, 16⅛in
(42cm) high.
£4,000–6,000 *HSS*

A bronze and ivory figure of a girl,
cast and carved from a model by
Ferdinand Preiss, unsigned,
6⅛in (16cm).
£1,400–1,600 *P*

*This model is known as 'The Necklace',
in this case the necklace she should be
holding is missing.*

l. A painted bronze and
ivory lamp, unmarked
but possibly by F. Preiss,
23in (58.5cm) high.
£1,000–1,500 *P*

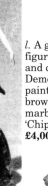

l. A gilt bronze and ivory
figure 'Old Style Dancer', cast
and carved from a model by
Demêtre Chiparus, cold
painted in dark olive green on
brown, black and green
marble base, inscribed
'Chiparus', 16in (40.5cm) high.
£4,000–6,000 *C*

r. A painted bronze
and ivory figure, 'Little
Cricketer', modelled as
a young boy wearing
pale brown short
trousers, signed
'F. Preiss' on base,
7in (17.5cm) high.
£1,000–1,500 *P*

A bronze figure 'A Lioness', cast after a
model by Demêtre Chiparus, signed in the
marble 'D. Chiparus', 22½in (57cm) long.
£1,000–1,500 *C*

l. A French cold painted, gilt bronze and ivory
figure of an exotic dancer, cast and carved
from a model by Demêtre Chiparus, the white
alabaster base signed 'D. Chiparus', early
20thC, 14in (36cm) high.
£3,500–5,000 *CNY*

A cold painted, bronze and carved ivory
dancing girl, signed 'Lorenzl', restored,
15in (38cm) high. **£700–900** *DSH*

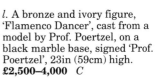

An ivory figure on an onyx base, c1930, 10in (25cm) diam.
£400–450 *JAD*

A bronze and ivory figure on a green marble base, 12in (30cm) high. **£2,500–3,000** *BWe*

A gilt bronze figure on a stepped marble base, 27in (69cm) high.
£1,200–1,800 *CSK*

l. A bronze and ivory figure, 'Flamenco Dancer', cast from a model by Prof. Poertzel, on a black marble base, signed 'Prof. Poertzel', 23in (59cm) high.
£2,500–4,000 *C*

r. A gilded and painted bronze figure, 'Venus', cast from a model by Edouard Drouot, on a mound base cast with waves and a rising sun, inscribed 'E. Drouot', 34in (86.5cm) high.
£2,000–3,000 *Bon*

l. A bronze figure, cast from a model by Lorenzl, patinated in green, on an onyx base, signed Lorenzl, 17½in (44cm) high.
£1,200–1,800 *P*

A bronze figure, 'Scarf Dancer', cast from a model by Demètre Chiparus, the marble base incised 'D.H. Chiparus', 27in (68cm) high.
£5,500–6,500 *C*

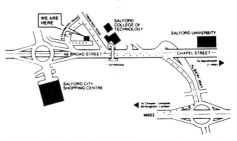

A bronze and ivory figure, 'Clown', cast and carved from a model by Jaeger, signed in the metal 'Jaeger R.v.M.', 10in (25.5cm) high.
£1,500–2,000 *C*

A bronze and ivory figure, 'The Courtier', cast and carved from a model by Lorenzl, signed in the bronze 'Lorenzl', 7in (17.5cm) high.
£600–900 *C*

An ivory figure, carved in the style of Ferdinand Preiss, 2½in (6.5cm) high.
£450–500 *CSK*

l. A bronze figure, by Philippe, signed, 8½in (22cm) high.
£1,500–2,000 *ASA*

A green-patinated bronze and ivory figure, 'Juggler', cast and carved from a model by Jaeger, signed in the bronze Jaeger and stamped 'Vrai Bronze Déposé', 36½in (93cm) high.
£2,000–3,000 *C*

l. A bronze and ivory figure, signed 'Philippe, 16in (41cm) high.
£4,000–6,000 *ASA*

A bronze and ivory figure, 'Page Boy', cast and carved from a model by Prof. Otto Poertzel, cold painted green cape, bronze foot and striated marble base, signed in the bronze Prof. O. Poertzel, 11½in (29cm) high.
£2,000–2,500 *C*

A bronze and ivory figure, by Tereszczuk.
£800–1,200 *ASA*

A bronze figure, 'Radha', by Philippe, 22in (56cm) high.
£3,000–4,000 *ASA*

l. An ivory figure, 'Girl with Skipping Rope', carved from a model by Ferdinand Preiss, signed 'F. Preiss', 6in (15cm).
£450–600 *P*

r. A bronze figure, by Philippe, 9in (23cm) high.
£600–1,000 *ASA*

An ivory figure, carved from a model by P. Philippe, on a brown onyx striated pedestal base, the base inscribed 'P. Philippe', 9in (23cm) high.
£1,200–1,800 *C*

A gilt bronze and ivory figure, cast and carved from a model by H. Keck, on an onyx base, signed in the bronze 'H. Keck', with foundry mark, 12in (30.5cm) high.
£650–800 *CSK*

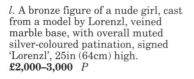

l. A bronze figure of a nude girl, cast from a model by Lorenzl, veined marble base, with overall muted silver-coloured patination, signed 'Lorenzl', 25in (64cm) high.
£2,000–3,000 *P*

An Art Deco bronze group signed 'H. Fugere', c1920, 18in (46cm) wide. **£1,000–1,500** *IHA*

A Lavroff patinated bronze figure of a young woman, on a stepped rectangular marble base, signed in the maquette, 1920s, 17in (43.5cm) high. **£1,200–1,800** *S*

A painted bronze and ivory figure with gilt, red and green costume, signed 'Gerdago', 'AR' founder's mark, 15½in (40cm) high. **£1,500–2,500** *P*

A Gori silvered and gilt-bronze and ivory figure of a young woman, in pyjama suit silvered and oxidised, with gilt design, base marked 'G. Gori', 1920s, 14in (30cm) high. **£1,500–2,000** *S*

A silvered and gilt-bronze figure, mottled red-green marble base, signed 'Guiraud Rivière', 1920s, 20½in (52cm) high. **£5,000–7,500** *S*

A bronze lamp, marked 'Guillemard', fitted for electricity, 1920s, 15½in (39.5cm) high. **£1,200–1,800** *S*

A bronze and ivory bust, by Agathon Leonard, on a green onyx base, signed 'A. Leonard', 6in (15cm) high. **£300–500** *P*

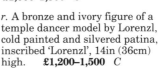

A polished bronze nude dancer, marked 'Lorenzl', 1930s, 16in (41cm) high. **£1,200–1,800** *S*

A Keck bronze and ivory figure, cold painted with metallic bronze-green, brown detailed hair, bronze base plate marked 'H. Keck fec', c1920, 13in (33cm) high. **£1,000–1,500** *S*

r. A bronze and ivory figure of a temple dancer model by Lorenzl, cold painted and silvered patina, inscribed 'Lorenzl', 14in (36cm) high. **£1,200–1,500** *C*

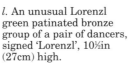

A dark bronze nude female figure cast from a model, inscribed Lorenzl, 17½in (44.5cm) high. **£1,200–1,500** *CSK*

l. An unusual Lorenzl green patinated bronze group of a pair of dancers, signed 'Lorenzl', 10½in (27cm) high. **£1,100–1,400** *P*

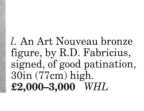

l. An Art Nouveau bronze figure, by R.D. Fabricius, signed, of good patination, 30in (77cm) high. **£2,000–3,000** *WHL*

r. A bronze figure, 'The Kicking Dancer', cast from a model by Bruno Zach, on green onyx base, bronze inscribed 'B. Zach', 12½in (31.7cm) high. **£750–950** *C*

A bronze figure, 'Con Brio', cast after a model by Ferdinand Preiss, with dull golden bronze patina, on black and green marble pyramid hase, signed on the base 'F. Preiss', 13½in (34cm) high. **£2,200–2,600** *C*

A bronze figure, 'Girl Skipping', cast from a model by Bruno Zach, signed in the bronze 'Zach', 14½in (37cm) high. **£1,000–1,500** *C*

A bronze group, signed in the bronze 'JB', 25½in (65cm) wide. **£2,300–£2,600** *C*

A gilt bronze figure of a girl with a dog, 12in (30cm). **£2,000–3,000** *C*

A large cold painted bronze figure of a young woman, by Bruno Zach, on a grey veined black marble plinth, signed, 36½in (93cm) high. **£10,000–12,000** *HSS*

A seated bronze study of Lucifer, 20thC, 8in (20cm) high. **£400–500** *CSK*

A bronze figure of a panther, cast from a model by M Prost, dark patina, inscribed 'M.Prost' and 'Susse Fres Editrs. Paris', 7½in (18.5cm) high. **£500–800** *C*

A green and gilt patinated bronze figure of a female archer, unsigned, 15in (38cm) high. **£500–800** *GC*

r. A French bronze figure, 'A Seated Monkey', cast from a model by Edouard Marcel Sandox, formed as a finial, inscribed 'Ed M Sandoz', early 20thC, 4½in (11.5cm) high. **£800–1,000** *GC*

l. A bronze and ivory figure, by Marcel Bouraine, on a marble base, 12½in (32cm) high. **£1,000–£1,500** *ASA*

A gilt bronze and ivory figure of a clown, signed 'C. Mimo', c1920, 9in (22.5cm) high. **£600–900** *S*

A bronze figure, 'Pert', on a bronze base, signed 'Roland Paris', 12in (30.5cm) high. **£800–1,200** *P*

A bronze figure of a nude dancing figure with a hoop, marble engraved 'Aurore Onu', 1930s, 19in (48.5cm) high. **£800–1,200** *S*

A bronze and alabaster bust, 'The Jester', signed 'Roland Paris', 10in (25cm) high. **£500–800** *P*

A cold painted ivory and bronze figure, on a stepped onyx base, signed 'M. Munk, Vienna', 14in (35.5cm) high. **£1,000–1,500** *SS*

A bronze and ivory group of a woman and 2 hounds, cold painted in red gold, marked 'Prof. Poertzel', with foundry mark 'PK', 1920s, 19½in (49.5cm) high. **£5,000–7,000** *S*

A gilt bronze figure of a nude, attributed to Philippe, on a marble pedestal, 1920s, 22½in (57.5cm) high. **£1,000–1,500** *S*

A bronze and ivory figure of a pierrette, signed in the maquette 'A. Gilbert', 1920s, 9in (22.5cm) high. **£1,800–2,200** *S*

A pair of ivory figures, 'Greek Maidens', 7in (18cm) high. **£750–850** *CSK*

A painted bronze and ivory figure, 'Sun Worshipper', signed on onyx 'F. Preiss', 7½in (19cm) high. **£2,000–3,000** *P*

A painted bronze and ivory figure, coloured in amber and gold, on a green onyx base, signed on onyx 'F. Preiss'. 14½in (37cm) high. **£4,000–5,500** *P*

r. An Art Deco figure, 'The Tennis Player', by F. Preiss, with gold/bronze costume, ivory head, limbs and tennis racket, on a signed onyx base. **£4,000–6,000** *GSP*

l. A bronze figure, 'Nocturne', cast after a model by Edward-Louis Collet, inscribed in the bronze 'Collet Scpt', stamped foundry mark 'E Colin & Co. Paris', 18in (46cm) high.
£600–800 *C*

r. A bronze figure cast after a model by Hugo Lederer, dark brown patina, on a stepped circular speckled grey marble base, signed in the bronze 'Hugo Lederer', c1925, 17in (43cm) high.
£1,200–1,800 *C*

A cold painted gilt bronze figure, in the style of Bruno Zach, on a green onyx base, 12in (30.5cm) high.
£500–700 *Bon*

r. A bronze Guiraud Rivière figure, 'Stella', inscribed on star 'Guiraud Rivière, Etling Paris', and 'Bronze, France', 11½in (29.5cm) high.
£1,500–2,000 *P*

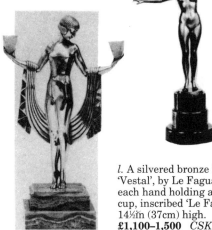

l. A German gilt bronze figure, by Schmidt-Hofer, inscribed 'Schmidt-Hofer', 16in (40.5cm) high.
£400–600 *P*

A Laurel silvered bronze figure, signed 'Pierre Laurel', stamped 'Marcel Guillemard 14', 17½in (45cm) high.
£1,500–2,200 *P*

l. A silvered bronze figure, 'Vestal', by Le Faguays, each hand holding an onyx cup, inscribed 'Le Faguays', 14½in (37cm) high.
£1,100–1,500 *CSK*

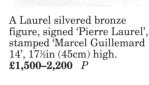

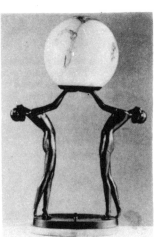

A pair of cold painted bronze figural bookends, 'Chinese Students', by H. M. White, on marble bases, signed 'H. M. White', 8½in (21.5cm) high.
£300–400 *P*

A bronze figure, 'Dancer of Olynthus', by D. Chiparus, signed on base 'Chiparus', 15in (38cm) high. **£1,000–1,500** *P*

A bronzed electric table lamp, with a mottled globular glass shade, on an oval base with an onyx stand, 20in (50.5cm) high.
£500–800 *AG*

A green patinated bronze figure, modelled as a nude female dancer, on a circular marble base, signed 'A. Bouraine, 17½in (45cm) high.
£800–1,400 *P*

A bronze and ivory figure of a dancing girl, on a pale green marble base, marked 'Gerdago', with founder's stamp, 1920s, 13in (33cm) high.
£1,800–2,400 *SB*

A bronze and ivory figure of a girl in Eastern costume, with carved ivory headdress set with red stones, some damage, marked 'B. Grundmann fec'.
£1,000–1,500 *SBe*

A cold painted simulated bronze, ivory and marble group, inscribed 'Limousin', 14½in (37cm) high.
£200–400 *C*

A polished bronze figure, on a rectangular marble base, signed in the maquette 'G. Lavroff', 1920s, 18in (45.5cm) high.
£1,000–1,500 *SB*

r. A bronze figure, cold painted silver, pink, and green, marked 'Lorenzl', 1930s, 12in (30.5cm) high.
£600–900 *SB*

A bronze and ivory figure in carnival costume, base marked 'Lorenzl', 1920s, 13in (33cm) high.
£1,500–2,000 *SB*

l. A bronze and ivory figure, 'The Champagne Girl', by F. Preiss, red cold painted, base marked 'F. Preiss', ivory glass broken, hat damaged, 16in (40.5cm) high.
£4,000–5,500 *SBe*

A cold painted bronze figure of a dancing girl, marked 'Lorenzl', 1920s, 16in (40.5cm) high.
£1,800–2,600 *SB*

A cold painted bronze figure of a dancing girl, by Lorenzl, 9½in (24cm) high. **£400–700** *SBe*

A bronze and ivory figure of a girl, engraved mark 'Le Faguays', 16½in (42cm) high.
£1,000–1,600 *SB*

A gilt bronze figure, cast from a model by Lorenzl, on a green onyx base, the bronze inscribed 'Lorenzl', 10in (26cm) high.
£500–600 *CSK*

A bronze and ivory figure of Harlequin, by Lorenzl.
£1,000–1,400 *ASA*

A cold painted bronze and ivory figure, by Lorenzl, enamelled in colours, on an onyx base, hairline cracks to base and one thumb lacking, signed 'Crejo', 10in (25cm) high.
£800–1,200 *CEd*

A bronze and ivory figure, by Lorenzl, c1930.
£700–1,000 *ASA*

A bronze figure, cast from a model by Le Faguays, signed on base, 25in (64cm) high.
£1,500–2,500 *CSK*

A cold painted bronze figure, 'Sword Dancer', cast from a model by Nan Greb, inscribed 'Nan Greb', 21 (54cm) high.
£1,500–2,000 *CSK*

l. A cold painted bronze figure, cast from a model by Nan Greb, inscribed 'Nan Greb', 11in (28cm) high.
£800–900 *CSK*

A bronze and ivory figure, 'Gamine', cast and carved after a model by Ferdinand Preiss, cold painted in green, on a green marble base, hairlines to head, arms and legs, inscribed 'F. Preiss', 13½in (34cm) high.
£4,000–6,000 *CEd*

A bronze figure, 'Hoop Girl', by D. H. Chiparus, 11in (28cm) high.
£1,800–2,600 *ASA*

A bronze figure of a dancer, by F. Preiss, c1930.
£1,800–2,200 *ASA*

A bronze and ivory figure, in the manner of F. Preiss, on a black marble plinth, 11in (28cm) high.
£4,000–5,500 *BWe*

l. A bronze figure of a motorcyclist, unsigned but attributed to Bruno Zack, the marble base applied with metal tag stamped 'B. Zach Sculp. Argentor Vienna', 8in (20cm) high.
£1,500–2,500 *P*

Locate the Source

The source of each illustration in *Miller's Art Nouveau & Art Deco Buyer's Guide* can be found by checking the code letters below each caption with the Key to Illustrations.

A bronze group, cast from a model by C. Kauba, dark gilt patina, signed in the bronze 'C. Kauba', on a marble base, 5½in (14cm) high.
£450–500 *C*

A figure lamp, by Le Verrier, c1930, 19in (48.5cm) high.
£1,000–1,500 *ASA*

A bronze figure, cast from a model by Jaeger, signed 'Jaeger', stamped 'Vrais-Bronze Déposé K', foundry marks, 26in (66cm) high.
£400–500 *P*

l. A bronze figure, 'The Racing Driver', cast from a model by Saalmann, inscribed 'Saalmann', stamped 'Echte Bronze', 11⅛in (28.5cm) high.
£1,800–2,200 *C*

A cold painted gilt bronze and ivory figure, c1930, 17in (43cm) high.
£550–650 *S*

A bronze figure, 'A Torch Dancer', cast after a model by Ferdinand Preiss, with dull golden bronze patina, on a black and green marble pyramid base, signed on the base 'F. Preiss', 13½in (34.5cm) high.
£2,000–2,800 *C*

A silvered bronze figure, 'A Huntress', cast from a model by G None, signed in the bronze 'G None Gorini Fres Ed teors, Paris' 13½in (34cm) high.
£1,500–1,800 *C*

l. A bronze figure cast from a model by Ferdinand Liebermann, in various cold coloured patinas, including gilt, dark gold and red, signed in the bronze 'F. Liebermann', 15½in (40cm) high.
£1,000–1,600 *C*

A bronze figure of a hunter, cast from a model by Pierre Le Faguays, bronze inscribed 'P. Le Faguays', 14in (35.5cm) high, and another similar bronze cast from a model by Le Faguays.
£700–1,000 *CSK*

A silvered bronze 'Messenger of Love' by Pierre le Faguays, c1930, 30½in (78cm) high.
£4,000–5,500 *ASA*

A bronze group, cast from a model by A. Boucher, dark patina, signed in the bronze 'A. Boucher' and with Siot-Paris foundry stamp, 19½in (50cm).
£3,000–5,000 *C*

A bronze and ivory figure, by F. Preiss, on a stepped green and black onyx base, lacking hands, signed in the maquette, c1930, 5in (13cm) high.
£300–500 *S(S)*

A bronze inkwell, by P. Tereszczuk, with a young girl crossing a stream, a basket in each hand, signed, c1920, 12½in (32cm) wide.
£300–400 *S(S)*

A bronze and ivory figure, 'Dancer', cast and carved from a model by Gerdago, her costume with gold patination and cold painted geometric decoration in red and shades of blue, on an oval green onyx base, decoration rubbed, signed in the bronze 'A. R. Gerdago', 13in (33cm) high.
£3,000–5,000 *C*

An enamelled bronze and ivory dancer, in red and black shoes, her dress decorated in orange, red, blue, green, black and gilt flowerheads, a wide-brimmed hat similarly painted, raised on a stepped oval green onyx base, incised 'Austria' on the base, 1920s, 12½in (32cm) high.
£1,500–2,000 *S(S)*

A chrome plated sculpture of a reclining figure, worn, stamped 'A. Reimann, Ges Gesch, Made in Germany', 5½in (14cm) long.
£400–600 *S(S)*

A Dutch brass model of a woman dancing, on an oval base, signed 'Th. A. Vos.', and 'Kunst-Bronsgieterij, De Kroon, Haarlem', 19in (48cm) high.
£300–500 *C(S)*

Thomas Vos was born in Groningen in the Netherlands in 1887. Having learned to sculpt in Brussels, he worked principally on figures of women, animals and children until his death in Haarlem in 1948.

An ashtray, with a figure of a boy, 6in (15cm) high. **£600–900** *ASA*

l. A silvered bronze figure, by Helène Grünne, indistinct foundry mark, 1920s, 1½in (29cm) high.
£700–800 *S (S)*

A silvered bronze and ivory figure of a dancing girl, painted with bell-formed blue flowers and green foliage, raised on a green onyx base, damaged, moulded mark 'Lorenzl', painted 'Crejo', 1920s, 14½in (37cm) high.
£1,500–1,800 *S(S)*

l. A bronze and polychrome marble figure, 'Reading', cast and carved from a model by Schumacher, signed in the bronze 'Henry', 10in (25cm) high.
£1,000–1,300 *C*

A bronze and ivory figure, 'Dancing Girl', from a model by Lorenzl, signed 'Lorenzl', 9in (22.5cm) high.
£700–900 *C*

l. A gilt bronze and ivory figure, 'Mystery', cast and carved from a model by V. Seifert, signed in the bronze 'V. Seifert', 11½in (29.5cm) high.
£1,000–1,500 *C*

A bronze figure, 'Spanish Flamenco Dancer', cast from a model by Sonher, inscribed 'Sonher', 13½in (34.5cm) high.
£1,000–1,200 *C*

A bronze figure, 'The Fencer', cast from a model by H. Müller, signed in the bronze 'H. Müller', 17½in (44.5cm) high.
£600–1,000 *C*

r. A bronze figure, 'Athlete', cast from a model by H. Henjes, signed in the bronze 'H. Henjes fec.10', 14in (35.5cm) high.
£600–900 *C*

A bronze and ivory figure, 'Feeding the Birds', cast and carved from a model by L. Barthelémy, signed in the bronze 'L. Barthelémy', 12in (30.5cm) high.
£2,000–3,000 *C*

A spelter and ivorine group, 'Pierrot and Columbine', cast from a model by D. Chiparus, on a striated marble plinth, 30in (76cm) wide.
£1,200–1,500 *C*

r. A bronze figure, 'Flower Girl', cast from a model by Tuch, a flower in her right hand, signed in the bronze 'Tuch', 17in (43cm) high.
£500–900 *C*

A silver patinated bronze figure, 'Amazon', by Marcel Bouraine, the stylised nude female warrior kneeling on a dark patinated base, signed in the bronze 'Bouraine, 7in (17.5cm) high.
£1,000–1,500 *C*

l. A marble and bronze figure, by Lothar, signed. **£2,000–2,500** *ASA*

A pair of bronze figures by Pierre Laurel, 11½in (29cm) high. **£1,500–2,200** *ASA*

A gold patinated bronze ivory group, 'Elegant', cast and carved from a model by S. Bertrand, on a bronze plinth and black marble base, slightly chipped, signed, 12in (31cm) high. **£2,500–3,000** *C*

A bronze figure, 'Speedskater', cast from a model by Carl Fagerberg, signed on the bronze plinth 'Carl Fagerberg, Stockholm' and dated 'April 1932', 20½in (51cm) high. **£2,500–3,500** *C*

This piece was commissioned for a competition and exhibition commemorating the 1932 Los Angeles Olympic Games, and bears its original exhibition label on the underside of the base.

l. A bronze and ivory figure, cast and carved from a model by Lorenzl, on green onyx base, stamped 'Lorenzl, Made in Austria', 13½in (35cm) high. **£1,500–2,000** *P*

A bronze and ivory figure of the poet Dante, signed in the bronze 'D.H. Chiparus', 28in (70cm) high. **£2,000–3,000** *C*

A bronze and ivory figure, cast and carved from a model by Boulard, the young girl wearing a green patinated short dress with puff sleeves, on green onyx base, signed in the bronze 'Boulard', 14in (34cm) high. **£600–700** *CSK*

A bronze and ivory figure by Lorenzl, 12½in (32cm) high. **£1,400–1,800** *ASA*

A gilt bronze figure, 'Beside the Missouri', cast from a model by Claire Jeanne Roberte Colinet, inscribed in the marble 'Cl. J.R. Colinet', 19½in (49cm) high. **£1,000–1,500** *CSK*

A cold painted bronze figure, unmarked but attributed as a model by Colinet, the girl poised on one leg with a green serpent entwined round her ankle, 20in (50cm) high. **£1,200–1,800** *P*

A cold painted bronze and ivory figure, cast and carved from a model by Lorenzl, on a geometric green and black onyx base, signed 'Lorenzl', 10in (25.5cm) high. **£1,000–1,500** *P*

l. A bronze figure, 'Cleopatra', cast from a model by D.H. Chiparus, signed in the bronze 'Chiparus', 19in (48cm) wide. **£3,000–5,000** *C*

SILVER AND METALWARE

The collector of silver and metalware from the Art Nouveau and Art Deco periods has an enormous range from which to choose, as the items illustrated on the following pages indicate. A vast array of forms, materials, makers and designers are available and, regardless of the depth of one's pockets, there is something for everyone.

Towards the end of the 19th century, forms and styles in silver and metalware began to move away from the elaborate medieval, baroque or rococo designs favoured during the mid-19th century. Christopher Dresser, a prominent designer for Elkington's from 1875 to 1888, was inspired by a visit to Japan in 1876. His work shows a cleanness of line that anticipated the styles of the 1920s and 1930s – the Machine Age – and are now highly sought after. A plated teapot made in 1879 sold for £40,000 in 1986, and another from the same group fetched almost £70,000 in 1994.

Other British designers/makers of note working in silver and representing the Arts & Crafts Movement were Charles Robert Ashbee (1863–1942) at the Guild of Handicraft Ltd., Omar Ramsden, Alwyn Carr and Gilbert Marks. They worked according to two principles: the rejection of mass-market machine-made items, and appreciation of the forms and styles of decorative pieces produced during the Middle Ages.

Liberty & Co. combined innovative design and a craft 'look' with mass-production. Founded by Arthur Lasenby Liberty in 1875, the company launched its Cymric range of silverware in 1899, and in 1901 Liberty & Co. (Cymric) Ltd was formed, in conjunction with the Birmingham-based silver firm of W. H. Haseler. Archibald Knox was one of Liberty's most important designers, producing designs for Cymric silverware, and for the Tudric pewter range introduced in 1903. Together with Rex Silver and Oliver Baker, Knox established the 'Liberty Style' in the early years of the 20th century.

The use of combinations of different metals became popular during this periods. A. E. Jones used silver and copper together and produced pleasing jewellery caskets, and W. A. S. Benson designed lamps using copper and brass that were retailed through William Morris & Co., as were embossed copper pieces by John Pearson who had spent time at Ashbee's Guild of Handicraft.

In Germany, the firm of WMF (Württembergische Metallwarenfabrik) created a range of metalwares which epitomise the popular conception of Art Nouveau. They produced machine-made, mass-produced vessels, cutlery and mirrors embellished with maidens, sinuous forms and motifs from nature, providing for a large clientele, and consistantly sought by collectors today.

A constant reminder of the past pre-eminence of Art Nouveau in France are Hector Guimard's Metro entrances, made from green-patinated bronze, emblematic of the power of growth exhibited everywhere in nature. Louis Majorelle of Nancy produced stunning ormolu mounts for his furniture, and there are examples of his collaboration with the glass factory, Daum Frères. Daum Frères and Emile Gallé also chose leading silversmiths of the day to fashion quality mounts for their glassware.

The 'Exposition des Arts Decoratif' of 1925 in Paris showed what was considered the best of the period, and later the name 'Art Deco' was used to categorise such pieces. In 1935, France launched the luxury liner *S.S. Normandie*, making her maiden voyage to New York. Her interior was a showcase of Art Deco, with the very best of French design, fittings, cuisine and crew: tableware by Puiforcat and Christofle, glassware by Lalique, Daum and St. Antoine, and furniture by Ruhlmann.

Technological advances in transportation and communications had considerable influence on architecture and design: steamlining became a prominent design feature, combining the principles of aerodynamic engineering and geometry. In addition, discoveries such as the tomb of Tutankhamun in 1922 encouraged the development of an Egyptian style.

The Art Deco metalwares of Swiss designer/maker, Jean Dunand (1877–1942), deserve a mention. He produced extraordinary patinated copper vases using a technique called dinanderie, often featuring strong angular lines and with a geometric bias.

Also working in this style was Claudius Linossier (1893–1955) who was noted for the elegant design and textured surfaces of his vases, bowls and plates. Pieces by these two designers are particularly sought after. Finely executed and designed silver cigarette cases and compacts with geometric motifs, were produced by Gerard Sandoz (b1902) and Raymond Templier (1891–1968) , reflecting the opulence of the very rich in the 1920s and 1930s.

When buying Art Nouveau and Art Deco silver, always buy what you find pleasing and can most afford. Never buy something which you have reservations about, however reasonable the price. Always ask advice from reputable sources if you are not sure.

Whatever your taste or collecting criteria, there will be surely something for the discerning collector from this most colourful, exotic and dynamic periods in Decorative Arts.

Keith Baker

A Liberty & Co. Tudric Pewter flower vase, possibly designed by Archibald Knox, stamped marks, Tudric 0441, 4in (10cm) high.
£600–800 *P*

A Bronze vase, signed 'J. Ofner', 13in (33cm) high. **£500–600** *CSK*

A pair of WMF figural metal vases, with glass liners, stamped marks on base, 14½in (36.5cm) high. **£2,000–2,500** *P*

A silver vase, maker's marks G & Co. Ld and Birmingham marks for 1963, 10½in (26cm) high. **£400–500** *P*

A silver backed brush set, embossed with kingfishers and water lilies, Chester 1909, cased by Oldfields, Liverpool.
£400–500 *P(CW)*

A Hagenauer plated hand mirror with linear decoration on one side, stamped on reverse 'WHW' in circle, 9⅛in (23.5cm) high.
£400–450 *P*

A hammered copper framed mirror, 21 by 15in (53 by 38cm).
£300–400 *ST*

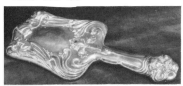

A silver backed hand mirror, 1907.
£50–70 *PC*

An Arts and Crafts mirror, with a moth enamelled in relief, 19 by 15 (48 by 38cm)
£300–400 *ST*

A silver and enamelled picture frame marked 'H & A', Birmingham 1904, 6½in (16.5cm).
£600–700 *P*

A brass flower, the petals remove to make individual ashtrays, c1900, 9½in (24cm) wide.
£120–150 *GAL*

A pair of Liberty & Co. silver and enamelled picture frames, marked 'L & Co.', Birmingham 1913, 5⅛in (13cm) diam., in original Liberty box.
£2,000–2,500 *P*

A pewter garniture by Margaret Gilmore, comprising an oval mirror and a pair of double candle sconces, each piece embossed with a Celtic interlaced design, each stamped 'M.G.', the mirror 30in (76cm) wide.
£1,000–1,400 *CEd*

A Hukin and Heath 'Japanesque' teapot and sugar bowl, heightened with silver colour against a warm copper ground, inscribed 'Designed by Dr. C. Dresser', teapot 4in (10cm) high.
£1,500–2,000 *P*

A beaten pewter and ebonised wood rectangular wall mirror, designed and executed by Margaret and Frances Macdonald, impressed 'Margaret Macdonald, Frances Macdonald, 1897', 27in (69cm) high.
£8,000–12,000 *C*

A heavy punch bowl in Art Nouveau style, by F. Fattorini & Son Ltd., Birmingham 1905, 12½in (31.5cm) wide, 37 oz.
£1,200–1,500 *L*

An Art Nouveau silver comport, chased with roses and foliage on a hammered ground, makers W. Walker and B. Tolhurst, signed 'L. Movio 1904', 13½in (34.5cm) high, 50oz.
£2,500–3,000 *GSP*

On graduation from the Glasgow School in 1894, the Misses Macdonald opened a studio at 128 Hope Street, Glasgow where they devoted themselves to the applied arts. The metal items produced by the 2 sisters were, apart from a very few examples, not only designed but worked entirely by themselves and although closely collaborating, few examples of their metal work now exist bearing both signatures. The studio closed when Frances Macdonald married Herbert MacNair in 1899.

A silver and enamel flared cylindrical vase, probably designed by Archibald Knox, indistinct stamped marks, 'Rd 467167', damaged, 7in (17.5cm) high.
£400–600 *C*

A Goldsmiths and Silversmiths Co. Ltd. silver and enamel presentation cup and cover, London 1902, 12in (30.5cm) high, 25½oz gross.
£1,000–1,200 *C*

A Guild of Handicrafts Ltd. silver toast rack, maker's mark for London, 1906, probably to a design by Charles Robert Ashbee, 5in (13cm) wide, 7oz.
£1,500–2,000 *P*

A Walker and Hall silver mounted jug, inspired by a design by Christopher Dresser, maker's mark, Sheffield, 1906, 9in (22.5cm) high. **£300–400** *S*

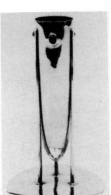

*r.*A William Hutton & Sons Ltd. silver dressing set, designed by Kate Harris, maker's marks, '1900/03/04', mirror 11in (28.5cm) high, 7oz. **£800–1,000** *S*

l. A Liberty & Co. silver vase, designed by Archibald Knox, the rim set with turquoises, maker's mark, stamped 'Cymric, Birmingham, 1903', 6in (15cm) high. **£1,200–1,500** *S*

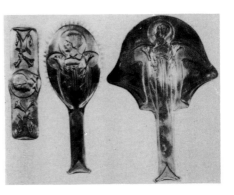

A Gold and Silversmiths Company silver box, maker's marks for London 1901, (10.5cm) high, 22oz.
£600–800 *P*

An Edwardian Art Nouveau rose bowl, makers Hamilton and Inches, Edinburgh 1902, 9in (23cm) diam., 38oz.
£800–1,000 *CDC*

An Art Nouveau claret jug, Birmingham 1905, 10½in (25cm) high.
£800–1,000 *CDC*

A silver tea set, marked 'GD.DF', London 1901, teapot 5½in (14cm) high, 35.5oz.
£260–340 *P*

A Hukin & Heath plated metal and glass biscuit barrel, marked 'H & H' and No. '1894', 5½in (14cm) high.
£250–300 *P*

A Hukin & Heath plated toast rack, H & H mark, lozenge registration mark for 9th October 1878, 'Designed by Dr. C. Dresser' and No. '1987', 5½in (13.5cm) high.
£2,000–3,000 *P*

A five-piece electroplated metal tea service, set on green ball feet on stepped bases, 1930s, 23in (60cm) wide. **£500–700** *S*

A plated Aesthetic Movement kettle, the design attributed to Christopher Dresser, maker's marks for R. & R. Hodd & Sons, and a design lozenge for 16th May 1878, 7½in (18.5cm) high.
£350–450 *P*

A Hukin & Heath plated sweetmeat bowl, stamped 'H & H No. 2047' and 'Designed by Dr. C. Dresser', 7in (17cm) wide. **£550–650** *P*

A Kewsick School of Industrial Arts silver buckle, 3in (8cm), each half stamped KSIA, in original case
£350–400 *DWB*

An unusual Dixon and Sons plated teapot, designed by Christopher Dresser, maker's marks, facsimile signature and No. '2277', 13cm high.
£6,000–8,000 *P*

A William Hutton and Sons Ltd. electroplated cruet set, inspired by a design by Christopher Dresser, maker's mark, c1900, 2½in (6.5cm) high. **£100–150** *P*

A Hukin & Heath plated sweetmeat dish, designed by Christopher Dresser, stamped 'H & H' and 'No. 2593', 7in (17cm) wide. **£200–300** *P*

A Georg Jensen hammered teapot, with grooved ebony handle, stamped '456', artist's monogram GS and London import marks for 1929, 6in (15cm) high, 16oz gross.
£800–1,000 *CEd*

A Hukin & Heath silver teaset, designed by Christopher Dresser, the teapot with wickered handle and domed cover with button finial, 4½in (11cm) high, and a milk jug and sugar bowl, both contained within the pot, maker's marks for Birmingham 1880, registration lozenge for 18th October 1879.
£1,500–2,000 *P*

A large pewter ale jug and cover, showing the influence of the designs of C. F. A. Voysey, unmarked, probably Liberty & Co, 14½in (36.5cm) high.
£600–800 *P*

An Orfèvrerie Gallia plated tea and coffee set, stamped factory marks, numbered '4643' and '4644', tray 20½in (52.5cm) wide.
£1,200–1,500 *P*

r. A silver goblet, Chester 1905, 8in (20.5cm) high.
£300–400 *TVA*

A Mappin & Webb silver coffee set, comprising: a hot milk jug and sugar bowl, coffee pot, 7in (18cm), maker's marks for Sheffield 1938.
£1,000–1,200 *P*

A Modernist teaset, the silver coloured metal stamped '800' and '210ff' in shaped punch, teapot 5in (13cm) high.
£800–900 *P*

A pair of pewter candlesticks, by Just Anderson, c1920, 9in (23cm).
£600–700 *GAL*

A pair of Liberty's Tudric pewter candlesticks, each with detachable driptray, No. 01769, 8in (20.5cm) high.
£200–300 *HCH*

A WMF pewter dish with figure, 9in (23cm) high.
£650–750 *GAL*

A German pewter bowl by Osiris, 5½in (14cm) high.
£300–400 *GAL*

A Guild of Handicraft Ltd plated copper Tazza to a design by Charles Robert Ashbee, 10⅓in (27.5cm).
£1,000–1,500 *P*

A Jean Després plated bowl, with overall hammer textured finish, signed on base and 'JD' poinçon on rim, 4in (10cm) high.
£900–1,200 *P*

l. An Arts and Crafts stemmed bowl, attributed to John Paul Cooper, inscribed 'In memory of a Labour of Love, Ascension Day 1914', 6in (15cm) high.
£1,000–1,500 *P*

A Liberty & Co. pewter and Clutha glass stemmed bowl, the mount marked 'English Pewter' and '0276', 6½in (16.5cm) high.
£600–800 *P*

A WMF silvered pewter covered two-handled punch bowl, and ladle, stamped, 21⅓in (54cm) high. **£650–750** *CAm*

A silver coloured metal bowl, stamped 'David Anderson 830S' and numbered '5485', 16½in (42cm) wide.
£600–800 *P*

An Omar Ramsden silver soup ladle, stamped 'OR' with London hallmarks for 1924, 10½in (27cm) long, 6oz.
£600–800 *P*

A 57 piece Georg Jensen Continental pattern table service, stamped marks, London import marks for 1934, 68oz.
£2,000–2,500 *CEd*

A 79 piece set of Georg Jensen Scroll pattern cutlery, designed by Johan Rohde, stamped in oval 'Georg Jensen' and 'Sterling Denmark', 136oz. gross.
£2,500–3,000 *P*

A set of 6 Georg Jensen silver coffee spoons, stamped maker's mark 'G.S.' and London import mark for 1925, cased.
£200–300 *CEd*

r. A 61 piece set of Cypress pattern cutlery, designed by Tias Eckhoff, stamped in oval 'Georg Jensen Sterling Denmark', 92oz gross.
£2,000–2,500 *P*

A Liberty pewter and enamel clock, c1903, 11in (28cm) high.
£1,000–1,500 *ZEI*

l. An Art Nouveau pewter mirror, 22in (56cm) high.
£1,000–1,500 *ZEI*

A WMF Art Nouveau plated pewter mirror, the surround cast in relief with the figure of a maiden in long flowing drapery, her hair adorned with flowers, stamped factory marks, 14½in (37cm) high.
£800–1,200 *P*

l. A Liberty pewter tea set and tray, c1910, tray 17in (43cm) wide.
£500–700 *ASA*

A Guild of Handicraft silver jam spoon, designed by C. R. Ashbee, set with turquoise, engraved 'Lorna', stamped 'G of H Ltd.', London hallmarks for 1904, 50gr.
£300–400 *C*

An A. E. Jones hammered silver rose bowl, decorated with a repoussé frieze of Tudor roses amid foliage, mounted on a wood plinth, stamped maker's marks 'A. E. J.', Birmingham hallmarks for 1909, 9in (23cm) diam., 990gr.
£2,000–3,000 *C*

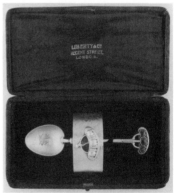

A Liberty & Co. silver and enamel christening set, comprising: a teaspoon and matching napkin ring, in original box, both with moulded floral design, heightened with blue and green enamel, maker's mark for Birmingham 1908, 4in (11cm) high.
£300–500 *P*

A WMF silver plated dessert service, with unusual box, 13in (33cm) wide.
£800–950 *ARE*

l. A pair of Liberty & Co. Cymric silver candlesticks, design attributed to Archibald Knox, maker's mark for Birmingham 1909, one repaired.
£2,000–3,000 *P*

A WMF silver plated pewter champagne bucket, signed and dated '1906'.
£1,000–1,500 *ASA*

A WMF silvered pewter bowl, with swing handle, and green glass liner, stamped marks, 10in (25cm) wide.
£500–700 *CSK*

A WMF round silverplate box, 5in (13cm) diam.
£300–400 *ASA*

A Liberty & Co. Tudric pewter clock, the arched top cast with heart-shaped leaves, their stems flanking the tapering rectangular body, the copper dial above 2 blue enamelled cabochons, stamped marks, 8in (20cm) high.
£1,200–1,500 *Bon*

A pewter bowl, moulded with female heads and swirling draperies, with a cut glass liner.
£250–300 *LRG*

A Liberty & Co. pewter and enamel clock, c1900, 7½in (19cm) high.
£1,500–2,000 *ASA*

r. A pair of Tudric candlesticks, attributed to Archibald Knox, 5½in (14cm) high.
£300–400 *NCA*

A Liberty & Co. pewter and enamel clock, 4½in (11cm) high.
£700–1,000 *ASA*

A Tudric pewter picture frame, with stylised honesty decoration, 10in (25cm) high.
£800–1,000 *C*

A Liberty & Co. pewter and enamel clock, 8in (20cm) high.
£1,500–2,000 *ASA*

Two Liberty & Co. silver and enamel cigarette cases, detailed in turquoise enamel, one stamped 'Cymric', Birmingham, 1902, 3½in by 3in (8 by 7.25cm). **£600–700** *S*

A set of 6 William Hutton & Sons silver salts, with, with spoons, maker's mark and hallmarks for London 1901, also Austrian importation marks, fitted case, 1½in (3.5cm) high, 5oz. **£700–900** *P*

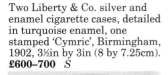

A shallow bowl by Georg Jensen, maker's mark, Denmark, stamped Sterling, silver coloured metal, 6½in (16cm) diam., 8.8oz. **£400–600** *L*

A WMF electroplated pewter tazza, c1900, 8½in (21.5cm) high. **£350–400** *S*

An Art Nouveau silver and enamelled christening set, each piece embellished with a blue enamelled plant form, maker's marks 'E. J. & S.', Birmingham 1905, cup 3in.(7cm) high, in a fitted case. **£300–400** *P*

A WMF standish, c1900, 13½in (35cm) high. **£200–300** *TA*

A WMF electroplated dish, marked, c1900, 8½in (21cm.) high **£800–1,000** *S*

A Hukin and Heath electroplate-mounted jug, attributed to Dr. Christopher Dresser, ebonised wood handle and hinged cover, manufacturer's mark, 1880s, 9½in (24cm). **£500–700** *S*

l. & r. A pair of German Art Nouveau wine coasters, stamped mark of Württembergische Metallwarenfabrik (WMF), 3¼in high (8.2cm). **£300–400**
c. A German Art Nouveau jewel casket, stamped mark of Württembergische Metallwarenfabrik (WMF), 7¼in (18.5cm) overall length. **£300–400** *L*

An Elkington Art Nouveau bowl, of pierced oval outline, with curved handles supported on 2 C-shaped stems above an oval domed base, stamped 'E. & Co.', with Birmingham hallmarks for 1910, 7in (17cm) high.
£400–500 *P*

A C. R. Ashbee hammered silver bowl, with pierced design of stylised fruit laden branches, stamped 'CRA' with London hallmarks for 1899, 8in (19.5cm) diam., 430gr.
£1,200–1,700 *C*

A Liberty & Co., silver rose bowl, designed by Bernard Cuzner, engraved with Golden Wedding dedication on one side, marked 'L & Co.', for Birmingham 1916, separate grille top for flower display, 6½in (16.5cm) diam.
£1,500–2,000 *P*

A Tiffany & Co. silver child's mug, the body decorated in low relief, with etched detailing, with a scene of children preparing a number of small dogs to jump through a hoop, stamped 'Tiffany & Co. 410SE', Sterling Silver 925-1000 M, 3in (7cm) high.
£350–400 *P*

An Art Nouveau preserve jar and spoon, George Lawrence Connell, with plain glass jar, hammered openwork trefoil frame and tripod handle to cover, Birmingham 1909, the spoon with heart shaped bowl and enamelled interlace motif terminal, spoon 1912, 5in (13cm) high, 12oz.
£1,500–2000 *S(S)*

A Georg Jensen silver vase and cover, of baluster form, on a small circular foot, the lip moulded with leaves, the overhanging cover with moulded piecrust edge, set with 4 cabochon amethysts in flower buds, impressed marks for Georg Jensen and import marks for 1924, 8½in (21cm) high.
£3,500–4,000 *P*

An Art Nouveau silver photograph frame, stamped in relief with entrelac scrolls, with enamelled hearts and ovals in mottled blue and green, on later wood mount and easel support, Birmingham 1904, 8in (20cm) high.
£500–600 *CSK*

A Guild of Handicraft hammered silver beaker, designed by C. R. Ashbee, with repoussé and engraved decoration of stylised flowers and leaves, stamped 'G of H Ltd' with London, hallmarks for 1904, 4in (11cm), 210gr.
£800–1,200 *C*

r. A silver plated tureen and cover, designed by Christopher Dresser, with ivory handles and raised on triple spike feet.
£1,200–1,500 *AAV*

This piece has been well used and is missing a ladle, which would have increased the value considerably.

Pricing Pointers

A popular maker or designer can affect price: a piece designed for Liberty & Co. for example, will have a relatively high value because there is a strong body of collectors for items by Liberty.

A Libert & Co. hammered pewter rose bowl, the design attributed to Oliver Baker, set with 5 green glass studs, on 5 curved legs and trefoil feet, stamped 'English Pewter made by Liberty & Co, 01130', 6½in (16.5cm) high.
£600–800 *C*

A German claret jug, with a pewter top, 11½in (29cm) high.
£300–500 *ASA*

A WMF pewter jug, 12in (30.5cm) high.
£200–300 *ASA*

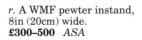

A WMF pewter dressing table mirror, 12½in (32cm) high.
£400–500 *APO*

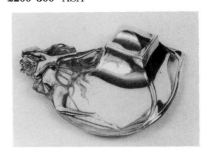

r. A WMF pewter instand, 8in (20cm) wide.
£300–500 *ASA*

l. A German green glass and pewter claret jug, 14in (36cm) high.
£250–300 *ASA*

r. Tudric pewter tea set, tray 18½in (47cm) wide.
£600–700 *APO*

A Continental pewter plaque, with central dished panel chased with the head of a Pre-Raphaelite maiden, flanked by curved uprights pendant with husks with stepped cresting, the reverse initialled 'EP' and stamped '279', 8½in (21cm) wide.
£200–300 *HSS*

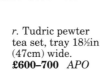

A WMF electroplated pewter tazza, 12½in (32cm) high.
£600–800 *HEW*

A Tudric pewter vase, cast in relief with sprays of honesty and bearing the inscription 'For Old Times Sake', stamped marks, 8in (20cm) high.
£300–400 *CSK*

A Liberty & Co. pewter biscuit barrel and cover, embellished with stylised buds and tendrils, having swing handle and domed cover, stamped marks and numbered '01167', 5in (12.5cm) high.
£300–500 *P*

A Liberty & Co. Tudric jardinière, with pink enamelled insets.
£600–700 *ZEI*

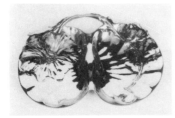

A Kayserzinn pewter dish, 11in (28cm) wide.
£275–325 *ZEI*

A Kayserzinn lidded pewter jug, 9in (23cm) high.
£300–400 *ZEI*

An Art Nouveau pewter desk blotter, 6in (15cm) wide.
£150–200 *ZEI*

Liberty

Liberty & Co. was the principal outlet for Art Nouveau designed in England. Arthur Lasenby Liberty (1843–1917) founded his furniture and drapery shop in 1875. Later he commissioned designs exclusive to his store, including Cymric silver and Tudric pewter, which gave rise to a distinctive 'Liberty Style'.

A Liberty & Co. Tudric pewter clock, with embossed copper face above a blue and green enamelled plaque, flanked and mounted by stylised scrollwork, impressed 'Tudric 0367', with key, 6½in (16cm) high.
£1,000–1,200 *I*

A pair of Liberty Art Nouveau pewter vases, 10in (25cm) high. **£400–600** *ASA*

A Liberty & Co. pewter salad bowl, designed by Rex Silver, with an openwork design of interwoven entrelacs extending to form 2 small handles, marked 'English Pewter Made by Liberty & Co.', numbered '0318', with original green glass liner, probably by Whitefriars, 10½in (27cm) diam.
£1,200–1,700 *P*

A Glasgow School pewter wall mirror, attributed to Margaret Gilmour, mounted in a wooden frame faced in pewter and embossed with a peacock at either end, united by branches with stylised leaves, enamelled with a blue/green panel, reserved against a textured ground, 12 by 24½in (31 by 62cm).
£900–1,200 *P*

Similar use of enamelling can be seen on a wall clock by Margaret Gilmour, illustrated in 'Glasgow Girls – Women in Art and Design 1880–1920'. and similar style leaves are shown in 'The Glasgow Style' by Gerald and Celia Larner, No. 182.

A WMF pewter lamp, c1900, 14in (36cm) high
£1,200–1,300

A Hukin & Heath plated spoon warmer, probably designed by Christopher Dresser, stamped 'H & H 2693', 5in (13cm) high. **£400–600** *P*

A Hukin & Heath electroplated soup tureen, designed by Christopher Dresser, with ivory finial and twin ivory handles, maker's marks and registration mark for 1875, 8in (29cm) high. **£2,500–3,000** *P*

A William Hutton silver faced oak photograph frame, the upper corners inlaid with blue/green enamel, London 1904, stamped mark, 7in (17.5cm) high. **£1,000–1,200** *CSK*

An Art Nouveau ladle, 6in (15cm) long. **£15–20** *ASA*

A Ramsden and Carr silver inkwell and cover, with glass liner, engraved 'Omar Ramsden et Alwyn Carr me Fecerunt', maker's mark, London 1912, 3in (8cm) high. **£800–1,200** *SB*

A Liberty & Co. silver stopper, the design attributed to Archibald Knox, maker's mark, stamped '2226', Birmingham 1906, 2½in (6.5cm) high overall. **£400–600** *SB*

A James Dixon & Sons electroplated teapot and cover, designed by Christopher Dresser, stamped 'J.D. & S 2272', registration mark for 25 November 1880, 7in (18cm) wide. **£1,000–1,500** *C*

r. A Guild of Handicraft Ltd. tea tray, London 1901, 21½in (54.5cm) wide. **£800–1,200** *SBe*

A set of 6 Liberty & Co. silver coffee spoons, maker's mark, dates between 1926–32, in original fitted box, 4½in (11cm) long. **£550–650** *SB*

A pair of Liberty & Co. silver vases, maker's mark, stamped 'Cymric', Birmingham 1902, 7in (17.5cm) high. **£1,000–1,400** *SB*

A fruit tazza, by Mappin & Webb, Sheffield, 1903, 12in (30.5cm) high. **£600–800** *SB*

A WMF electroplated vase, maker's mark, 16in (40.5cm) high. **£400–600** *SBe*

r. An Art Nouveau silvered metal sweetmeat dish, stamped 'AK & Cie', 9½in (24cm) high. **£300–400** *CSK*

l. A spelter figure of a young girl, cast from a model by L. Alliot, inscribed by L. Alliot, 30in (76.5cm) high. **£1,000–1,200** *C*

A WMF green glass claret jug, with pewter mounts, stamped marks, 16in (41cm) high.
£500–700 *P*

A pair of pewter two-branch candelabra designed by Albert Reimann and manufactured by Gerhardi & Cie., 15in (38cm) high.
£1,200–1,500 *C*

An Art Nouveau pewter sweetmeat centrepiece, 8½in (21.5cm) high.
£250–300 *LEX*

An Art Nouveau pewter mirror, stamped '120', c1905, 21½in (54.5cm) high.
£600–800 *SB*

A pair of silvered pewter wall plates, stamped mark 'as', 9½in (24cm) diam.
£400–600 *SBe*

A Jean Dunand wrought metal vase, inlaid in contrasting metals, marked 'Jean Dunand 1913', 7in (17.5cm) high.
£250–300 *SB*

A Guild of Handicraft Ltd. silver and enamel box and cover, maker's mark 'London 1901', 4⅓in (11cm) diam.
£1,500–2,000 *SBe*

A WMF electroplated triform basket, with clear glass liner, WMF monogram, 28cm high.
£300–400 *SBe*

A Guild of Handicraft Ltd. silver tea caddy, maker's mark London, 1906, 3in (7.5cm) high.
£500–600 *SB*

A Ramsden and Carr silver ciborium, maker's mark, engraved 'Omar Ramsden et Alwyn Carr me Fecerunt', London 1905, 7in (17.5cm) high.
£1,200–1,500 *SB*

Two Guild of Handicraft Ltd. silver loop-handled stemmed cups, after a design by C. R. Ashbee, each with maker's mark, London 1904, 4in (10cm) high.
£2,000–3,000 *SB*

A Guild of Handicraft Ltd. silver and enamel two-handled dish and cover, the design attributed to C. R. Ashbee, maker's mark, London 1902, 10⅓in (27cm) wide.
£3,000–4,000 *SB*

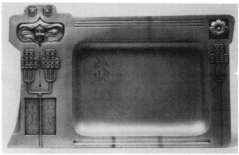

A Heath & Middleton silver pepper pot, attributed to Christopher Dresser, maker's marks 'JTH. JHM', Birmingham 1892, 3½in (9cm) high, 1.5oz. **£600–700** *P*

A Russian Art Nouveau rectangular pen tray, by O. Korlyukov, Moscow 1899–1908, 10⅓in (26.5cm) wide. **£700–800** *C*

An Arts & Crafts metal and enamelled triptych, by Nelson and Edith Dawson, all panels signed with 'D' and 2 dated '1901', 10⅓in (26.5cm) high. **£2,500–3,000** *P*

An enamelled cigarette case, after a design by Eugène Grasset, maker's mark 'MZ', French poinçons, c1900, 3in (8cm) wide. **£600–800** *S*

Pewter

Pewter is an alloy, consisting mainly of tin, which has been used in Britain since Roman times. When no lead is used in the alloy, pewter tends to remain bright and almost like silver; the higher the proportion of lead, the darker the colour.

Largely ousted during the 19thC, pewter was revived as a material by exponents of the Arts & Crafts movement, and their contemporaries and successors, followers of the Art Nouveau.

In Britain and Germany particularly, Art Nouveau pewter work achieved great popularity and high standards of craftsmanship. Liberty's 'Tudric' range of pewter wares decorated with motifs taken from the Celtic, included tea and coffee services as well as clocks, tableware, bowls and vases. The chief German exponent was Engelbert Kayser (1840–1911), whose range was as extensive as Liberty's, but fashioned in the 'high' Art Nouveau style.

A William Hutton & Sons silver faced photograph frame, with blue and green enamelled panels, stamped maker's mark, London 1903, 8in (20cm) high. **£1,000–1,200** *CSK*

A polished pewter photograph frame, the design attributed to Archibald Knox, with oak back, 7in high. **£800–1,000** *CSK*

A Jugendstil electroplated pewter mirror frame, by Kayserzinn, c1900, 18in (46cm) high. **£800–1,000** *S*

An Art Nouveau silver faced mirror, stamped maker's mark 'W.N.', Chester 1903, 12in (30.5cm) high. **£300–400** *CSK*

An Art Nouveau WMF white metal mirror, stamped marks, 20in (50.5cm) high. **£1,500–2,000** *CSK*

Silver & Metalware

What does 'white metal' mean when it looks like silver?

The British Hallmarking Council, which has jurisdiction over the selling of silver in Britain, does not recognise foreign marks indicating a standard below Sterling (925 parts per thousand), and as such they cannot be considered as approved standard marks. Consequently, such items cannot be called silver legally, or sold as such, hence the rather ambiguous term 'white metal'. A piece that has been assayed in Britain and found to be of the necessary standard will have the relevant marks stamped and will then be saleable legally, and referred to as silver.

A Ledru bronze pitcher, cast with grotesque fish, the handle in the form of a naked nymph, singed in the maquette 'Ledru, c1900, 13½in (34.5cm) high.
£1,000–1,500 *SB*

An Art Nouveau copper tray, 22in (55.5cm) wide.
£100–150 *HM*

A bronze hand mirror, from a model by A. Bartholomé, gilt patina, inscribed 'A. Bartholomé' and stamped 'P.39 Siot, Paris', 14in (35.5cm) high.
£1,500–2,000 *C*

A silver and copper tea caddy and cover, by Albert Edward Jones, stamped maker's initials, Birmingham, 1913, 5in (12.5cm) high.
£300–400 *CSK*

A St. Lerche gilt bronze vase, signed in the maquette 'H. St Lerche', stamped 'Louchet', c1900, 5in (12.5cm) high.
£500–600 *SB*

An Art Nouveau copper inkstand, 8in (20cm) wide.
£60–80 *ASA*

An oval Art Nouveau copper dish, 12in (30.5cm) wide.
£80–100 *HM*

A pair of Art Nouveau hand hammered copper candlesticks, 10in (25cm) high.
£100–150 *ASA*

l. An Art Nouveau hand hammered copper candlestick, 6½in (16.5cm) high.
£50–60 *ASA*

r. An Art Nouveau hand hammered copper vase, 5in (12.5cm) high.
£60–70 *ASA*

A Liberty & Co. 'Tudric' pewter box and cover, designed by Archibald Knox, underside stamped '9 Tudric 0194', c1905, 4½in (11.5cm) wide.
£400–600 *SB*

A WMF pewter matchbox cover.
£30–40 *ASA*

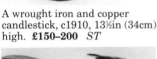

A set of silver buttons.
£80–130 *ASA*

An Arts & Crafts copper candlestick, with 3 garnets inset on the stem.
£150–200 *ST*

A pair of Edwardian Arts & Crafts candlesticks, by James Dixon, Sheffield 1907, 8½in (22cm) high.
£700–750 *HCC*

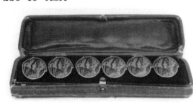

A pair of copper candlesticks, c1910.
£150–200 *ST*

A pair of pewter WMF candelabra, decorated with nymphs entwined around tendrils forming the sconces, on spreading bases, 10in (25cm) high.
£1,200–1,500 *P(M)*

A wrought iron and copper candlestick, c1910, 13½in (34cm) high. **£150–200** *ST*

A Liberty & Co. silver bowl, stamped 'L & Co.', London hallmarks for 1998, 2½in (6.5cm) high, 247gr.
£600–650 *C*

An Arts & Crafts copper bowl, possibly by the Birmingham Guild of Handicraft, 7½in (19cm) high.
£325–375 *ST*

A pair of WMF pewter candlesticks, 8½in (22cm) high.
£800–1,000 *ASA*

A copper bowl, by Keswick School of Industrial Arts, 16in (40.5cm) wide.
£250–300 *ST*

l. A German pewter fruit comport, with glass liner, marked, 12½in (32cm) wide.
£300–400 *ASA*

A Guild of Handicraft electroplated muffin dish and cover, designed by C. R. Ashbee, 8in (21cm) diam.
£400–600 *C*

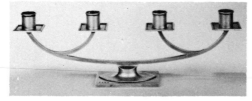

A pair of Hawksworth Eyre & Co. silver four-light candelabra, stamped maker's marks, Birmingham, 1913, 15in (38.5cm) wide, 35oz. **£800–1,000** *C*

An Art Nouveau silver-faced photograph frame, stamped 'W.A.', Birmingham 1902, 'Rd 40047', 4⅛in (12.5cm) wide. **£350–450** *C*

A pair of silvered-metal candlesticks, designed by Gallé, unmarked, 9½in (24cm) high. **£1,000–1,500** *P*

An Arts & Crafts silver-faced double photograph frame, glazed, mounted on a blue plush covered wood, stamped 'W.J.H.', Birmingham 1904, 4⅛in (12.5cm) wide. **£400–600** *C*

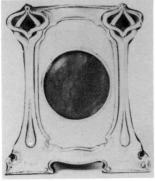

A pair of Art Nouveau silver frames, maker's mark 'W.N', Chester, 1907, 12in (30.5cm) high. **£1,000–1,400** *S*

An Art Nouveau silver and enamelled picture frame, embossed and hammer-textured with green and violet enamelling, W. Hutton & Sons, maker's mark for London, 1902, 8in (20cm) high. **£800–1,200** *P*

r. An Art Nouveau silver-faced photograph frame, enamelled in turquoise and violet, maker's mark 'G.A.D.W.D.', Chester 1905, 6¼in high. **£400–500** *CSK*

A Georg Jensen 64-piece part table service, designed by Gundorph Albertus in the cactus pattern, all with firm's stamped marks, weight without table and luncheon knives and salad servers 84oz. **£2,000–3,000** *C*

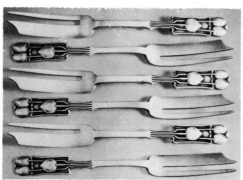

A set of 6 pastry forks by Liberty & Co., Birmingham, 1930, in original case. **£350–400** *L*

A Georg Jensen 50-piece part table service designed by Johan Rohde in the acorn pattern, all with firm's stamped marks, weight without knives 52oz. **£2,000–2,500** *C*

A Hutton and Sons silver and enamelled picture frame, heightened with blue and green enamelling, maker's marks and hallmarks for London 1904, 8in (20cm) high. **£1,200–1,500** *P*

A pair of Leuchare silver and shagreen candlesticks, stamped maker's mark 'WL' and 'Leuchare, London and Paris', London 1887, 8in (20cm) high. **£600–800** *CSK*

An Art Nouveau electroplated mirror, stamped 'V.S.', 19½in (49.5cm) high. **£800–1,000** *CSK*

An Art Nouveau WMF electroplated and glass jardinière, stamped marks, 18in (45.5cm) wide. **£600–800** *CSK*

An Art Nouveau silver on pewter bowl, 21in (53cm) wide. **£600–800** *CDC*

A brass, wood and glass punch set, comprising: 12 brass cups with glass liners, and a twin-handled tray, stamped with crossed swords and 'C.D.E.' in shield, 30in (76.5cm) high overall. **£600–800** *P*

An Arts & Crafts wrought iron and copper hearth set, possibly made by the Birmingham Guild of Handicrafts. **£500–600** *P*

A spun brass mounted glass punch bowl and ladle with brass tipped glass stem, c1910, 14½in (37cm) wide. **£350–400** *S*

An Art Nouveau pewter and green tinted glass claret jug, mounted on a pewter pedestal foot and overlaid with trailing leaves and flowers, 12in (30.5cm) high. **£400–600** *CSK*

A Wiener Werkstätte silver-coloured metal dish mount, designed by Josef Hoffmann, maker's and designer's monograms, Austrian poinçons, c1905, 1in (3cm) wide. **£3,000–4,000** *S*

l. An Art Nouveau claret jug, by WMF, the green glass with pewter mounts, stamped 'WMF EP 1/10' and small 'as', 16½in (42cm) high.. **£600–800** *WHL*

A WMF electroplated pewter
three-piece coffee set, comprising:
coffee pot, cream jug and
sugar basin on trestle feet,
stamped, coffee pot 8in
(19.5cm) high.
£500–700 *C*

A martelé inkstand with
removable glass liner, the
stand repoussé and chased
with serpentine ribs and
flowers, on three ball feet, by
Gorham, Providence, marked
'Martelé 9584', c1905, 10in
(25.5cm) wide, 9.5oz.
£1,200–1,500 *CNY*

A Liberty muffin
dish, designed by
Archibald Knox,
11½in (29cm) diam.
£400–500 *ABS*

A mixed metal sugar bowl and
cream jug, applied with copper
castings of foliage, birds and
insects, sugar bowl with 2 bronze
handles and cream jug with one,
each cast in the form of a stylised
elephant's head, with traces of
gilding on the interiors, by
Gorham, Providence, both
marked, '1882', sugar bowl 4in
(10cm) diam., 11.5oz gross.
£2,500–3,500 *CNY*

A Tiffany fruit bowl, of fluted
circular form on spreading base
with lightly hammered surface,
mid-20thC, 10½in (27cm) diam.
£2,000–2,500 *CNY*

An Art Nouveau silver photo
frame, Birmingham, 1902.
£275–300 *DSA*

A Mappin and Webb Art Nouveau
silver and enamelled frame, on
easel support, cast in relief with
shamrocks, stamped 'M & W,
Sheffield', 1904, 8in (20cm) high.
£700–800 *CSK*

A silver and copper box, by
Birmingham Guild of
Handicraft, signed 'B.G.H.',
c1900, 8⅝in (22cm) wide.
£1,200–1,300 *DID*

A silver toast rack, by Georg
Jensen, c1930, 6in (15cm) wide.
£1,200–1,300 *DID*

An Art Nouveau style malacca
walking stick, the white metal
handle modelled with a figure
of a young woman kneeling
amidst reeds.
£350–450 *CSK*

A hammered silver raised bowl,
by A. E. Jones, the frieze cast
with foxes chasing geese, on a
raised foot, Birmingham 1915,
4in (10.5cm) diam.
£300–350 *P(M)*

A Tudric vase, the design attributed to Archibald Knox, 7½in (19cm) high.
£300–400 *BLO*

A Guild of Handicraft toast rack, designed by C. R. Ashbee, the end panels with repoussé decoration of stylised trees, stamped 'G of H Ltd.', with London hallmarks for 1906, 5in (13cm) wide, 220gr.
£1,500–2,000 *C*

A laminated copper frame, c1900.
£25–50 *BLO*

An ormolu and hand-cut coloured glass lantern, 16in (41cm) high.
£400–600 *HAE*

A WMF dish, with a female figure, 10½in (27cm) diam.
£300–500 *ASA*

A silver hand mirror, with embossed cherubs, London 1896.
£150–250 *PCh*

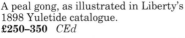

A Tudric pewter muffin dish and cover, stamped 'Tudric C293', 9½in (24cm) diam. **£300–400** *P*

A peal gong, as illustrated in Liberty's 1898 Yuletide catalogue.
£250–350 *CEd*

A WMF pewter dish, 14in (36cm) wide.
£200–300 *ASA*

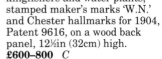

A silver repoussé picture frame, decorated in relief with kingfishers and water plants, stamped maker's marks 'W.N.' and Chester hallmarks for 1904, Patent 9616, on a wood back panel, 12½in (32cm) high.
£600–800 *C*

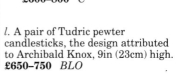

l. A pair of Tudric pewter candlesticks, the design attributed to Archibald Knox, 9in (23cm) high.
£650–750 *BLO*

A four-piece chrome tea service.
£45–50 *CIR*

A chrome picture frame,
10½in by 7½in (27 by 19cm).
£40–60 *DEC*

A chromium plated cruet, 2½in
(6cm) high.
£30–40 *CIR*

A chromium plated cake stand, 8in
(20cm) high.
£15–20 *CIR*

A chrome novelty aeroplane
cruet, c1950, 4½in (11cm) high.
£80–100 *DEC*

A Dunhill shagreen
cigarette lighter,
c1930, 2in (5cm) high.
£40–50 *ASA*

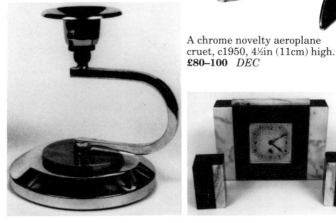

A pair of chrome candelsticks,
trimmed with green Bakelite, 5in
(13cm) high.
£80–100 *DEC*

A clock garniture.
£200–250 *SH*

A chrome desk lamp, 18in (46cm).
£90–120 *DEC*

A chrome cruet set, 8in (20cm) wide.
£40–60 *DEC*

A chrome cake basket with etched
glass, 11½in (29cm) wide.
£40–60 *DEC*

A pair of American bronze book ends, by Chase, 6in (15cm) high. **£200–300** *GAL*

A chrome and enamel cigarette box, 9½in (24cm) wide. **£75–100** *GAL*

A set of 6 Liberty & Co. silver and enamel handled cake forks, Birmingham 1931. **£300–400** *HCH*

A French electroplated tea and coffee service, with rosewood handles and finials, stamped 'GM', tray 21in (53cm) wide. **£1,000–1,200** *C*

A four-piece tea service, by Edward Barnard and Sons Ltd., London, 1934, 54oz. **£1,200–1,500** *DN*

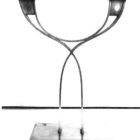

A pewter candlestick, c1955, 8½in (22cm). **£100–150** *GAL*

A pair of candlesticks, with carved oak barley-twist stems, hammered silver square bases and circular nozzles, A. E. Jones, Chester, 1922, 9in (22.5cm) high. **£450–500** *Bea*

A four-piece Art Deco style Walker & Hall tea set, Sheffield 1944, 50oz. **£450–500** *WIL*

A Guild of Handicraft silver chalice, lightly hammered, stamped marks 'G of H Ltd.', London hallmarks for 1902. 8½in (22cm) high. **£1,200–1,500** *C*

r. A pair of chrome Art Deco style uplighters, 75in (190.5cm) high. **£300–400** *RG*

A silver tea and coffee service, by Mappin & Webb, with ivory handles, 1937 and 1939. **£2,500–3,000** *SWO*

l. A Hukin & Heath electroplated toast rack, designed by Christopher Dresser, stamped with maker's mark, 5in (12.5cm) high. **£2,000–3,000** *CSK*

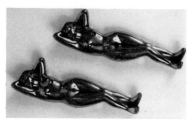

A pair of chrome posy holders, 6in (15cm) long. **£20–30** *CIR*

A WMF silver plated punchbowl and ladle, on a stepped base, each side with figure of Minerva in high relief, dedicated to Rev. Joseph Larzan, bowl and ladle impressed with firm's marks, 20in (51cm) high.
£2,000–2,500 *CNY*

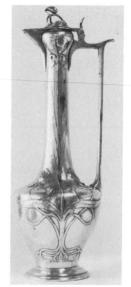

A WMF pewter jug, c1900, 15in (38cm) high.
£400–500 *ASA*

A pewter mirror, probably Osiris, c1900.
£800–1,200 *DID*

An Art Deco lamp, with a silver and gold plaster figure of a lady.
£100–150 *LRG*

A Danish 3-piece demitasse service, by Georg Jensen, comprising: coffee pot, sugar bowl and cream pitcher, with side bone handles and knop finials with beaded joins, c1945, 18.5oz gross.
£2,000–3,000 *CNY*

l. A pair of Asprey chromium plated cocktail shakers, each dumb-bell shaped, with strainer, one end forming the lid, one dented, stamped mark 'A & Co. Asprey London 6333 Made in England', 10½in (25.5cm) high.
£600–800 *C*

A Hagenauer brass bowl, the shallow hammered bowl on a tapering foot with openwork decoration of horses, stamped mark 'wHw Hagenauer Wien Made in Austria', 12½in (32.5cm) diam.
£1,500–2,000 *C*

A three-piece Art Deco style silver tea service, Birmingham 1935, 20oz gross.
£600–800 *GAK*

r. A Hagenauer brass sculpture of a bird and a golfer, the stylised forms on circular bases, stamped 'Hagenauer wHw Made in Austria' golfer 15in (38.5cm) high.
£700–900 each *C*

An internally decorated vase, with applied vertical grips, engraved 'G. Dumoulin', c1930. **£1,800–2,500** *C*

An enamelled glass vase, by G. Argy-Rousseau, gilded mark, 1920s, 6in (15cm) high. **£3,000–4,000** *S*

A Venini bottle vase, designed by Fulvio Bainconi, acid stamped mark, 9in (23cm) high. **£7,000–8,000** *C*

A set of 6 Liberty & Co. silver and turquoise enamel buttons, with entrelac Celtic design, stamped 'L&Co., Cymric', Birmingham 1907, in original fitted case. **£500–600** *C*

An Art Deco brooch, by Cartier, set with calibre cut black onyx and round diamonds, mounted in platinum. **£25,000–30,000** *CNY*

A Pforzheim plique-à-jour pendant, c1910, 2⅜in (6cm) high. **£800–1,200** *DID*

An Art Deco jade, rock crystal, diamond and enamel desk clock, signed 'Cartier', c1930. **£28,000–32,000** *CNY*

r. An Art Deco carved emerald, diamond and enamel bracelet, by Cartier. **£45,000–50,000** *CNY*

Three Liberty & Co. silver pendants. **£200–300 each** *DID*

Two Liberty & Co. pendants, and one by Murrle Bennet & Co. **£200–300 each** *DID*

A Georg Jensen silver coloured metal necklace, monogrammed 'GJ', c1910, 9in (23cm) long. **£1,000–1,500** *S*

A white metal brooch, by Henry Wilson, the domed seven-sided form of cast stemwork with a central flowerhead and pale turquoise enamel detail. **£400–600** *C*

An Arts & Crafts circular clip brooch, attributed to Sibyl Dunlop, with gold leaves, tourmalines and mother-of-pearl. **£400–600** *P*

A Guild of Handicraft white and yellow metal brooch, designed by C. R. Ashbee, set with blister pearls, pearls, sapphires, 2 paste replacements, tourmalines and moonstones. **£8,000–9,000** *C*

A yellow metal and enamelled bracelet, designed by James Cromer Watt, formed as a snake, of blue-green enamel, set with opals, stamped monogram 'JCW'. **£2,500–3,000** *C*

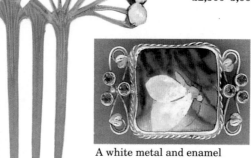

A white metal and enamel brooch, set with citrines, stamped 'G. Hunt 1922', and another set with amazonite. **£600–800** *C*

A yellow metal, enamel and rock crystal brooch, by Henry Wilson or Henry G. Murphy, set with opals and a central cabochon amethyst. **£1,800–2,000** *C*

A horn hair comb, by Fred T. Partridge, set with baroque pearls in white metal, formed as an umbellifer, slight damage, signed. **£800–1,000** *C*

A Liberty & Co. yellow metal and enamel ring, by Archibald Knox. **£2,500–3,000** *C*

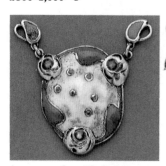

A green and mottled white enamel pendant, designed by Sir Frank Brangwyn for La Maison de l'Art Nouveau, Paris, with monograms 'F.B., W.B.' **£2,500–4,000** *C*

A yellow metal, ivory and enamel brooch, by George Hunt, set with opals and pearls, stamped 'Medusa, G.H.' **£1,500–2,000** *C*

A yellow metal and sapphire ring, by Henry Wilson, with pierced decoration. **£2,000–2,500** *C*

A Guild of Handicraft silver peacock brooch, designed by C. R. Ashbee, set with enamel, abalone and a ruby, stamped, maker's marks, London hallmarks for 1907. **£1,800–2,000** *C*

l. A two-division frame, Birmingham 1901, 3in (7.5cm) high.
r. An Edward VII Art Nouveau photograph frame, by F. J. Hall, decorated with stylised foliate motifs and whiplash on a textured ground, Birmingham 1903, 12in (30.5cm) high.
c. A plain photograph frame, Birmingham 1914, 7½in (19cm) high.
£800–1,000 *Bea*

A Georg Jensen 155-piece Acorn pattern table service, with stamped marks.
£5,000–7,000 *CSK*

A WMF silver plated centrepiece, c1905, 33in (83.5cm) high.
£2,500–3,000 *ZEI*

A Hukin & Heath electroplated toast rack, designed by Christopher Dresser, convex base on bun feet, wire frame with 7 supports joined by small spheres, the central support raised to a handle, stamped 'H&H 2556', with date lozenge for May 1881, 5in (13cm) wide.
£400–600 *C*

A Hukin & Heath plated spoon warmer, designed by Christopher Dresser, with open top, sealed hot water reservoir, straight ebonised handle and 4 spiked feet, maker's mark and '2693', 6in (15cm) wide.
£650–700 *P*

A silver and enamel rouge pot, c1930.
£30–50 *ASA*

An Art Nouveau brass and copper vase, by Fisher Strand, 6in (15cm) high.
£50–80 *KNG*

A tortoiseshell and silver powder compact, 2in (5cm) diam.
£50–60 *HOW*

A silver tea set, with Bakelite handles, made in India.
£850–950 *JJIL*

A Liberty & Co. Cymric bowl, designed by Oliver Baker, set with Connemara marble discs, Birmingham 1901, 8½in (21cm) diam.
£3,000–3,500 *DID*

A Mappin and Webb vase, the handles with heart shaped terminals, the base with inverted hearts in relief with inscription, maker's mark, London 1903, 5in (13cm) high.
£250–300 *P*

A plated pewter pen and inkstand, 8½in (22cm) high.
£150–200 *P*

A Liberty & Co. silver pen tray, each end decorated with a cabochon turquoise, with owner's initials 'A.M.W.' stamped marks 'L & Co.' and Birmingham hallmarks for 1912, 7in (17cm) long, 60gr.
£250–300 *C*

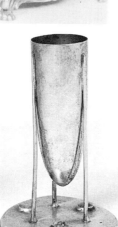

l. A Liberty & Co. Cymric silver vase, designed by Archibald Knox, the base with 3 turquoise cabochons and 3 wire supports, maker's marks, Birmingham 1903, stamped 'Cymric 2126', 4½in (11cm) high.
£1,500–2,000 *P*

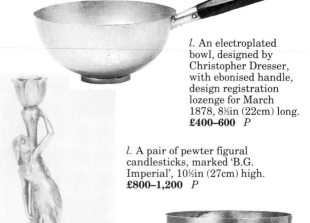

l. An electroplated bowl, designed by Christopher Dresser, with ebonised handle, design registration lozenge for March 1878, 8½in (22cm) long.
£400–600 *P*

l. A pair of pewter figural candlesticks, marked 'B.G. Imperial', 10½in (27cm) high.
£800–1,200 *P*

A hammered silver goblet, by C. R. Ashbee, the foot with a radiating repoussé pattern of stylised buds, stamped 'C R A' with London hallmarks for 1899, 5in (12cm) high.
£1,000–1,500 *C*

A WMF silvered metal tea set, comprising: a teapot, coffee pot, covered sugar bowl and creamer, with two-handled lobed tray, all cast with curvilinear foliage, tray 24½ (62cm) diam.
£1,500–2,000 *CNY*

WMF

Short for the German Wüttembergische Metallwarenfabrik, one of the principal producers of Art Nouveau silver and silver plated objects during the early 20thC.

l. A William Hutton and Co. five-piece silver tea set, comprising a teapot, coffee pot, milk jug, sugar basin and sugar tongs, the teapot and coffee pot with ebony handles, all pieces en suite, each piece stamped with maker's marks 'WH & Co' and London hallmarks for 1904, teapot 6½in (17cm) high, 57ozs 11dwts gross.
£1,900–2,100 *C*

r. A Liberty & Co. Cymric silver vase, attributed to Archibald Knox, marked 'L & Co.', Cymric Birmingham hallmarks for 1903 and numbered '2020', 5½in (14cm) high.
£1,500–2,000 *P*

l. A Tiffany & Co. cup and saucer, embellished against a copper ground, marked 'Tiffany & Co.', Sterling silver and other metals, pattern numbers 5623, c1879-1880, cup 2⅛in (6.5cm) high.
£480–550 *P*

A Liberty & Co. silver biscuit box, marked 'Cymric' and 'L & Co.', with Birmingham hallmarks for 1902, 20oz 14dwt, 5½in (14cm) wide.
£1,200–1,500 *C*

A Tiffany & Co. hammered white metal and parcel-gilt 3 piece tea-set, comprising a teapot, milk jug and sugar bowl, engraved Tiffany & Co maker's mark, sterling silver and other metals and various numbers, c1890, teapot 6½in (17cm) high.
£3,700–4,200 *C*

l. A Tiffany & Co. Japanesque jug, applied with copper and brass against a 'martelé'-textured ground, stamped 'Tiffany & Co.', makers, Sterling silver and other metals, pattern no. 5051, c1878, 8½in (22cm) high.
£3,000–4,000 *P*

An Art Nouveau silver overlay decanter.
£350–450 *Vin*

An Art Nouveau dressing table tray, maker's mark 'R.P.', Birmingham 192, 14in (36cm) wide, 13.5ozs (420gms).
£600–700 *Bea*

l. An Art Nouveau silver condiment set, all with green liners.
£400–600 *Bon*

A silver box, with inserted miniature on ivory, signed, hallmarked 1904.
£150–250 *PJ*

r. A German four-light candelabra, stamped with crown, crescent and '800', maker's marks for probably Bruckmann and retail mark for M. Stumpf & Sohn, 17½in (44cm) high.
£1,000–1,400 *P*

An Edwardian rose bowl, H. E. Ltd., Sheffield 1901, 9in (23cm) high, 17.75 oz. **£400–500** *CSK*

r. Two copper vases, by Keswick School of Industrial Art, 7½in (19cm) high. **£275–300** *ST*

A set of Liberty silver teaspoons, marked Liberty & Co., Birmingham 1908, in silk lined wooden box. **£400–500** *OBJ*

A set of 6 WMF pewter tea glass holders, each with scrolling handle and pierced entrelac and ivy decoration, stamped with WMF marks, 3in (7.5cm) high. **£350–400** *CA*

A Georg Jensen 131-piece Acorn pattern table service, designed by Johan Rohde, stamped marks, 7010gr. gross, in original fitted case. **£4,000–6,000** *C*

A pewter photograph frame, 8in (20.5cm) high. **£120–150** *ASA*

A German pewter mirror, 18in (45.5cm) high. **£500–700** *ASA*

A Danish silver dish-on-stand, marked, 5½in (14cm) high. **£250–300** *ASA*

An electroplated mirror-on-stand, the cartouche form decorated with maidens and trumpets amid scrolling foliage, 16½in (42.5cm) high. **£300–500** *C*

l. A Georg Jensen silver tazza, 7½in (19cm) high. **£800–1,200** *ASA*

A Liberty & Co. silver and enamel inkwell, with design by Archibald Knox, marked 'Liberty & Co.', hallmarked Birmingham c1906, 2in (5cm) high. **£250–300** *OBJ*

A pair of silver picture frames, Chester hallmark, 12in (30.5cm) high.
£700–1,000 *ASA*

A bronze inkwell, 8½in (22cm).high
£300–400 *ASA*

An Arts &Crafts tobacco jar, c1900.
£225–275 *ST*

A German pewter inkstand and well, 11in (28cm). wide
£40–80 *ASA*

A pewter wall plaque, 5in (12.5cm) diam.
£30–50 *ASA*

A spelter figure on a tray, 6½in (16.5cm).wide.
£30–50 *ASA*

A WMF jug with lid, 13½in (34cm) high.
£200–400 *ASA*

A WMF wall plaque, 12½in (32cm) diam.
£400–600 *ASA*

A Newlyn School copper plate, stamped 'Newlyn', c1900, 10in (25.5cm) diam.
£150–300 *OBJ*

A pewter wall plaque, 5in (12.5cm) diam.
£30–50 *ASA*

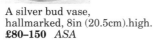

A WMF tray with figure in relief, 15½in (39cm) wide.
£300–450 *ASA*

A silver bud vase, hallmarked, 8in (20.5cm).high.
£80–150 *ASA*

A Tiffany & Co., Japanesque hip flask, stamped 'Tiffany & Co.', '325M8903', Sterling silver and other metals, 5½in (14cm) high.
£1,500–2,000 *HSS*

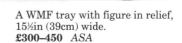

A Scottish pewter teapot stand, 7in (18cm) square.
£20–40 *ASA*

A Wiener Werkstätte plated fish knife, designed by Josef Hoffmann, stamped with registered trademark, 'WW' monogram, Hoffmann's monogram and 'JF' in circle, 7½in (19cm) long.
£200–250 *P*

A pair of pewter candlesticks, stamped 'Kayserzinn 4521', c1900, 12in (30.5cm) high.
£350–400 *C*

A pair of pewter candelabra, with geometric decoration, and a central holder, probably Dutch, c1900, 18in (45.5cm) high.
£350–400 *C*

An eight-light bronze chandelier, cast after a design by Carlo Bugatti, c1910, 65in (165cm) high.
£1,300–2,000 *C*

An Arts & Crafts brass hanging chandelier, glass shades missing, 25in (62cm) wide.
£180–220 *P*

A German 48-piece part canteen of cutlery, comprising: 12 forks, spoons and fish knives and forks, silver coloured metal stamped with '800' and maker's mark for A.C. Frank of Hamburg. **£700–800** *P*

A set of 6 Liberty & Co. silver and enamelled coffee spoons, with shaded blue/green enamels, marked 'L & Co' with Birmingham marks for 1937, in original fitted case, 4½in (11.25cm) long.
£280–320 *P*

l. A dressing table set, of lignum vitae, with decorative Art Nouveau silver mounts and the initials 'MH' in monogram with red enamelled background, 1926–27.
£600–700 *P*

A silver caddy spoon, marked 'RS' for Robert Stebbings, London 1903, 4⅛in (11.75cm) long.
£60–70 *P*

A silver caddy spoon, marked 'RS' for Robert Stebbings, London 1903, 4⅛in (11.75cm) long.
£60–70 *P*

l. A bronze figure of Circe, by Bertram Mackennal, incised on the base with artist's signature and foundry mark of Gruet Jeune, verdigris patches, 23in (58.5cm) high.
£13,000–15,000 *Bon*

A bronze statuette of Daphne, signed 'Raoul Larche', 37½in (93.5cm).high
£2,000–2,500 *Bon*

A pewter and coloured enamel dressing mirror, in the Art Nouveau style, attributed to the March Brothers, 20in (50cm) high. **£300–400** *L*

A WMF silver plated pewter mounted green glass decanter, stamped 'WMF' and other usual marks, c1900, 15½in (38.5cm) high. **£600–800** *C*

A green glass Art Nouveau wine jug, with pewter swirling mounts and handles and feather pattern stopper, 11in (27.5cm) high. **£300–400** *CDC*

A Walker and Hall silver mounted claret jug, after a design by Christopher Dresser, maker's marks for Sheffield 1904, 9½in (24cm).high **£300–400** *P*

A silver Liberty Coronation spoon **£250–300** *JJIL*

A WMF pewter centrepiece, in the form of an Art Nouveau maiden, her dress flowing outwards to form 4 dishes, stamped marks, 10in (25cm) high. **£300–400** *P*

Silver and Metalware

By law, all British silver must be hallmarked. The date, maker and provenance of a piece can be checked by referring to a catalogue of marks.

The letter 'F' added to a British hallmark indicates that the piece is a foreign import which has met the British silver standard.

A brass standing table mirror, impressed 'WMF' c1900, 16in (40cm). high. **£400–600** *C*

A set of 4 Hukin & Heath silver salts with salt spoons, decorated in silver, copper and silver gilt, marked 'H & H', Birmingham hallmarks for 1879, 1½in (4cm) high, 6oz. **£850–950** *C*

An Art Nouveau silver photo frame, Birmingham 1902. **£250–300** *PC*

l. A WMF silvered metal dressing mirror, 14in (35cm) high. **£800–1,000** *Re*

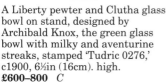

A Liberty pewter and Clutha glass bowl on stand, designed by Archibald Knox, the green glass bowl with milky and aventurine streaks, stamped 'Tudric 0276,' c1900, 6½in (16cm). high.
£600–800 *C*

A Liberty & Co. Tudric-Moorcroft cake tray, stamped 'Tudric Pewter 0357', 12in (30cm) wide.
£500–700 *P*

A Barnard Aesthetic Movement silver gilt christening set, comprising: a tankard, a knife, fork and spoon, all engraved and gilded, stamped 'W.B.J.', maker's marks for London 1879, 9oz, in original Goldsmith & Silversmith Company box, tankard 3½in (9.5cm) high.
£600–800 *P*

A WMF electroplated pewter tea and coffee set, all pieces with usual impressed marks, c1900, 25in (64cm) wide.
£1,200–1,500 *C*

A Georg Jensen silver tazza stamped marks, 7½in (19cm) high.
£750–850 *CSK*

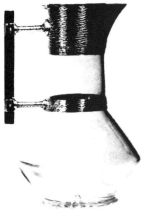

An Art Nouveau bronze, 'Seagull and Sail', by Guy Edouard, on a marble base.
£450–500 *Ksh*

A Hukin and Heath silver-mounted claret jug, designed by Dr. Christopher Dresser, with ebony handle, stamped with maker's monogram 'JWH & JTH', London hallmarks for 1884, 9in (23cm) high.
£800–1,200 *C*

A Heath & Middleton silver and glass claret jug, in the manner of Christopher Dresser, maker's marks 'JTH/JHM' and Birmingham 1892, 15in (38cm) high.
£500–700 *P*

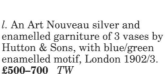

l. An Art Nouveau silver and enamelled garniture of 3 vases by Hutton & Sons, with blue/green enamelled motif, London 1902/3.
£500–700 *TW*

A William Hutton & Sons silver and enamelled picture frame, heightened with blue and green enamelling, fabric backed, maker's marks for London 1905, 5½in(14cm) high.
£800–1,000 *P*

A Guild of Handicrafts silver beaker base, designed by Charles Robert Ashbee, set with 7 oval garnet cabochons, marked 'CRA' in shield and London hallmarks for 1900, 4½in (11.5cm), 6.50ozs.
£2,000–3,000 *P*

An Art Nouveau silver frame.
£400–450 *JJIL*

A pair of French Art Nouveau pewter, vases, inscribed 'H. Sibeud', 12in (29.50cm) high.
£600–800 *P*

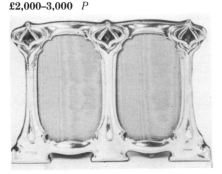

A William Hutton & Sons silver and enamelled double picture frame, maker's marks for London 1903, 8in (20cm) high.
£1,200–1,400 *P*

An H. Meinhardt silver coloured metal vase, 25½ in (63cm) high.
£550–650 *Re*

An Arts & Crafts movement toast rack, set with turquoise stones, by the Guild of Handicrafts, one end split, London 1904, 5in (12.5cm), 7½ozs. **£1,400–1,600** *DWB*

A hammer textured silver-coloured metal four piece tea service, by Tiffany & Co., the tray inlaid in green, yellow and red coloured metals, maker's marks and '5176M1781, 5291/2633', c1890, tray 15in (37.5cm) wide, 70oz gross.
£2,700–3,000 *N*

A Hukin & Heath plated letter rack, designed by Christopher Dresser, marked 'H & H', numbered '2555' and registration mark for 9th May 1881, 5in (12.25cm) wide.
£350–400 *P*

l. A Victorian three piece Aesthetic Movement teaset, inscribed by Messrs Barnard, 1877, teapot 8in (20cm) high, 39.5oz.
£800–1,000 *P*

A set of 6 Liberty silver and turquoise enamel coffee spoons, stamped 'L & Co.', Birmingham 1930, in a fitted case.
£400–450 *C*

A pair of silver and enamelled spoons, marks for George Lawrence Connell, London 1904, 7in (17.5cm) long.
£300–400 *P*

An American ivy-chased jug by Tiffany & Co, later inscribed 'Corrie Cup won by Burnswark, nos. by David Bell Irving Esq. 1886', c1870, 9in (23cm), 27.5oz.
£2,300–2,800 *P*

Above right. A copper and brass kettle on stand, by W A S Benson, stamped 'Benson', 34in (86cm) high. **£300–400** *C*

A Hukin and Heath silver condiment set, designed by Dr Christopher Dresser, stamped maker's marks and London hallmarks for 1881, 5½in (14cm).
£1,200–1,600 *C*

A pair of large WMF pewter mounted green glass vases, 19in (48cm).
£800–1,000 *ASA*

A white metal hors d'oeuvres dish, 14½in (36.5cm) wide.
£500–600 *CSK*

A silver coloured metal centrepiece, with an alpaca liner, unmarked, possibly Austrian or German, 22½in (57.5cm) wide.
£1,500–2,000 *P*

A WMF pewter dish by, 9in (23cm) wide.
£300–400 *JJIL*

A Hukin and Heath electroplated picnic teapot, designed by Dr Christopher Dresser, stamped maker's mark, 'H & H, 2109 Designed by Dr. C. Dresser' with registration lozenge for 18th October 1879, 3½in (9cm) high.
£800–1,000 *C*

A large French white metal vase with 2 scantily clad females draping the body, with various marks, signed and dated '1902', Marcelle Devuit foundry seal, 26½in (66cm) high.
£800–1,200 *ASA*

A William Hutton and Sons silver toast rack, maker's marks and Sheffield hallmarks for 1902, 5in (12.5cm), 11oz 5dwt.
£250–300 *C*

A pair of copper and brass vacuum flasks, attributed to W A S Benson, with pewter liners, brass strap hinges, wooden lids and brass carrying handles, 19in (48cm).
£300–500 *C*

A WMF electroplated pewter drinking set, comprising: a lidded decanter, 6 goblets and a tray, all with usual impressed marks, c1900, tray 19in (48cm) wide.
£1,000–1,500 *C*

A silver cup and cover, by John Paul Cooper, stamped with beetle mark, dated '1903', 6½in (16.5cm) high.
£200–300 *P*

A set of 6 Art Nouveau silver teaspoons, in a fitted case, Birmingham 1900.
£200–300 *FHF*

A seven-branch brass candlestick, the design attributed to Bernhard Pankok, with a raised circular base and central column on which the arms pivot, with case decoration of concentric rings, 12in (29.5cm) high.
£2,000–1,600 *C*

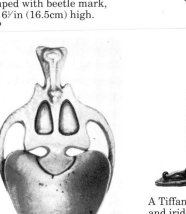

An Art Nouveau silver caddy spoon, by Liberty & Co., Birmingham, 1911.
£200–300 *SBe*

A Tiffany Studio bronze and iridescent glass candlestick, with separate pendant snuffer, having overall greeny-brown patination, stamped 'Tiffany Studios New York 1212', 10in (25cm) high.
£1,000–1,200 *P*

l. An Art Deco cocktail shaker, and tray with glasses.
£150–200 *LEX*

An Arts & Crafts plated metal cross, in the manner of Omar Ramsden, engraved with a memorial to 'Frederic Wilkins, Preist', dated '10th January 1937', 22in (56cm) high.
£1,000–1,500 *P*

A pair of bronze firedogs, 24in (61cm) high.
£150–200 *C*

A Benham and Froud copper and brass kettle on a wrought iron and copper stand, designed by Christopher Dresser, stamped 'Benham and Froud' mark, 26in (65.5cm) high.
£500–700 *C*

JEWELLERY

At the end of the 19th century, the design and construction of jewellery was to undergo a dramatic change from the styles of the previous 100 years. The fantastic creations of French masters such as René Lalique, Lucien Gaillard, the Vever Brothers and Georges Fouquet, raised the craft to a level of originality and excellence of execution that has probably not been superseded. The intrinsic value of the jewellery lay in the originality and workmanship of the piece, rather than the amount of valuable gemstones used. Lalique, for example, used semi-precious stones which were sometimes carved. These he complemented with often translucent enamels, in a decorative technique known as *plique-à-jour*. He also used moulded glass in his creations, which eventually led him to a career in glass production for which he is better known.

Like Lalique, British designers and manufacturers of the Arts and Crafts period often used natural or organic forms as a source for inspiration. They were also inspired by the work of the medieval Guilds – groups of skilled workers who believed in the principles of trueness to materials, the integrity of manufacture, and the direct involvement of the artist in the craft.

William Morris and John Ruskin's teachings and ideologies inspired a whole group of artists and craftsmen in Britain, the rest of Europe, the United States and Australia. One important figure was Charles Robert Ashbee, who founded the Guild of Handicraft in Britain in 1887. His workshops produced foliate brooches and pendants, with wirework embellishment set with chrysoprase (a green stone) or mother-of-pearl, amethysts or enamel. A favourite subject was the peacock, which appeared in many forms, with the body and the tail feathers set with stones. The sailing boat was also popular, a motif that amusingly came to be known as the 'craft' of the Guild. Tiffany in the United States produced exquisite work in enamels and gemstones, as did Marcus & Co. Simple but effective embossed silver brooches of girls' faces were made by the Unger Brothers and William B. Kerr.

In Europe we see the bold and curvilinear designs of Henri van de Velde in Germany and Belgium, and the formal but striking pieces by Bert Nienhuis in Holland. Theodor Fahrner and Murrle Bennett in Pforzheim, Germany, mass-produced good quality and well-designed jewellery. The high degree of stylization in the designs of Josef Hoffmann and Koloman Moser of the Weiner Werkstätte (Vienna Workshops) in Austria (and to some extent the designs of Charles Rennie Mackintosh in Glasgow), influenced jewellery design in an exciting way. Geometry played a greater part, with the use of materials with contrasting shapes and colours anticipating the styles to come in the 1920s and 1930s.

After the harsh realities of World War I, jewellery design took on a whole new look: the somewhat frothy styles of the Belle Epoque and Art Nouveau periods must have seemed overly sentimental to post-War emancipated women. There were simpler variations of natural forms, which finally became completely abstracted and geometric. The 1925 Exposition des Arts Decoratifs in Paris was the showcase of the new style and gave it the name we now recognise – Art Deco.

The 'Roaring Twenties' saw the first mass-produced motorcars and air travel, the radio and the 'movies', all influencing everyday design. Jewellery complemented other products of this 'machine age' with the sweeping lines of aeroplanes and railway carriages, and shapes reminiscent of cog wheels or other mechanical components.

The use of newly-created materials in everyday life was also reflected in jewellery manufacture, with recently-developed plastics set with stones, and silver cufflinks plated in 'genuine chromium plate'. It seems hard to believe that many of these materials are now commonplace, and regarded as inappropriate for jewellery.

There was room for fun with amusing costume jewellery – playful Scotty dog brooches with paste-set bodies, Chinamen, deer leaping through foliage, and enamelled tennis players. Of course there was also the superb quality of design and workmanship of major jewellers such as Cartier, Van Cleef and Arpels, Boucheron and their contemporaries, available for the very wealthy.

The most useful advice for the contemporary buyer must surely be to choose the best quality at a price one can afford. Never buy something that you are indifferent about just because the price is right. Look out for good design: a well-designed piece in an inexpensive material is often more pleasing than an ill-conceived piece made from precious stones or metals. If you are unsure when buying a piece of jewellery, do not be afraid to ask about condition and authenticity. Many items of jewellery the collector may encounter will have a makers' mark, monogram or signature, but beware – this is not a foolproof means of identification as marks on fakes are known. There is no shortcut to knowledge, but perseverance will show results – learning is a very gradual process, and experienced collectors and dealers will usually be pleased to advise you.

Keith Baker

A gold and opal brooch, shaped with arc of gold beading above, set with central opal, marked 'IX', c1905, 1in (2.5cm). **£70–100** *SB*

A silver and enamel brooch, after a design by G. Slatin, with large dragonfly wings detailed in blue, turquoise and green enamels, indistinct maker's mark, French poinçons, with box for Lefèbvre, Paris, 3½in (9cm) long. **£200–300** *SB*

A part-oxidised silver coloured metal buckle, with lily between French poinçons, maker's mark 'E (?) F', c1900, 3¼in (8cm). **£125–200** *SB*

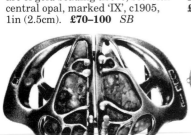

A Theodor Fahrner silver and stone buckle, maker's mark of Murrle Bennet & Co., London, 1902, 2½in (6.5cm) wide. **£250–350** *SB*

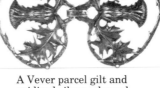

A Vever parcel gilt and oxidised silver coloured metal buckle, marked 'FE', c1900, 5in (12.5cm) wide. **£350–450** *SB*

A German Jugendstil brooch, in the style of Patriz Hubert, silver coloured metal set with lapis cabochon and hung with triangular lapis cabochon, c1900, 1½in (3.5cm) wide. **£130–180** *SB*

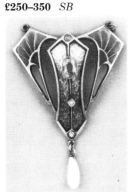

An Art Nouveau plique-à-jour pendant, enamelled in mauve and yellow green and amethyst plique-à-jour enamels, with freshwater pearl drop, 2¼in (5.5cm). **£180–230** *P*

A Charles Horner pendant, enamelled green, turquoise and yellow, stamped 'C.H.' and Chester marks for 1909, 1½in (3.5cm) wide. **£60–90** *P*

An Art Nouveau silver coloured metal belt. **£20–30** *ASA*

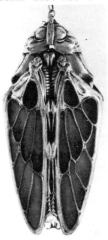

An electroplated metal and plique-à-jour enamel scent phial, the cicadas heads forming the removable cap, c1900, 2in (5cm) high. **£250–300** *SB*

An Art Nouveau hair comb, with embossed openwork scrolling foliage set with blue stained chalcedony cabochons and blue enamelling, probably Scandinavian, 5½in (14cm) wide. **£350–400** *P*

A navette shaped gold wirework brooch, by Murrle Bennet, with turquoise matrix and 3 seed pearls, stamped 'MB' monogram, and '15ct.' on pin, c1900, 1½in (4cm) wide. **£180–220** *C*

An Art Nouveau silver and enamelled pendant, picked out in coloured enamels, stamped 'M & B', Birmingham 1909. **£80–100** *P*

An Art nouveau pendant brooch, with central circular plaque of mother-of-pearl flanked by enamelled leaves of shaded blue and white, 5cm across, sold with Liberty & Co. fabric covered oval box and cover
£400–600 *P*

A necklace, set with 3 plaques of Tiffany iridescent 'cypriote' glass, flanking a rose-cut diamond, with glass drop below and suspended on chains spaced with further mounted segments of Tiffany glass, the catch also set with glass, 17in (44cm) long.
£1,000–1,400 *P*

A Danish Art Nouveau hammered silver brooch, set with lapis lazuli, Continental silver marks, c1910, 4½in (11cm) high. **£150–200** *C*

A silver, enamel and paste brooch/clip, c1920.
£150–200 *ABS*

An American gold and turquoise necklace, with teardrop-shaped cabochons of turquoise matrix, stamped 'Im' and '14k', 16in (40.5cm) long.
£450–500 *P*

An Arts & Crafts chalcedony, amethyst and mother-of-pearl openwork pendant with matching drop and neck chain; and a chalcedony, chrysoprase and marcasite articulated, drop boooch/pendant
£400–450 *CSK*

A Mexican silver and inlaid semi-precious stone necklace designed by Ladesma, c1945.
£150–200 *ABS*

l. A citrine single stone and diamond pendant/brooch, with frosted crystal and diamond surround to a diamond and gemset suspension, with detachable fittings for conversion to a clasp.
£400–450 *CSK*

A silver and enamel brooch, by Phoebe Anna Ramsay Traquair, the central plique à jour enamel panel with 2 lovers in medieval costume embracing, coloured in blue, green, pink, brown and yellow with touches of gold, enclosed within a silver mount with single bar pin, the enamel inscribed to the reverse 'The Kiss' and with P.R.T. monogram, the silver mount for Edinburgh 1935, 2in (5cm) diam.
£1,800–2,200 *C(S)*

r. An 18 carat gold clip, with rubies, c1940.
£600–800 *ABS*

A silver and enamel pendant, c1900.
£50–100 *ASA*

A silver and turquoise
pendant, with baroque
pearl drops and diamonds.
£200–300 *ASA*

An Arts & Crafts pendant, in the
medieval style, with rubies,
sapphires, emeralds and pearls
and picked out in enamels, 6in
(15cm) long overall.
£400-450 *P*

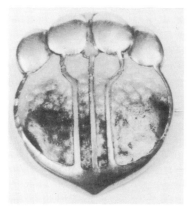

A silver and green enamel brooch,
signed and dated c1900.
£50–100 *ASA*

A pendant with amethysts.
£80–150 *ASA*

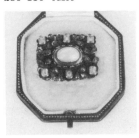

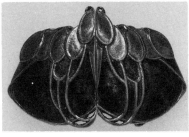

A green paste and
tourmaline brooch, by
Arthur Gaskin, c1900.
£600–800 *DID*

A Liberty & Co. Cymric enamelled
silver belt buckle, decorated with
pendant honesty against a blue/green
enamel background, with stamped
mark 'L. & Co. Cymric', and
Birmingham hallmarks for 1903.
£400-500 *C*

l. An Austrian silver and plique-à-
jour enamel brooch, stamped '800
Silver', c1905, 1½in (4cm) wide,
and a silver and plique-à-jour
enamel bar brooch in the form of a
scarab, turquoise enamel and
plique-à-jour details, maker's
mark 'G.K.', stamped 'Real Silver',
c1910, 2in (5cm) wide.
£250–300 *S*

A Liberty & Co. gold enamel and
mother-of-pearl pendant
necklace, maker's mark, stamped
'15ct', c1910, 3in (7.5cm) long.
£350–400 *S*

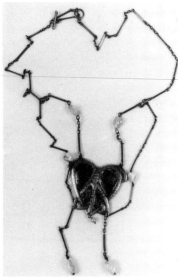

An Art Nouveau necklace, by
Murrle Bennet, in enamel and
silver, c1900.
£400–450 *DID*

A German Art Nouveau 15ct.
pendant, with ruby, diamond
and pearl, Pforzheim in the style
of Kleeman.
£400–450 *DID*

An Art Nouveau silver, enamel
and pearl necklace, by Murrle
Bennet & Co.
£250–300 *DID*

A 15ct. gold
pendant, with
turquoise, by
Murrle Bennet.
£350–400 *DID*

A silver, gold and enamel
pendant necklace, c1910,
2in (5cm) long.
£300–350 *S*

An Art Nouveau carved horn
pendant of a butterfly, on a woven
silk cord with 2 blue glass beads
between wooden spacers, 3in
(7.5cm) long.
£150–200 *CSK*

A pair of costume jewellery clips,
by Boucher, c1940.
£200–300 *ABS*

A horn and
turquoise necklace,
signed 'Bonté.
£300–400 *OBJ*

An Art Nouveau
tortoiseshell comb, in
silver and olivine, by Wm.
Soper, 5½in (14cm) high.
£400–500 *DID*

A Guild of Handicraft white metal
cloak clasp, designed by C. R.
Ashbee, each piece with repoussé
decoration of pinks. **£400–600** *C*

A Guild of Handicraft white metal
and enamel waist clasp, designed
by C. R. Ashbee, each piece with
pierced floral decoration and set
with turquoises, the centre with
green/blue enamel.
£800–1,200 *C*

r. An Argentinian bracelet, stamped 'Axel Giorno? – Buenos Aires', 8in (20cm) long.
£200–300 *P*

l. An Art Nouveau plique-à-jour brooch, stamped 'Déposé' and '900', 1½in (3cm) wide.
£700–900 *P*

r. A powder compact and 2 lipstick holders, the compact marked 'Boucheron, London, no. 875012. Made in France', one lipstick holder marked, 'Boucheron Paris', the other 'Boucheron, London 875012', compact 3in (7.5cm) high.
£400–450 *C*

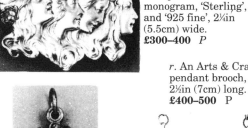

l. An Unger Brothers Art Nouveau brooch, stamped with maker's monogram, 'Sterling', and '925 fine', 2¼in (5.5cm) wide.
£300–400 *P*

A silver and enamel circular brooch, signed 'Omar Ramsden Me Fecit', London silver marks, 2¼in (5.5cm) diam.
£600–800 *P*

r. An Art Nouveau enamelled pendant, the sliding front revealing a mirror, stamped '900', 'Déposé', and dragonfly maker's mark, probably Austrian, 1⅜in (3.5cm) wide.
£250–350 *P*

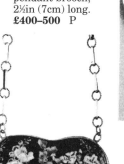

r. An Arts & Crafts pendant brooch, 2½in (7cm) long.
£400–500 *P*

An Art Nouveau necklace, 21½in (54cm) long.
£300–400 *P*

An Arts & Crafts enamelled pendant, painted in naturalistic enamelled colours, signed on reverse 'Pegram', 2¼in (5.7cm) wide.
£250–300 *P*

l. A Liberty & Co. 'ship' pendant, designed by Bernard Cuzner, the hull set with a pale blue tourmaline cabochon, unmarked, 2in (4.5cm) wide.
£600–800 *P*

r. A Liberty & Co. enamelled silver pendant, designed by Jessie M. King, marks for W. H. Haseler and 'Silver', 2in (4.5cm) wide.
£600–800 *P*

l. A German Art Nouveau pendant of red and green paste, stamped with '900', a wolf's head and 'W' maker's mark, 2¼in (5.5cm) wide.
£300–400 *P*

r. A Murrle Bennet & Co. gold and mother-of-pearl pendant, designed in the manner of Knox, stamped 'MB&Co', monogram and '15ct', 2¼in (5.5cm) wide.
£400–500 *P*

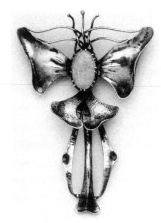

A Guild of Handicraft white metal brooch, designed by C. R. Ashbee, in the form of a winged insect with an articulated body formed by an opal, in original case.
£600–800 *C*

Two Guild of Handicraft white metal brooches, one designed by C. R. Ashbee with openwork repoussé decoration of stylised foliage, set with moonstone and turquoise, stamped marks 'G of H Ltd.', and one with wirework design in the form of a flower set with baroque pearls and turquoise enamel and a pear drop.
£1,000–1,200 *C*

Three white metal brooches, by Bernard Cuzner, one with a pierced and chased design of birds amid foliage, one with pierced decoration of leaves and berries, set with a central amazonite, and another with wirework heart shaped design set with a central Ruskin Pottery circular plaque, all with maker's mark.
£700–800 *C*

A Liberty & Co. silver and enamel waist clasp, designed by Jessie M. King, with circular openwork decoration of stylised flowers and birds with blue/green enamel details, stamped 'L & Co.', Birmingham hallmarks for 1906.
£1,200–1,500 *C*

Two Guild of Handicraft brooches, one designed by C. R. Ashbee, with an openwork design in the form of a tree, with repoussé details set with turquoise enamel and baroque pear drops, in its original fitted case, engraved 'LC', and another with a wirework scrolled design, set with turquoises and turquoise enamel.
£600–900 *C*

A white metal and cloisonné enamel buckle, and 2 white metal brooches, all by Nelson and Edith Dawson.
£700–800 *C*

Two sets of 6 Guild of Handicraft white metal buttons, each of stylised foliage motif, set with agate and chrysoprase, one set in original fitted case.
£600–800 *C*

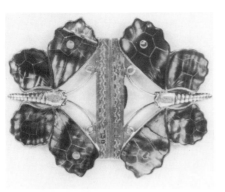

A silver buckle, each piece in the form of a butterfly with shaded mother-of-pearl wings, marked 'R.P.', Birmingham 1910, 3½in (9cm) wide.
£300–400 *P*

A Liberty & Co. silver belt buckle, in the style of Archibald Knox, with stylised spade-shaped flowers, supported on entwined entrelacs, the surface beaten, stamped marks 'L & Co.' Cymric, Birmingham 1901, 2in (5cm) wide.
£300–400 *S(C)*

A plique-à-jour and diamanté pendant, the ivory and mother-of-pearl bust mounted in a gilt white metal setting, the wings and fan tail with shades of green and turquoise plique-à-jour enamel, set with white and pink gems, in fitted leather case, 13in (33cm) high.
£3,800–4,000 *C*

A hammered silver, turquoise and blue enamel belt, by William Hutton & Son, each plaque with hallmarks, buckle with full hallmarks for 1904, maker's monogram 'W.H. & S.Ld.' within shaped surround, 28in (69cm) wide. **£600–700** *C*

A French 18ct gold brooch, the sculpture effect hand finished, c1900.
£600–800 *DID*

A 9ct gold pendant, by Murrle Bennet & Co., set with an opal flanked by 2 pale aquamarines and 2 citrines, c1900.
£700–900 *DID*

A rose diamond and plique a jour enamel butterfly brooch, with baroque pearl, untested, rose diamond and gem body.
£2,500–3,000 *CSK*

A diamond and rose diamond cluster brooch, the pierced and chased floral scrollwork shoulders each set with 2 rose diamonds. **£400–500** *CSK*

l. A Liberty & Co. silver and enamel belt buckle, attributed to Archibald Knox, enamelled in mottled blue and green, some enamel replaced, stamp marks 'L & Co.' Cymric, Birmingham 1901, 3in (8cm) wide.
£350–500 *S(C)*

r. An 18ct gold lady's cocktail watch, with synthetic rubies and diamonds, c1940.
£800–1,000 *ABS*

l. A Mexican silver and semi-precious stone bracelet, c1945, 7in (17.5cm) long.
£200–300 *ABS*

A Liberty & Co. Cymric silver and enamel waist clasp, designed by Archibald Knox, stamped maker's mark, Birmingham 1905. **£600–800** *CSK*

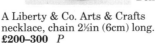

A Liberty & Co. enamelled pendant, of flower form, enamelled in blue and green with wirework stamens and mother-of-pearl centre, 1½in (3.5cm) long. **£300–400** *P*

An Art Nouveau German style pendant, probably by Murrle Bennett. **£200–300** *P*

A Liberty & Co. Arts & Crafts necklace, chain 2½in (6cm) long. **£200–300** *P*

A George Hunt cruciform pendant, marked 'GH', 4in (10cm) long, on a chain. **£350–450** *P*

A German Art Nouveau brooch, pierced and set with a plaque of amethyst flanked by 2 ovals of mother-of-pearl with a faceted amethyst drop, stamped '900', monogram for Carl Hermann of Pforzheim, 1½in (4cm) wide. **£350–400** *P*

A brass 'posy' brooch, fashioned as a butterfly, stamped with design lozenge for 1868 and 'Perry & Co. London', 2in (5cm) wide. **£300–400** *P*

This piece may have been designed by Christopher Dresser, as in 1854 he married Thirza Perry, a lecturer at South Kensington.

A gold, turquoise and pearl necklace, stamped 'Reg 422909', 16in (40.5cm) long. **£300–400** *P*

l. An Arts & Crafts pendant, set with amandine garnet cabochons, and another drop, 1½in (4cm) long. **£350–450** *P*

The leaf motifs show the characteristics of the work of Sibyl Dunlop.

From left.
1) An Arts & Crafts gold and lapis lazuli ring, showing affinities to the work of John Paul Cooper or Henry Wilson. **£300–400**
2) An Arts & Crafts ring, characteristic of the Birmingham School work under the influence of Gaskin. **£200–300**
3) A Theodor Fahrner opal ring, stamped '925 FAHRNER' and 'TF'. **£350–400**
4) A George Hunt ring, marked 'GH' in shield. **£200–300**
5) An Arts & Crafts ring, with lapis lazuli cabochon, stamped 'Sterling'. **£200–300** *P*

l. An Arts & Crafts pendant, with turquoise cabochon and drop, 1½in (4.5cm) long. **£80–120** *P*

From top.
1) An Arts & Crafts pendant, with oval plaque of lapis lazuli, set with a blister pearl, freshwater pearl drop, on a chain, 1½in (4cm) wide. **£150–200**
2) An Arts & Crafts necklace, characteristic of the work of the Birmingham School under the influence of Gaskin, 2in (5cm) long. **£350–400**
3) A Liberty & Co. gold, amethyst and pearl necklace, designed by Archibald Knox, 15in (38.5cm) long. **£1,000–1,200**
4) A Liberty & Co. Arts & Craft necklace, 16in (41cm) long. **£400–600** *P*

l. An Arts & Crafts gold, silver, plique-à-jour and opal hair ornament, attributed to Henry Wilson, 6½in (16.5cm) long. **£1,400–1,700** *P*

l. An Arts & Crafts pendant, with turquoise cabochon and drop, 1½in (4.5cm) long. **£80–120** *P*

A Charles Horner silver opal and turquoise enamel brooch, maker's mark, Chester 1907, 1in (3cm) wide. **£70–90** *S*

A Georg Jensen silver bracelet, designed by Henning Koppel, formed by 5 amoebic-like openwork plaques linked together, Danish maker's marks and London import marks, 8½in (21cm) long.
£600–800 *P*

A Liberty & Co. silver cloak clasp, with foliate design set with seed pearls, stamped 'L & Co.', Birmingham hallmarks for 1905.
£300–400 *C*

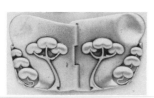

A Liberty & Co. Glasgow style silver and enamel waist buckle, with openwork decoration of stylised foliage with enamel details, stamped 'L & Co.', Birmingham hallmarks for 1902.
£900–1,200 *C*

Two Liberty & Co. silver waist clasps, one from a design for a bell push by Arthur Penny, each section of stylised honesty decorated with a central turquoise, marked 'LCCUD Cymric' with Birmingham hallmarks for 1903, and another stamped 'L & Co. Ltd.', with Birmingham hallmarks for 1899.
£600–800 *C*

A white metal and enamel brooch, by Ernestine Mills, with polychrome foil enamel decoration of a bird perched on a branch of flowring prunus, signed with 'EM' monogram, and a set of 6 enamel buttons, by Beatrice Cameron, in green, turquoise and purple scrolling foliate cloisonné enamel decoration, in original fitted case, damage to enamel.
£500–600 *C*

Three white metal brooches, by Mary Thew, one brooch with blister pearl and chrysoprase, one with abalone shell with wirework decoration set with blister pearl, another with openwork decoration of a sailing vessel, set with baroque pearls, citrine and amethyst and the hatpin set with agate.
£700–800 *C*

l. An Artificers Guild yellow and white metal pendant, by J. H. M. Bonnor, of a Viking ship in full sail, with wirework details and decoration of sea creatures, suspended from a loop with the North Star, set with enamel, opals and garnet, with monogram 'J.H.M.B.'
£1,000–1,200 *C*

An Art Nouveau hair comb, the gilt floral openwork head set with 3 opals within curvilinear frame to the blonde tortoiseshell comb, the reverse with stamped signature, in maker's case stamped 'Ch. Dubret, 83 rue de la Liberté, Dijon.
£800–900 *CSK*

r. A yellow and silver pendant on a chain, by Joseph A. Hodel, the wirework foliate design set with a black opal, baroque pearls and 2 modelled and cast yellow metal maidens, stamped 'Hodel'.
£1,200–1,500 *C*

A white metal and enamel pendant, by Nelson and Edith Dawson, the central floral enamelled medallion mounted in an octagonal frame, suspended from an earlier wirework bow set with crystal, and crystal drop, inscribed 'ND'.
£1,000–1,200 *C*

A silver coloured linked bracelet. **£50–100** *ASA*

A silver buckle. **£20–25** *ASA*

A chrome necklace, with red beads. **£40–80** *ASA*

l. A silver necklace, set with green stones. **£40–50** *ASA*

l. A chrome necklace, with green beads. **£40–80** *ASA*

l. A chrome and red beaded necklace. **£40–80** *ASA*

GLOSSARY

Acid-cutting A method of decorating glass by which an object is coated with wax or another acid-resistant substance, then incised with a fine steel point and dipped in acid.

Aesthetic Movement An artistic movement prevalent in Britain c1860–80, which advocated a return to a harmony of form and function in design and decoration.

Appliqué The decorative application of a second fabric to the main fabric ground.

Arts & Crafts A late 19thC artistic movement led by William Morris, which advocated a return to medieval standards of craftsmanship and simplicity of design.

Bauhaus A German school of architecture and applied arts founded in 1919 by Walter Gropius.

Bentwood Solid or laminated wood, steamed and bent into a curvilinear shape. First used in 18thC, it was favoured by Wiener Werkstätte craftsmen.

Britannia metal A 19thC pewter substitute, which was an alloy of tin, antimony and a trace of copper.

Cameo glass Decorative glass formed by laminating together two or more layers of glass, often of varying colours, which are wheel-carved or etched to make a design in relief.

Cased glass (overlay) Similar to cameo glass, but with the design on the outer layer cut away rather than in relief.

Chasing A method of embossing or engraving metal, especially silver.

Chryselephantine An expensive combination of ivory and a metal, usually bronze.

Cire perdue ('lost wax') The French term for a process of casting sculpture that results in unique casts.

Cold painting A technique for decorating bronze whereby coloured enamels are annealed or painted on to the metal.

Crackled glaze A deliberate cracked effect achieved by firing ceramics to a precise temperature.

Dinanderie The application of patinated enamel to non-precious metals such as copper and steel.

Electroplating The process whereby silver is electronically deposited on a copper, nickel silver or Britannia metal base.

Entrelac A type of interlaced decoration used on jewellery. Of Celtic origin, its use was revived by Arts & Crafts designers.

Favrile From the Old English word meaning hand-made.

Federal style A chronological rather than stylistic term applied to American arts of the period from the the the establishment of the Federal Government in 1789 to c1830.

Hallmarks The marks stamped on silver or gold pieces when passed at assay (the test of quality).

Impressed Indented, as opposed to incised.

Incised Decoration or maker's mark cut or scratched into the surface, rather than impressed.

Intaglio carving A type of carving whereby forms are sunken into , as opposed to moulded on to, a surface.

Jardinière A plant container made from a variety of materials, including glass or pottery.

Jugendstil The term for German and Austrian design in the Art Nouveau style. Named after the Munich-based publication, *Jugend*.

Lustreware Pottery with a polished surface produced using metallic pigments, usually silver or copper.

Macassar A rare form of ebony.

Maquette A rough wax or clay model for a sculpture.

Marquetrie-de-verre A glass making process whereby pieces of coloured glass are pressed into the warm, soft body of a piece and rolled in. The insertions are wheel-carved.

Marquetry Furniture decoration in which shapes are cut into a sheet of wood veneer and inlaid with other woods or materials.

Martelé The French for 'hammered'; the term for silverware with a fine hammered surface produced first in France and revived by the American Gorham Corporation during the Art Nouveau period.

Millefiori A glass-making technique whereby canes of coloured glass are arranged in bundles so that the cross section creates a pattern. Slices of millefiori canes can be used as decoration or fused together to form hollow wares.

Modernism/Functionalism
International movement in 1930s
furniture design. Clean lines and the
cube shape were emphasised.

Opalescence A translucent white
quality in glass; a reddish core is visible
when held up to the light.

Pap-boat A small boat-shaped vessel,
usually of silver or pottery, used for
feeding infants.

Pâte-de-cristal Near transparent glass
made of powdered glass paste which has
been fused in a mould.

Pâte-de-verre Translucent glass
similar to pâte-de-cristal but with a
lower proportion of lead.

Pâte-sur-pâte A form of ceramic
decoration developed at Sèvres whereby
white slip is applied and fired in layers,
building up a cameo effect.

Patina The fine layer or surface sheen
on metal or furniture that results with
time, use or chemical corrosion.

Plique-à-jour An enamelling method
whereby a backed, many-celled mould is
filled with translucent enamel of
different colours. When the backing is
removed, the finished piece resembles
stained glass.

Pontil mark The mark left by the iron
rod upon which some glass is supported
for final shaping after blowing.

Pressed glass Glass items produced in
a mechanical press mould.

Repoussé The term describing relief
metalwork decoration created by
hammering on the reverse side.

Rock crystal A form of engraved lead
glass cut and polished to simulate the
natural facets of actual rock crystal.

Sand-cast A method of casting bronze
in a mould made from pounded quartz
and sand.

Secessionist The term for the
movement formed in opposition to
established artistic taste which surfaced
in Munich, Berlin and Vienna toward
the end of the 19thC, and which
initiated the Art Nouveau movement.

Sgraffito A form of earthenware
decoration incised through slip,
revealing the ground beneath.

Shagreen A type of untanned leather,
originally made from the skin of the
shagri, a Turkish wild ass, soaked in
lime water and dyed. By the 19thC it
was made mainly of sharkskin.

'Silvered' glass Items produced by
injecting silver between two layers
of glass.

Slip A smooth dilution of clay and
water used in the making and decoration
of pottery.

Slip-trailed decoration A form of
ceramic decoration involving thin trails
of slip trailed across the body of a piece.

Slipware Earthenware decorated with
designs trailed in or incised through slip.

Stilt mark The mark left on the base
of some pottery by supports used
during firing.

Stipple engraving A technique of
decorating glass with designs made up of
incised dots of varying density, giving an
appearance of light and shade, and a
much richer effect than line engraving.

Stoneware Non-porous pottery, a
hybrid of earthenware and porcelain,
made of clay and a fusible substance.

Studio glass One-off pieces made by
designers and glass makers in
collaboration.

Triple soufflé (blow-out) glass
A variation of mould blowing, this
method involves the overlaying of glass
in the mould and then pumping in air at
very high pressure, pressing the glass
into the recesses of the mould.

Tube-lining A form of ceramic
decoration whereby thin trails of slip
are applied as outlines to areas of
coloured glaze.

Underglaze The coloured decorative
layer applied under the main glaze.

Vase parlante A form of vase produced
by Emile Gallé, the decoration of which
includes an engraved quote from a
literary work.

Vaseline glass A cloudy, yellow and
oily-looking glass, similar in appearance
to vaseline, developed during the 19thC.

Vitro porcelain British art glass, made
from slag, crysolite and glass metal,
giving a streaked opaque green effect,
with purple veining.

Verdigris The green or bluish patina
formed on copper, brass, or bronze.

Ziggurat Stepped pyramid-shaped
pedestal of marble or onyx for small
bronze figures.

Zinc or Spelter A hard, brittle bluish
white metal, alloyed with copper to
make brass.

DIRECTORY OF SPECIALISTS

If you would like to contact any of the following dealers, we would advise readers to make contact by telephone before a visit, therefore avoiding a wasted journey.

Arts & Crafts
London
New Century Art Pottery,
69 Kensington Church
Street, W8 4BG.
Tel: 0171 937 2410

U.S.A.
Rago, David,
9 South Main Street,
Lamberville,
New Jersey, 08530.
Tel: (609) 397 9374

Suffolk
Zarins,
Wrentham Antique Centre,
Wrentham, NR34 7HB.
Tel: 01502724569

Bronze & Ivory Figures
Manchester
A S Antiques,
26 Broad Street,
Pendleton,
Salford, M6 5BY.
Tel: 0161 737 5938

Clarice Cliff
Hampshire
Bona Arts Decorative Ltd,
19 Princes Mead
Shopping Centre,
Farnborough, GU14 7TJ.
Tel: 01252 372188

London
Beverley,
30 Church Street,
Marylebone, NW8 8EP.
Tel: 0171 262 1576

Sussex
Witney and Airault,
Prinny's Gallery,
3 Meeting House Lane,
The Lanes,
Brighton, BN1 1HB.
Tel: 01273 204554

Warwickshire
Art Deco Ceramics
The Stratford Antique
Centre, Ely Street,
Stratford-upon-Avon,
CV37 6LN.
Tel: 01789 204351

Rich Designs,
1 Shakespeare Street,
Stratford upon Avon,
CV37 6RN.
Tel: 01789 261612

Yorkshire
Hewitt, Muir,
Halifax Antiques Centre,
Queens Road, Gibbet
Street, Halifax, HX1 4LR.
Tel: 01422 347377

Decorative Arts
Cheshire
Nantwich Art Deco,
87 Welsh Row,
Nantwich,
CW5 5ET.
Tel: 01270 624876

Hampshire
Bona Arts Decorative
Ltd,
19 Princes Mead
Shopping Centre,
Farnborough,
GU14 7TJ.
Tel: 01252 372188

Lincolnshire
Art Nouveau Originals,
Stamford Antiques
Centre,
The Exchange Hall,
Broad Street,
Stamford,
PE9 1PX.
Tel: 01780 62605

London
Abstract 20th Century
Decorative Arts,
58-60 Kensington Church
Street,
W8 4DB.
Tel: 0171 376 2652

Beverley,
30 Church Street,
Marylebone,
NW8 8EP.
Tel: 0171 262 1576

Collector, The,
9 Church Street,
Marylebone,
NW8 8EE.
Tel: 0171 706 4586

Jesse, John,
160 Kensington Church
Street,
W8 4BN.
Tel: 0171 229 0312

Shapiro & Co,
Stand 380,
Grays Antique Market,
58 Davies Street,
W1Y 1LB.
Tel: 0171 491 2710

Style,
1 Georgian Village,
Camden Passage,
N1 8DU.
Tel: 0171 359 7867

Sylvia Powell Decorative
Arts 1860–1960,
28 The Mall,
Camden Passage,
N1 0PD.
Tel: 0171 354 2977
Wednesday & Saturdays

Titus Omega,
Shop 18,
Georgian Village,
Camden Passage,
N1 8DU.
Tel: 0171 226 1571
Wednesdays & Saturdays

Van den Bosch,
Shop 14, Ground Floor,
Georgian Village,
Camden Passage,
N1 8DU.
Tel: 0171 226 4550
Wednesdays & Saturdays

Zeitgeist Antiques,
58 Kensington Church
Street, W8 4DB.
Tel: 0171 938 4817

Shropshire
Antiques on the Square,
2 Sandford Court,
Sandford Avenue,
Church Stretton,
SY6 6DA.
Tel: 01694 724111

Surrey
Church Street Antiques,
15 Church Street,
Godalming, GU7 1EL.
Tel: 01483 860894

Sussex
Witney and Airault,
Prinny's Gallery,
3 Meeting House Lane,
The Lanes,
Brighton, BN1 1HB.
Tel: 01273 204554

Wales
Paul Gibbs Antiques,
25 Castle Street, Conwy,
Gwynedd, LL32 8AY.
Tel: 01492 593429

Warwickshire
Art Deco Ceramics
The Stratford Antique
Centre, Ely Street,
Stratford-upon-Avon,
CV37 6LN.
Tel: 01789 204351

Rich Designs,
1 Shakespeare Street,
Stratford upon Avon,
CV37 6RN.
Tel: 01789 261612

Yorkshire
Country Collector,
11-12 Birdgate,
Pickering, YO18 7AL.
Tel: 01751 477481

Hewitt, Muir,
Halifax Antiques Centre,
Queens Road,Gibbet
Street, Halifax,
HX1 4LR.
Tel: 01422 347377

Dutch Ceramics
London
Pieter Oosthuizen,
1st Floor, Georgian
Village, Camden
Passage, N1 8DU.
Tel: 0171 359 3322/376
3852

Furniture
London
Art Furniture (London)
Ltd, 158 Camden Street,
NW1 9PA.
Tel: 0171 267 4324

Glass
London
Gould, Patrick & Susan,
Stand L17, Gray's Mews
Antique Market, Davies
Street, W1Y 1LB.
Tel: 0171 408 0129

Jewellery
London
Didier Antiques,
58-60 Kensington Church
Street, W8 4DB.
Tel: 0171 938 2537

Moorcroft
Kent
Hearnden, Peter,
Corn Exchange Antiques
Centre, 64 The Pantiles,
Tunbridge Wells,
TN2 5TN.
Tel: 01892 539652

London
Rumours,
10 The Mall,
Upper Street,
Camden Passage,
Islington, N1 0PD.
Tel: 01582 873561

Doulton
Cleveland
Market Cross Jewellers,
160 Linthorpe Road,
Middlesborough,
TS1 3RB.
Tel: 01642 253939

London
Collector, The,
9 Church Street,
Marylebone, NW8 8EE.
Tel: 0171 706 4586

Heritage Antiques,
Unit 14 Georgian Village,
30 Islington Green,
Camden Passage,
N1 8DU.
Tel: 0171 226 9822